Culture and Language at Crossed Purposes

Culture and Language at Crossed Purposes

THE UNSETTLED RECORDS
OF AMERICAN SETTLEMENT

Jerome McGann

The University of Chicago Press   Chicago and London

The University of Chicago Press, Chicago 60637
The University of Chicago Press, Ltd., London
© 2022 by The University of Chicago
All rights reserved. No part of this book may be used or reproduced in any manner whatsoever without written permission, except in the case of brief quotations in critical articles and reviews. For more information, contact the University of Chicago Press, 1427 East 60th Street, Chicago, IL 60637.
Published 2022
Printed in the United States of America

31 30 29 28 27 26 25 24 23 22   1 2 3 4 5

ISBN-13: 978-0-226-81845-0 (cloth)
ISBN-13: 978-0-226-81846-7 (paper)
ISBN-13: 978-0-226-81847-4 (e-book)
DOI: https://doi.org/10.7208/chicago/9780226818474.001.0001

Library of Congress Cataloging-in-Publication Data

Names: McGann, Jerome J., author.
Title: Culture and language at crossed purposes : the unsettled records of American settlement / Jerome McGann.
Description: Chicago ; London : The University of Chicago Press, 2022. | Includes bibliographical references and index.
Identifiers: LCCN 2021050920 | ISBN 9780226818450 (cloth) | ISBN 9780226818467 (paperback) | ISBN 9780226818474 (ebook)
Subjects: LCSH: American literature—Colonial period, ca. 1600–1775—History and criticism. | Treaties in literature. | Ethnic relations in literature.
Classification: LCC PS195.T74 M34 2022 |
DDC 810.9/001—dc23/eng/20220217
LC record available at https://lccn.loc.gov/2021050920

FOR FIONA, SKYLAR, AND LUCA
AND SOFIA AND OWEN, BECAUSE THEY ASKED

Give me your tired, your poor,
Your huddled masses yearning to breathe free
EMMA LAZARUS (1883)

but not the Canaanites
"A modell of Xtian Charity" (1630)

Speak truth to truth.
CHARLES BERNSTEIN, "The Truth in Pudding" (2013)

CONTENTS

List of Figures ix   Preface xi

Introduction

1: Scope and Method 3
2: The Exceptional Encounter 8
3: On Native Grounds: North American Treaty-Making
(ca. 1609–1721) 15

Part I: Puritan Enlightenment: *Via Dolorosa*

Prologue 31
4: William Bradford: The Diary (1620–21), the History
(*Of Plymouth Plantation*), and the Hebrew Studies 35
5: John Winthrop: From Journal to History 50
6: Anne Bradstreet: The World Elsewhere 67
7: Cotton Mather's *Magnalia* 79

Interchapter 1. Covenant Chain Treaty-Making and Franklin's Folios 102

Part II. Secular Enlightenment: The Importance of Failure

8: Franklin's *Autobiography*: Composition as Explanation 129
9: The Education of Thomas Jefferson 150

Interchapter 2. The End of *Kaswentha*:
A Brief History 166

Part III. Truth and Method

10: The *Arbella* Sermon: A Case Study 183
11: The American Scholar in the Twenty-first Century 200

Acknowledgments 219   *Notes* 221   *Index* 257

FIGURES

1: The Skidi Sky Chart (seventeenth century?) xii

2: William Bradford, "Hebrew Exercises" (ca. 1652) 48

3: Thomas Parkhurst, *An Exact Mapp of New England and New York* (1702) 84

4: John Thornton, et al., *A New Map of New England, New York, New Iarsey...* (1685) 85

5: John Sellers, *A Mapp of New England* (1675) 85

6: Benjamin Franklin, *The Treaty Held with the Indians of the Six Nations...* (1742) 103

7: Vandalia (late-eighteenth century) 143

8: "A modell of Xtian charity" (late seventeenth century?) 184

9: Francis Bayard Winthrop, "Donation List" (1809) 191

10: John Cotton, *Gods Promise to His Plantations...* (1634) 192

11: Isaac Ambrose, *Redeeming the Time. A Sermon...* (1674) 194

PREFACE

> a proposition about our use of language
> LUDWIG WITTGENSTEIN, *Philosophical Investigations* no. 58

Claude Lévi-Strauss thought that "men have always been concerned with only one task—how to create a society fit to live in."[1] For broad guidance in pursuing that goal, people have regularly turned to religion, to philosophy, to science. Although he neglected none of those traditional institutions, Lévi-Strauss argued that Rousseau's anthropological "model" would prove "more fruitful."[2] Being drawn from a study of daily human practices, it would escape the abstractions of philosophy, the arbitrary claims of religion, and—perhaps for him most dangerous of all—science's ideology of progressive human development, "the secular imaginary."[3] Though an ideal model,[4] Rousseau's served him as a device for measuring and judging social conditions and imagining how to change them for the better.

How to explicate the documentary record of those conditions has been this book's overriding procedural focus. In every case I have turned to the discipline that takes the media of language exchange not only as its critical purview, but as its source and end and test. Using language to study the language practices in any and all forms of expression and modes of transmission, philology cannot make the kind of Enlightenment claim that bedevils so much of religion, philosophy, and science. As conceived by August Boeckh, philology is a capacious field of related disciplines in the humanities: anthropology, archaeology, bibliography, cartography, paleography, codicology, ethnography, geography, history, lexicography, linguistics, literary studies, and semiotics.[5] Once upon a time the lost Library of Alexandria was its great Western exponent. The *lost* library.

In approaching the human record, each of those disciplines recognizes it as broken and scattered to the winds. So is the presence of the past

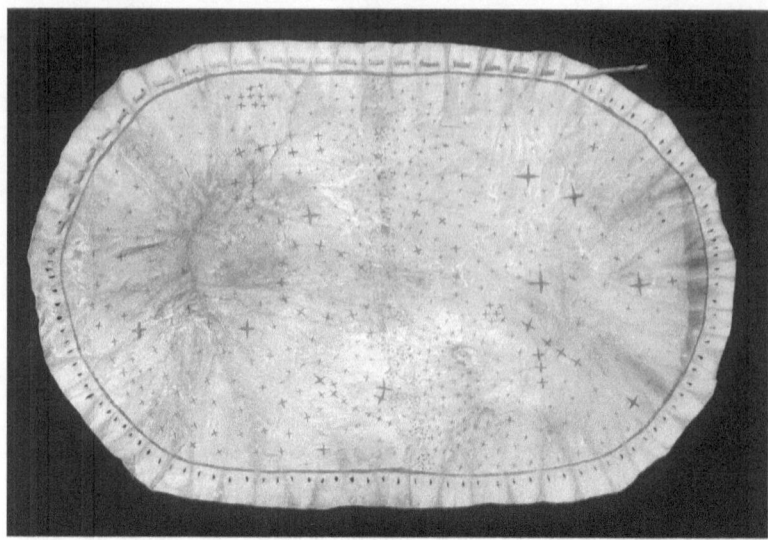

FIGURE 1. The Skidi Sky Chart (seventeenth century?), oriented with north at the top. Photograph: Field Museum of Natural History, Chicago. Photograph: © The Field Museum of Natural History (CSA16231/71898).

difficult to place or parse, as Reiner Smolinski suggested when he pledged allegiance to historicist method and the one thing needful for any philological investigation: "so far as possible, to see things their way." "So far as possible" is always far short of what one wants and, especially, what one needs. Not only are the records fractured, but we necessarily approach them with blinders. In a crucial sense, any present perspective is far more difficult to manage than even the most alienated subject matter exactly because our perspectives come shrink-wrapped. That's why materials intractable on their face are so important for critical inquiry. No disciplinary method, certainly not a philological method, can be trusted unless it is braked at crisis by its subject matter.

All that being the case, I have tried throughout to keep in mind an essay by the geographer William Gustav Gartner that I read ten years ago as I was beginning to work on this book. Gartner set himself the task of explicating a document far more recondite than any I have taken up in this study: the Skidi Sky Chart (see fig. 1), a Pawnee star map made on an ovoid piece of soft deerskin measuring approximately twenty-two by fifteen inches.

As Gartner observes, "We cannot begin to comprehend American Indian maps unless we attempt to see them from American Indian eyes."[6] But while that foursquare historicist view leads Gartner to a remarkable set of fact-based judgments and conjectures about the Sky Chart, the keynote of the essay, set down at the beginning, is that "the Skidi Star Chart is a map of all that we cartographers do not know."[7] When he closes his investigation and turns to "end in a conclusion," Gartner swerves and declares simply that "I cannot do [it]." He can't because what he wrote at the beginning remains true at the ending: "The Skidi Sky Chart is, and always will be, a graphic reminder of all that we do not know."[8]

It is a "Sky Chart," it is "a map," it is "a graphic reminder": as Gartner struggles to explain, he keeps revising his descriptors. It isn't exactly a map at all, least of all a "photograph." It is more like an "exegesis" of the night sky.[9] And when he comes to parse its ceremonial functions ("performative cartography"), that characterization also falls short, for the Sky Chart is much more like a user's manual,[10] laying out the "spatial syntax of Skidi rituals."[11] As Gartner's study proceeds, the problems multiply, and understanding itself becomes at once more clear and more strange. Pressing at various contradictory features of the Sky Chart, Gartner realizes that one of the most accepted scholarly judgments—that it is a map of the night sky as seen from a particular position on the Skidi earth—is itself misleading. Indeed, Gartner realizes, the Sky Chart is closer to what the Skidi priest Roaming Scout once told the anthropologist James Murie: it is a projection "from a vantage point on the vault of the heavens looking down through the celestial sphere."[12] It is the view of "the Father Tirawahat"[13] of "World Creation"[14] as imagined and now reprojected from a human world below. So Gartner also calls the Sky Chart a "transcendental expression" of Tirawahat's divine action of renewing the existence of the world in recurrent seasonal cycle and the ritual performances that give them their local, human, Skidi *habitus*.[15]

How is all that—there is much more to Gartner's rich discussion— "*all that* we do not know" about the Sky Chart?[16] In part, Gartner means that the more one investigates the Sky Chart, the more one exposes matters that have escaped explanation or generated conflicting explanations. Identifying and explaining its features multiplies the negative space of any picture one's analysis is producing. Philology is a fallible social enterprise ("of making many books there is no end" [Ecclesiastes 12:12]). More profoundly, Gartner's interpretations of the buckskin's minute material and contextual particulars do not explicate the knowledge that comes into play when the Sky Chart is put to ceremonial use. His second-order secular projection succeeds by exposing all that it will never know about the Sky Chart. Although he has no idea how to use the Sky Chart, he does know that there were, and still are, human beings who knew and know how to use it according to its ritual intention: to recreate a world fit for the Skidi to live in. Philosophy and science are too enlightened to make Gartner's move, which sets the Sky Chart free to judge the limits of secular knowledge, including Gartner's own. And while any number of religions might recognize the specifically Skidi pretension, none would possess the authority assumed by the Sky Chart. They have their own sacraments to confess and maintain.

Religion, philosophy, and science have projected many heroes: Jesus through the days of his Passion and death, Socrates in his last hours speaking with his friends, Galileo before the Inquisition, Newton's "mind forever / Voyaging through strange seas of Thought, alone."[17] But philology? Albrecht Dürer was himself long virtually alone in having fashioned an iconic image of the pedant as hero: Jerome at his desk scouring the *Vetus Latina* documents for their Vulgate reincarnation and, Dürer thought, dreaming of the Renaissance. But after Dürer, pedants would be seen mostly as a comical or sorry lot: Jonathan Oldbuck, Teufelsdröckh, Casaubon. There is as well the tragic figure of Nietzsche, the philosophical philologist sinking into dementia as he was stripped of his linguistic function, both studied and commonplace.

Thinking perhaps of Scott or Carlyle, Emerson thought he might reshape the philologist as a modern American hero when he spoke to Harvard's Phi Beta Kappa society in 1837 on "the American scholar." But what he holds up is not a man or woman, unless he is exalting himself: it is a thought, the idea of "Man Thinking." Emerson's thinking about that thought is that "the true scholar [is] the only true master." That mastering thought gives him pause in his speech only once, and only briefly, when he thinks that "perhaps" he has been "tediously" flogging "this abstraction of the Scholar." So he makes a final rhetorical turn through the idea that Man Thinking is "the only true master" by giving it a "nearer reference to [this] time and to this country." For all that, his closing remarks are not notably less abstract:

> Patience,—patience; with the shades of all the good and great for company; and for solace the perspective of your own infinite life; and for work the study and the communication of principles, the making those instincts prevalent, the conversion of the world. Is it not the chief disgrace in the world, not to be an unit; not to be reckoned one character; not to yield that peculiar fruit which each man was created to bear, but to be reckoned in the gross, in the hundred, or the thousand, of the party, the section, to which we belong; and our opinion predicted geographically, as the north, or the south? Not so, brothers and friends,—please God, ours shall not be so. We will walk on our own feet; we will work with our own hands; we will speak our own minds. Then shall man be no longer a name for pity, for doubt, and for sensual indulgence. The dread of man and the love of man shall be

a wall of defense and a wreath of joy around all. A nation of men will for the first time exist, because each believes himself inspired by the Divine Soul which also inspires all men.[18]

Do we see in such high-minded rhetoric what Emerson doesn't—that it has succeeded in distracting itself and, more successfully, that his language has let that distraction be known? The scholar as true master? On the contrary, for the philologist in particular, the scholar is apprentice to the sorceries of language. So did Wallace Stevens, who called his work "the scholar's art," dress the master in loving motley and call him by various comic names—sublimely, major man. For another modern American scholar-poet, Laura Riding, such joking words were not enough. She renounced poetry and turned herself into a serious, and a seriously eccentric, philologist. From the pedantic rag-and-bone shop of her voluminous late writings came a simple warning about "the common risks of language": that "failure stalks in every word."[19]

Gartner's essay would be a fine gloss on that remark. For myself, I wrote this book to try to illustrate Riding's insight, and to recall Samuel Beckett's late word and testament when we shrink from recalling what we've done and undone: "Fail better."[20]

Introduction

The Past is another country; they do things differently there.
L. P. HARTLEY

CHAPTER ONE

Scope and Method

For scholars of North American colonial literature, nothing is more widely recognized than its "practical" character. That *utile* focus prevailed from the first years of colonial settlement to the founding years of the republic, producing a corpus of functional writings firmly oriented to the world of social, religious, and economic purpose. Declarative and often polemical, its representations summoned reflection and judgment from the conflicted world that it purposed to engage. Aesthetic and formal criteria were thus secondary considerations, rhetorical moves reinforcing the truths being proposed for the conditions being addressed. Almanacs, sermons, practical manuals of all kinds, books of theology and religious instruction, histories, treaties, institutional documents, even poetry—*The Bay Psalm Book*, Anne Bradstreet, Michael Wigglesworth: all of it was literature prosecuted in a context of public purpose and instruction. Intentions, everywhere in play, were rarely playful. Many have thought, with good reason, that the greatest works of the colonial period—perhaps the greatest of all American literary works—were those culminating documents that announced its termination: the Declaration of Independence and the Constitution.

Utile works propose for themselves a correspondence theory of truth, not a coherence theory. Works like the *Arbella* sermon and the *Magnalia Christi Americana*, or Benjamin Franklin's *Autobiography* and Thomas Jefferson's *Notes on the State of Virginia*, are organized according to complex public intentions. They engage conflicted fields where their forays toward truth are judged not by the grace of art, but by the merciless standards of a reality they struggle to control. In such a context, we may improve understanding if we shift our framework of investigation from aesthetics to axiology, where a coherence theory of truth will not suffice.[1] The significance of cultural records that were so conceived and so dedicated entails studying what they set out to do in saying what they say, and then trying to assess the significance of their inevitably unresolved condition.[2] In the cases we will be dealing with here, we'll want to examine carefully just how telling these exchanges turned out to be.

In the field of American studies, Hugh Amory and William Charvat set impressive models for that kind of approach. What Amory called "ethnobibliography" is essentially what August Boeckh 150 years ago called *Sachphilologie* ("thing philology") and what Don McKenzie, working in British studies, called the "sociology of texts."[3] Like a great many scholars who came before, they judge that the sign system and even the discursive fields of language were shaped in the first instance by the materials, means, and modes of the records' production. More media than text, language so prosecuted organizes itself through acts of social exchange and the institutional mechanisms that make communication possible.

In 1972 Quentin Skinner wrote a seminal essay on the interpretations of texts in which he insisted "that *amongst* the interpreter's tasks must be the recovery of the writer's intentions *in* writing what he writes."[4] Implicit in Skinner's focus is the (so to speak) negative space of intentional acts: the array of conditions and agents—adverse, transverse, diverse, and converse—in which intentional moves take place. Bearing witness to that implied order of forces and actions, the documents record much more than a set of authorized intentions.

I judge that Skinner's classic historicist formula—"[t]o see things their way"—is most usefully read in its most embracing compass.[5] Purpose-driven in asymmetrical social fields, documentary records expose not just certain intentions and beliefs, declared or not, but the eccentric conditions in which they were undertaken. "To see things John Winthrop's way," or Anne Bradstreet's, or Thomas Jefferson's, is to be plunged into particular networked wildernesses and their differently revealing traversals.

Indeed, such works need not involve singular authors at all. But whether so authored or not, they always take place in a field full of folk with whom they are variously engaged, directly or indirectly. So in this study I will not be reading colonial works primarily for what they mean in what they say, but—to pick up on a formulation I still find pertinent—for what they mean to do in saying what they say.

Nothing is richer or stranger than our records of the impertinent gone world. That's why, in approaching our documentary archive, we should take seriously James Sidbury and Jorge Cañizares-Esguerra's warning against "generalizations [that] leap ahead of the careful empirical mapping of experience on which they should be based." As they go on to reflect on ethnogenesis in the early modern Atlantic, "Many of our histories of cultural change in the Atlantic world are overtheorized."[6]

But if we take our cue from the intransigent character of our documentary archive, we might want to write "undertheorized." Sidbury and Cañizares-Esguerra are protesting against theoretical methods that aim to draw synthetic maps of complex scenes and records. But there is a long-established model for media studies—philology—that moves through its documentary field in the opposite direction. Its aim is not to generalize but to fill out what Wallace Stevens called "the course of a particular." It is the tale of the long tail—the "science of exceptions" grounded in the Lucretian swerve[7]—that monitors all moves toward unified theories of cross-purposed fields. When the philologist encounters the documentary record, what she sees is what Marianne Moore said in "The Steeplejack" of his world: "It is a privilege to see / so much confusion."

Documents are obdurate because those who made them and those who passed them forward were caught up in treacherous cross-purposes. So do traditional philological methods remain crucial even for the most *engagée* cultural criticism. Over the past three decades we have been blessed with a significant recovery of such work throughout the humanities at large. The shift was perhaps most clearly signaled in 2013, when the Mellon Foundation began resourcing the Rare Book School's efforts to found the Society of Fellows in Critical Bibliography, where media and book history, philology, memory studies, and bibliography have made a notable disciplinary convergence.[8]

Similar changes have been overtaking American studies for some years, as my notes will show.[9] Some of the most consequential have come in specially focused scholarship or digital ventures—Marta Werner's close textual studies, Ryan Cordell's Viral Texts Project—or in focused essays whose broad relevance can escape attention.[10] Michael Ditmore, for instance, makes an important general point when he presses the importance of an historicism that pays close attention to the downstream contexts that have shaped the character of colonial documents.[11] Or consider how Vincent Carretta's detailed scholarship reset the agenda for how we read Gustavus Vassa's *The Interesting Narrative of the Life of Olaudah Equiano* (1789).[12] More than that, his essay helped to promote the kind of careful attention needed for a faithful view of the complicated scene of early transatlantic Black history and—certainly in my case—even beyond.

The *Arbella* sermon (1630), which I will later take up in detail, is an especially interesting case, because it is about as seminal an American work as we have. But though regularly studied and taught, it remains full of mystery.[13] For lack of a close examination of its documentary condition, we do not know what we do not know about it, including even its authorship. Or consider the significance of the "new light" Thomas McElwain threw on Logan's speech in Jefferson's *Notes on the State of Virginia* (1785).[14] Because the *Notes* winds so relentlessly between special pleading and exacting inquiry, it begs for the gift of McElwain's cool philological eye. Few scholarly works expose so economically the importance and the difficulty of disentangling the American dialectic of enlightenment.[15]

That kind of work has been the frame of reference for this book, whose historical purview is the period in North America from roughly 1620 to 1790, when British colonial settlement passed through two phases of American Enlightenment, the first religious, the second secular. In each case, the practicality that marks all colonial literature shifts into high, purpose-driven—even messianic—gear in the influential documents I will be looking at. Such works expose the conflicted scenes of colonial Enlightenment history—both the Enlightenment of grace and the Enlightenment of secular modernity—in especially dramatic ways.

Part I situates these works on their native grounds and then tracks them through four key exponents of the Enlightenment of grace: the works of William Bradford, John Winthrop, and Anne Bradstreet, along with Cotton Mather's *Magnalia Christi Americana*. Then comes an interchapter, where I examine a set of Covenant Chain treaties as they were represented in Benjamin Franklin's Treaty Folios. The chapter is important for exposing the political and cultural continuities that persisted in the colonies after the break marked by the Salem witch trials and the founding of Penn's colony, when the American Enlightenment project began to take a decisive shift. Looking at two exemplary documents of the eighteenth-century secular Enlightenment, Benjamin Franklin's *Autobiography* and Thomas Jefferson's *Notes on the State of Virginia*, part II offers an account of what persisted and what changed after the watershed of the 1690s.

Because the Enlightenment of modernity is such a central concern of both Franklin and Jefferson, those chapters begin the turn to part III, where I address directly the issue of critical method and its relation to the ethics of humanities scholarship. But first comes a second interchapter, where I discuss the final and most dispiriting period of colonial treaty-making—the years when Franklin was writing his *Autobiography* and when Jefferson began his *Notes*.

The first essay in part III, on the *Arbella* sermon, lays out an argument that is primarily addressed to a professional community. But I hope that nonspecialist readers may be interested in its less spectacular view of the American scholar than Emerson gave in his famous essay. This tour of a humanist's foul rag-and-bone shop is a field report on the uncertainties of knowledge and the status of what we may take to be familiar facts. As such, it means to set a workaday context for the second essay's more general reflections on the work of educators at all levels, from primary school to graduate programs—a special company of men and women who have made a vocational pledge to promote the advancement of learning and habits of truthfulness.

Like all educators, the most consequential work we do is day by day, working with students and colleagues in our classes and other academy-related settings. But because what is happening in society at large hovers over and intrudes upon even our tight little island, educators are sometimes called to a more public address. Such action has rarely seemed more urgent than at a time when we in America elected a president and were governed by an administration of unexampled and shameless dishonesty.

Sometimes it's important to speak truth to power. For educators, it is always even more important to try speaking truth to truth,[16] lest we fail the promise we have made to society. As Robert Calef said of Cotton Mather's moving and disastrous pursuit of enlightenment, a "prejudice of education" imperils the resolute commitment to knowledge and truth.[17] That is as true of our own regimes of knowledge—to which this book pledges allegiance—as of the regimes I want to examine. Only a habitual commitment to truthfulness will sustain the work of educators. Scholars cultivate such habits in our workshops where our watchwords are those common, everyday virtues—accuracy, thoroughness, and candor—that are now in such need of modest yet resolute example.

CHAPTER TWO

The Exceptional Encounter

For quite some time we have known that so-called classic American literature is haunted, and that the haunting of our cultural works has scarcely ceased to this day. Everyone cites the scandal of slavery—"America's original sin"—as at least one of the "unseen somethings haunting the day,"[1] and not a few have recognized a demon driving the wars to seize the lands of Native Americans and destroy their civilizations (1610–1890). Largely focused on later, less primal nightmares, Modern argued that they all reflect a philosophical ground he calls "the secular imaginary." "More than an ideology"—by which he means more than a constellation of related ideas—"the secular imaginary" is a quasi-religious faith, "a moral force, a connective tissue, a widely shared and massively intricate set of epistemological assumptions. And like anything in excess of ideology, secularism defies logic, particularly its own."[2]

It seems true, perhaps by definition, that this secular imaginary "defies logic," not least of all the logic of John Modern's critical account. But because that secular imaginary is, as he also points out, "a language"—indeed, a living language—it is far from defying use and expression. It certainly doesn't defy exposure or description. In that perspective, one may gain a notable advantage from a philological rather than a philosophical approach to the issues he addresses. Philology argues that one neither could nor should stand aside from one's subjects. I occupy the inner standing point where my American language forces me to stand. From here I can try to turn a small screw on the prevailing logic of critical method in order to seize the great privilege of close philological encounter, where failure stalks in every word.

I say "a small screw" because I take my bearings from what treatymaking between the Americans and the colonials shows us about our culture and history.[3] This book is heavily indebted to the remarkable work in

Native American studies that has emerged since the late 1960s. The focus I take here, however, while narrowly pivoting off colonial treaty-making, is historically extensive in two respects. The first is strictly chronological: the more than 150 years of conferences and formal treaties made between the Americans and the settlers from the early seventeenth century through the founding of the republic in the late eighteenth century. The second is ethnographic, for the treaty-making was conducted within two different space-times. Marshall Sahlins tracked a cognate space-time asymmetry in his brilliant study of Captain Cook's voyages to the Sandwich Islands.[4]

Karl Marx's famous essay "The Eighteenth Brumaire of Louis Bonaparte" underscores the importance of that differential. "Men make their own history," he wrote, "but they do not make it as they please; they do not make it under self-selected circumstances, but under circumstances existing already, given and transmitted from the past." When he then wrote of "the tradition of all dead generations weigh[ing] like a nightmare on the brains of the living," he disclosed his strictly neo-European perspective.[5] It is the same perspective that all the colonials, including the English, carried with them to the New World.

But the New World was already steeped in complex and radically different histories. That novel encounter—that *exceptional* situation—exposes the importance of the American condition for all the people involved. It marks an exceptionalism that has never been adequately considered in the obsessive discussions of American exceptionalism.[6]

If we consider just the people in the English colonies—the focus of this book—we see how seventeenth-century immigrants were trying to make a new history athwart their English homeland and its European context. Because of the fraught religious and political conditions in England, those transatlantic roots created problems for the colonies, particularly in New England. But the settlers would be yet more severely tested, for they had entered an historical network transmitted from a past about which they were all but completely ignorant. Insofar as they recognized a native presence, what they knew or thought they knew came from other, equally ignorant European sources. Because their very survival, as they themselves recognized, depended on their intercourse with native peoples, they had to work at establishing practical modes of accommodation. Many of the early colonial writings carry instructional reports—implicitly, user's manuals—for managing relations with the Indians.

This explains why Constance Rourke launched her discussion in *The Roots of American Culture* from a consideration of Indian treaties of the seventeenth and eighteen centuries. Not only were the treaties a model of pragmatic enterprise ("Quite strictly they belong to practical letters [and] were created for practical ends"); even more important, they were decisively *American*. As Rourke observes, "[N]othing like them exists in our own literature or any other."[7] Because formal and informal treaty-making has a long history, we might demur from that judgment. But it is in large measure justified because the treaty-making Rourke had in mind—*kaswentha*—was a uniquely North American settlement practice largely dominated by rules laid down by the Americans, not the settlers.

Although the first known formal *kaswentha* treaty dates from the early seventeenth century, its procedures had been worked out much earlier by the Iroquois (Haudenosaunee) to negotiate conflict between Native Americans living in the Haudenosaunee orbit. In Jon Parmenter's now classic description of *kaswentha*, its salient concept "emphasizes the distinct identity of the [the negotiating parties] and a mutual engagement to coexist in peace without interference in the affairs of the other."[8] *Kaswentha* protocols were the foundation for uniting the Iroquois League (later the Iroquois Confederacy) into a body for cooperative action of five (later six) nations.

Kaswentha deploys the ceremonial Maussian gift exchange practices that were fundamental to neolithic civilizations generally. In his classic study *Stone Age Economics*, Marshall Sahlins explicated Mauss's theory of gift giving through an extended comparison with Hobbes's *Leviathan*.[9] For both Hobbes and Mauss, because "the understructure of society is war,"[10] mechanisms for avoiding its destructive inertia were imperative. Hobbes's first law of nature "is to seek Peace, and follow it."[11] "So in structure, [Hobbes's] argument unites with Mauss's. . . . Hobbes understands the suppression of Warre neither through the victory of one nor by the submission of all, but in a *mutual surrender*."[12] That is the equivalent of Mauss's total prestation, the giving of gifts laying upon the receiver the obligation of reciprocity. In Sahlins's summary: "The Gift transposes the classic alternatives of war and trade from the periphery to the very center of social life, and from the occasional episode to the continuous presence. . . . [P]rimitive society is at war with Warre, and . . . all their dealings are treaties of peace. All their exchanges, that is to say, must bear in their material design some political burden of reconciliation."[13]

Besides working out elaborate ritual procedures, *kaswentha* made its condolence ceremony a pivotal treaty-making action. It was the crucial feature of the "mutual surrender" that *kaswentha* was practicing. Condolence was achieved as a ceremony of grieving that the conflicted parties offered as a gift to each other, the sign of an amity grounded in a confession of shared suffering. A win-win condition emerged from an acknowledgment of lose-lose. *Kaswentha* fostered a politics radically at odds with zero-sum war and realpolitik.

When *kaswentha* operated in the unusual conditions that prevailed in the North American settlement territories, however, its drive toward mutual surrender faced unusual difficulties. First and most important, the lifeways of the treatying parties were worlds apart: to adopt a vocabulary we have to use with care, one was Western European and early modern, the other was American and neolithic. Equally significant, the European parties were compelled to engage with the Americans according to rituals—both linguistic and ceremonial—that were of native design. Since the settlers largely regarded the Americans as "savages," the authority of the negotiations was rarely felt as strongly by the settlers as by the Americans.

Kaswentha required the colonists to treat with native people "under circumstances existing already" and within protocols "given and transmitted from [a] past" that the immigrants could barely appreciate or feel a deep relation to. Bad faith often corrupted even their best efforts and intentions—how could it not, given their own recent, brutal Anglo-European history?—and after the Revolution the former colonials, the United States, apostatized altogether. Thence followed the "Century of Dishonor" too late lamented by Helen Hunt Jackson.[14]

Yet for the republicans and especially for their postcolonial children, the memory of a glimpsed civilization preserved a secret life. It survives in the Franklin folios, his Albany Plan, and the *Autobiography*; in Crèvecoeur's *Letters from an American Farmer* (1782); and not least in Jefferson's *Notes on the State of Virginia* (1785) and the tormented fictions of Charles Brockden Brown. But it is the career of James Fenimore Cooper where the dark truth of cultural loss—native and nonnative—first becomes completely visible. At that point, what we call American literature began in earnest.

Before that, what we had was an American literature before American literature—a literary corpus all but completely occupied with practical, often day-to-day, economic, political, and religious concerns. Because none were more pressing or difficult—or more dangerous—than the settlers' relations with the Americans, treaty-making, and especially *kaswentha*, quickly assumed decisive importance for everyone.

As such, treaty-making is also this book's heuristic focus because it compels one to recognize and deal with the complexity and precariousness of settlement conditions. Many agents were interacting in pursuit of their different—often radically different—plans and purposes. Colonial North America was an unusually decentered world. Individual colonies were at odds with one another, often sharply so, and as they grew they developed further internal tensions, not least between the colonies' established eastern centers and their restless western peripheries.

Furthermore, because of the colonies' distance from imperial London, they were moved to follow independent courses that increasingly put them at odds with Crown authorities. From time to time the Crown moved to take greater control, its last effort coming with its victory in the Seven Years' War. When George III announced the Proclamation Line in 1763, his decision proved both impossible and disastrous. Thirteen of the twenty British colonies—even New York—resisted, and when England reacted with further colonial restrictions, opposition grew to a concerted push for complete independence.

Decisively, those stressed colonial relations met and mirrored a contentious array of native peoples operating from their different *habitus*, and conflicting interests were pervasive even within a particular colony, nation, or confederation of nations.[15] If a treaty was made between a very small subset of people—one colony, say, and one nation or alliance of nations—many others not directly involved were nonetheless implicated because their interests were being neglected or positively excluded. The scandalous Treaty of Fort Stanwix (1768), which we shall examine closely later, was perhaps the prime example of colonial mendacity. In addition, all the treaty-making by the English colonies with the native peoples had profound effects upon New France and vice versa, and the native nations had to suffer and deal with similar blowback conditions among themselves.

In this sense, treaty-making constantly exposed the differential forces that New World contact involved. The treaties and their records make a good display of their incongruent features because the network of alienations is recognizably pervasive. As diverse companies of immigrants swelled the English colonies, the people and their governing institutions were faced with repeated and wildly different emergencies, so volatile was this mongrel social and political scene.

The unsettled conditions of colonial settlement inform the approach taken in this book: to use treaty-making and its records as a template for parsing out a small corpus of English canonical writings from the period. Though by no means the only way to read these materials, my approach has its humanities. All seriously practical works, the canonical writings of the period engaged a web of conflicted agents as tangled as the web exposed by the treaties. The "discovery" of America by imperial Europeans and, most decisive of all, its complex North American settlement put the reawakening dreams of Western European enlightenment, both religious and secular, to the severe test of objectively adverse conditions. Reading English colonial documents as a record of prosecuted dreams, often as blind or brutal as they were venturous and intrepid, we typically shuttle between Frederick Jackson Turner's frontier thesis or Richard Slotkin's tale of regeneration through violence, modifying the picture with records that expose the impact of racism, slavery, and the slave trade.[16]

But the dream records look significantly different when they are examined in the context of *kaswentha* treaty-makings, which were undertaken to keep fraught or menacing conditions under mutually agreed-upon controls.[17] Disputes that would be difficult if not impossible to resolve under bewildering real-world circumstances could be, and were, held—at least for a time—in equable if precarious abeyance by the different treatying agents.

But the treaty-makers never doubted the uncertainties—the unsettled character—of what they were prosecuting, and a similar ethos pervades the canonical and strictly English works of the period, such as Bradford's and Winthrop's histories or Mather's *Magnalia Christi Americana*. As practically focused as the treaties, those works also deliberately tested themselves against exacting, because objective, measures of truth and accomplishment. Paradoxically, as we track the limits, the contradictions, and the failures of such works' purpose-driven collisions with reality, we may see them gain a new birth of freedom, uplifted to a view that does not expect them to appear either more or less than fallibly human.

My subjects and materials pick up on a familiar set of scholarly keywords: encounter and settlement, enlightenment (both religious and secular), exceptionalism, and empire. Each names a set of conditions that was forcibly carried into a New World by strangers in a strange land. The invasion created problems for both the Americans and the colonials, as we know, and while this book necessarily engages with the Native situation, its focus is on how the colonials, specifically the English colonials, managed the experience. Because nothing brought those topics into sharper focus for me than the Indian treaties that the Americans and the colonists negotiated between 1620 and 1778, treaty-making set the conditions for the particular view of colonial literature presented here. Colonial treaty-making throws into relief the extreme, the *exceptional*, contradictions that shaped the works of English colonial literature.

In pressing this argument I am far from looking to debunk American dreams or thrill to American nightmares, or for that matter to salute the glories of Native American history. The Narragansetts betrayed and helped destroy the Pequots, the Iroquois broke faith with and humiliated their dependent Delawares, native nations splintered; nor were the colonists alone in perpetrating acts they knew were shameful. Yet the struggle to maintain social order under complex and dangerous conditions, and to persist in the struggle against all odds and in the continual experience of unsuccess and disappointment, nonfeasance and outright malfeasance, seems to me a tale of considerable, even inspiring significance.[18] That the efforts did not and have not and probably could not succeed, and that yet they continued, seems to me something to know and remember: according to the Native American formula, "so long as the sun and moon shall last." Not at all the greatest story ever told—the tale is too fearful and faithless, too pious and self-deceived—but it is perhaps one of the world's bravest, most sobering, and most naked.

CHAPTER THREE

On Native Grounds: North American Treaty-Making, circa 1609–1721

While historians differ about when the Iroquois League was founded—dates range from the middle of the twelfth, the fourteenth, and the fifteen centuries CE—it was certainly powerful and functioning in the middle of the sixteenth century, and its *kaswentha* protocols were being adopted and adapted by other neighboring nations. Those diplomatic ceremonials were initially worked out to forge civility between different native peoples. The earliest recognized treaty between the Iroquois League and a European colonial power dates to 1613, the Treaty of Tawagonshi with New Netherland. A Dutch document said to be a record of the treaty-making has been the focus of sharp scholarly dispute. Whatever the status of that object—it is certainly a late copy in what may have been an extensive line of lost earlier documents—the actual treaty event seems well attested.[1] The different dates for the event that have been proposed (1609, 1613, 1618, 1623, 1634, 1643) almost certainly indicate one of the characteristic features of *kaswentha* treaty-making: that it called for frequent face-to-face renewal.

It's worth pausing to comment on an important passage in the document: the formula declaring that the treaty will remain in force "so long as the grass is green" (*soolangh t' gras groen is*). This clearly echoes similar formulaic expressions found in later authentic treaty documents. But the document's critics read it as inauthentic: "a metaphor familiar to present-day Americans from film and fiction [and] not a seventeenth century form."[2] The criticism argues that the phrasing isn't like (for example) "so long as the sun and moon shall last" or "so long as the sun shines." But that reading, I think, misses the real force of all such expressions, which emerge from a profound sympathy with cyclic and seasonal phenomena. Grass for a good part of the year is *not* green, and the sun and moon do not always shine but cycle into and out of presence, appearing and disappearing over the course of the seasonal year and, if one is attuned to such matters, shape-shifting in complex ways. "So long as the grass is green" measures the treatied duration in two salient respects: it will endure as a recurrent "green" event and, when the grass is not green, as will inevitably happen, it will—inevitably, seasonally—turn green again.

In his "Analysis of the 1613 Tawagonshi Treaty," Robert Venables pointed out that it was a "Two-Row Wampum Belt" treaty specifying "Separate Paths, Separate Sovereignties, [and] Mutual Cooperation" in trade and political relations. That arrangement, he went on to say, "stands in stark contrast to the negotiations with other Indian nations made by the English in 1587 at Roanoke, in 1608 in Virginia, and 1622" (sic) in Plymouth.[3] Venables is correct to call the native-colonial intercourse at Roanoke and Jamestown "negotiations" rather than treaty-making because the early Virginia colonists did not recognize native sovereignty, and "negotiation" in Virginia was not amicable. But as we shall see, the Plymouth event was a treaty involving a full-blown set of *kaswentha* protocols. Not least significant, because the Plymouth treaty was made with the Wampanoag Confederacy, it shows just how influential Haudenosaunee *kaswentha* treaty-making had become. The Wampanoag were an Algonquin people, and the Algonquins and the Iroquois were often in conflict.

Before we consider the Plymouth treaty, one other *kaswentha* treaty of the period demands attention: the 1645 Treaty of Trois-Rivières with New France that William Fenton called "The Earliest Recorded Description."[4] The treatying began in early July 1645 with a gift of seventeen belts of wampum presented to the French by the chief spokesperson for the Iroquois ambassadors, Kiotseaeton, who explained the significance of each belt.[5] The gifts were accompanied by "appropriate" ritual "gestures," song, and dance. Two days later the French reciprocated with "fourteen gifts, all of which had their meanings and carried their own messages."[6] The initial ceremonies concluded with elaborate reciprocal salutes.

About a month later, in order "to secure peace in this new world, it was necessary that [the parties] should meet all together" again and continue the gift-exchange ceremonies.[7] It took several days for the various Indian nations to arrive and assemble, at which point a French ambassador delivered eighteen belts of wampum and presented them to the tribes along with highly expressive explanations. As the Jesuit recorder explains, "[W]ords of importance in this country are presents,"[8] which is to say that the beautiful wampum presents are themselves "words of importance" cast in a nonlinguistic medium.[9] As the French reciprocated Kiotseaeton's gifts in the first ceremony, now the Indians also reciprocated, and the assembly closed.

About a week later, however, all the parties gathered for yet a third meeting, where a final set of gifts was exchanged,[10] this time between the Iroquois, the French, and the other tribes involved in the negotiations. The treaty involved "four different languages . . . French . . . Huron . . . Algonquin, and . . . Hiroquois."[11] Particularly notable at this third meeting was the explicit enactment of the condolence ceremony, where the "bond" of friendship was decisively executed.[12]

Unlike the English when they treated with the Americans during these early years of settlement, the French were fascinated by the exacting Iroquois spectacle, perhaps because their Roman Catholic heritage gave them easier access to the expressive power of sacred ritual and its panoply. From 1677 on, when the English became invested in Covenant Chain treaty-making, they were forced to pay closer attention to the ceremonials, but even then, as we shall see, they were frustrated that things did not move more expeditiously.

Nothing shows their indifference more clearly that Governor John Winthrop's *Journal*. Although Winthrop is a meticulous reporter of the colony's trying and recurrent religious tensions and disputes, his engagements with native Americans could scarcely be more perfunctory.[13] In 1639 Massachusetts Bay Colony gift exchanges with the Indians had been going on for "two years," but Winthrop reports them as if they were brief business transactions: "he had received from the Indians, in presents, to the value of about £40, and that he had spent about £20 in entertainments of them" (*J*, 296). Even more striking is a brief entry in the summer of 1642, when the colony was seriously concerned about the threat of Indian violence. Massasoit, "the great sachem of Pokanocott, . . . came . . . to visit the governour." On the face of it this was an event of considerable moment, as Massasoit's entourage showed (he was "attended with many men and some other sagamores accompanying him"). All that Winthrop had to say of the visit, however, is that he "entertained him kindly, etc." (*J*, 399). The "etc." is particularly striking.[14]

As Jon Parmenter has shown, from 1701 to 1760—the period when the Covenant Chain treaties were being regularly renewed—the French "came far closer than did the English to fulfilling the Iroquois vision of *kaswentha*."[15] The Iroquois found treating with the English difficult partly because the English colonies were often at odds with each other, and partly because, unlike the French, the colonies were bent upon acquiring Indian land and displacing the natives. In both respects New France took a different approach to their colonial affairs: the French worked through a highly centralized authority, and their principal interest was in trading rather than land acquisition. But even though English colonials came to recognize the Americans' fierce insistence on their sovereignty, they did so with great reluctance and often in bad faith.

English colonial truculence toward the Americans was strongest in the two most important seventeenth-century colonies, Virginia and Massachusetts Bay. In each case, when treaties were made they were imposed by the colonial authorities, though the forms of imposition were quite different. The settlement of Plymouth, as we shall see, was another matter entirely and produced an extended (twenty-five-year) period of cooperative relations that only ended when the Massachusetts Bay Colony's aggressive approach pulled Plymouth into the New England Confederation in 1643.

In Virginia, suspicion, conflict, and finally widespread violence dominated relations between the Americans and the colonials from the first. Despite Captain John Smith's notoriously confused (and multiple) accounts of the Jamestown settlement, the point at issue was clear: sovereignty and, even more, the ritual and public demonstration of sovereignty. Powhatan had no intention to make treaties in regular ways with the immigrants until his sovereignty was clearly acknowledged. He proposed to accomplish this very early through the 1608 ceremonial marriage of Smith to the American's daughter Pocahontas. Smith and his people could not have understood the great significance of this ritual event when Powhatan organized it. Later, when he wrote his retrospective *Generall Historie*, Smith misrepresented both its spirit and its letter in the mythic tale of his being saved from death by the smitten Pocahontas.

Yet Smith's demonic account of his ceremonial adoption underscores how complete was Powhatan's assumption of authority. Dressed "in the most fearfullest manner that he could . . . more like a devil than a man," Powhatan married Pocahontas to Smith and declared that, after a final gift exchange, "he would give [Smith] the country of the Capohawosick, and for ever esteem him as his sonne Nantaquod."[16] But as Alfred Cave laconically remarks about the promised gift exchange, Smith "had no intention of keeping" his promise to complete the ritual expectation.[17] Smith recognized Powhatan's power and admired the character of (at least some of) his people. But finally they were all "salvages" who had to be dealt with even more severely than Smith dealt with his rude companion settlers.

Resisting or violating the gift-exchange rituals that Powhatan insisted upon, the earliest Virginians pursued a mercantile relation with the Powhatan Confederacy. The offerings of the settlers struck Powhatan as perfunctory. He despised even the exchange of the consumables the Virginians needed and would not so much as consider land cessions.[18] For Powhatan, only Smith's ritual adoption would have established a proper basis for future cooperative relations with people who wanted residence and resource usufruct in his domains.

After the deadly surprise attack on the colonists that Opechancanough launched in 1622, Smith decided that a policy of "vanquishing the salvages" was "now" the best course since "our [previous] gentlenesse and faire comportments"[19]—he was writing about his economic overtures—had failed to establish peaceful relations. Indeed, while the attack by the "treacherous and rebellious Infidels" was judged by "some [to] be good for the Plantation, because now we have just cause to destroy them by all meanes possible," Smith thought "it had beene much better it had never happened."[20] For Smith, the event signaled the end of the promise of cooperation based on economic exchange. His entire approach to the settlement of Virginia was driven by the promise of the material wealth he saw in Powhatan's world ("the goodnesse and commodities [that] may be had in Virginia)."[21]

Because those were the terms Smith and the Virginians kept pressing, Powhatan and, later, Opechancanough remained on a permanent war footing with the English, and the bloody violence of the Powhatan Wars dragged on, with occasional breaks, from 1610 to 1646.[22] A general reflection by Smith in the aftermath of 1622 expresses his changed view of future colonial policy toward Indian relations. Given the situation, he reasoned, "it is more easie to civilize them by conquest then faire meanes; for the one may be made at once, but their civilizing will require a long time and much industry."[23] That the nations of America were high-functioning, civilized communities was a very late discovery on the part of the settlers and their leaders. By the same token and given the circumstances, one can understand how Powhatan and Opechanconough would have reached exactly the same conclusion when they decided to launch their 1622 attack. Everything depends on your view of civility and what counts as "gentlenesse and faire comportments." The 1622 massacre was the Indian move to end once and for all the continuing state of hostility that the settlers had, in the Americans' view, created.

Violence only ended finally in 1646, when the colonists destroyed the Powhatan Confederacy. Opechanconough, then ninety-two years old, was captured and murdered by the colonials, and the new *werowance*, Necotowance, submitted to the English and their imposed treaty arrangements.[24] The tribes were made subject to the protection and authority of the Crown, their *werowances* would "be appointed or confirmed by the King's Governour," and they were ordered to occupy and use only the lands set aside for them. They were forbidden on pain of death to travel in any other part of the colony without permission and identifying "badges."

Meanwhile, in the north, the Americans in the New England region were being imposed upon in different ways. When the Massachusetts Bay Colony treatied in 1634 with the Pequots and in 1636, after the Pequot War, with the Narragansetts, there were reciprocities, but no *kaswentha*. Puritan treaties from 1634 on were not "imposed" in the manner of the 1646

Virginia treaty or, later, its renewal as the Treaty of the Middle Plantation (1677). Though based on a fair effort to meet the parties' mutual trade interests, the Puritan treaties were shaped by colonial authorities, and they established the Massachusetts Bay Colony as the adjudicating authority of the treaty arrangements.[25] So Governor Winthrop used the 1634 peace and trade agreement to mitigate, if not resolve, the hostility of the Narragansetts toward the other major regional native power, the Pequots. The parties were enjoined from committing violence against each other, and the colony would mediate disputes.

But the treaty itself created further tensions. Growing apprehensive at the spread of settlements and, even more, at the power and authority the colony gained with the treaty, the Pequots resisted when the colony charged them with murder and treaty violation. Had a thorough investigation been pursued, the truth might have emerged: that the charges were raised by the Narragansetts in order to seize regional power from the Pequots. When the Pequots refused the Massachusetts Bay Colony's demands, the colony prepared to move against them for violating the treaty and repudiating colonial authority. The Narragansetts then convinced the English to make the preemptive strike against the Pequots—the notorious Mystic massacre—and agreed to take part in the operation. They would play a major role in the dreadful event, just as they were themselves deeply implicated in the murders that precipitated the attack in the first place.[26]

After the war, the Narragansetts, led by the sachem Miantunnomoh, spent two days working out a peace and trade treaty with Boston's governor and magistrates. Though not imposed, it was an agreement clearly fashioned to colonial specifications and even with an eye toward founding the Confederation of New England Colonies that the Bay Colony had begun—to this point unsuccessfully—to push. It declared a commitment to "[a] firm peace" with the Indians that would include "us and our friends of other plantations (if they consent)." It was to last "to the posterity of both [the American and the colonial] parties" (J, 191–92), a formulation notably different from the *kaswentha* formulas. Two years later, in 1638, the agreement was reinforced when Miantunnomoh and the Narragansetts made a treaty at Hartford with the colony of Connecticut and the Mohegans under the leadership of Uncas. A peace and trade alliance built on the spoils of the Pequot War, it divided up the Pequot lands, with the Pequot survivors being sold as slaves or dispersed among the Narragansetts and Mohegans.[27]

Since 1634 the Massachusetts Bay Colony had been trying to manage the trade rivalries between the regional tribes. Initially the discussions involved the Narragansetts and the Pequots, a rivalry that was settled in 1636 with the destruction of the Pequots. But with the emergence of Miantunnomoh and the Narragansetts in a position of power, another rivalry developed with Uncas and the Mohegans, who had initially sided with the Narragansetts against the Pequots. Winthrop reported the charge, brought by Uncas and his supporters, that Miantunnomoh was violating the treaties of 1634 and 1636 and seeking to unite the regional tribes in a war against the colonists (J, 408–12). Miantunnomoh successfully defended himself when, in September 1642, he was called to the Bay Colony to answer the Mohegan charges. But from that point the Narragansetts and the Mohegans were repeating the struggle of 1634–36 between the Pequots and the Narragansetts. Massachusetts's treatying statecraft was helping to create other wars among the Americans.

This volatile situation finally allowed the Bay Colony to persuade the other colonies of the region to establish the New England Confederation for their mutual defense in May 1643. When open war between the Narragansetts and the Mohegans broke out that summer, the colonists were persuaded by Uncas that Miantunnomoh was pursuing a treacherous plot against the colonies like the one he had previously carried out against the Pequots—"a general conspiracy among the Indians to cut off all the English" (J, 472). In a decisive battle, Uncas defeated the Narragansetts and captured Miantunnomoh. Because the charges against Miantunnomoh were unproven and in fact probably false, the colony could not legally act against him and certainly could not execute him. In what may have been its most disgraceful public act, it turned Miantunnomoh over to Uncas, who murdered the sachem in August 1643 on the road "between Hartford and Windsor . . . clav[ing] his head with a hatchet, some English being present" (J, 473).

Two years later, in August 1645, New England history repeated itself in a treaty that the New England Confederation, led by the Bay Colony, made with the Narragansetts, the Mohegans, and the Niantics (allies of the Mohegans at that point). Mirroring the treaty the Bay Colony made in 1634, it aimed to halt the violent tribal rivalries that were threatening the stability of the colonies.[28] By now Uncas had replaced Miantunnomoh as the colonial ally, and the Narragansetts were put on notice that the colonies were prepared to deal forcefully with any threat to the stability of their plantations.

Internal and external conditions in New England were very different from those in Virginia. The Bay Colony took a strong line with the fractious Americans, but they resorted to "Conquest" only after they had tried to work out other means of coexistence. Conquest proved an attractive option in Virginia because the colonists were dealing with a more consolidated American presence.[29] But for all their differences, Virginia and Massachusetts adopted Indian policies that exacerbated the problems they were trying to control. Between 1634 and 1676 native Americans discovered that the New England colonies—Massachusetts Bay in particular—were unreliable treatymakers, though of course the colonists judged that the Americans were at fault. So the colonists' recurrent fear of a consolidated native resistance drew out a matching native realization of the colonies' expansionist plans. Both colonial fears and native misgivings climaxed in the Great Narragansett War, now almost always called King Philip's War. But its Indian name is more pertinent because it underscores the shape of the region's history from the founding of Plymouth in 1620. The war was led by Metacom—the second son of Massasoit, the Wampanoag sachem who engineered the first (1621) treaty with New England colonists—and Canoncet, the son of Miantunnomoh.

From 1634 on treaty-making in the New England region was not imposed, but its authority was decisively colonial. So while the colonies—in particular the Bay Colony—assumed responsibility for maintaining regional order, the treaty-making actually kept stoking violence by exploiting and even reinforcing tribal differences. When Massasoit and a band of his people were arrested and tried for trespassing in 1649, Metacom and the tribes allied with the Wampanoag Confederacy could not imagine that the treaty Massasoit arranged in 1621—a *kaswentha* treaty—still had any force. At the same time, with the execution of Miantunnomoh and the emergence of Uncas and the Mohegans as the colonists' chief native ally, the Narragansetts, the Niantics, and other regional tribes could see how far colonial expansionist policies had advanced.

Both the Great Narragansett War in New England and Bacon's Rebellion in Virginia broke out in mid-1675 and precipitated major changes in the English approach to treating with the Americans from Casco Bay to the Cape Fear River. Perhaps even more significant was the final Anglo-Dutch War, which was carried on for ten years until in 1674 the Dutch surrendered their New Netherland colonies to British control. The war in New England and the civil war in Virginia caught the Crown's attention by exposing the dangerously fragile relations that prevailed between her colonies and the American nations. From the Crown's point of view, Virginia and the New England colonies had clearly failed to treat successfully with the Indians. Having for decades left these colonies largely to their own devices, the king and his ministers began working toward more centralized control from London.

In addition, with the New Netherland colonies now in English hands, the king established the proprietary colony of New York and appointed Edmund Andros governor in 1674. From the beginning, Andros continued to cultivate close relations with the Iroquois League, which for years had been treating with the Dutch in the *kaswentha* model first established at the Treaty of Tawagonshi. The upshot was a series of treaty negotiations that began shortly after the English first took power in 1664 and carried forward into the 1680s. These were the first of the Covenant Chain treaties that would dominate British colonial treaty-making for the next hundred years.[30] After his appointment, Andros quickly drove a series of complex negotiations with the League and other tribes in their orbit of power as well as with the authorities of New England, Maryland, Virginia, and the American nations of their regions.

In 1677 Albany was the seat of the Council Fire for Covenant Chain treaty-making, but it moved to eastern Pennsylvania after the Iroquois League turned to William Penn and his agents for treaty-making leadership. Penn's treaty-makings, particularly with the Delaware nation, set a model for fair dealing that proved broadly influential for both the native Americans, especially the Iroquois League, and the fractious colonies. Indeed, Penn's treaty-makings achieved legendary status quite early, as we know from the story of the Penn Treaty Elm, the mythic account of Penn's negotiations in the early 1680s with the Delaware chief Tamenend. But like Massasoit's lament over the legend of the Plymouth settlement, Tamenend would regret the land arrangements he was making for his people.[31] Both of those obscure(d) events throw a useful light on how John Modern's "secular imaginary" has made a clearer view of American history difficult to achieve.

We also get a better view—in this case, a more uplifting view—from the early documents preserved in *The Livingston Indian Records, 1666–1723*. Their picture of colonial and American intercourse differs dramatically from nearly all British colonial accounts of the previous fifty years.[32] Treatyings in these records do not gravitate toward stipulative documentation; rather, they come as pressing and quite elaborate conversations—treaty*ing* events—between parties eager to address and solve common disputes. The earliest records come from a moment, 1666–77, when the Dutch and the English were negotiating together in a region where colonial authority was passing from the Dutch to the British. Though the records are in English, they are all noted as having been "translated from the Dutch." The history of Dutch treaty-making with the Iroquois League and other regional nations is manifest.

The very first document, dated February 1666 from Albany, is a "[p]roposal made by the Chiefs of the Maquas [Mohawks]," the keepers of the Eastern Gate of the Iroquois League.[33] Warning the Dutch and the English that the French and their Indian allies are "on their way" south with a war party from Canada, the Maquas ask for help from their colonial allies. "Brethren," they say, "we do not wish to insist, but you cannot desert us now," because the entire "country is in danger." This is so because, they point out, "the French have let us know through the Senecas that they want to make peace with us" and hence undermine the security of the Dutch and the English, their colonial allies. But "[w]e do not believe" their peace overtures, they declare, and so they remain loyal to their past promises.

Although this proposal is not itself part of an immediate treaty-making, it clearly picks up on previous treaty-making (what it calls "a covenant [?]... promised last year in July").[34] The initial documents in the Livingston Papers dating from 1666–77 underscore how invested the different parties are and continue to be in treaty arrangements that are not only ongoing, but require the kind of personal, face to face engagements here on display.[35] In July 1677 the Onondagas directly addressed the colonials who had come from Maryland and Virginia to attend the Albany conference. "Exhort[ing] us to ye peace," they declare,

> we are so mynded, bot doe acknowledge yt wee have killed of yor Christians & Indians formely.... Bot wee desyre now yt all wch is past may be hurried in oblivion and doe make now ane absolut Covenant of peace wch we shall bind wth a chayn for the Sealing of ye Same doe give ane band [of wampum] of Therten deep.[36]

Even more personal is the record of the Mohawks' August 1677 treaty declaration:

> wee are one, and one hart and one head, for the Covenant that is betwixt ye Govr: Genll: and us is Inviolable yea so strong yt if ye very Thunder should break upon ye Covenant Chayn it wold not break it in Sunder.[37]

And to underscore the depth of their commitments,

> They Sing a song after thar maner being thar method of a new Covenant: maid wch they doe undertake to hold firm beeing ye first tym they have Seine any Authorized from Mary Land and Virginia, and... They doe Sing ane oyr Song The meaning whereof is yt ther people might not forgett what is past.[38]

Exchanges of this kind would soon become a regular feature of Covenant Chain treaty-making, though they were not always recorded in the colonial records. As the British imperial drive took over in regions where they had earlier had little presence, the English were learning new ways of treating with their American neighbors (and unlearning habits that had been ingrained in Virginia from the start, and that the Massachusetts Bay Colony quickly acquired).

As it happened, the experience of the Plymouth settlers might have taken the New England colonies in a very different direction, for the settlers had a full encounter with *kaswentha* treaty-making in 1620–21. But as T. S. Eliot might have said, although they had the experience, they mostly missed the meaning. With the founding of the Bay Colony in 1630, separatist Plymouth was slowly drawn to see New England through Massachusetts's more stern and expansionist eyes. This change is clearly recorded in the second part of William Bradford's *Of Plimoth Plantation*,[39] which he began writing in 1644, by which time his assessment of the Puritan errand had grown quite dark.

The Indian wars of the seventeenth and eighteenth centuries show how proprietary control of the land could change hands and that the extent of one's control could shift, grow, or shrink. Control was often gained by the exercise of power, whether military, political, or both. But it could be acquired as well if a recognized authority such as Massasoit "willingly" granted either usufruct rights—which is what Massasoit was doing—or even surrendered ruling prerogatives, which the Iroquois and other eastern tribes would do in the period of the Covenant Chain treaties.

But even under those conditions, the autonomy of the parties was a recognized—and for many, perhaps most, of the English, an unfortunate—fact on the ground. The Indians could and did swiftly reassert their own rights and obligations, often with violence, if they saw their way of life imperiled. The Powhatan Wars, the Pequot War, the Great Narragansett War: in each case the English claim was denied, and the Indian counterclaim did not lose force or relevance when the resistance failed. When the Canajoharie Mohawks renounced the Covenant Chain itself—in 1753, almost seventy-five years after the Chain was first forged—the Crown was so disturbed that it immediately summoned seven of the nine colonies and the Iroquois League to the Albany Congress of 1754.[40] The Crown was desperate to restore the Chain, since France and England were on the brink of their decisive imperial struggle—the Seven Years' War—over the continent their empires wanted to control.

The last historical record we have of Massasoit shows how quickly the character of English emigration and settlement changed between 1621 and 1649. In treating with Massasoit the settlers finessed an issue of great consequence for everyone involved: land sovereignty. Everything we know of Bradford suggests how little attention he gave to this matter, although for the merchants who funded the Plymouth adventure and their agents it was of paramount importance. For Massasoit it was simply a nonissue.

Every native cultural document—story, legend, myth, history—assumes or positively argues that land was not an alienable commodity in the native economies of America.

Nothing shows more dramatically Massasoit's view of the world as what happened to him in 1649. He was arrested and tried for trespassing on his own land.[41] The treaty he had made almost thirty years before did not mean what he thought it had meant: that he and the English settlers would share the use of the land so long as the sun and moon should last. He was arrested because land was not the Earth, it was property. "What is this you call property?" Massasoit asked the Crown authorities. "It cannot be the earth. For the land is our Mother . . . the woods, the streams, everything on it belongs to everybody and is for the use of all."[42] Like nearly every Indian spokesman who would come after him, Massasoit did not recognize the European concept of sovereignty at all. For Massasoit, the land itself was a sovereign source. A sachem could assign administrative authority over land in his dominion, which is what was involved in the 1621 treaty, and he could make outright gifts. In each case, however, he was granting a privilege—he was not relinquishing shared use.

The incident is also the first instance where we see the important difference between treaty-making—especially with respect to the *kaswentha* treaties—and the documents that the settlers fashioned from them. While these white and European American records were regarded as "the treaties" by the men who drew them up, they did not reflect what the Indians understood from their face-to-face negotiations. And while the settlers often made these records in good faith, they also often used them to modify what had been agreed to. Such duplicity would come to be called by the Indians "pen and ink witchcraft."[43]

Massasoit's querulous reflection on the unforeseen consequences of his treaty-making with the English exposes just how fortuitous the initial success of the Plymouth plantation had been. The colonists in 1620–21 were fulfilling obligatory native ceremonial negotiations, even though they did not fully understand the significance of what they were doing or how it was being interpreted by the Wampanoags. Soon enough, however—the founding of the Bay Colony was decisive—the dangers implicit in the drive to settle the country became clear.

Covenant Chain treaty-making developed in the late 1670s in the Middle Colonies as an effort to address these problems on a broad scale. It would prove remarkably successful for some forty years. But like all the treaty-makings that came before, the Covenant Chain model harbored its own contradictions, as we see in both Massasoit's 1649 lament and Tamenend's 1685 regrets. *Kaswentha*'s promise of maintaining "separate but equal" cooperation with the Europeans was a native-born invention designed to mitigate violence among peoples with shared neolithic lifeways. The dismal fate of the 1620–21 treaty at Plymouth, recorded in a 1649 New England court, would echo through all the Covenant Chain treaty-makings, faintly at first but far more loudly as time passed. Its perfect expression came when the betrayal of the Delaware nation by the United States was recorded in the Treaty of Fort Pitt (1778). But in this history of land and violence, the Indian nations never ceased to resist land encroachment or to assert their claims of sovereignty.

Few events bring greater clarity to this often dreary history than the early eighteenth-century dispute between the Wabanaki (Abenaki), the French, the Bay Colony, and the English Crown.[44] Briefly, conflict arose following the Treaty of Utrecht in 1713, which ended Queen Anne's War (the War of the Spanish Succession). Although the Wabanaki took no part in the treaty-making, the French and English settled between themselves their rival claims to what were Wabanaki lands. The Wabanaki protested the settlement and finally called a meeting of the various parties in July 1721. When Governor Samuel Shute of the Massachusetts Bay Colony refused to attend, the Wabanaki wrote him a letter stating their claims and grievances.[45]

The letter reveals two matters of great importance to this discussion, one relating to the Wabanaki, the other to the English. First, it shows that while the Wabanaki did not oppose English settlement as such, they denied the English claim that settlements had been ratified by legal purchase. The settlement land was permitted as a gift exchange: "our lands have [not] been purchased," they wrote to Governor Shute; "what has been alienated was by our gift." In a series of vigorous representations to the English authorities—"insolent," in the English view—the Wabanaki made it clear that they alone had the authority to decide whether and where settlement could happen.

Second, when the English received the letter it contained a Wabanaki claim about "my land which I have received from God only, my land which no King or foreign power could have or can dispose of against my will." But as Saliha Belmessous remarks, "In the English translation kept in the Colonial Archives, that claim has...been...simply deleted."[46] The move was one that the English came regularly to adopt in what John G. Reid has described as "a full-blown system of parallel diplomacies."[47] In this case, English "pen and ink witchcraft" for modifying oral treaty agreements turned state's evidence of their own malpractice.

In his many essays that address the frontier, Frederick Jackson Turner does not mention Indian treaties. The closest he comes is a brief discussion of the Albany Congress of 1754.[48] Accepting the colonial view that the frontier was "the meeting point between savagery and civilization" in a "land which has no history," Turner imagines Americans acquiring an exceptional character through repeated struggles to civilize a howling wilderness. He argues that the colonies that stood against England in the Revolution were exploiting their "previous cooperation in the regulation of the frontier." What he means is that the frontier served as "a military training school, keeping alive the power of resistance to aggression, and developing the stalwart and rugged qualities of the frontiersman."[49] It is entirely, perhaps even ludicrously, appropriate that Turner would represent a company of New World invaders as the victims of aggression. Many of the colonial leaders in New England and Virginia had seen long service in the military training schools of Europe—for the English colonials, in England's long-running campaigns to subjugate the "savage" Irish.

Not only did Turner imagine America as a land without a history; it was "a zone of free land" that could be had for the taking.[50] But those ideas, as we know, were brought to America from Europe, as was the expertise in prosecuting war, including total war. But cooperation in frontier violence was not an exceptional event for any of the players, neither the Americans nor the European invaders. The rise of the power of the Iroquois League was significant for precisely that reason. *Kaswentha* treaty-making was an innovation not only for the American nations but even more for the English immigrants trying to establish settlements in America.

When the colonists consciously adopted *kaswentha* as their vehicle for political negotiation, they were explicitly working with a neolithic institution to advance their early modern Western economic and political goals. I use that enlightened term "neolithic" to underscore the truly exceptional difficulties, and opportunities, that such an arrangement created for the English colonials. The fundamental European distinction between what could count as "savage" and what as "civilized" was compromised by the form of intercourse that the parties were adopting. Notably, however, the native party did not labor under a burden in the exchange, because their points of social and political friction—their violent encounters—did not map onto a binary view of savage versus civilized.

A political mechanism based in subsistence economics and forged by Stone Age peoples proved an imperative for the practice of English colonial settlement in the New World. That political organization, which reflected a polytheistic belief in the sovereignty of the biosphere, was at odds with monotheistic conceptions and institutional practices, especially as they were being recalculated after Karl Polanyi's "Great Transformation."[51] Negotiation became both more difficult and more complex over time and, after King William's War, more urgent and dangerous.

Because circumstance rather than ideology brought the colonials to treaty-making, their participation in the native ceremonies required conformity but not faith. Belief in European progress and civilization—both religious and secular—remained and in colonial society even outgrew its place of origin. When circumstances changed after 1776, the colonists began almost at once to turn away from treaty-making to the extravagant violence of "the first way of war" they had brought to America from Ireland and Europe.[52] The end of clasped-hands treatying was unmistakably signaled with the Sullivan Campaign of 1779, when Washington ordered an invasion of the Iroquois heartland "to lay waste all the settlements around with instructions to do it in the most effectual manner, that the country may not be merely overrun but destroyed."[53]

But the native peoples of North America remained committed to a different view of civilization. Fundamental to this view was a subsistence-oriented political economy grounded in seasonal rhythms, cyclic temporalities, and the sovereignty of the natural world. Drawn as they were into the European fur trade and—even more threatening—land cessions, the native populations grew increasingly complicit in the destruction of their traditional habitat and *habitus*.

At the same time, the emigrants to America would be increasingly affected by a nativist ethos. The influence was almost inevitable, for the colonists had been forced to treat directly with the Americans on native terms for almost two hundred years. The influence did not begin to gain serious traction until the emerging republic made the destruction of Indian civilizations public policy. At that point critical reflection on the significance of native American civilizations became both a practical necessity and an imaginative option.

James Fenimore Cooper realized that the documents of American barbarism—the gift-exchange rituals and clasped-hands treaties—were transmitting important messages to downstream America, messages that Cooper, in the subtitle of *The Pioneers*, rubricated as "The Sources of the Susquehanna."[54] In deploying that riverine figure, Cooper was thinking less about a complex river system and more about a territory where violent American history unfolded. But still, he was thinking of the watershed. Indeed, his environmental consciousness is in certain respects deeper than Thoreau's because it was much more attuned to, or at least more explicit about, the contentious political issues. Human and ecological loss in Cooper cannot be turned to transcendental or personal account because, as his American tales repeatedly show, the natural and the human losses are inseparably connected.

Consider *The Last of the Mohicans*, which ends with an elaborate condolence ceremony that underscores both its native authority and now—alas for Cooper—its mythic character. Presiding over the ceremony is the Delaware sachem Tamenend (ca. 1625–ca. 1701), whose negotiations with

William Penn would be fashioned into a pious American legend of Indian and colonial treaty-makings of peace and friendship. But in *The Last of the Mohicans* Tamenund (as Cooper spelled it) is a ghost, having died a half century before the date of Cooper's "Narrative of 1757." The reenactment of the Iroquois condolence ceremony that closes the book is itself a spectral event, as we see when Colonel Munro, mourning the deaths of Uncas and of his own child Cora, addresses the assembly. "The time shall not be distant," Munro dreams, "when we may assemble ... without distinction of sex, or rank, or color." To this Cooper appends Leatherstocking's mordant gloss: "The scout listened to the tremulous voice in which the veteran delivered these words, and shook his head slowly when they were ended, as one who doubted their efficacy. "To tell them this," he said, "would be to tell them that the snows come not in the winter, or that the sun shines fiercest when the trees are stripped of their leaves" (chap. 33). *The Last of the Mohicans* ends in a *kaswentha* condolence ceremony of peace and friendship that Cooper's work remembers but disbelieves, and his career from *The Last of the Mohicans* (1826) to *The Crater* (1847) follows an arc of deepening skepticism. A long line of American imaginative reflection will inherit and rework the unhappy conscience that pervades Cooper's work, not least of all signal works from the great sentimental tradition stretching from *Hobomok* and *Hope Leslie* to *The House of Mirth* and *My Ántonia*. In "Edgar Poe's Significance," Whitman discovered in Poe's "dark romanticism" a diagnosis of "the malady of America."[55] Poe, Melville, Twain, Henry Adams, the late Henry James of *The American Scene*: in each we read the tormented renunciation of the exceptional American Dream unexpectedly revealed with aboriginal contact and then carried forward through the racist economics that sustained the plantations of America.

Paradoxically, the Dream would survive and mutate wonderfully through those confessions of betrayal and disbelief. Even the Belle of Amherst made her work a mirror, and herself an index, of her Strange Nation's contradictory estrangements.[56] We do not forget her letter of June 11, 1852 to her beloved Susan. Reflecting on the Whig convention in Baltimore being torn apart over the question of slavery, Dickinson added a mordant postscript: "'Delenda est' America, Massachusetts and all!" And then came the letter's famous last words, warning Susan to "open me carefully" lest her forlorn testament shock her friend or, perhaps, her father, who was attending the convention and was carrying the letter to Susan. A great American Apostate's Creed, those two sentences could be an epigraph for the internal exile she chose, the world elsewhere she imagined and lived.[57]

PART I
Puritan Enlightenment: *Via Dolorosa*
Prologue

Because the New England colonial reformers were so preoccupied with "spiritual things"—matters of life and death—the practical and always conflicted demands of "ciuill and ecclesiasticall" institutions set mortal measures for their realization. Isaac Ambrose's oft-reprinted *Media: The Middle Things in relation to the first and last things* (1637) is typical of the reform ethos that shaped the Puritan archive.[1] *Media* is an enormous how-to manual for managing a religious life in a day-to-day world: "the Means, Duties, Ordinances, both Secret, Private, and Publick; for Continuance, and Increase of a Godly Life." On the specific topic "Reading the Word" (chap. 15), Ambrose writes that "[t]he end of studying the Scriptures is not only knowledge, but practice."[2] He then unfolds an extended discussion—under nine "heads" and with numerous examples—"Of the Use of these Collections" of scripture.

Ambrose was describing the common practical pursuit of the Puritan errand and its literary Media: the establishment of covenantal communities. He calls this work "Media," which includes his own book so named, because it is carried out within the framework of universal prophetic history ("first and last things"). No matter what happens in the occasional *now*, at any given *now* the "modell" of God's redemptive work is finished. That is one of the Puritans' firm perspectives on their place in the world. It was less a mortal experience of the world, however, than a confession, a testimony to the evidence of things not seen.

The Puritans had another, very different perspective. Within the pragmatic horizon of immediate experience, nothing is finished. Indeed, everything important and practical—the spiritual errand—seems at stake and in constant peril. No one has read Puritan literature without registering that peculiar spiritual intensity, the aptly named Puritan Ordeal.[3] Immediate life is driven by divine promise and threatened by absolute failure. As the foundations are laid in and built up, individuals and their communities struggle with their own internal contradictions and uncertain historical circumstances. The spiritual life of the Puritan reformers is a quotidian emergency.

To say that a work such as "A Modell of Christian Charity" is "the first great communitarian statement in American literature" or that the *Magnalia Christi Americana* "is an important work of the figural imagination" is to mark both as what Matthew Arnold called cultural "touchstones."[4] But to read them that way is to edit out some of their intransigent truth. Far better to approach them as that profound bibliophile Walter Benjamin did when he wrote about our "documents of civilization."[5] Although from a certain perspective a seventeenth-century view of these works could be judged a dead-letter view, they might matter most to us now if we tried to read them as they mattered to their authors. Every word of their Puritan truth and address is either stalked by fear or haunted by failure.

We have often been told that this is an impossible way to read, and the charge is true. But it is also an imperative way to read, and not merely because it was the way of these strange men and women of that time and place. Andrew Delbanco writes so movingly of the "fleetingness" of the Puritan aspiration because he knows this so well. Thinking specifically of John Winthrop and the Bay Colony, he tells us that the *Arbella* sermon is itself "the best measure of how quickly and how far [they] fell" from the sermon's "great communitarian statement": "That man can truly be remade . . . into an image of a generous God."[6] Delbanco was recalling the colony's plunge into the politico-religious conflicts that would splinter the New England settlements, as well as the more ominous later events involving Quaker persecutions and, finally, the Salem witch trials. Though "A Modell of Christian Charity" is a promise of Christian love, far more severe things would fall out from the Puritan errand, and not only for the anathematized American Canaanites. In lamenting that plunge, Delbanco was pleading for the resurrection of what he judged the "true" Puritan commitment to a generous, rather than a jealous, God. But the generosity of that God, his saving grace, could not be known, only believed. There is no evidence for things not seen; there is only testimony.

That is why disputes over the published word, whether preached or printed, are a regular, even dominant feature of seventeenth-century colonial intercourse. That is also why, for Protestant reformers, no biblical text was more important, more uplifting, than 2 Corinthians 3:3–6. Paul celebrates the Church at Corinth by saying that its members are the living words of Christ's truth, "written not with ink, but with the Spirit of the living God; not in tables of stone, but in fleshy tables of the heart." Paul's Corinthians are themselves "the new testament; not of the letter, but of the spirit; for the letter killeth, but the spirit giveth life."

But as that exemplary Puritan Isaac Ambrose repeatedly insisted, the spirit's letters were delivered not only in traditional oral and documentary media and "ciuill and ecclesiasticall" ordinances, but on the fleshy tablets of the human heart, which was, as God Himself had declared, "only evil continually" (Genesis 6:5). "Are... Prayers, Mournings, and other Divine Exercises in any sort sinful?" Ambrose asks. "Yes," he says, for there is some mixture of Man's Infirmity in them; "for *all our righteousness is as filthy rags... Albeit our good Works are perfect, in respect of the Spirit... yet are they polluted when they pass from us, because they run through our corrupted Hearts and Wills, as Fair Water runs through a dirty channel.*"[7]

Being mortal and therefore fallible instruments, all the Puritan documents, ordinances, and institutions distort divine truth, the Living Word secreted away within the dead letter. Inspired by Paul's poetic figure, the Reformers assumed an impossible task: to build a spiritual city on an actual American hill, to lift regenerate life out of frail and corrupt flesh.[8]

"The letter killeth": for the Puritan heart, and perhaps even more for the Puritan mind, focused as they were on *sola scriptura*, that famous text is a strait gate. It calls to attention the daily—the spiritually imperative—experience of the killing failures of a practical mortal life. Access to the living spirit of the reformers' errand had to be through a literal gate of Ambrosian media that they were duty bound to reinscribe in hearts that were faint without the free gift of God's grace. "It is a sign that a Man rests in his Duties," Ambrose wrote, "if he never came to be sensible of their Poverty, and utter Emptiness of any Good in them."[9] Has there ever been a better, more succinct, or more piteous description of the spirit driving the Puritan errand?

CHAPTER FOUR

William Bradford: The Diary (1620–21), the History (*Of Plymouth Plantation*), and the Hebrew Studies

Bradford's daybook runs from September 6, 1620 to June 18, 1621, with the core account beginning on November 13, 1620, two days after the pilgrims landed at Cape Cod. It has a kind of coda or appendix: a letter of December 11, 1621 written from the colony by Edward Winslow to an English supporter of the *Mayflower* expedition, almost certainly George Morton. "Bradford's Relation" and Winslow's letter were composed in situ during the first year of colonial settlement (November 1620–December 1621). Both were included with five other texts printed in 1622 in *Mourt's Relation*, which printed the daybook from Bradford's manuscript.[1] But while the printed diary reproduced Bradford's text, the two documents were very different. This is apparent even though Bradford's manuscript, which was setting copy for the print text, is not extant. Bradford composed the daybook as an aide-mémoire for an event he saw as a momentous one for reformed religion. His daybook and Winslow's letter presented a sanguine account of the first year. Bradford enthused over the region's resources and took special care to show the "savages" as helpful and accommodating to the settlers. The daybook thus presented a sharp contrast to the grim reports coming back to England about the disasters in the Virginia colony. Therefore, when the merchant adventurers who were financing Plymouth read Bradford's daybook, they commissioned Morton and another Leiden agent, Robert Cushman, to compose promotional copy—the other five documents in *Mourt's Relation*—advertising Plymouth as an attractive commercial opportunity. But Bradford's relations with those investors were never friendly, because he knew they were interested in money, whereas for him Plymouth was a religious venture. After the founding, as is clear from *Of Plymouth Plantation*, he deplored how many of the new emigrants were largely coming with mercenary rather than religious goals in view.[2]

Two other features of the daybook are even more arresting: its narrative of the colony's relations with the Indians and the treaty that emerged from their intercourse. Because of the daybook's seriatim and day-by-day focus, we can now see a remarkable truth about Bradford's report: for some three months he was recording events that, while they appear in the diary as random, were part of a design orchestrated not by God—though that was Bradford's belief—but by the Wampanoag sachem Massasoit. It was a careful scheme to settle an unresolved six-year blood feud in which these new colonists, as Englishmen, had been unknowingly involved even before they landed.

To appreciate the secret history recorded in Bradford's diary, we have to respect the immediacy of the narrative. Our later perspective lets us see what escapes Bradford in his day-by-day account.

Here is what Bradford reports. During the first month of arrival the emigrants see evidence of native presence everywhere: food caches, burial grounds, deserted villages and agricultural fields. But the Indians avoid the settlers, and the daybook finds their behavior puzzling because the Indians' absence seems deliberate. In early December the uneventful first month is suddenly broken when a party of Indians attacks the settlement. However, it is a brief event, there are no casualties, and afterward the colony quickly returns to its basic routines. The diary records no more hostile acts against the settlers.

After the December attack the diary resumes its uneventful record: reports of stormy weather; of Indians heard but not seen, or seen but not heard ("We saw great smokes of fire made by the Indians, about six or seven miles from us"; *MRJPP*, 68); of the settlers gathering thatch, shooting an eagle, "finding alive upon the shore a herring," fishing for cod; of different plans for building houses, of people falling sick; of two settlers getting lost in the forest, being searched for in vain, and eventually finding their way back:

> Saturday, 20th [of January, 1621], we made up our shed for our common goods.
> Sunday, the 21st, we kept up our meeting on land.
> Monday, the 22nd, was a fair day. We wrought on our houses; and in the afternoon we carried up our hogsheads of meal to our common storehouse. The rest of the week we followed our business as usual. (*MRJPP*, 78)

Two months later, on February 16, there is a surprising event. A party of "twelve Indians" is seen near the plantation and "many more" are heard "in the woods." Something important seems afoot, and the diary grows more expansive. When Myles Standish and Francis Cooke return from the forest, they find that "their tools were taken away" from their houses, and the community determines to "keep more strict watch" for native presence. The next day two Indians suddenly appear "on the top of a hill, over against our plantation . . . and made signs unto us to come unto them." But when Captain Standish and Stephen Hopkins "went towards them . . . the savages would not tarry their coming" and quickly disappeared (*MRJPP*, 79–81).

An event that briefly seemed significant passes into apparent inconsequence. What the events of February 16–17 *meant*, if anything, is unclear to Bradford, and the daybook proceeds to record another uneventful month. But on the morning of March 16, as the company is preparing certain military arrangements, suddenly "there presented himself a savage . . . [who] very boldly came alone" into the plantation, where he bade the emigrants "*Welcome*" (*MRJPP*, 82–83).

Because we are reading a diary, the significance of its recorded events typically emerge after the fact. Only much later in the daybook do we learn this man's name, Samoset, and his mission. He is an advance diplomatic agent sent to "welcome" the English strangers to the domain of Massasoit, the Wampanoag sagamore. Thus the significance of his visit begins to emerge. Samoset is himself a notable sachem, he says, but "was not of these parts" (he was in fact a Wabanaki and only contingently allied with the Wampanoag Confederacy). Nonetheless, though from an adjacent region, he is Massasoit's initial representative to the English and therefore—a point that we have to infer and that Bradford will have to learn to appreciate—one of Massasoit's dependent subjects. As such, he is a living index of Massasoit's extensive power. The boldness of Samoset's entrance and address leads to another inference: that he is unintimidated by the settlers and confident of the authority he represents.

Besides welcoming the English and introducing them to Massasoit's domain, Samoset gives an account of a recent plague that decimated the native population (thus finally explaining the deserted fields and villages reported earlier in the daybook). Most important, Samoset wants to recall and explain "the *huggery*, that is, [the] fight" the pilgrims had with Indians in December. The attack, Bradford now learns, was part of a long and complex history of violent encounter. It was carried out not by the Wampanoags but by "The Nausites" who were "ill affected toward the English by reason of one [Captain Thomas] Hunt," a disreputable trader who six years earlier had seized some two dozen Nausets and sold them into slavery, a crime the Nausets had neither forgotten nor forgiven. Indeed, Samoset explains that several months before the pilgrim landing, being once again "incensed and provoked" by certain English traders, the Nausets "slew three Englishmen" and sent two others to flight. Like the "huggery" in December, the murder was revenge for the unforgotten and—most important—unrequited Hunt atrocities of 1614. Samoset also recalls a smaller, more recent incident: the Nauset theft of Standish and Cooke's tools (*MRJPP*, 85–86).

Because Bradford gives an extensive report of what Samoset says, we know he is eager to divine Samoset's meaning and intentions. At the same time, because he doesn't offer an interpretation (either in the daybook or later in *Of Plymouth Plantation*), we only know for certain that Bradford recognized the visit as a welcoming one. But he must have begun to understand the deeper import of Samoset's declarations, meanings that a reader now is even better positioned to see: that the English bear a responsibility for what the Nausets had done, that Massasoit and the Wampanoags are not directly responsible, and, crucially, that Massasoit's position is such that he has both the authority and the willingness to step into this hostile scene and perhaps defuse it.

Although in early 1621 Bradford could hardly have grasped the native politics implicit in Samoset's report, succeeding months threw them into much sharper focus and, as the daybook shows, led Bradford to appreciate the value of Massasoit's initiative and the treaty-making that it had set in motion. Although the Nausets were Wampanoag tributaries, each tribe in native confederacies had considerable independence in matters that affected them directly. At the same time, as head sachem Massasoit was expected by the tribes to protect the interests of the entire league.

In *Of Plymouth Plantation*'s later narrative, the Americans are a secondary concern for Bradford, even when they figure prominently in the action.[3] Unlike his diary, Bradford's history book focuses on the pilgrim community and on what Bradford sees as its historic religious struggle and mission in the world. The contemporary 1620–21 daybook account is completely different. It focuses on how the pilgrims made their way in a strange socioecological environment and how they established relations with the even stranger people who lived there. Bradford made it clear that the settlement would have failed had the natives not come to its aid. While he saw providential assistance in repelling the Nauset attack in December, God does not figure in his 1621 account of the key subsequent events. But a design was certainly operating. It was initiated by Massasoit and subsequently recognized and actively supported by Bradford in 1621.

The daybook provides a detailed if also an unglossed record of ritualized native American treaty-making. Various ceremonial events and gift-exchange rituals are recorded in the daybook, though not systematically. Because retaliatory acts of blood violence provided the occasion and rationale for Massasoit's ten-month cultural operation, it almost certainly involved a condolence ceremony that went unrecorded in the daybook.[4]

The first event in this drama was the attack on the settlers in December by which the Nausets announced that the blood feud involving the English remained unresolved. The next was Samoset's welcoming arrival in February to introduce the settlers to Massasoit as the region's chief political power. So machinery was being set in motion to introduce protocols of peace and friendship in a scene of inherited violence. That scene was not so much the Plymouth colony as the large domain of the great chief Massasoit, which required his attention.

Samoset was well received and was sent away with presents. He soon returned with a much larger company of natives. After another exchange of gifts, they again left, but they returned a few days later, this time with Tisquantum (Squanto). Sent—by Massasoit—to function as principal interpreter between the parties, Squanto "was one of the twenty captives who by Hunt were carried away" (*MRJPP*, 86–87). That detail is particularly striking because Squanto would be such an important presence in the continuing events. Like the director of a theatrical performance, Massasoit meant to keep Squanto a focus of attention, since his history implicitly explained what had happened and what was happening. Squanto and the latest envoys from Massasoit brought more gifts and then announced a decisive moment in the action, the most dramatic yet: "their great Sagamore, Massasoyt, was hard by" (*MRJPP*, 91).

Massasoit's visit would have been impossible without these diplomatic preparations and gift exchanges. After Samoset's second visit, according to the daybook, Edward Winslow had been sent by the colony to beg the sachem's indulgence with an array of English gifts. The success of Winslow's mission now became apparent. Accompanied by "his train of sixty men," Massasoit made a dramatic descent from a "high hill," entering the plantation with great pomp and ceremony. An elaborate reception ensued, complete with speeches, musical fanfare, and acts of obeisance. Then Bradford appeared "with drum and trumpet after him, and some few musketeers." After Massasoit and Governor John Carver kissed each other, the two "sat down together" in a ritual exchange of food and drink with "their followers" (*MRJPP*, 92–93).

At that point, in the words of the daybook, the parties began to "treat of peace," and Bradford wrote up what would be the first English documentary record of treaty-making with an American nation (*MRJPP*, 93–94). But the truth is that the treaty-making had already been operating for two or three months, and the daybook, along with Winslow's letter, would keep reporting its operation over the next eight months, culminating in November when the Bradford/Winslow record stops. Bradford's treaty document testifies to his understanding of how the relationship that Massasoit was offering had to be executed. So in June Bradford, now governor after Carver's recent death, decided to "continue the league of peace and friendship" by traveling with gifts "to Packanokik, the habitation of the great king Massasoyt." Imitating the Massasoit model, the colony sent Stephen Hopkins and Edward Winslow ahead as advance diplomatic couriers bearing gifts and an elaborate, ingratiating message (*MRJPP*, 98–100).

After they returned, the full colonial contingent set out in early July. They were welcomed and feasted along the way by the Wampanoag villages they passed through, Massasoit evidently intending to make their journey a lavish spectacle and sign of his power and glory. When the colonists arrived on July 4, the pageantry continued all day and into the next with feasting, games, and gift exchanges. Done in by Massasoit's ritual extravagances, the Puritans soon told him that they couldn't "stay any longer [lest] we should not be able to recover home for want of strength." "Grieved and ashamed that he could no better entertain us," Massasoit reluctantly let them depart (*MRJPP*, 109).

The next event recorded in the diary is the episode of John Billington, the boy who had "lost himself in the woods" (*MRJPP*, 112) apparently sometime in July.[5] In a shrewd commentary on the incident, Betty Booth Donohue shows that the rescue operation took place within a larger Indian ceremonial action.[6] The boy had been found by a party of Nausets, adopted into the tribe, and finally returned to the colonists both as a gift and as a living message of brotherhood: what Donohue calls "another, and possibly better, way of life."[7]

When we fold this event into the peace-and-friendship treaty-making that Massasoit had been arranging since December, we can see its significance. The Nausets—almost certainly with Massasoit's encouragement if not under his explicit direction—are closing the account of 1614. They had taken revenge on some English settlers a few months before the Pilgrims arrived, and now they are "deliver[ing] to us the boy, behung with beads [to] make peace with us" (*MJRPP*, 115). On the June trip to Pokanoket the colonial visitors were greeted along the way with a series of ritual celebrations in the Wampanoag villages they passed through, and now, returning to Plymouth with the sacred boy, they observe a similar pageantry of "women . . . singing and dancing" (*MRJPP*, 116).

Although "Bradford's Relation" only extends into September 1621, Edward Winslow's letter of 11 December added an important contemporary coda. The letter shows that the treatying in March–April, ratified in July, was sealed once again in November by another peace-and-friendship ceremony. Bradford organized this event—"The First Thanksgiving"—"at which, amongst other recreations, we exercised our arms, many of the Indians coming amongst us, and among the rest their greatest king, Massasoyt, with some ninety men, whom for three days we entertained and feasted" (*MRJPP*,133).

This extraordinary record of native American treaty-making has another matter of great significance hidden in plain view of its text.[8] To see it, we have to watch how Bradford used the daybook when, in 1644, he wrote up what happened on that momentous day in early spring 1621. The daybook and *Of Plymouth Plantation* both give a text of the spring treaty document and set it in its ceremonial context. But the account Bradford composed for *Of Plymouth Plantation* in 1644, which I reproduce now, differs from the daybook text.

> Being, after some time of entertainments & gifts, dismist, a while after he came againe, & 5. more with him, & they brought againe all ye tooles that were stolen away before, and made way for ye coming of their great Sachem, called *Massasoyt*; who, about 4. or 5. days after, came with the cheefe of his friends & other attendance, with the aforesaid *Squanto*. With whom, after frendly entertainment, & some gifts given him, they made a peace with him (which hath now continued this 24. years) in these terms.
>
> 1. That neither he nor any of his, should injurie or doe hurte to any of their people.
> 2. That if any of his did any hurte to any of theirs, he should send ye offender, that they might punish him.
> 3. That if any thing, were taken away from any of theirs, he should cause it to be restored; and they should doe ye like to his.
> 4. If any did unjustly warr against him, they would aide him; if any did warr against them, he should aide them.
> 5. He should send to his neighbours confederats, to certifie them of this, that they might not wrong them, but might be likewise comprised in ye conditions of peace.
> 6. That when ther men came to them, they should leave their bows & arrows behind them. (*OPP*, 115)

The 1621 and 1644 reports of this event both reflect a general understanding of the "sophisticated information systems" that Massasoit had activated.[9] But when Bradford copied his 1621 treaty document in 1644, he changed it, and one of those alterations was radical. The 1644 document removed the final item in the treaty document of 1621: "Lastly, that doing this, King James would esteem of him [Massasoit] as his friend and ally" (*MRJPP*, 94). Fundamental to native American treaty-making throughout the colonial period was the assumption of an equal authority between the treaty-making parties. In 1621 Bradford made sure that his English record reflected that assumption. But by 1644, as we shall see when we examine

Of Plymouth Plantation, Bradford and the Plymouth colony had begun to adopt the Bay Colony's assumption of its supremacy. In 1649 the colony authorities convicted and jailed Massasoit for trespassing on what in 1621 was part of his eminent domain.[10]

The History (*Of Plymouth Plantation*) and the Hebrew Studies

It's apparent that Bradford kept his diary partly as a detailed factual record that he might consult later should he write a more comprehensive account of the Plymouth venture. So ten years after landing in the New World he began composing *Of Plymouth Plantation* as a general history of the colony's founding. It is organized in two books. The first ten chapters were composed in 1630, the second part—chapters 11–36—fourteen years later, in 1644–46. Those different moments of composition are deeply pertinent to the testimony they present.

Book 1 tells the story of the religious wars and controversies of the late sixteenth and early seventeenth centuries; of the emigration of the Scrooby separatists from England to the Netherlands, where they hoped to find conditions favorable to their religious liberty; of the disappointment of those hopes; and finally of their second emigration, this time to the New World. It is written as a continuous narrative.

Book 2 could scarcely be more different. Abandoning the continuous history of book 1, which he wrote in 1630, Bradford in 1644 switches to a serial account arranged by years beginning "Anno 1620." The intention is to narrate the "principal things ... as they fell in order of time" (*OPP*, 180). Furthermore, while book 1 is a completed narrative, book 2 breaks off at the end of 1646, closing the work with the empty headings "Anno 1647 And Anno 1648." He returned briefly to the manuscript in 1650 to add a list of names of the original pilgrims and, sometime after that, to include the "Hebrew Exercises" I shall discuss below.

Those last words of book 2—"Anno 1647 And Anno 1648"—signal more than an accidentally truncated narrative of the kind we have, for example, in John Winthrop's *Journal*, which also broke off abruptly. While illness and then death stopped Winthrop's history in early 1649, Bradford deliberately abandoned his work while his health was good and his mind as lively as ever. So why did he stop writing? He stopped, I judge, because the story had grown too dark in the telling—"tragic" and "elegiac" are typical descriptions for Bradford's tale of "loss and failure."[11]

Book 1's narrative of the exilic years in the Netherlands proved that sojourn was a trying time. But if Leiden offered no escape from either sinful church or sinful state, it brought spiritual clarification and a revitalized faith. In Leiden the Scrooby separatists discovered what true separation from Europe and England had to mean: "deliverance," the keyword in the final pages of book 1.

Shortly after landing, the small company of pilgrims was beset with an assault of "Indians wheeling about upon them," but "it pleased God to vanquish [these] enemies and give them deliverance" (*OPP*, 104–5). The attack, in Bradford's 1630 view, was the final sign of a continuing providential oversight. When the Indians were driven off, the company "gave God thanks for His mercies in their manifold deliverances" (*OPP*, 104)—from England, from the Netherlands, from the fearful sea passage, and now yet again in a truly God-ordained place, for on setting out they were bound for Virginia. So they "sounded the harbor and found it fit for shipping, and marched into the land and found divers cornfields and little running brooks, a place ... fit for situation." It is not paradise but rather "the best that they could find," and as such "did much comfort their hearts" because "they arrived safe in this harbor." prepared for them by God (*OPP*, 106).

Bradford in 1630 fashioned this final episode of book 1, as he fashioned all of chapter 10, by drawing on his daybook, on his now more extensive memory, and on his faith. When he resumed the history in 1644, book 2's opening chapters, 11 and 12, drastically rework the years reported in the daybook. Two subjects not in the daybook were introduced that would figure prominently throughout book 2: intertribal rivalries in the settlement region, and the arrival of new settlers, "many of them wild enough, who little considered whither or about what they went" (*OPP*, 128). Around these two subjects spin nearly all the "principal things" that occupy Bradford's attention in book 2. Although Plymouth had to deal with both of these problems in the 1620s, they only became seriously dangerous in 1630s and 1640s, that is, when Plymouth began to come under the influence of the Bay Colony's more severe approach both to colonial government and settler relations with the Americans.

Bradford augmented his daybook account of Indian relations with extensive reports in chapters 11, 12, and 13 (1621 and 1622) of Narragansett threats to the colony and bloody disputes between regional nations. These reports cut back against the daybook's largely benign account of relations with the Americans and the central event in the daybook, the treaty with Massasoit. Bradford altered the treaty text as originally reported, dropping the final crucial declaration that Massasoit and the English king would be "friend and Alie" to each other. By 1644 all of New England had become contested ground and stability was largely driven by Massachusetts *realpolitik*, as we shall see. Native rivalries continued well beyond the Pequot war, driving Plymouth into the United Colonies military alliance that

Massachusetts Bay had wanted to establish since the mid-1630s and that Bradford finally ceased to resist.

The chapters also plaintively recollected the arrival, beginning in late 1621, of new settlers who were not obliged to work for the religious mission of the colony: "particulars" they were called because they came "on their own particular."[12] Especially troublesome were the parties organized by Thomas Weston, who tried and failed to found a new colony called Wessagusett, some twenty miles north of Plymouth. The venture would cause Bradford and Plymouth much grief until it failed in 1623. Replying to a captious letter Weston had sent to Governor Carver, Bradford does not hide the exasperation that runs throughout his reports on Weston and the "particulars": "[I]t is our calamity that we are (beyond expectation) yoked with some ill conditioned people, who will never do good, but corrupt and abuse others" (*OPP*, 132).

One of book 2's most plangent episodes involved "Massasoit their friend," who, Bradford learned in 1623, had fallen seriously ill (chap. 24, 1623). Bradford inserted this event in the midst of his ongoing narrative of the trouble that Weston's purely economic venture was bringing to the young settlement. Sending "to visit him [Massasoit]," Bradford wrote that he "gave him great content and was a means of his recovery." "Upon which occasion," Bradford immediately added, "he [that is, Weston] discovers the conspiracy of these Indians,"

> how they were resolved to cut off Mr. Weston's people, for the continual injuries they did them, and would now take opportunity of their weakness to do it; and for that end had conspired with other Indians their neighbours thereabout. And thinking the people hear would revenge their death, they therefore thought to do the like by them, and had solicited him to join with them. He advised them therefore to prevent it, and that speedily by some of the chief of them, before it was too late, for he assured them of the truth hereof. (*OPP*, 158)

But Weston was lying, Bradford laconically observes, for "they [Bradford and Plymouth] took it into serious consideration, and found upon examination other evidence to give light hereunto, too long here to relate" (*OPP*, 158).

Bradford began writing *Of Plymouth Plantation* in 1630 as a story of deliverance, but when he resumed it in 1644 he could see how rife with tares were the wheat fields of the Lord, for "a 'mixed multitude' came into the wilderness with the People of God out of Egypt of old (Exodus xii. 38)" (*OPP*, 477). So his history turned into a dark book of revelation: "And thus, in 20 years' time it is a question whether the greater part [of the colonial emigrants] be not grown the worser" (*OPP*, 477).

Bradford posed that question at the end of chapter 32 (1642). Chapter 33 (1643) opened with a long encomium for "my dear and loving friend Mr. William Brewster" (*OPP*, 487), whom Bradford was uplifting as a saintly example of one who "had borne his part in weal and woe with this poor persecuted church above 36 years," that is, from the Scrooby years to Brewster's death in 1644. Then came Bradford's general tribute to "the marvelous providence of God" for raising up the whole separatist company, who are presented as models of good church government, personal holiness, and theological purity (*OPP*, 494). The third and final section of the chapter then comes as a shock: "By reason of the plottings of the Narragansetts ever since the Pequots' War the Indians were drawn into a general conspiracy against the English" (*OPP*, 496). In response, the several English colonies "enter into" the military alliance that Bradford had long resisted, and Bradford recounts the tangled web of conflict in which the Narragansetts, the Mohegans, and the colonies were caught up.

As Bradford pointed out, this narrative reached back to the ugly events of 1634–38 (chapters 26–28) that ended in "the subduing of the Pequots" (*OPP*, 505), a war for which the Bay Colony bore considerable responsibility. Though they were induced to contribute to Massachusetts' war effort, Bradford and Plymouth knew they had been both deceived and betrayed by the Bay Colony. Bradford annotated Winthrop's account of the perfidy of the Pequots (in his letter of March 1634) with a note: "There is little trust to be given to [Winthrop's account of] their [the Pequots] relations in these things" (*OPP*, 417). Indeed, since 1634 Massachusetts had been secretly trying "to make [the Connecticut region] Massachusetts' exclusive possession," openly supporting French encroachments on Plymouth's early trading post in Connecticut ("and so have continued to do till this day," Bradford commented in his 1635 annal [*OPP*, 401]).[13]

Bradford's accounts of the runup to the conflict and to the war itself were heavily in debt to the reports passed along to him by Winthrop and others in the Bay Colony. His central report came in chapter 28, half of which is made up of Winthrop's far from accurate view of the war.[14] Here we register one of the most striking features of Bradford's history: his habit of augmenting his own narrative with substantial documentary material drawn from others. It was an especially shrewd move when, as often happened, Bradford was uncertain of the factual truth of the events being reported to him. So in chapter 28 he pointed out that "I shall only relate [what happened] as it is in a letter from Mr. Winthrop" (*OPP*, 427). Similarly, more than half of chapter 26 is composed of supporting documents that bear on the dismal machinations of the Bay Colony in the Connecticut valley in 1635. Bradford's summary comment—that Massachusetts' "unkindness [was] not so soon forgotten" (*OPP*, 407)—explains why

Plymouth was so reluctant to enter cooperative arrangements with the Bay Colony.

Perhaps even more striking from our later point of view, these materials are the most explicit markers of how many forces and agents were driving the events. *Of Plymouth Plantation* reflects that larger regional—and also imperial—history. It recorded how Bradford was involved in that history—accommodating, resisting, moving independently, stepping away. *Of Plymouth Plantation* is the record of Bradford's purposeful actions as they were shaped and changed by the purposes and actions of many others. The importance of those nonauthorial materials leaps to attention when we look at the many editions of the history that either remove them altogether or, as with Samuel Eliot Morison's otherwise fine (and influential) scholarly edition, relegates them to a set of appendices. The move seriously distorts our view of Bradford's work, which is one of the few colonial documents that lays bare its own intentions by nesting them in documents where other intentionalities are summoned to make clear the full range of purposes in play.

Of Plymouth Plantation is for the most part a darkening tale because the "deliverance" foreseen in 1620 and then faithfully attested in 1630 became even more sorely tried by 1644, when Bradford resumed his tale of Plymouth's response to God's providence. The leitmotif word in book 2 is "tedious," never more strikingly applied than at "the conclusion of that long and tedious business" Bradford records at the end of chapter 32 (the annal for 1642; *OPP*, 477). He was referring to the long-running dog's-meat squabble "between the partners here and them in England" over the colony's financial obligations to the merchants who were still funding the venture (*OPP*, 477). The episode made a fittingly woeful capstone to the tale Bradford set down of "the breaking out of sundry notorious sins (as this year, besides other, gives us too many sad precedents and instances)" (*OPP*, 459).

The record was so dreadful to Bradford that he offered an explanation of how these things could happen in a company living under the direction of "the powerful work and grace of God's Spirit." "Rather [than] think . . . that Satan hath more power in these heathen lands, as some have thought, than in more Christian nations," he gives three reasons for why "wickedness did grow and break forth here: first, because the devil has a "greater spite against the churches of Christ . . . here"; second, because "wickedness" being more "dammed up" in New England than elsewhere, it breaks out with especially violent "noise and disturbance"; and finally—the reason that most persuades him—because New England rectitude is so strict that it "look[s] narrowly to [its] members" and "ma[kes] public" sin that would rather lie hid (*OPP*, 459–60).

While we might now reasonably judge this as theological special pleading, it brings real insight into the touching honesty of Bradford's character. Especially striking is the way he formulates his third reason: "Besides, here the people are but few in comparison of other places, which are full and populous, and lie hid, as it were, in a wood or thicket, and many horrible evils by that means are never seen nor known; whereas here they are, as it were, brought into the light, and set in the plaine feeld, or rather on a hill, made conspicuous to the view of all" (*OPP*, 460). Though celebrated as a "sweet-tempered and heavenly minded" man,[15] as indeed the records all testify, Bradford's faith was such that he could imagine—in his judgment, had to imagine—New England as simultaneously one of the wicked cities of the plain (Genesis 13:12) *and* the city "on a hill" (Matthew 5:14) that George Phillips preached for John Winthrop and the *Arbella* colonists before they sailed in 1630.[16]

The last chapter in Bradford's history (anno 1646) has two brief records, both lamentable. The first involved the arrival into Plymouth harbor of "three ships ... in warlike order," the small pirate fleet of the "desperate fellow" Thomas Cromwell. Their brief stay brought only violence and manslaughter. Bradford closed the episode by recording how Cromwell, having "returned rich into the Massachusetts," died suddenly by what Bradford saw as "the hand of God." The second event, perhaps even more dispiriting, told of Edward Winslow's mission to seek Crown help with "some discontented persons under the government of the Massachusetts" who were "troubl[ing] their peace."[17] Here are the last words of Bradford's narrative: "he has now been absent these four years, which hath been much to the weakening of this government, without whose consent he took these employments upon him" (chap. 36). Having been Bradford's chief partner in the founding of Plymouth in 1620–21, Winslow undertook a commission from Massachusetts Bay and eventually abandoned Plymouth altogether to join with Oliver Cromwell in England. With Winslow gone, Bradford stopped writing *Of Plymouth Plantation*, though he continued as governor for ten more years.

Bradford twice returned to add supplementary materials to the history, once in 1650 and then probably two years later. One of these—the 1650 addition—is sometimes included in editions, but the other has never been, though its existence has been known and noted. Both make clear calls to bring the history back into touch with its secular and spiritual origins, and in that respect they implicitly comment on the history of Plymouth that he no longer intended to continue. In 1650 Bradford added a name list of the original passengers on the *Mayflower*, a document that recalls Bradford's eulogy of Brewster and the small company that founded the colony.

The 1652 addition is perhaps even more significant. An eight-page set of

Though I am growne aged, yet I haue had a longing desire, to see with my owne eyes, something of that most ancient Language, and holy tongue, in which the Law and oracles of god were write; and in which god, and angel's spake to the holy patriarks of old time; and what names were giuen to things, from the creation. And though I cañot attaine to much herein, yet I am refreshed, to haue seen some glimpse hereof: (as moyses saw the land of Canan afarr of) my aime and desire is to see how the words, and phrases lye in the holy texte; and to discerne somewhat of the same, for my owne contente.

חֶסֶד וַיהֹוָה מָלְאָה הָאָרֶץ	The earth is full of ye mercie of Jehouah
וַיַּרְא אֱלֹהִים כִּי טוֹב	And god saw that it was good
לֹא טוֹב הֱיוֹת הָאָדָם לְבַדּוֹ	It is not good that man should be alone
כַּבֵּד אֶת אָבִיךָ וְאֶת אִמֶּךָ	honour thy father, and thy mother
וּשְׂמַח מֵאֵשֶׁת נְעוּרֶיךָ	And rejoyce with the wife of thy youth
זְנוּת וְיַיִן וְתִירוֹשׁ יִקַּח לֵב	whordome, and wine, a new wine take away the harte
קוֹל דְּמֵי אָחִיךָ צוֹעֲקִים אֵלַי	The voyce of thy brothers blood crieth unto me
דָּן יָדִין	lying Iudge the ...

שָׁם פָּחֲדוּ פַחַד לֹא הָיָה פָחַד	Ther they feared a fear wher no fear was
הוֹן יוֹסִיף רֵעִים רַבִּים	Riches gather many friends
רַע רַע יֹאמַר הַקּוֹנֶה	It is naught, it is naught, saith the buyer
מָצָא אִשָּׁה מָצָא טוֹב	he that findeth a wife findeth good
וַאֲנִי בְּרֹב חַסְדְּךָ אָבוֹא בֵיתֶךָ	But I in multitude of thy mercies, will come into thy house
וְהָיָה כְּעֵץ שָׁתוּל עַל פַּלְגֵי מָיִם	And he shall be as a tree planted by the brooks of waters
חַכְמוֹת נָשִׁים בָּנְתָה בֵיתָהּ	A wise woman buildeth her house
נְקִי כַפַּיִם וּבַר לֵבָב	Innocente in ...

FIGURE 2. William Bradford, "Hebrew Exercises" (ca. 1652). From *Of Plimoth Plantation* (Manuscript 197). Photograph: Special Collections Department, State Library of Massachusetts.

exercises shows Bradford turning to the study of Hebrew, the language, it was believed, in which God spoke to his people.[18] It consists of a vocabulary of elementary words and phrases, a list of some key Old Testament expressions that caught his attention, and a demonstration of his efforts to script Hebrew characters. Embedded in these materials is Bradford's testament to his purpose: "[T]o see, with my owne eyes, something of that most ancient language . . . in which God and angels spake to the holy patriarchs of old time" (see fig. 2).

> Though I am growne aged, yet I have had a longing desire, to see with my own eyes, something of that most ancient language, and holy tongue, in which the Law, and oracles of God were write; and in which God, and angels, spake to the holy patriarks, of old time; and what names were given to things, from the creation. And though I canot attaine to much herein, yet I am refreshed, to have seen some glimpse hereof; (as Moses saw the Land of canan afarr of) my aime and desire is, to see how the words, and phrases lye in the holy texte; and to dicerne somewhat of the same for my owne contente.[19]

"As Moses saw the Land of canan afarr of": that comment about his elementary knowledge of Hebrew reflects as well how differently he was applying the standard providential biblical signs in 1652 from the texts he was writing in 1630. Here the land of Canaan—"afarr of" yet[20]—is figured in personal terms, the errand of the individual soul. Given Bradford's late, darkening view of the condition of Plymouth after the founding of the Bay Colony and then the departure of Winslow, this inward and spiritual perspective might well "comfort [the] hearts" of second- and third-generation pilgrims, or indeed anyone trying to inflect their secular world with spiritual values.

CHAPTER FIVE

John Winthrop: From *Journal* to *History*

Bradford's abandoned history and his late effort to learn the language of God and angels is a touching emblem of a separatist response to "the Puritan Dilemma"—"the paradox that required a man to live [and work] in the world without being of it."[1] Edmund Morgan had good reason to see the most perfect realization of that dilemma in the story of John Winthrop. Like all Puritans, Bradford and Winthrop understood that "[t]he kingdom of God is within you" (Luke 17:21), and both assented as well to the Geneva Bible's gloss on that text: that the regenerate must not, like the Pharisees, "[look] for an earthly kingdom of Messiah." But for Winthrop, a firm and authoritative church institution based in messianic belief and commitment was essential given political conditions in Europe and England. When Winthrop entered into founding the Bay Colony, he never wavered from building a complex, even a quasi-imperial, theocratic state apparatus.

Puritanism taught both Bradford and Winthrop "that a man [must] devote his life to seeking salvation but told him he was helpless to do anything but evil." It also "required that he reform the world in the image of God's holy kingdom but taught him that the evil of the world was incurable and inevitable."[2] Everything about *Of Plymouth Plantation* testifies to how dispiriting and "tedious" Bradford's duties came to seem. Winthrop's embattled and often disturbing account is different. Called by God, as he believed, to "reform [a] world [whose] evil . . . was incurable and inevitable," he made that call the unwavering pursuit of his life.[3]

The allies, opponents, and bystanders of his pursuit have left us a substantial documentary archive that exposes Winthrop's intrepid life and character. But his own account has imperative significance, because his convictions forbade him to present it, or us to read it, as triumph or catastrophe or even as the forecast of some coming resolution of achievement or disaster. "History must tell the whole truth" (*J*, 376), he wrote, and readers have justly admired his candor even when his prose is vilifying others or minimizing his faults. But he was often far from candid, and his sharp legal mind produced remarkable sophistries. He was also a religious bigot. So his own record shows him by turns admirable and despicable, clear-eyed and painfully benighted. How do we read such a work? For that matter, how could he even write it, knowing his dilemma as well as he did?

A useful way, I believe, is to try to read it as literally as Winthrop and the Puritans tried to read scripture. That would be to seek something we now judge more fundamental than *ipsum verbum*, the Word of God. The object in view would be rather *ipsae tabulae*, the documents created by men at a certain time and under specific circumstances, where all is put at risk and failure stalks in every word. James Savage was the first scholar to attempt that kind of approach to Winthrop's work when he set about creating his 1825 edition, *The History of New England from 1630 to 1649 by John Winthrop*.[4] Continuing his work in our own day, Richard Dunn and Laetitia Yeandle produced another great edition. But it comes with a very different title: *The Journal of John Winthrop*. Between those competing titles lie several questions that those scholars recognized as fundamental to what Winthrop had done and what he intended to do. First of all, are we to read his work as a journal or as a history? Second, however we deal with that question, what exactly is Winthrop's subject? And third, how are those questions pertinent to the work as we have it?

The first is no mere pedantic question—indeed, it is at once the most fundamental and the most intractable. Winthrop's work comes down to us in three manuscript volumes, volumes 1 and 3 being autograph, volume 2 being an editorial copy and reconstruction from an autograph destroyed by fire in 1825. Volume 1 is untitled and covers the years from the departure in March 1630 to 1636. Volumes 2 and 3, however, are headed "A Continuation of the History of New England." Keying on that, Savage felt entirely comfortable titling his edition as he did. It didn't matter that volume 1 was left untitled. Volumes 2 and 3 were authoritatively a "History," and Winthrop applied that title retrospectively to volume 1.

Responding to the unfinished character of Winthrop's manuscripts and its style of presentation, Dunn and Yeandle argue that the work is more a journal than a history. Two features of the manuscripts are pertinent for them. First, all three volumes are clearly still in process of composition: additions and revisions are made regularly, gaps appear from time to time, and queries are left for further attention. Dunn and Yeandle also stress that even when Winthrop is narrating retrospectively, the prose handles the events under a horizon of immediacy. Besides, the first third of volume 1—the opening that sets up the work—is notably elliptical. It is not merely that incidents and details don't get elaborated as they do later, especially in volumes 2 and 3. More striking is the absence of a relevant context that—like Bradford's book 1—would establish what set the venture going in the first place. The work simply leaps off from a diary entry for March 29, 1630, made on board the *Arbella* as it was about to sail from England.

These issues with the title remain unresolved, as is often the case with important philological problems. But the work of these and other scholars has been important for sharpening our view of the problems and for suggesting different approaches to them. So Lee Sweninger argued that "in part it is a journal ... but it is also a reflective history."[5] That's right but, I think, not right enough, because although the work begins as a journal, historical reflection comes in very soon. The key point to realize is that the two forms feed off each other throughout. It is a reflective history, Sweninger argues, because "it is a record of facts written after their occurrence and with the advantage of hindsight." The diaristic form dominates volume 1, which lacks the narrative amplitude of volumes 2 and 3. But while the work ceases to be a daybook and gaps of time stand between events and their recording, the compositional presentation is aggressively journalistic throughout, which is why Dunn and Yeandle ended up calling it a journal. As I shall be arguing, to see the work as a "Journal/History" can improve our view of what is one of the most important and least discussed features of the work: how Winthrop argues the presence of providential design.

Savage noticed another interesting problem with the title: that Winthrop made an "improper appropriation" of the name "New England" for his *History*.[6] Savage rightly argued that the other colonies figured in Winthrop's work only as they stood in relation to Massachusetts, a relation that was often only secondary or even altogether severed. For Savage, the appropriation reflected Winthrop's ambition to see the entire colonial region joined in a Congregational allegiance under Massachusetts leadership. Winthrop appropriated the title "New England" for his *History* of Massachusetts Bay because his colonial vision was from the start politically ambitious and, as settlement grew, expansionist—a small-scale model of Old England's imperial ambitions.[7] Plymouth never had such enterprising designs. But Winthrop is intensely focused on the 1643 alliance of the United Colonies of New England and, beyond that, on seeing the 1648 Cambridge Platform implemented.

Winthrop's ambition for Massachusetts may have also been less narrowly self-serving yet even more grandly imperialistic. When he oversaw the translation of the Massachusetts Bay Colony from a private investment enterprise to a Crown colony—a change he worked hard to achieve—the American venture became an international undertaking. The title *The History of New England* implicitly calls out a distinction, and a relation, between New and Old England that was not present in Britain's other colonial ventures at Plymouth or the Virginia Crown colony.[8] The charter, the *Humble Request . . . of his Majesties loyall Subjects* (1630), and the *Arbella* sermon all declare allegiance to the Crown, and those declarations are no more perfunctory than the appropriation of "New England" as the subject of Winthrop's history. Unlike Plymouth, the Bay Colony was conceived as an attempt to refound Old England along reformed civil and religious lines. So the appropriated title perhaps signals Winthrop's secret hope—was it even a founding plan?—to establish in America a model of a "New" England that might even help to accomplish a true reformation in Old England.

One other feature of the work's title, one that has not yet been addressed by scholars, also seems significant: the fact that volume 1 has no title at all, even though Winthrop declared it was the first part of his *History of New England*. Of course all three volumes were left in compositional flux, including the third. But if Winthrop left his work unfinished at the end of volume 3, he didn't leave it incomplete. First of all, as a serial record it closes with an opening to the future. Second, and perhaps even more important, the last significant event recorded in the work—it is nearly the final entry—is the establishment of the Cambridge Platform, which made Congregationalism New England's established religion in all the colonies except Roger Williams's Rhode Island. Even more than the military alliance of 1643—the United Colonies of New England—the Cambridge Platform actually brought Winthrop's history to a culminant moment in his idea of the American errand.

But volume 1 is uniquely unfinished. Begun as a diary, it launched Winthrop into starting with an adventitious text. One great virtue of journalistic writing is that it nurtures a posture of attention. But to be read as a history, a certain amount of material has to be laid in before the writing can turn reflective and, in taking that turn, selective. Like Bradford when he turned in 1630 to write book 1 of *Of Plymouth Plantation*, Winthrop could have reorganized the diaristic materials of volume 1, giving them a more determined shape and introducing crucial information about the idea and design of the colony as it developed, especially in 1628–29. If the work was to be a history of Massachusetts or New England, it doesn't need an ending, but it does need a context that explains its beginning. Yet Winthrop didn't supply it.

Volume 1 differs from volumes 2 and 3 because, considered as a history, it hasn't really begun. Volumes 2 and 3, though unfinished, are coherent and organized, and their prehistory is implicit throughout both volumes.

But Winthrop never decided how or perhaps even whether he should define and frame that prehistory—that is, how the details of volume 1 might be synthesized and perhaps elaborated, and what might or should be added. Why did he leave volume 1 unsynthesized with the "Continuation" of the later volumes?

That is both an impossible and an important question. It's impossible because we can't know "the answer." It's important because it helps us see what is happening in volumes 2 and 3 and, after that, what might have been more thoroughly presented in volume 1. Two things here are especially interesting. First, while the context that Winthrop left out of volume 1 is present in volumes 2 and 3, it is scattered across their serial reports. Second, aspects of that context are revealingly problematic for the settlement project of New England as Winthrop conceived it. In an important sense, Winthrop couldn't give a thorough presentation of the founding context of his "Journal/History" because to do so would have compromised his polemic with the many other agents working at colonization and plantation, often in conflict with the Bay Colony and Winthrop personally.

We have already seen how Winthrop helped to manage Massachusetts' engagements with the Americans. (Like nearly every colonist—Williams is the notable exception—Winthrop took an imperial European view of American land, which he just assumed could be appropriated ad libitum.) Here we have to consider how the "Journal/History" was engaging with those other agents. That means parsing the significance of his decisive view—it is central to the work's argument—that colonial government should be organized on a Congregational church model.

That institutional apparatus highlighted a contradiction that pressed the settlement community from two very different directions. Congregationalism's commitment to self-governance created tensions with the Crown and a Parliament operating within the religious authority of the Church of England. But the "Civll or foedoral" authority arrogated by Winthrop and the colony's first founders created serious intracolonial conflicts (J, 587). Winthrop and the church magistrates were adamant that unconditional authority on all local matters rested in a Congregational General Court, to be elected by regenerate church members only. As a result, the charge of arbitrary authority was raised from several quarters, not all of them religious, as early as 1631 and continued as late as 1646. Because the colony's Crown charter was often the focus of these disputes, I shall begin with the problems it caused.

Or I should say that Winthrop himself caused by his decision to take the charter with him to Massachusetts and keep its provisions secret from all but his inner circle of church authorities. Scholars regularly point out that Winthrop did this in order to insulate the colony from Crown interference in its affairs, especially from meddling with its plans for Congregational self-government. While that is certainly the case, equally certain is that he wanted the Massachusetts churches to keep firm local control of all policy and governance. Because the king's charter did not limit the colonial franchise to church members only, Winthrop kept the colonists in the dark about its provisions and moved quickly to establish the rule that only regenerate church members would have a vote in governance.[9]

Winthrop's clandestine manipulation of the Crown's charter was exposed in 1631, when a Freeman's Oath was declared the instrument for establishing the colonial franchise. When the General Court met at its second session in May 1631 and promulgated the "Oath of a Freeman," sharp controversies immediately arose.[10] They would not be resolved until the Oath went through a series of revisions that took three years to work out (1631–34) and that ensured certain liberties for the people that Winthrop and the magistrates had secretly tried to curtail. An explicit statement was added to the Oath in 1634 declaring that it would not abridge freedom of conscience: "[W]hen I shal be called to give my voyce touching any matter of this State, in which Freemen are to deal, I will give my vote and suffrage as I shall iudge in myne owne conscience may best conduce & tend to the publique weale."[11] A conscientious objection could be raised against the authorities' policies or decisions. But it remained true that if the General Court found against the complainant, the only recourse was either submission to the judgment or excommunication. So the Bay Colony would continue to be whiplashed by the unresolved juridical contradiction implicit in that revision.

As Massachusetts' power and population grew, these kinds of tensions persisted and even grew more acute. Though the institution of the Cambridge Platform and the Westminster Confession in 1648 created a broad Congregational unity (again, Rhode Island excepted), a mere ten years later the General Court was executing Quakers for their religious beliefs. It was not simply that "[a]s people increased, so sin abounded"— Winthrop's lament as the Great Migration was in full swing in 1642 (J, 374). The problem was that the distinction between divine and human authority was especially difficult to maintain in colonies subject to the ultimate authority of the king, the empire's representative of God on earth. The authority of the chartered colonies was by Crown dispensation and subject to review or revocation, as eventually happened in 1684. Complaints against arbitrary Bay Colony authority were lodged by various colonials with the Plantation Commission in London in 1635, in 1638–39, and again in 1646, and each time the colony was told to send back its original charter. But each time it refused and temporized, and each time events conspired to aid the colony in its disobedience.[12]

In 1638 Winthrop wrote a "Humble Petition to Lords Commissioners for Foreign Plantations." On one hand it is a plea not to revoke its charter, arguing that the colony would suffer great damage if the charter were compromised. On the other, as in the *Humble Request* of 1630, it made an elaborate public reaffirmation of the colony's subservience. In neither case was Winthrop being disingenuous about the colony's allegiance to England, but he was seriously equivocating. In private he and the ruling magistrates had always been working to ensure that they, and not the Crown, would be the supreme authorities in the colony. Their 1646 reply to Robert Child's charges against their authority—the reply was never made public—was explicit: "our Allegeance bindes vs not to the Lawes of England, any longer then while we live in England: for the Lawes of the Parliament of England reache no further: nor doe the kings writtes under their great Seale goe any further" (*J*, 663).

Winthrop's long-running struggle to control the charter throws important light on the received condition of the "Journal/History." Volumes 2 and 3 are relatively coherent narratives, so Winthrop titles them part of his "History of New England." But volume 1 is almost entirely journalistic, and if it were to have been reorganized as part of that "History," Winthrop would have had to address the colony's founding documents and conditions—most important of all, the king's charter. When composing volumes 2 and 3, Winthrop had clearly shifted from a diaristic to an historical method, but the problem of the first volume had, if anything, become more clear. As Winthrop struggled to defeat Child's 1646 "Remonstrance and Petition . . . to Massachusetts General Court," he worried "that our secrete Counsells were presentlly known" in England and urged the magistrates to make certain "that our present Consultations might be kept in the brest of the Court, & not divulged abroad" (*J*, 647). Winthrop never had any compunction about operating in secret. The tumultuous events in England of 1646–49 made the situation in Massachusetts inconsequential from London's point of view. Circumstance intervening once again, Winthrop kept the charter in the colony.

The documentary state of volume 1 helps us see more clearly a significant, and long-recognized, colonial problem. The Puritan Dilemma was not the only contradiction that troubled the lives of the reformed colonists. Equally pressing was the question of freedom of conscience that Roger Williams and Anne Hutchinson brought to dramatic attention. In founding Rhode Island, Williams proved that a practical governmental order in a reformed religious world did not require an established religion. That existential proof exposed the fault line in Winthrop's argument for limiting the colonial franchise to regenerate citizens and resting civic authority in an executive that bound itself to Congregational Church ordinance. Representative government and executive authority by select persons did not require, as Winthrop argued, a state religion. But Williams's position went further. He argued that binding the operation of religious practice to a state apparatus, and vice versa, was ipso facto to institute the pharisaical pursuit of an "earthly kingdom of Messiah."[13]

The question of the claims of individual conscience versus institutional authority was far more pressing for a Congregational ordinance than it was for either an Episcopal or a Presbyterian one. That is why Winthrop kept having to deal with it and, eventually, address it more formally: first in his justification of the ruling council's "Negative Vote" (1643); next in the "Discourse on Arbitrary Government" (1644); and most famously in the "litle speeche" on liberty (1645).[14] All three of those discourses should be set and read beside "A Modell of Christian Charitie" to see the differences between ministerial and magisterial thinking.

Winthrop dealt with the strictly secular issue of a representative rather than a democratic ordinance in the 1643 and 1644 tracts. The "Little Speech on Liberty" (1645), as it is now called, addressed more directly the question of "the proper ende & obiecte of Authoritye," which Winthrop saw as an imperative obligation of the colonial leadership. So essential was this obligation that Winthrop could declare that "if your magistrates should erre here, your selues must beare it" (J, 587). In this very case, as he admitted and the Court agreed, the governor had indeed "erred." The Court accepted his admission, exonerated Winthrop, and reaffirmed what Dunn describes as the governor's and the magistrates' "God-given authority over the people" (J, 584 n.).[15]

Winthrop grounds his judgments on a legal distinction between two kinds of liberty, "Naturall (I mean as our nature is now corrupt) & Civill or foederall." The former "is common to man with beastes & other creatures," whereas the latter has "reference to the Covenant betweene God & man, in the morall Lawe, & the Politicke Couenantes & constitutions among men themselues" (J, 587): "This Libertye is the proper ende & obiecte of Authoritye, & cannot subsist withoute it, & it is a Libertye to that onely which is good, just & honest: this Libertye you are to stand for, with the hazard (not onely of your goodes but) of your lives, if need be [for] it is of the same kinde of Libertye wherewith Ch[r]ist hath made us free" (J, 587–88). Winthrop's "little speech" is developing a model of Christian polity, not "A Modell of Christian Charitie." The *Arbella* sermon's overriding concern is with "Justice and Mercy" and the rule of Christian love. Its subject is not authority but community.

> There is ... a double Lawe by which wee are regulated in our conversacion one towardes another: in both the former respects, the lawe

of nature and the lawe of grace, or the morrall lawe or the lawe of the gospel... By the first of these lawes man... is commaunded to love his neighbour as himselfe.... the former propounds one man to another, as the same fleshe and Image of god, this [latter] as a brother in Christ allsoe, and in the Communion of the same Spirit and soe teacheth to put a difference betweene Christians and others. ("Christian Charity," MS pp. 5–6; *The Winthrop Papers*, 2:283–84)

In specifying the "difference betweene Christians and others," the *Arbella* sermon anticipates the social conditions that the Bay colonists would enter when they arrived. It foresees intercourse with the Plymouth separatists and the fledgling Salem Congregationalists, with the colonials from France, the Netherlands, Sweden, and Spain, and of course with the Americans. So drawing on what would become for the Puritans a ubiquitous Old Testament analogy, the sermon sketches a practical rule for how the members of a "household" living under the "law of grace" are to conduct themselves in the New World: "Doe good to all, especially to the household of faith; vpon this ground the Israelites were to putt a difference betweene the brethren of such as were strangers though not of the Canaanites" ("Christian Charity," MS p. 7; *The Winthrop Papers*, 2:284). This "Modell" of "Christian Charity" holds for the good of "all," though the law of grace creates a special bond of love in the "household of faith." After that regenerate company come the other Christian "strangers" who will be or were even then sojourning in the land of the Americans. Beyond that pale, however, lay a world of ultimate difference where the ground of difference itself appeared: "though not the Canaanites." Where matters of social intercourse were concerned, neither the law of nature nor the law of grace applied to the Americans.[16]

As a Congregationalist like George Phillips, Winthrop would have honored and assented to that argument of the *Arbella* sermon. But it was not something he would have presumed himself qualified to deliver. The three tracts on personal liberty, institutional authority, and civic ordinance, on the other hand, were exactly his responsibility and suited to his expertise.

The "Little Speech on Liberty" was responding to what Dunn and Yeandle call "the most dramatic power struggle between the people and their church authorities since the Antinomian controversy of 1637" (J, 578 n.). Although those two events were indeed the most dramatic, such conflicts persisted and kept having to be engaged. Winthrop regularly comments on "occasion[s that increase] the people's jealousy of their magistrates" (J, 294) and their continual fear of "Arbitrary Gouernment" (J, 561), and he draws a sharp distinction between the leaders of the colony and "the common sort of people who eagerly... embrace" the deplorable views of persons like Roger Williams or, worse yet, Anne Hutchinson (J, 281).

Although similar tensions arose in Plymouth, the size of the colony protected it from the serious wrangles that shook Massachusetts. These were exacerbated by the ambitious lines along which Winthrop's venture had been planned. Besides, and unlike the Plymouth colonists, Winthrop and his alliance of founders were notable English citizens, accustomed to command and control. Through the 1630s Winthrop deplored the founding of the breakaway colonies and, even worse, the departure of many out of New England altogether.[17] Faced with the increasingly complex Indian situation—an instability that Massachusetts, as we've seen, had unwittingly helped to create—he promoted the 1643 founding of the United Colonies of New England as a way to secure a measure of centralized authority. The threats of violence from Indians, France, and Spain made the other, smaller colonies incline to a military alliance, but for Winthrop and the Bay Colony a federation of Congregational church institutions under its leadership was the greater and even more important goal. It was in large measure achieved in 1648 with the institution of the Cambridge Platform.

While Winthrop broadcast his legal and theological arguments for strong colonial authority, one of the most salient motifs of his "Journal/History" shows that those arguments had to be more deeply—more divinely founded. Though the work is certainly a record of key events in the earthly kingdom of Messiah, Winthrop made it much more than that. The work lays out a series of dramatic accounts of Winthrop's relentless search for evidence that God was presiding over the colony's daily life. Indeed, all of Winthrop's secular arguments for magisterial authority depended on such evidence. Only if God's providential presence could be demonstrated as fact would the position of the governor and the magistrates be patently, so to say, God-ordained.

Winthrop's "Journal/History" begins in medias res, thus: "Anno domini, 1630: march 29: mundaye. Rydinge at the Cowes, near the Ile of wight in the Arbella, a Shippe of 350 tu. whereof Capt. Peter Milborne was master" (J, 1). If the work were conceived as an epic poem or perhaps a modern novel, that opening, and all of the daybook that it signals to follow, would have established this rhetoric of immediacy as the work's narrative rationale. But a dramatic narrative is not the only form feeding off Winthrop's rhetoric. The daybook succeeds to a highly polemical composition meant to justify the "New England" way to the world. At once a story and an argument, the "Journal/History" works up a demonstrative proof of a God-ordained venture "Anno domini." His subject is the providential history of Massachusetts and New England. More important, his subject is also an argument for the truth of his report on a miraculous history.

That focus makes his work a far more dynamic, argumentative, and often tormented record than Bradford's. The "Journal/History" is dominated by two regular preoccupations. The first, which I've just surveyed, concerns his struggles with a host of persons—a diverse company—who resisted the authority he and the magistrates of the Bay Colony wielded. The second, which is related to the first and at least as compelling, appears in his many fascinated reports on extraordinary natural and human events. These run from briefly noted to elaborately detailed episodes from the colony's history and, often, from places beyond. They all reflect Winthrop's obsessive concern to register and interpret the signs of providential and satanic action. He reports earthquakes, storms, and other natural phenomena because they reflect a vast and often mysterious design. It was not just a meteorologist or navigational historian who gave that meticulous account of the weather conditions on the initial crossing. "The winde" was such a daily, ubiquitous, and infinitely variable presence on the voyage that we find ourselves watching a man studying the action of the awful Spirit of God, whose presence throughout the Atlantic passage Winthrop is reporting.

The first of many providential deaths recorded by Winthrop came on May 27, 1630 on the *Jewell*: "a moste profane fellowe, & one who was verye iniurious to the passangers though muche against the will of the [ship's] master" (*J*, 24). As all readers have noted, Winthrop not only worked out sacred interpretations of even such small events, he assiduously sought them out to make his work a repository of spiritual signs recorded elsewhere. One of the most famous is the anecdote of the mouse and the snake reported out of the Watertown church in July 1632.

As so often in the "Journal/History," that story came into Winthrop's record immediately after his account of a contentious worldly event: a "st[r]ife in Waterton Congregation" raised by the separatist John Masters, who objected to a person recently admitted to church membership whom he judged unfit. Masters eventually "submitted himselfe" to the judgment of the Watertown magistrates and "was received in againe" to the congregation (*J*, 71–72). Winthrop then inserts the story out of Watertown of "a great combate between a mouse & a snake" that glosses the previous one and resonates for the entire community of Bay Colony churches.

> the mouse prevayled & killed the snake: the Pastor of Boston mr willson, a very sincere, holy man hearinge of it, gave this interpretation, that, the snake was the devil, the mouse was a poore contemptible people which God had brought hether, which should overcome

Sathan here & dispossesse him of his kingdome. upon the same occasion he tould the Gouernor that before he was resolued to come into this Countrye, he dreamed he was heere, and that he saw a church arise out of the earthe, which grewe vp & became a merveylous goodlye church. (J, 72)

Perhaps the most striking of these kinds of report are those Winthrop recorded in such considerable detail that the events escaped confident explanation. Take, for example, this haunting tale from the church at Weymouth.

> February 6 [1637]. A man of Weymouth (but not of the church) fell into some trouble of mind, and in the night cried out, "Art thou come, Lord Jesus?" and with that leaped out of his bed in his shirt, and, breaking from his wife, leaped out at a high window into the snow, and ran about seven miles off, and being traced in the snow, was found dead next morning. They might perceive, that he had kneeled down to prayer in divers places. (J, 209)

Though "not of the church" marked the man as unregenerate, the import of the story is left uncertain. Was he deranged? By Satan? Or had he perhaps been smitten with a fearful test of faith ordained by God? As a pitiful monitory record for the community of both saints and strangers? And why would Winthrop, having left the point of the anecdote dubious, introduced it anyway?

Because Winthrop was a reformed man devoted to prudential works and the duty and necessity, especially in worldly leaders, of practical foresight in taking action, he felt a special urgency in seeking signs of God's providence in the community. We therefore find repeated entries in his "Journal/History" of imprudent behavior in the community and, reciprocally, of God's brooding presence. As the episode of the mouse and the snake shows, the significance of these incidents is often very clear. But other incidents that call for simple prudential judgment fit into the more spectacular theophanies—for instance, the "young man a tanner in Boston," who "going to wash himself in a creek, said, jestingly, I will go and drown myself now." And so it "fell out accordingly," Winthrop remarks, "for by the slipperiness of the earth" he went "beyond his depth [and] was drowned, though company were at hand, and one in the water with him" (J, 354). Winthrop hardly even needed the loaded reference to "the slipperiness of the earth" to let himself (and us) know what happens to people who treat God's gift of life so lightly.

A confident report on some other godly mice is also arresting.

About this time there fell out a thing worthy of observation. Mr. Winthrop the younger, one of the magistrates, having many books in a chamber where there was corn of divers sorts, had among them one wherein the Greek testament, the psalms and the common prayer were bound together. He found the common prayer eaten with mice, every leaf of it, and not any of the two other touched, nor any other of his books, though there were above a thousand. (J, 341)

In this case Winthrop was altering the incidental facts in order to establish his providential application, as the recent editors of the *Journal* have noted.[18] But Winthrop's lapse here is perhaps less important than the entry that immediately follows: "Quere, of the child at Cambridge killed by a cat." Saying nothing further, Winthrop simply leaves one, including himself, to speculate on the incident's spiritual import.

Strange births and deaths are regularly recorded and make insistent calls for providential explanations. These are also the events that most terrorize Winthrop's narrative, as we know from his account of the "monster[s]" born to Mary Dyer and Anne Hutchinson (J, 253–54). It's impossible to overstate just how deeply the Puritan mind—men's and women's alike—were menaced by the myth of Eve's original commerce with Satan. Winthrop's extensive tales of Anne Needham Hett (J, 229–30, 391–92, and 469) and Dorothy Talby (J, 271–72) are appalling and complex little prose masterpieces because they deliver such exacting reports on a shared affliction of sin.

The Hett and Talby stories are both presented "as revelations from God" (J, 230) of satanic "delusions." Although "[s]he had been a member of the church of Salem, and of good esteem for godliness, etc." (J, 272), Talby in 1638 twice tries to murder her daughter, succeeding the second time. Hett makes three attempts at murder (first in 1637, twice more in 1642), but each fails. Both women are overcome with murderous impulses and both are temporarily rescued back to authorized religious communion. And while the community keeps working to save these women and their families, Winthrop's narrative describes all the turns and counterturns as sudden and inexplicable. Talby is finally executed for her crime, while "the church received [Anne Hett] in again" in 1643.

[T]he Lord was pleased so to honor his own ordinance, that whereas before no means could prevail with her either to reclaim her from her wicked and blasphemous courses and speeches, etc., or to bring her to frequent the means, within a few weeks after her casting out [of the church of Boston], she came to see her sin and lay it to heart, and to frequent the means, and so was brought to such manifestation of repentance and a sound mind, as the church received her in again. (J, 469)

But given these impulsive swings from normalcy to violence and back again, Hett's return to the social order is precarious, as Winthrop's reports make clear.

> [H]aving been long in a sad melancholic distemper near to phrensy, and having formerly attempted to drown her child, but prevented by God's gracious providence, did now again take an opportunity, being alone, to carry her child, aged three years, to a creek near her house, and stripping it of the clothes, threw it into the water and mud. But, the tide being low, the little child scrambled out, and taking up its clothes, came to its mother who was set down not far off. She carried the child again, and threw it in so far as it could not get out; but then it pleased God, that a young man, coming that way, saved it. (J, 391–92)

"She would give no other reason for it," Winthrop adds, "but that she did it to save it from misery"—the same reason that Talby had given[19]—"and withal that she was assured, she had sinned against the Holy Ghost, and that she could not repent of any sin." What exactly is she saying? Is the foreseen "misery" hell and damnation, or is it simply life in the colony? And does she mean that she cannot repent of her attempted murder because at some time previous she had sinned against the Holy Ghost? And in any case, why persist in the attempted murder? Winthrop has no answers to the questions he leaves hanging fire, so he closes the tale by reflecting that "Thus doth Satan work by the advantage of our infirmities, which should stir us up to cleave the more fast to Christ Jesus, and to walk the more humbly and watchfully in all our conversation" (J, 392).

While the comment applies to every soul, including the governor, it carries an added inflection when he delivers it in this history of the colony, and when he writes it, as here, in 1642. Alert to surrounding dangers of every kind—natural, political, spiritual—Winthrop's chief focus as governor has been from the start to maintain order. The task is demanding because the colonials are immigrant settlers, because other imperial powers—France, Spain, and the Netherlands—threaten their venture, and most of all because the colonial company itself is a complex and diverse group, many godly, many bestial, and most fiercely independent. Indeed, the most independent spirits of all are those closest to Winthrop—Hooker, Davenport, Wheelwright, Williams, Cotton, even Hutchinson—who came to the New World to escape the authoritarian orders of the Church of Rome and the Church of England, which they either denied or questioned. That left Congregational Massachusetts with the task of showing that its own authority was divinely sanctioned. How seriously Winthrop felt that obligation is apparent throughout his "Journal/History," and not least when he recorded the climactic event in the founding of his messianic enterprise.

On August 13, 1648 the Cambridge Synod met for a third (and last) time in Cambridge to establish "the framing of a Confession of Faythe &c. & a forme of Church discipline" (J, 715) for the United Colonies of New England: "For the first they wholly Agreed with that which the Assembly in England had lately sett forthe: for the other viz. for discipline they drewe it by itselfe, according to the generall practice of our Churches. so they ended in lesse than 14: days" (J, 715). With the institution of the Platform, nearly everything that Winthrop had hoped for Massachusetts and the New England colonies was achieved. Though the Westminster confession of faith was not Congregational, it was firmly Calvinist, and, most important, it left the colonies free to work out their local forms of church government. Congregationalism was colonial orthodoxy, with the churches of Rhode Island, chartered in 1644 and committed to tolerance of dissenters, Catholics, and Jews, excluded from the New England Confederation. In 1648 Massachusetts and—by Winthrop's extended argument in his "Journal/History"—"New England" had formally established their theocratic order.

Because the synod marked the institutional climax of Winthrop's "Journal/History"—a nearly twenty-year narrative of trial and often sharp intramural conflict over issues of faith and church government—we might be surprised that he reports it in such brief, almost perfunctory, terms. But the founding of the messianic kingdom was less significant for Winthrop than the sign that marked the event as godly. So while the fourteen conference days are only briefly summarized, a single dramatic event on the first day is handled *in extenso*. It is the culminant divine revelation of the "Journal/History."

> It fell out, about the middest of his Sermon, there came a snake into the seat where many of the Elders sate behind the preacher. It came in at the doore where people stood thicke upon the staires, diverse of the Elders shifted from it but mr Thomson, one of the Elders of Braintree (a man of muche Faythe,) trode vpon the head of it, & so held it with his foote & stayle with a small paire of Graines, vntill it was killed: this beinge so remearkable, & nothinge fallinge out but by divine Provi-

dence, it is out of doubt, the Lord discovered somewhat of his minde in it. The serpent is the devill; the Synod the Representation of the Churches of Christ in N: E: England. The devill had formerly & lately attempted their disturbance and dissolution, but their Faithe in the seed of the woman overcame him & Chrushed his head. (J, 715)

Here is a great moment in church history being providentially framed and glossed. God has arranged the scene so that a man of faith can choose to act out the truth of a central Calvinist text, Genesis 3:15, and so that Winthrop can make a record of it: "I will also put enmity between thee and the woman, and between thy seed and her seed. He shall break thine head, and thou shalt bruise his heel." "Thee" is Satan, the serpent, and "the woman" is the Church of Christ. Satan's power shall be broken, but in the struggle—this is the Geneva gloss—"Satan shall sting Christ and his members [i.e., the Church], but not overcome them." "Thy seed and her seed" draws a fundamental distinction between the offspring of natural procreation—the seed of the woman who, through Satan, brought sin into the world—and the offspring of spiritual regeneration—the seed of the Holy Mother, the Congregational Church of Christ.

Coda: *The Bay Psalm Book* and the Unearthly Kingdom

For Winthrop, the establishment of the Cambridge Platform in 1648 was the culminant achievement of his Congregational errand. For Roger Williams and Rhode Island, however, who did not sign on, it was the declaration, appropriately institutional, of the colony's commitment to an "earthly kingdom of Messiah."

But the history of the Bay Colony's fierce internal disputes, Winthrop's fears and secrets and, perhaps even more, his own spiritual trials show how surely their City on a Hill never entirely turned away from a less worldly vision of that City. Perhaps the most striking evidence of this is the single most important early American literary work we have, the first book published in America: *The Whole / Book of Psalmes / Faithfully / Translated into English / Metre* (also known simply as *The Bay Psalm Book*).[20] Remarkably, its conception has much in common with Bradford's late interest in Hebrew language and poetry.

The Bay Psalm Book was created by colony scholars, who had set an unusual goal for themselves: to fashion a translation for a community that might aspire to address God in a language He would be most likely to hear and understand—a language as close to the language of God himself as still exists in the fallen world.[21] This would be an English metrical translation that sought to echo the original poetry of the Hebrew Bible. The result was the work's often deplored and notoriously forbidding prosodies, such as these lines from its translation of Psalm 137.

> Because there they that us away
> led in captivitee,
> Requir'd of us a song, & thus
>   askd mirth: us waste who laid,
> Sing us among a Sions song,
>   unto us then they said.
> . . .
> O happie hee shall surely bee
>   that taketh up, that eke
> thy little ones against the stones
>   doth into pieces breake.

As John Cotton, one of the translators, observed, "pretty paraphrase" and smooth versification were out of the question.[22] What was sought was extreme literality. Because the Hebrew "verses observe a certain number and measure of syllables," the Bay psalter set itself the daunting task to give a literal English equivalent of "that tongue in which they were written."[23] So in defending *The Bay Psalm Book* against the charge that the translation was "framed . . . more to the Meeter, than the Prose" sense, Cotton declared that such framing was simply what the task demanded: the translation should "expresse the Holy Art of the Originall Hebrew Poetry, which the Prose doth not attend unto."[24] The criterion of literality could scarcely have been set at a greater extreme. When Zoltán Haraszti remarked that the Bay psalter's obdurate verses often strike one as "almost as mystic as the allegories of the Schoolmen," one can scarcely demur. On the other hand, one might justly observe in passing that such metrical means would later find glorious realization in a great deal of American verse from Poe and Dickinson through Hart Crane and on to Susan Howe.[25] It is a style of address that we recognize in what is arguably Anne Bradstreet's greatest single work: "Contemplations."

CHAPTER SIX

Anne Bradstreet: The World Elsewhere

John Winthrop didn't think women should involve themselves in public affairs, and if—like Anne Hutchinson—they presumed to speak authoritatively on faith and morals, he was seriously unpleased. Ann Hopkins's depressions, he was certain, came because she had "giv[en] her selfe wholly to readinge & writinge . . . [and] gone out of her waye & callinge, to meddle in suche things as are proper for men, whose mindes are stronger &c." (*J*, 570). Perhaps he would have felt differently about Anne Bradstreet's poetry, had he seen it. Entering the world in 1650 to a chorus of masculine salutes, its stylistic posture, while often free, was loving and deferential to celebrated male persons, including her father and husband. Furthermore, when she spoke *in propria persona*, as came out in her posthumous collection of *Several Poems* . . . (1678), her domestic world was the haunt and main region of her song. Perhaps best of all, her focus on the vanity of the quotidian world would have marked her, for a man like Winthrop, as a woman of admirable religious discretion.

But in the great recovery of her work that followed John Berryman's belated poetic encomium *Homage to Mistress Bradstreet* (1956), the subtlety of the masks she wore exposed how a gifted and intense woman of her place and time not only expressed herself, but cultivated her coterie of readers and managed her work when it gained an unforeseen public address. Her brother-in-law John Woodbridge marshaled a small male company in England to introduce her to the world in *The Tenth Muse* (1650), a book published, Woodbridge averred, "without [her] knowledge, and contrary to her expectation" (*The Tenth Muse*, [i]).[1] That shrewdly equivocal comment leaves open the possibility that she could have had neither knowledge nor expectation of the actual publication and yet have been hopeful for and even complicit in the final event.

And note that arresting title. Whether or not approved or supplied by

Bradstreet, it made a brave declaration to the courtly muses of Europe not only that Puritanism was inspired by a new spiritual Muse, but that it would be first heard in the voice of a woman. Bradstreet—and presumably her brother-in-law as well—would have known it was Plato's sobriquet for the great Greek erotic poet Sappho, a model who on the face of it could scarcely be less like Bradstreet.[2] It's difficult not to think it was meant for a deliberately ironic reflection of a very different poet and a very different kind of poetry "[l]ately sprung up" in Congregational America. Especially in the first period of her writing, when she makes such a display of her learned and witty address, Bradstreet was quite capable of such a move, and she never repudiated the style of verse that she later, in the 1660s, left behind.

Bradford's book was not published in London until three years after Woodbridge left the colony with whatever manuscripts she had given him. The hiatus is quite unusual and suggests that Woodbridge had to work at the publication.[3] All but one of the encomia printed in the book are from men living in England. So although Bradstreet surely knew of her brother-in-law's plans at least in a general way, we don't know how much of the book's specific form, arrangement, and contents was left to Woodbridge's discretion.[4] Its title, prefatory tributes, and arrangement constitute an elaborate piece of theater that he and perhaps others in England managed and that she clearly did not repudiate. Her prologue to the poems is an important testimony that, if she did not actively work to see her book printed, she viewed the writings entrusted to Woodbridge as a body of work.

Indeed, the cunningly understated prologue is the perfect introduction to the poetry it announces, especially because it follows the train of patriarchal praise and, most important, her act of homage "To her most Honoured Father *Thomas Dudley* Esq; *these humbly presented.*" Her grandiose quaternions, she lets us know, walk in her father's ways.

> I bring my four; and four, now meanly clad,
> To do their homage unto yours most glad

In fact Bradstreet would bring five, not four: "The Foure Elements," "Of the foure Humours in Mans constitution," "The Four Ages of Man," "The four Seasons of the Yeare," and finally "The Foure Monarchies." Is she being cheeky? Well yes, but deferential too. Her father's quaternion, now lost, was the work not of a poet but of a man bound to his worldly obligations. Though she sometimes deprecates her work as "home-spun" ("The Author to her Book") and unworthy of the literary works of a male tradition—she indited, and included here, acts of homage to Guillaume de Salluste Du Bartas, Philip Sidney, Edmund Spenser and others—she was a learned woman who knew how to practice their cultivated European styles.

Such is her skill that she can manage the most nuanced changes of register. The prologue opens on a light, knowing tone, and the eulogy for Queen Elizabeth, while "serious," is also self-consciously "fantastick." Even the quaternions have their playful moments. "Water," for example:

I need not say much of my Haile and Snow,
My Ice and extream cold, which all men know.
Whereof the first, so ominous I rain'd,
That *Israels* enemies, therewith was brain'd. (*The Tenth Muse; Several Poems*, 17)

Having begun and carried out the whole ambitious project under the example of her father, she breaks off the first four with a droll epilogue that complements them both:

My Subjects bare, my Brain is bad,
Or better Lines you should have had:
The first fell in so nat'rally,
I knew not how to pass it by;
The last, though bad, I could not mend,
Accept therefore of what is pen'd,
And all the faults that you shall spy
Shall at your feet for pardon cry. (*The Tenth Muse; Several Poems*, 68)

That kind of arch complacency is the prevailing attitude until the book's last two poems, "Davids Lamentation for Saul, and Jonathan, 2 Sam 1.19" and then the much-celebrated final work, which has no title (though in 1678 it would be given one, *The Vanity of All Worldly Things*). No other poem in *The Tenth Muse* so clearly predicts Bradstreet's later work, where her great subject—worldly vanity—overtakes everything.

But the subject is already at the heart of *The Tenth Muse*, as the grandiose quaternions, especially "The Foure Monarchies," shows. Dating them to an Old Testament chronology is as telling a move as *The Bay Psalm Book*'s turn to Hebrew poetry, especially when she gives "the fourth and last"—"the Roman Monarchy"—a notably abbreviated treatment. Even more interesting, she closes it with the semilegendary tale of Lucrece, the "mirror of chastity" whose rape and suicide, according to Livy, led to the founding of the Republic. In this context, however, Bradstreet is clearly thinking of the Christian interpretation of Lucrece, begun in Augustine's

City of God and carried on through the Middle Ages, as "a mirror of chastity" and secular type of the Church of Christ. The whole of "The Foure Monarchies" is nothing less than an allegorical forecast of the coming of the Tenth Muse.

I would not say the quaternions are overblown, but they are surely pretentious, in the full double meaning of that useful word. As such, they implicitly involve a cautionary tale on the central subject of her prologue: "preheminence." After imagining an unfavorable reception of her work ("They'l say it's stoln, or else, it was by chance" [*The Tenth Muse; Several Poems*, 4]), she pivots to a reflection on the nine classical Muses, all women, and then delivers a set of mischievous comments suggesting that her male Christian readers might pull down their vanity by measuring themselves against the "milde" pagan Greek worthies:

6.
But sure the antick *Greeks* were far more milde,
Let *Greeks* be *Greeks*, and Women what they are,
Men have precedency, and still excell,
It is but vaine, unjustly to wage war,
Men can doe best, and Women know it well;
Preheminence in each, and all is yours,
Yet grant some small acknowledgement of ours. (*The Tenth Muse; Several Poems*, 4)

"Have precedency," "still excel," and "can doe best" are artfully equivocal—"and Women know it well," as certainly Bradstreet does. And "what ... are" women anyhow in the man-managed world lately sprung up in America? "Preheminence" is both "yours" and "ours," and beyond that, whatever "preheminence" men may seek seems to depend upon some kind of mutual exchange. Besides, she's not trying "to wage war," just to keep things in perspective. If they try, men *can* do best. (Would that be "*the* best" or "*their* best"?) So the stanza pivots on that Bradstreetian keyword "vaine." Is she suggesting—surely she is—that without "some small acknowledgement of ours," the "preheminence" of men might be thought a vain show?

The prologue thus makes a kind of witty love, not war, on male achievement and so is an apt introduction to a book that is an *ave atque vale* to the monumental literary and cultural past. In such a theatrical work the quaternions bring a spectacular demonstration of Bradstreet's powers of classical poetic *imitatio*. But they are not the book's most nuanced or trenchant works. That comes in her little masterpiece *In Honour of that High and Mighty Princess, Queen Elizabeth*, where another act of homage delivers an explanation of how to negotiate the vain world of patriarchal "preheminence."

Presenting Elizabeth as a model of Christian sovereignty, Bradstreet fashions a little poetic manifesto, a model of Christian poetry. It is the sheerest vanity to take (or imagine!) anything in the sublunary world as real or true. The greatness of Bradstreet's Elizabeth lay in her decision to "play the Rex" and in that move to make a show of the dumb show of monumental history and its earthly kingdoms: "The World's the Theatre where she did act" (*The Tenth Muse; Several Poems*, 211). In the famous royal play that Elizabeth directed (and lived), kings were vanquished, lesser queens exposed, and great men, wittingly or unwittingly, performed their required parts. Elizabeth's "fantastick" career becomes the exponent of a deathless life, a "Phoenix Queen" because a being as pure and transcendent as the broadcast "Fame" that, investing her, translates her to "a higher sphere."[5]

Learned and ingenious as she was, Bradstreet was an orthodox Congregationalist. Indeed, all of her work centers in her religious commitments. If vanity is another name for woman, as a long patriarchal tradition has it, then Bradstreet might be the very person to make it her great subject, as she did. So *The Vanity of All Worldly Things*—an extended critical reflection on the vanity of "preheminence"—deploys her signature poetic move: to make a poetic show of appearances that the shows of the world may be seen for the vanities they are.

Bradstreet writes to expose the trappings of power and ambition as second-order illusions draped upon the "brittle Earth." In the poem's climactic move she speaks directly to the proud men of reformed Puritan communities in terms they ought to understand but may not, having in their time on earth worked so hard to erect an "earthly kingdom of Messiah" in both New and Old England:

This pearl of price, this tree of life, this spring,
Who is possessed of, shall reign a King.
Nor change of state, nor cares shall ever see,
But wear his Crown unto eternitie,
This satiates the soul, this stayes the mind,
The rest's but vanity, and vain we find. (*The Tenth Muse; Several Poems*, 234)

Her poetical kingdom is most definitely not of this world's scene of vain shows. "This pearl of price, this tree of life, this spring": none of those things are possessable things. More pertinently, here they are not even to be valued as poetic ornaments worked up by a poet's "mind." They are empty signs uplifted in a world of "change" and "cares" that point to an unknown condition of grace, in "eternitie," where the soul's longing will be satiated and the struggling mind put to rest. Bradstreet's demanding argument strips even those traditional religious figures of their vanity.

A key line in her first epitaph for Queen Elizabeth makes the point with unnerving intellectual economy: "The greater was our gain, our loss the more" (*The Tenth Muse; Several Poems*, 214). He that would gain "preheminence" must lose it. As Jesus told an inquiring young man, to have "treasures in heaven" he must "sell that thou hast" (Matthew 19:21). Also, note the verse grammar which both augments the import of the phrase and cancels it out. Poetic inversion, one of Bradstreet's—and *The Bay Psalm Book*'s—regular moves, are especially effective devices for gaining that effect, as Rosamond Rosenmeier noted in commenting on a similar passage in *The Vanity of All Worldly Things*. There the subject is something unpossessable and indeed literally impossible in time and space, "that living Christal Fount": "Who drinks thereof, the world doth nought account." Because "[t]he sentence reads both ways," Rosenmeier observes, the verse "manages to erase as it portrays [so that] the scene and the participant in it, indeed the world itself, become 'nought.'"[6]

The focus of Bradstreet's religious poetry—it dominates the later period of her life—is the conflicting authorities of the "mind" and the "soul." Vanity is a condition that enslaves the mind to an imagination of mortal and fleshly permanences. As a consequence, it is thrown into those torments of "conscience" that Bradstreet suffers and that are on such disturbing display in Winthrop's "Journal/History."

> The sensual senses for a time they please.
> Mean while the conscience rage, who shall appease? (*The Tenth Muse; Several Poems*, 234)

Perhaps the chief object of her verse is to demonstrate what will appease the raging conscience birthed by a seriously reformed Puritan religion. The primal engine of vanity is not the "sensual senses"; it is the mind that vainly imagines ways to turn the spectral forms of both the flesh and the spirit into permanence and even "preheminence.'" So Bradstreet's poetry means to "stay the mind" and discover the utterly, the queenly, "fantastick" region of the "soul."[7]

Though Bradstreet is often celebrated, in one sense justly, as the first poet of America, her work is thoroughly of a piece with her fractured European time, when a Renaissance of learning collided with intense and even fanatic religious upheavals. She had an excellent education and was raised in a well-born and well-bred social circle that took its learning as seriously as its reformed religion. Brought to the New World in Winthrop's fleet, she called the place New England. She never used the word "America," and the one time she seems to acknowledge the presence of the Americans, her discourse and vocabulary are strictly Puritan.[8] Bradford, Winthrop, and the men who settled up and down the Atlantic coast all had Indian neighbors who were troublesome, hostile, sometimes even friendly. Bradstreet's neighbors are her family and, beyond that, the noble living and the noble dead conceived and recalled in an Elizabethan/Calvinist universal history. As for the Indians and their land—a wilderness to the Europeans but to the Americans a living world—Bradstreet pays them little attention.

That ethos is what makes her work such a trenchant reflection of the New World to which her new husband—she married Simon Bradstreet in 1628—brought her. Ann Stanford, one of Bradstreet's earliest and best readers, sees her as "the civilized European facing the wilderness [and] gradually gaining roots in the new land and finally sloughing off the old world."[9] The comment is exact, I believe, if we read certain of its key words—"wilderness," "new land," and "old world"—in biblical and even Calvinist terms, which is how Bradstreet framed her existence. Bradstreet's new world—even the "wilderness" of America—is not a natural and real biosphere; rather, it is strictly typological (see her "Meditations Diuine and morall," 21), and the terms "new" and "old" are filtered through a key Pauline text of reform theology (Ephesians 4:22–24). Except in her unpublished domestic pieces, the quotidian world scarcely exists in Bradstreet's work.[10]

All that comes out clearly in the poem many readers judge her masterpiece, the late "Contemplations" (ca. 1664–65).[11] It opens in a generalized natural scene, a "collocation of place" characteristic of Renaissance poetries of meditation. But playing across the first nine stanzas is a certain vague uncertainty. Is it a good thing that her senses are "rapt" at sights "gilded" and "painted" by Phoebus? Has Bradstreet in stanza 2 confused Phoebus with God himself?

> I wist not what to wish, yet sure thought I,
> If so much excellence abide below;
> How excellent is he that dwells on high?
> Whose power and beauty by his works we know.
> Sure he is goodness, wisdome glory, light,
> That hath this under world so richly dight:
> More Heaven then Earth was here no winter & no night.

If she were sure, would she write "Sure he is"? And who has "so richly dight" the world she is observing? Phoebus? The sun? God? If Bradstreet were confident of herself and the "wandring feet" (stanza 8) of her poem, if her mind were spiritually clear, ought she to have written this?

> Then higher on the glistering Sun I gaz'd,
> Whose beams was shaded by the leavie Tree,
> The more I look'd, the more I grew amaz'd,
> And softly said, what glory's like to thee?
> Soul of this world, this Universes Eye,
> No wonder, some made thee a Deity:
> Had I not better known, (alas) the same had I. (stanza 4)

The question "what glory's like to thee?" might be an oblique way of declaring the difference between divine and sublunary glory, but that isn't what happens here. Bradstreet is so "amaz'd" by immediate appearances that her writing confesses a certain loss of spiritual confidence. The placement of "(alas)" is not quite right, and brilliantly so. If she wanted to avoid all ambiguity in that line, "(alas)" ought to have been put after "the same."

Such disorientations accumulate in stanza 8, where she finally declares her desire to magnify "my great Creator." But the wish comes to expose her "imbecility." She doesn't know how to build her Magnificat because "in pathless paths I lead [the] wandring feet" of her verse. The poem's execution is out of joint, she wants to sing but feels "mute," even less in tune with the Creator than the grasshopper and the cricket.

At that point the poem virtually collapses as a steady composition: all continuity is lost in the broken transition between stanzas 9 and 10. The abrupt shift from space to time, from immediate experience to memory, introduces a disorientation that grows into a narrative interpolation (stanzas 11–16) which further fractures the poetic continuity even as it argues a direct and "long descent" (stanza 16) from her dreadful tale of Genesis to the present. The story so dispirits Bradstreet that she grasps at edifying tags about the difference between mere natural phenomena and human being:

> By birth more noble than those creatures all,
> Yet seems by nature and by custome curs'd (stanza 19)

> Nay, they shall darken, perish, fade and die...
> But man was made for endless immortality. (stanza 20)

Self-conscious platitudes launch the poem into its two final movements, both struggling to "lead my Rivolets to rest" (stanza 23). The rivers she conjures (stanzas 21–25) lead her to "Neptune's Glassy Hall," where his creatures "take the trembling prey before it yield, / Whose armour is their scales, their spreading fins their shield" (stanza 25).

From that vision of nature red in tooth and claw Bradstreet turns quickly (stanzas 26–28) to a poetic memory of "sweet tongu'd Philomel," the nightingale. This is the most dire and most brilliant sequence in "Contemplation," especially for Bradstreet, who knows only too well the tale—perhaps worse even than her tale from Genesis—of Tereus, Procne, and Philomela, and beyond that, of the ancient world's identification of Sappho, another tenth Muse, with the nightingale. But exactly because Bradstreet represents a Philomel with "no sad thoughts, nor cruciating care," the tale bears down remorselessly on the verse. Nothing could be less true than a Philomela imagined by a Bradstreet as a creature who "[r]eminds not what is past, nor what's to come dost fear."

After that Bradstreet might well declare that "Man at the best" is simply "a creature frail and vain" (stanza 29), as this brilliantly bewildered poem shows. There is no "cessation" of the "sorrows, losses, sickness, [and] pain," "But day and night, within, without, vexation, / Troubles from foes, from friends, from dearest, near'st relation." Like the orthodox dogmatic phrases that follow—living in "hope of an eternal morrow," avowing that "[o]nly above is found all with security"—these reflections seem even more ineffectual than the chaotic movements that have led to this point. These are artfully if painfully clear expressions of what it means to see through a glass darkly.

But the final stanza—surprising and metrically irregular—shows that the poem's hitherto "wandring feet" have all been deliberately anticlimactic movements.

> O Time the fatal wrack of mortal things,
> That draws oblivions curtains over kings,
> Their sumptuous monuments, men know them not,
> Their names without a Record are forgot,
> Their parts, their ports, their pomp's all laid in th' dust
> Nor wit nor gold, nor buildings scape times rust,
> But he whose name is grav'd in the white stone
> Shall last and shine when all of these are gone. (stanza 33)

The dark tale Bradstreet left inexplicit in the Philomela passage forecasts this brief and cryptic revelation. "Commanded," according to the Geneva gloss, "to write those things which the Lord knew" but which are otherwise hidden, John speaks to the suffering churches: "Let him that hath an ear, hear what the spirit saith unto the Churches. To him that overcometh, will I give to eat of the Manna that is hid, and will give him a white stone, and in the stone a new name written, which no man knoweth, saving he that receiveth it" (Revelation 2:17). To this the Geneva glossators add that "such stones did in old times witness the quitting of a man" ("the old man is killed"). The stone is, they add, "the bread of life, invisible, spiritual, and heavenly, which is kept secretly with God, from before all eternity." In making the equation of stone and bread, the text calls up a startling and unexpected reference, Matthew 7:9: "Or what man is there of you, whom if his son ask bread, will he give him a stone?"

Bradstreet has here put a remarkable set of terms and texts in play, the import of which is the poem's final and most confoundingly splendid moment. No consolation will come—no escape from "vexation"—that does not recognize the radical paradoxes involved in trying to speak of transhuman things. The message comes "from before all eternity," an astonishing conception, especially for a Christian. It says: do not ask for bread, ask for a stone. The stone will have on it a word that is an unreadable redemptive name. The name will be a death—it is "grav'd"—for in this vision, the "letter [that] killeth" is also "the spirit [that] giveth life" (2 Corinthians 3:6).

Thinking of Bradstreet writing "Contemplations" in her Bay Colony home, Michael Ditmore is struck by its "thorough evasion... of what we must assume to have been Bradstreet's decades of actual New England wilderness experience."[12] But the American world, as we know, never enters any of her works, at least not on its own terms, as it does, however abrasively, in Bradford, Winthrop, and other more secular men, like Smith, who all struggled in it. Nonetheless, "Contemplations" is an impressive "wilderness" poem. For all her exquisite powers of perception, Bradstreet did not see the American world at all, at least so far as we can see. She registered wilderness only—yet profoundly too—in a spiritual and typological sense. For Bradstreet, wilderness is a condition of psychic and emotional bewilderment for which "vexation" was a favorite, and entirely apt, term.

If she doesn't even see the American world, she also pays scant attention to the "swift Annual, and diurnal" (*The Tenth Muse; Several Poems*, 222) course of the world of John Winthrop, her father, and her husband, all prominent figures in the attempt to build its earthly city. With one exception (and that only in part an exception, as we'll see)—"A Dialogue between Old *England* and New; concerning their present Troubles, *Anno*, 1642"—the colonial world appears significant in her verse when it disturbs or fractures her domestic peace, most dramatically when her husband or son are away from home doing the colony's business.

Unlike Anne Hutchinson, Bradstreet never directly calls the Bay Colony to a spiritual account of itself. But as so many of her readers know, Bradstreet's public status as a woman shapes much of her best work with its clear view of the vanities of the earthly city she lived in and the illusions of masculine "preheminence." The ironic wit of her earlier work succeeds to the more severe spiritual focus of the later verse, "Contemplations" being the premier example of the quest that takes over her writing: the turn from Coriolanus to Richard Poirier's "World Elsewhere" (or, in Baudelaire's more stringent formula, "[a]nywhere out of the world").[13]

Bradford's separatist venture and, perhaps even more, his late "Hebrew Exercises" are turns from the world quite like Bradstreet's. Winthrop's case is different—a brave plunge to bring radical change to a real world about as complex and dangerous as one can imagine and as he was himself. He saw it in the global and imperial terms—political as well as religious—that he brought with him from England. But his was also a world elsewhere, for it was, as he knew, in constant pursuit even after he finally engineered the Cambridge Platform. His "Journal/History" is bedeviled with his search for definitive signs of the colony's election. In a spiritual sense, Winthrop's world is often even more ominous than Bradstreet's, because he never exhibits the inner certitude that led her to pen the final astonishing stanza of "Contemplations."

But all three are together in never having grasped that there was another world elsewhere, the native American world, that might have brought some enlightenment to the spiritual and secular imaginings they brought with them from monotheist Europe. Of the three, Bradford alone glimpsed it when fate or God or Massasoit laid it in his way. Bradstreet is the one whom it touched hardly at all. We can see why it didn't in the climactic movement of "A Dialogue between Old *England* and New," New England's message of comfort to an Old England suffering religious and political turmoil in 1642.[14]

Following an extended imagination of an all-England destruction of "*Romes* whore, with all her trumpery" (*The Tenth Muse; Several Poems*, 200), Bradstreet's vision grows global.

> This done with brandish'd Swords to *Turky* goe,
> For then what is't, but English blades dare do,
> And lay her waste for so's the sacred Doom,
> And do to *Gog* as thou hast done to *Rome*.
> Oh *Abraham*'s see[d] lift up your heads on high,
> For sure the day of your Redemption's nigh. (*The Tenth Muse; Several Poems*, 202)

And after that happy day of apocalyptic wrath,

> Then follows dayes of happiness and rest;
> Whose lot doth fall to live therein is blest:

> No Canaanite shall then be found i'th' Land,
> And holiness on horses bells shall stand. (*The Tenth Muse; Several Poems*, 202)

This cleansing of the land of the Canaanite natives recalls the *Arbella* sermon's argument for "Christian Charity." "Though not the Canaanites" is the sermon's shorthand reference to various Old Testament texts, especially Deuteronomy and Joshua, where the dreadful tales of Canaanite expulsion and extermination are told. More even than Bradford and Winthrop, Bradstreet has inherited that vision and vocabulary. Peering into the promised "days of happiness and rest," Bradford knows that "no Canaanite shall then be found i'th' Land." She knows this because she has thoroughly internalized the Word of God, in this case Zechariah 14:20–21.

> In that day shall there be upon the bells of the horses, Holiness Unto The Lord . . .
> and in that day there shall be no more the Canaanite in the house of the Lord of hosts.

Fortunately, that day has never come. Blessedly, those who imagined and even worked to achieve it would be held in check, at least for a time, by a less imperial if no less consequential power that would work its will in New World history: "[c]ircumstance, that unspiritual God."[15] Circumstance, not ideology, brought the invaders to trade and treaty-making.

CHAPTER SEVEN

Cotton Mather's *Magnalia*

Model cases of practical letters, Puritan writings expected to be judged by measures as absolute and objective as God Almighty. Beyond that unconditional standard of judgment, they submitted to another set of objective, applied measures. The *Magnalia*, for example, was a commission that the Massachusetts Church issued and that Mather took up in the shambles of the witch trials of 1692–93. But the work's religious stock fell precipitately in the colonial world of Benjamin Franklin and the republican world of Jefferson and Adams and beyond. A latitudinarian theology and ecclesiology and a more secular ethos disparaged the *Magnalia*'s supreme Puritan spirit and its correspondingly difficult and spectacular prose. Conceived as a monumental testament to the achievements of reformed religion, the *Magnalia* fell upon stony Enlightenment soil.

Few periods in Western history are more fraught with "cultural change" than the American colonial centuries, and no document of English colonialism before the Declaration of Independence is more revealing of the early modern years than the *Magnalia*. Yet this great and pivotal American work remains little known and hardly read. It is not even included in the Library of America. Though published more than three hundred years ago, in 1702, there has never been a complete scholarly edition.[1]

Sacvan Bercovitch launched his distinguished academic career in 1966 by putting the *Magnalia* at the front and center of his work.[2] In the new historicist map he sketched for traversing its terra incognita—his map remains authoritative—the *Magnalia* emerged as the first comprehensive argument for the idea of America as the "redeemer nation."[3] Drawing on Ernest Lee Tuveson's earlier studies in American history of ideas, Bercovitch shifted the focus slightly but decisively to the *Magnalia*'s formal and literary features. Through Bercovitch, the *Magnalia*'s redeemer nation emerged less as Tuveson's imaginative idea than as a literary—a rhetorical and aesthetic—invention. Transcending its historical particulars, Bercovitch's *Magnalia* had, he argued, the mythic power and coherence of a "New England epic."

But Bercovitch's approach obscured the *Magnalia* by making it a far more orderly and internally consistent work than in fact it is. The light that suffuses it is incoherent, like every daylit world, and so is the light that scholarship throws back upon it. That's why literary and historical documents such as the *Magnalia* have to be addressed through rigorous attention—time- and date-stamped—to their minute historical particulars. In representing the *Magnalia*, Bercovitch, like many new historicists, neglected or turned away from traditional philological theory and method, whose specialized investigations, it was judged, missed the forest for the trees. When Nietzsche's *The Birth of Tragedy* brought that charge against philology in 1872, the book opened up a greatly consequential line of strongly theorized humanist studies. But not all of the strengths of that line proved to be virtues, as a case like the *Magnalia* shows.

That is the framework where the significance of Reiner Smolinski's work becomes apparent. It has "the privilege of its historic"—its philological—"backwardness."[4] Though never specifically cited, Bercovitch's unified field theory of the Puritan ethos, and of the *Magnalia* in particular, is Smolinski's chief critical target. Bercovitch argued that the *Magnalia* transcended its "outdated" history by "infus[ing] the word ['American'] with the imaginative power it has carried ever since": "the redemptive meaning of America." By contrast, Smolinski's *Magnalia* is a polemical action supporting Reformed religion's "struggle for survival" under its special menacing conditions.[5] For Smolinski, scanting attention to those menacing conditions, Bercovitch's symbolic meanings remained mystic meanings.

Nor does it signify for Smolinski whether the actions and the records seemed glorious or benighted, the best or the worst that may have been thought or urged. That's why he sets the *Magnalia* in relation to three histories of New England that put forward very different views. What signifies are the different existential purposes and truths that each work was advancing and the conditions that shaped those differences.[6]

Smolinski's method asks us to get as deeply as possible into the weeds of the *Magnalia*'s "Ecclesiastical History of New-England, from its first planting, in the year 1620, unto the year of Our Lord 1698." The misrule of historical events—Satan is the prince of Mather's world—propels what is surely a primary feature of the *Magnalia*: its tormented rage for order. We see this, for instance, in the fragile artfulness of the final chapter of book 7, where Mather recalls the Virgilian mode on which it set forth. Coming at the end of the *Magnalia*'s vast heap of broken images and memories, the move is moving precisely because its call for "Reformation" (*M*, 2:680) simultaneously represents such a willful resistance to reformation.[7]

Equally striking is how Bercovitch's millenarian parallel is made to arc across the *Magnalia*. Mather opens his work by pointing out that at "the beginning of the *sixteenth century*" there were "*three* most memorable things ... aris[ing] unto the world": "the *resurrection of literature* ... the opening of America ... the *Reformation of Religion*" (*M*, 1:42). But written at the end of the seventeenth century and on the verge of the eighteenth, the *Magnalia* also opens under the sign of three alarming historical factors: King William's War, when papal France and American Canaanites entered an alliance to destroy God's plantations; the continuing threats to the Congregational experiment from new antagonists within the spreading colonial communities; and perhaps most dreadful of all, the catastrophe of the Salem witch trials.

The *Magnalia* is so fretful and distressed throughout that to see it clearly requires what Milman Parry called "a picture of great detail."[8] Thick description is needed because documentary records are never transparent as to meaning. Of few works is this truth more true than of the *Magnalia*. It was written as a vast and, Mather hoped, a summary account of the great—even epochal—significance of Congregational Christianity in colonial America. Mather struggled with his own documents of record, including contemporary works, because they carried meanings and views he resisted and often deplored. In working to organize and control his unruly materials, both Mather and colonial New England swing into clearer, if also far more contentious, view. The case of the *Magnalia* reminds us that literary records always have more than "merely historical" or symbolical significance. Mather's afflicted righteousness seems as alive and well today as it was then and as it would continue to be throughout the subsequent three hundred afflicted years of New World history.

I

The received *Magnalia*, commissioned in March 1693 and published in 1702, unfolds through shifting and volatile circumstances. Michael Mages's standard account argues that it was substantially "complete" either in early 1696 or early 1697.[9] But the *Magnalia* was far from finished in 1696 or even 1697. Indeed, it was essentially reconceived in mid-to-late 1697, when Mather first began to address the witch trials. All of "Ecclesiarum Praelia" (book 7) was written in 1698, much of it late in that year, and it remained incomplete until January 1699. Even more interesting, various events, some dated by Mather himself, show that he was making substantial additions to the work through 1699 and even into early 1700, only shortly before the manuscript went to London for publication. Furthermore, several works separately published between 1697 and 1700 were eventually placed in the *Magnalia*, suggesting that some or all were written and added very late. The crucial sections of "Thaumatographia Pneumatica," on demonic presences in New England—the "Thirteenth Example" from John Bailey's diary, "Sadducismus Debellatus," and "A Token for the Children of New England" (*M*, 2:470–86)—were all no earlier than late 1797.

Because an extended composition history (1693–1701) unsettled the *Magnalia*'s original organizational design, we need a schedule of the changes it underwent between 1696 and 1702. Updating our knowledge will show how the *Magnalia* embroils itself in its own contradictory circumstances, and why it is all the more impressive as a result. Whether viewed at the macro level of its overall structure or through the microfeatures of its extravagant style, the *Magnalia*'s incoherences are marks of honor. To assess those unsettled energies, we want a clear view of its "outdated" documentary details. The *Magnalia* is rich in particulate matter.

A SCHEDULE OF THE *MAGNALIA*'S REVISIONS

Book 1: addition February 1698, "The Bostonian Ebenezer" (15 pages, 23 percent of book 1)

Book 2: addition, probably mid-1697, *Pietas in Patriam* (76 pages, 52 percent of book 2)

Book 3: addition, early 1698, *A Good Man Making a Good End* (24 pages, 7 percent of book 3)

Book 5: addition, 1699, *Thirty Important Cases . . .* (28 pages, 19 percent of book 5)

Book 6: additions in late 1697, 1698, 1699, and 1700, "Mantissa"; *Humiliations follow'd with deliverances . . .* [the Swarton captivity narrative]; the "Terribilia Dei" sermon; *Pillars of Salt*; "Thaumatographia Pneumatica" ("Thirteenth Example" and "Sadducismus Debellatus"); *A Token for Children* (67 pages, 47 percent of book 6)[10]

Book 7: additions in 1699 and 1700, "Wolves in Sheeps Cloathing" (originally published as *A Warning to the Flocks . . .*); *Decennium Luctuosum*, including the Dustan captivity narrative from *Humiliations follow'd with deliverances . . .* ; the 1698 sermon *Observable Things* (102 pages, 52 percent of book 7)

From this we see that (1) the early to mid-1697 *Magnalia* was much shorter than the first edition; (2) the text was more coherently organized; and (3) except for a brief foray in mid-1694 (with the "Brontologia Sacra" sermon; *M*, 2:361–72), its history carried only into mid-1691 (*M*, 1:602). It avoided any discussion of the witch trials and hadn't begun its account of King William's War. Because Mather wrote his biography of Governor William Phips in 1696, it's likely that he began to conceive a massive augmentation of the *Magnalia* as he was writing the Phips piece, which was eventually placed in book 2.[11] The biography forced open the subjects of the witch trials and King William's War, the two events that dominate the changes and additions that come into the expanded *Magnalia* of 1697–1700. Both figure prominently in the central sections 16–18 of *Pietas in Patriam* (*M*, 1:204–22) where they are introduced with an arresting passage that calls ahead to book 6, chapter 7: "Reader, prepare to be entertained with as prodigious matters as can be put into any history! And let him that writes the next *Thaumatographia Pneumatica*, allow to these prodigies the chief place among the wonders" (*M*, 1:205). "Him that writes the next" is a quirky forecast of the crucial "Sadducismus Debellatus" section of book 6, chapter 7, which Mather had yet to lift from John Hale and copy into the *Magnalia*.

The schedule also suggests that when Mather decided—probably in 1697—to organize the *Magnalia* by books, he was codifying a formal structure present from the outset: accumulating materials by block addition. Changes are introduced as "appendices" to already "finished" books. The sectional organization of the *Magnalia* supports its seriatim presentation of exempla, which Mather definitely augmented at various times. An appendix itself could accumulate a block addition, as happens in books 6 and 7. At some point Mather even seems to have "interpos[ed]" (*M*, 1:25) an entire book (book 6) into the encyclopedic history he had initially conceived.

Against that compositional background, one further late addition—the last addition of all—needs attention. This is the unsignatured foldout object *An Exact Mapp of New England and New York* that is set before the seven books of the *Magnalia* in the first 1702 London edition (see fig. 3).[12] It is the final bibliographical preliminary, following the testimonials, Mather's introduction, and the table of contents.

The map was chosen and placed as the *Magnalia*'s frontispiece by the London publisher Thomas Parkhurst, who did not consult Mather about it.[13] Like the text on the cover sheet of the *Arbella* sermon, the map shows that Parkhurst wanted to supply the work with an interpretive aid, in this case visual, that set an explanatory preface before Mather's "Ecclesiastical History of New-England, from its first planting, in the year 1620, unto the year of Our Lord 1698."[14]

The map shows that Parkhurst read the *Magnalia* with care. We can see this best if we exploit our historical (dis)advantage and try to close the distance between ourselves and Parkhurst's Cheapside. Like so many maps, this one is a reconstruction from two maps that were created earlier,

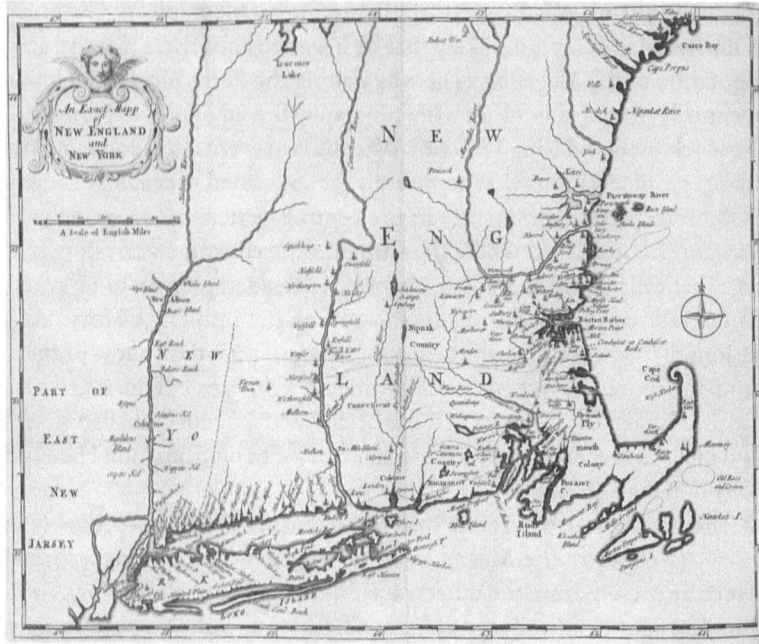

FIGURE 3. *An Exact Mapp of New England and New York* (London, 1702). Foldout map printed by Thomas Parkhurst in the first edition of Mather's *Magnalia Christi Americana*. Photograph: Yale University Library.

the most important one being augmented as it went through several editions.[15] The maps, reproduced in figures 4 and 5, are John Thornton, Robert Morden, and Phillip Lea's *A New Map of New England New York New Iarsey Pensilvania Maryland and Virginia* (London, 1685) and John Seller's *A mapp of New England* (London, 1675).

The publisher's *Exact Mapp* speaks eloquently through what it takes from its exemplar maps and in what it leaves out. Parkhurst extends the region of the larger and more detailed 1685 map with the 1675 map's representation of the northern region to Casco Bay. At the same time, he erases almost everything in the 1685 map's regions that extends to the west of New York's Hudson River valley. He apparently does this in order to expand a view of the area discussed in Mather's account of King William's War.

An especially interesting feature of Parkhurst's map is the sense of emptiness it conveys for all the regions that lie beyond New England as Mather's history represents it. The beautiful 1685 Thornton-Morden-Lea map is dramatically different, filling its uninhabited regions with small decorative features that help to create an image of civilized possibilities:

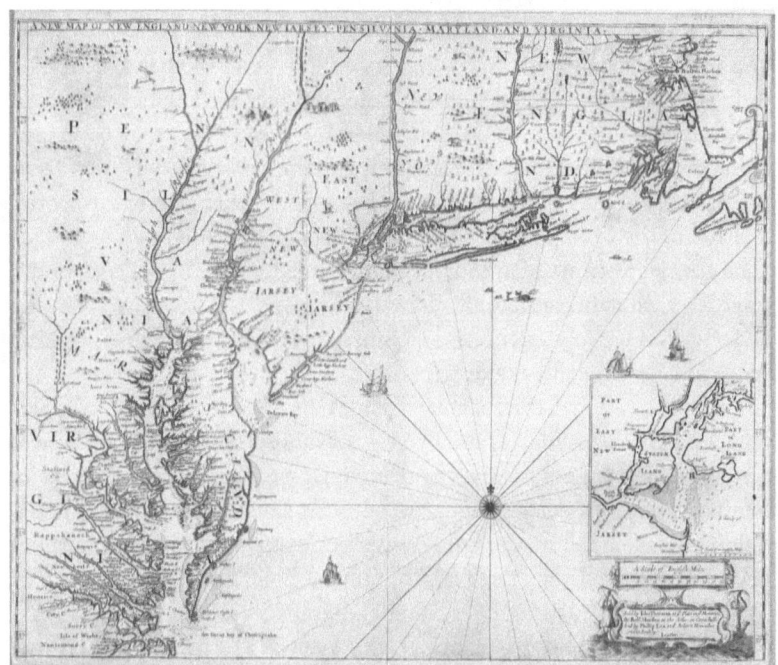

FIGURE 4. John Thornton, Robert Morden, and Phillip Lea, *A New Map of New England and New York, New Iarsey, Pensilvania, Maryland, and Virginia* (London, 1685). Photograph: Norman B. Leventhal Map Center Collection.

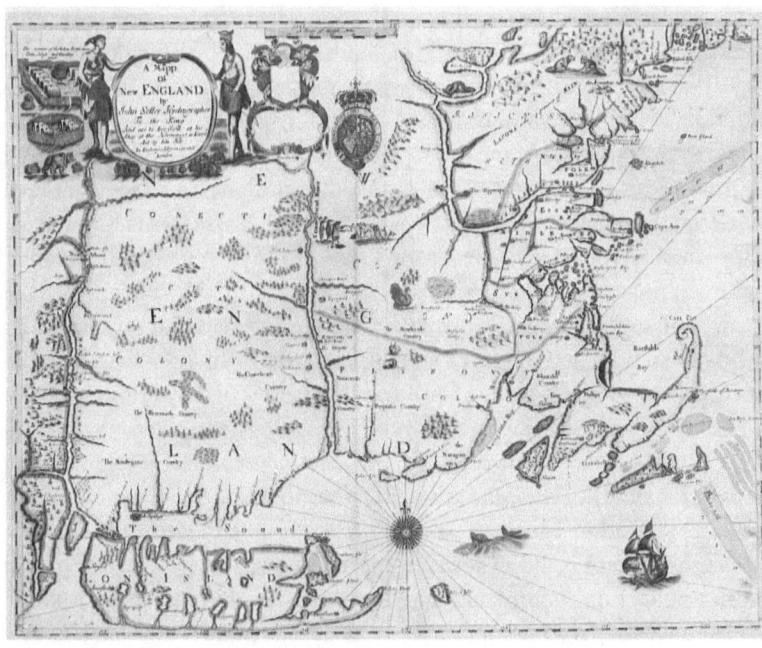

FIGURE 5. John Sellers, *A Mapp of New England* (London, 1675). Photograph: Norman B. Leventhal Map Center Collection.

"To the ambitious person, the map would have presented an enticing vista: it displays a loose federation of colonies, between and beyond which there appears to be ample unclaimed land. It creates an image of an area comfortingly linked by civilization but still containing much open territory."[16] Parkhurst's *Magnalia* map focuses on Mather's narrower world. Neither of the exemplar maps displays the New England town icons that are a special feature of Parkhurst's map. Indeed, with but one exception, only New England settlements have these icons, which convey—in the otherwise relatively featureless expanse of Parkhurst's map—a strong sense of New England as a restricted locale.[17]

Equally striking in the Parkhurst map is the absence of Virginia, Maryland, and Pennsylvania, especially Pennsylvania. To Mather, Virginia was a secular enterprise, and Maryland, a papist enclave. But the absence of Pennsylvania is especially important because, since the founding of Philadelphia in 1682, Penn's very differently conceived religious community had quickly established itself as a significant colonial venture, a fact that Mather acknowledges in his severely critical account of "Foxian Quakerism" (*Magnalia*, book 7, chap. 4). But even as Mather noted the "*new turn* [that] MR. PENN" gave to the Quaker movement in Pennsylvania (*M* 2:523), he by no means abjured what he calls Quaker "pride, and hypocrisie, and hellish reviling against the painful ministers of Christ" (*M*, 2:531).[18]

But most striking of all is the difference between Parkhurst's map of New England, which is drawn from commercial exemplars, and the purely textual "MAP of the Country" that Mather lays into his work (*M*, 1:27–28). This is what Mather meant when he proposed, in his "General Introduction," to replace "Strabo's cloak" with a "Christiano-graphy" (*M*, 1:42–43): "an *Ecclesiastical Map*," that is, a tabular list of the Reformed Church communities and their clergymen. Mather underscores the difference between these two modes of mapping when he remarks that although for more than twenty years, "the blasting strokes of Heaven upon the secular affairs of this country have been such, as rather to abate than enlarge the growth of it; yet there are to be seen in it, at this present year 1696, these ... Christian Congregations, now worshipping our Lord Jesus Christ, in the several Counties of New England, and the Names of the Ministers."[19]

With these bibliographical facts in hand, we can begin to investigate how the *Magnalia* organizes itself, how the new materials fold into the 1693–97 state(s) of the *Magnalia*, and what the new organization means both from Mather's point of view and from ours. Though Mather's autograph for the 1702 printing does not survive, we can see how it was built up from a collection of print and manuscript material, some his own, some collected from his contemporaries or gathered from records ancient and modern, some from first-person oral report.[20] The first book, "Antiquities," sets down "A Field Prepared for Considerable Things to be Acted Thereupon"—that is to say, for the "Hecatompolis; Or, A Field Which The Lord Hath Blessed"—into a spiritual *mappa mundi*, "an Ecclesiastical Map of the country, thus undertaken" by the planting fathers (*M*, 1:86).

That the *Magnalia* means itself to be "acting thereupon" in 1702 is declared repeatedly. Mather's long bibliography, long a world's wonder, is no mere curriculum vitae. His works are both weapons taken up in a spiritual war and the records of when and why they were used. Nearly all the publications are urgent and occasional, and they are multiply published because the war is ongoing and the urgent occasions ever present.

The massive set of materials added to the *Magnalia*'s opening and closing books (1, 6, and 7) brings all that into sharp focus. The two framing sermons are especially striking. Mather caps book 1 with "The Boston Ebenezer," delivered on February 7, 1698, then quickly broadcast in print for the larger New England community, and finally included in the *Magnalia* (*M*, 1:90–104) for long-term inspiring recollection. Reprising 1 Samuel 7:12, the sermon reminds the people of Boston how the Lord delivered them from the calamities of King William's War. Although the Treaty of Ryswick was signed in late September 1697, news of the war's end did not reach the colonies until the end of the year.[21] "Thus we have been this day," Mather says, "setting up a STONE, even an *Ebenezer*, among you" (*M*, 1:104). "This day" here encompasses date and place, stamped for three occasions, as a sign that "this day" is the emergency of the everyday: the day of the sermon (April 7, 1698); the day the sermon was subsequently published, late in 1698; and 1702, when the *Magnalia* was published.

The *Magnalia* ends with the "Observable Things" sermon (July 27, 1698) that Mather subsequently printed to "improve" his *Decennium Luctuosum* pamphlet, begun in August 1698.[22] For Mather, there cannot be too much writing, speaking, and publishing. So he makes this sermon a hortatory finale to *Decennium Luctuosum*, which is largely an historical narrative of events from the calamitous ten-year war "with Indian savages" (*M*, 2:580). The sermon is also a more ominous reprise of "The Boston Ebenezer" sermon delivered five months before, as its insistent refrain drives home. "Whoso is wise, will observe" that the calamities of the war, the descent of the witches on Salem, and the arrival of Quakers and "imposter" ministers (*M*, 2:659 and 537), Reformed as well as Anglican, plainly declare that the community must guard its righteousness if it is to preserve God's protection. The sermon and the *Magnalia* finish on a "demand for REFORMATION" (*M*, 2:680) in the Puritan community. That watchword clearly means to recall the "three most memorable things" from which Mather launched the *Magnalia*, and in particular "the opening of America [to] the Reformation of Religion (*M*, 1:42). Given the *Magnalia*'s extravagant history of Congregational institutions, including its demonological accounts of the Puritan record from the 1630s through the 1690s, the "Reformation" Mather calls for is a return to the imagined purities of a history darkly and deeply marked by what Robert Calef, reflecting critically on the witch trials, would call the "prejudice of [Congregational] education."[23]

Those framing sermons were among the many "prints" that Mather incorporated into the *Magnalia* from his own works, sometimes without acknowledging his authorship.[24] One is especially important. After the original *Magnalia* reached its (second or perhaps third) projected finish in 1698, Mather opened it again to add further materials. Like the works from the past on which he reflected so relentlessly, the *Magnalia* would have to be an unclosable book until the millennium—which Mather believed was near—closed the mysterious history in which he was living.

The sermons also set the context for the extensive late addition *Decennium Luctuosum*. Mather's chronicle of the war with papal France and its Indian allies follows directly on its precursor history, book 7, chapter 7, where he rehearsed the Indian conflicts from the Pequot War (1636) to the end of King Philip's War (1678). Indeed, *Decennium Luctuosum* is a response added to the problem left hanging in the final sentence of chapter 7: "God knows what will be the END" (*M*, 2:580). The "end" will be another, equally devastating war that itself portends further peril and conflict.

Also ongoing are the struggles with other, equally familiar, dangerous, even demonic enemies. The historical forces that emerged in the 1630s with Roger Williams and spread through the activities of the Antinomians, Anabaptists, and Quakers raised up formidable agents in Mather's world of the 1680s and 1690s. Most notable were the new and more powerful Quaker communities in and near New England (*M*, 2:644–52) and the appearance of "imposter" ministers in Massachusetts (*M*, 2:537–51). Especially interesting 1697 additions were the Hannah Dustan and Hannah Swarton captivity narratives (*M*, 2:634–36 and 357–61), which drew a connection between the Indian wars and the Reform communities' religious struggles. Swarton's narrative focuses on the threat posed by Catholic France. Its placement in book 6 reflects the religious issues of these communities, and its forecast of the *Decennium Luctuosum* history, the secular ones. Adding Dustan's narrative to book 7, Mather subtitles it "Dux Femina Facti" to echo the "Dux Femina Facta" title set above his astonishing tale of Anne Hutchinson and Mary Dyer in book 6, chapter 3 (*M*, 2:516–20). Placed near the end of the narrative of King William's War, he links the Dustan episode to his history of the ongoing threats to the "church order" of the Reform communities.

But *Decennium Luctuosum* addressed more than King William's War. Events from 1695 to 1697 led Mather to address once again the danger posed by the Society of Friends, for "if the Indians... prey[ed] upon the *frontiers* and *out-skirts* of the Province, the Quakers have chosen the very same *frontiers* and *out-skirts* for their more *spiritual assaults*" (*M*, 2:644). The Quakers had been the focus of book 7, chapter 4, written early. But the celebrated trial and acquittal of Thomas Maule led Mather to renew his attack (*M*, 2:644–52). His focus was Maule's "volume of *nonsensical* blasphemies and heresies," *Truth Held Forth and Maintained*, published in December 1695, in which he attacked both the current war and the witch trials (*M*, 2:644). Imprisoned for a year and finally tried late in 1696 for blasphemy and sedition, Maule was acquitted by the jury, even though the judges advised conviction.

The English Crown established an Anglican church (King's Chapel) in Boston in 1688—the same year, coincidentally, that Maule helped to found a meetinghouse, the first in the New World. For Mather, these religious and political threats seemed worse than those faced in the 1630s, since the Crown was also now seriously restricting the colony's long-enjoyed self-governance. The situation inspired Mather to some of his most energetic prose. In "Quakers Encountered" he gives thanks for the "special *favour* of God, that the number of Quakers is no greater; for if they should multiply, not only would *Christianity* be utterly extinguished, but *humanity* it self exterminated" (*M*, 2:652).

Particularly impressive is the artfulness of an earlier commentary on the Quakers. He quotes verbatim two colorful pieces of Quaker vilification against the Congregationalists—including one from "Penn the Quaker" (*M*, 2:531)—to underscore their scurrilous character.[25] First comes a splendid passage from Samuel Fisher's attack on "the great John Owen": "Thou fiery fighter and green-headed trumpeter; thou hedgehog and grinning dog; thou bastard that tumbled out of the mouth of the Babilonish bawd; thou mole; thou tinker; thou lizzard; thou bell of no metal but the tone of a kettle; thou wheelbarrow; thou whirlpool; thou whirlegig. O thou firebrand; thou adder and scorpion; thou louse; thou cowdung; thou moon-calf; thou ragged tatterdemalion; thou Judas" (*M*, 1:524). "And then," Mather remarks, "let Penn the Quaker add": "Thou gourmandizing Priest, one of the abominable tribe; thou bane of reason and beast of the earth; thou [least] to be spared of mankind; thou mountebank priest" (*M*, 2:531).[26] Here Mather's rhetorical move is particularly brilliant: quoting the prose of his enemies in order to dress them up in their own motley and, in his appropriation, turn their rags to riches.

A related attack on Congregational enemies, "Wolves in Sheep's Cloathing" (book 6, chap. 5), was incorporated into the *Magnalia* sometime early in 1700, only months before he sent his manuscript to London. Its narrative "History of several impostors, pretending to be Ministers" starts in 1624 and reaches forward to 1699. Mather augments these materials with several documents, including an official letter dated December 28, 1699 of "Faithful Advice from several Ministers of the Gospel" to warn "the Churches of New-England" of the dangers they continue to face (*M*, 2:537). The letter echoes the "Certain Proposals" signed by eight Harvard ministers in 1693, the document that launched the *Magnalia* project. The 1699 letter is signed by ten ministers, including Mather, who quotes the stories of other "impostor" ministers—Dick Swayn and Eleazer Kingsberry are named—culminating in the tale of Samuel May/Samuel Axel (*M*, 2:543–51).[27] The letter artfully reinforces the sense of the continuing emergency that is the central theme of the *Magnalia*, whose incorporated documents—in this case, correspondence within the community—establish the *Magnalia*'s expanding factual record.

II

When Mather called the *Magnalia* "The Ecclesiastical History of New-England," he presented it as an objectively truthful record. Though "objective" might seem the wrong word for a work pervaded by "Mather's ever present narrative voice,"[28] it is the most pertinent descriptor, if by "objective" we mean either grounded in a transcendental norm, like Plato's, or attested by a preponderant body of independent witnesses. "The Ecclesiastical History" implicitly declares that both measures apply to the *Magnalia*.

The secondary, empirical argument is based in the *Magnalia*'s archive of corroborated facts and first-person testimonies. This empirical data set is somewhat restricted, however, as Mather himself admits. Because "it is not the work of an historian, to commemorate the vices and villainies of men," Mather writes, "I have left unmentioned some censurable occurrences in the story of our Colonies" (*M*, 1:30). His intention, he declares, is less to generate "'indignation'" at wickedness than "'emulation'" of "'just . . . fair [and] honest actions'" (*M*, 1:30). The composition history here shows that among those "unmentioned . . . occurrences" were the witch trials. The original *Magnalia*—the 1697 version—was to have been a celebratory and inspiring record.

At that point Mather began a series of late revisions that added approximately 30 percent to the work in progress and more than 40 percent to books 6 and 7. At every stage, the *Magnalia*'s most generous empirical horizon would be monotheist religious communities, though papists don't really count and Quakers, scarcely.[29] Mather focuses on Reform congregations whose spirit lives through the four religious "classes" defined in book 3. He explicitly leaves out a class he calls the *"anomalies of New England"*'s Reformers because, while a few exhibited "godly" lives—even one Quaker!—they were in general "disagreeable to the *church order* for which the country was planted" (*M*, 2:242).

But Mather's principal address has a transcendental ground: the unimpeachable word of God sets his Model of Christian History, just as John Winthrop had appealed to the unimpeachable acts of God in his "Journal/History." The *Magnalia* reflects an eschatology more objectively true for him and the Christian world, regenerate or not, than the shadow world of contentious Europe, America, and New England. The *Magnalia* is a contemporary record built up from the textual ground of the *Biblia Sacra*, for which he was simultaneously composing a vast commentary (only now being published three hundred years later).[30] The model set a firm epistemological ground beneath his readings from the ancient world, sacred and secular; from the New England records; and from the contemporary events in which he himself was still taking part. Mather's method operates under the daring formula *"scriptural*, and therefore... *rational"* (*M*, 2:493).

But implementing the method was not only difficult, it was dangerous. Reform meant that fallible humans were expected to "divine" the meaning of eternal truth. That demand differs sharply from the task of fallible secular philologists studying fallible human works. A later, Enlightenment perspective would locate the Bible itself in that secular horizon. The rules *sola scriptura* and *sensus literalis* brooded over the Reformation like the Holy Spirit over sacred scripture, setting an absolute limit on the corruptions that frail humans—papists in particular, in the Reformer's view, with their despised *"mass-book"* (*M*, 1:35)—might lay upon the Word of God.

Indeed, because the Reformers laid such stress on scripture, they were especially attentive to the textual *cruces* pervading the universal history it projects. "Explaining and reconciling apparently contradictory passages" was the methodological ground of the Reformers' studies,[31] and it affected all Puritan discourse, including exploration and captivity narratives and reports of military campaigns against native peoples, such as the celebrated accounts of the Powhatan, Pequot, and Narragansett wars.[32] Everyone was under pressure to show how the tangled current world was part of revealed (and consummated) scriptural history.

So while Mather knew that his ecclesiastical history was incorporate with Christian eschatology, he also knew that different persons would have views that varied more or less from his own. He often cites them. But for him and for those divergent readers as well, the differences were not merely textual; they were, so to speak, textonic. They drew upon different practical beliefs that shaped different behaviors and drove different, seriously consequential actions. Objectively, the world the *Magnalia* records is a living scene of contested religious purpose. Mather underscored the deadly seriousness of that purpose in one of his late additions, the eulogy on the death of John Bailey (*M*, 1:602–26), with which the first volume of the *Magnalia* closes. The sermon rings the changes on the "peril" of the soul unprepared for death and judgment (*M*, 2:605).

So the style of the *Magnalia* is regularly ad hominem, whether the men and women are judged good or bad. Though he protests that he will avoid dealing "with fury and reproach on all who differ from him" (*M*, 1:30), the ferocity of his attacks is infamous. At his right hand are the hagiographical biographies of books 2, 3, and 4, at his left the denunciations of book 6 and especially book 7.[33] It required all of his considerable imaginative resources to fashion the eulogy for Governor Phips (*M*, 2:164–230), whose life might well have been differently presented.[34] But Phips was Mather's hero of contemporary Congregational Massachusetts, just as the "monster" Anne Hutchinson was its greatest villain. The misogynist attack on Hutchinson (*M*, 2:516–21)—a glorious piece of American prose—needs special attention because of what it shows about the *Magnalia*'s cultural and political importance and aesthetic power.

Like so much of Mather's prose, the passage builds itself from a complex set of literary allusions and references, both sacred and secular. Starting from Tertullian's *Prescription against Heretics* (chap. 41, sec. 5) and Paul's letter to Timothy (2 Timothy 3:6), Mather glances at the Eve of Genesis, the mother of all seducers, and moves quickly through related allusions to "Simon Magus... with his Helena, and Montanus with his Maximilla, for the more effectual propagation of their heresies, as Jerom[e] long since observed, and Epiphanius tells us" (*M*, 2:516). That gathering of historical references—signature Matherian rhetoric—suggests the manifold appearances of Hutchinson's demonic type. Mather's encapsulated mythohistory next calls up the Anabaptist "Munster tragedy" of 1534–35, which ushers in Mather's true contemporary subject: the threatening "*seditions* raised... by... this *Virago*" (*M*, 2:518), who came to Massachusetts from Lincolnshire, "a woman, a gentlewoman" with—Mather now begins to quote from John Winthrop, who will return in Mather's climactic paragraph—"an haughty carriage, busie spirit, competent wit, and a voluble tongue" (*M*, 2:516). The paragraph climaxes on a misogynist text from Juvenal, because even natural man recognizes the special character of such people: *Nulla fere causa est, in qua non femina litem moverit.*[35] Or in Mather's transliteration: "a *poyson* does never insinuate so quickly, nor operate so strongly, as when *women's milk* is the *vehicle* wherein 'tis given" (*M*, 2:516).

The next three paragraphs recount Mather's version of the central events, an argument he reshapes from Hutchinson's "call[ing] herself another *Priscilla*" (*M*, 2:517), the friend and companion of Paul (Acts 18). But Mather sees her as the Jezebel of Revelation 2:18–29, whose "claims to be a prophetess" the church at Thyatira was "tolerating," as Massachusetts was being "seduced" by Hutchinson. Hutchinson's career is a record of her "dangerous and *enchanting* extravagancies" (*M*, 2:518): her conventicles for women, her preaching, and the storm of enthusiasm and disapproval that followed; the official condemnation "of the *court*, as well as the *church* upon her" and, at trial, upon her "canting harrangue about her 'immediate revelations'"; her banishment from the colony, the court and church "finding no hope of reclaiming her from her scandalous" ways; and finally the death of her and her children "in a Dutch plantation called *Hebgate*," after her flight from Massachusetts to Rhode Island, "not liking," Mather laconically remarks, "to stay there" (*M*, 2:518).

Mather's great final paragraph plays monstrously with the thought, intimated earlier, that Hutchinson was a woman with power from the devil ("spreading *fascination* the *doctrines* did *bewitch* the minds of people" [*M*, 2:517]). Her children become an emblem of the "damnable doctrines ... hatched at her meetings" that went "crawling like vipers about the country" (*M*, 2:517). Echoing the "Sadducismus Debellatus" materials added to book 6, Mather raids the tabloid tales that followed Hutchinson out of Massachusetts—particularly John Winthrop's account—to build his final, amazing prose tour de force.

> The *erroneous gentlewoman* her self, convicted of holding about *thirty* monstrous opinions, growing big with child, and at length coming to her time of travail, was delivered of about *thirty* monstrous births at once; whereof some were bigger, some were lesser; of several figures; few of any perfect, none of any *humane* shape. This was a thing generally then asserted and believed; whereas, by some that were eye-witnesses, it is affirmed that these were no more *monstrous births*, than what it is frequent for women, labouring with *false conceptions*, to produce. (*M*, 2:519)[36]

The passage launches Mather into his shocking tale of Mary Dyer, "nearly related unto this gentlewoman, and infected with her heresies" (*M*, 2:519). She was "on October 17, 1637, delivered of as hideous a *monster* as perhaps the sun has ever lookt upon." This was a demon child: "It had no forehead, but above the eyes it had four horns; two of above an inch long, hard and sharp" (*M*, 2:519). Brought into the world by a "midwife ... strongly suspected of *witchcraft*"—Mather is obliquely recalling that Hutchinson practiced midwifery—the monster raises pandemonium among everyone nearby: "and about the time of the monster's death, which was two hours before his birth, such an odd *shake* was by invisible hands given to the bed as terrify'd the standers-by" (*M*, 2:519). When the child's grave was later opened, Mather has Virgil give the report of what was found: "*Monstrum, horrendum, in forme, ingens.*"[37] Mather does not mention Dyer's name or the fact that she was put to death as a witch.

Mather closes the section with an uncanny and suggestive coda.

> But of this monster, good reader, let us talk no further: for at this instant I find an odd passage in a letter of the famous Mr. Thomas Hooker about this matter; namely, this: "While I was thus musing, and thus writing, my study where I was writing, and the chamber where my wife was sitting, shook, as we thought, with an earthquake, by the space of half a quarter of an hour. We both perceived it, and presently went down. My maid in the kitchen observed the same. My wife said, it was the devil that was displeased that we confer about this occasion." (*M*, 2:519–20)

The passage illustrates one of Mather's most significant claims: the community maintains seismographs of the invisible world, and he is one of them. His prose reports on spirits malign and benevolent and testifies to their reality.

Mather's declarative ad hominem address was the required discourse of truth because actual persons were, willy-nilly, agents in a life-and-death spiritual war running *in saecula saeculorum*. To situate the work in Bercovitch's "realm of the imagination," then, whatever the virtues of that approach, is manifestly *not* to read it in the same spirit in which the author wrote it. More, it drains the work of its literary energy and diminishes its cultural importance. When Kenneth Silverman argues that "what unifies this seven-vault archive of fact, reminiscence, document, verse, and legend is Mather's ever present narrative voice," he explicitly invokes Bercovitch's Romantic reading of the *Magnalia*.[38]

Mather's voice is inescapable, but it is not, even in Mather's view, what unifies the *Magnalia*. It testifies that he stands by the *Magnalia*'s claims about a fateful religious and political struggle. But his testimony draws upon transpersonal sources. Jan Stievermann shows that the independent authority of its documentary materials turns the *Magnalia* into a medium for two other "voices" that are its source and end and test. One is "the voice of New England's Puritan orthodoxy speaking through Mather," the other is the voice of God himself speaking through all the "voices [of] a homogenous choir directed by the single divine truth."[39]

For Mather and his community, these voices are neither abstract nor figural; they are living and real. (For ourselves, if the voices seem dead and gone—if they have a "merely historical interest"—we will have expelled them from our hearing as surely as Hutchinson was expelled from Boston.) In the *Magnalia*, that first voice is beleaguered, the second is sure. The mission of the *Magnalia* is to arouse and comfort that beleaguered voice and to clarify that mysterious one. Those moves lay Mather's work on the anvil of his own prose. Stievermann notes the "semantic interferences" that necessarily spin off "the sheer number of . . . semantic and cultural connotations dragged along by the citations."[40] Such materials impose a weighty burden on Mather, who struggles to fashion a rhetoric that will testify not to his imaginative powers but to the truth of the two greater voices he is channeling: the voice of his militant, struggling community and the voice of God.

The *Magnalia*'s literary character becomes clear when we put it to the test posed, for example, by a work such as Philip Sidney's Aristotelian "The Defence of Poesy." Neither truth nor consequences apply in Sidney's "realm of the imagination," which is played in the optative mood. A work like the *Magnalia*, being declarative, chooses to meet more stringent demands. Its force rises from the danger it knows it is facing—or, in Mather's first-person testimony, "the difficulties and all the temptations with which my writing is attended" (*M*, 1:252). The "beast" Samuel Gorton (*M*, 2:505), the (unnamed) "monsters" Hutchinson and Dyer (*M* 2:518), the Quaker "madmen" (*M*, 2:525), the impostor ministers: all test and threaten his judgment and the order of his mind, but none more so than the demonic "Wonders of the Invisible World" presented in book 6, chapter 7, the "Thaumatographia Pneumatica."

III

Mather took up the scandal of the 1692–93 witch trials in "Thaumatographia Pneumatica," but in late 1697 or early 1698 he made a substantial addition—comprising almost 40 percent of the finished chapter—to his initial account. The entire section was carefully edited from the start. He included only a brief, relatively uncontroversial excerpt—the Joseph Beacon tale (*M*, 2:468–69)—from the 1693 pamphlet that brought him such opprobrium, *The Wonders of the Invisible World: Being an Account of the Tryals of Several Witches, Lately Executed in New-England*. Robert Calef, who authored a response to Mather in *More Wonders of the Invisible World*, is also never mentioned—a notable omission, since *More Wonders* was much on Mather's mind in 1697, the year Calef finished the compilation. Indeed, except for one brief and defensive reference to his "*adversaria*" (*M*, 2:469), Mather doesn't recall, much less directly address, the reproofs made against what he wrote and did at the time. Because he remained convinced that the community was threatened by demons, he was seeking new support for his fears and convictions. It came from Hale's *Modest Enquiry into the Nature of Witchcraft*, a report on the events by a participant who offered a chastened retrospective version of Mather's own contradictory responses to the trials. "Sadducismus Debellatus" is largely a direct quotation lifted from Hale's book.

Calef had vilified Mather's defense of the trials and executions as "ambidexter," which it was.[41] Indeed, the contradiction was broadcast by the two pamphlets issued at the height of the trials by Mather and his father: Mather's *Wonders of the Invisible World*, published on October 15, 1693, and his father's *Cases of Conscience Concerning Evil Spirits*, published shortly before. Silverman describes the problem with dramatic economy: "The drift of *Wonders of the Invisible World* is that devils have broke loose in New England, of *Cases of Conscience* that at Salem innocent people are being killed."[42] Father and son were not troubled by their different approaches, but they *were* dismayed at how shrewdly Mather's enemies exploited them in public. Given the apparent evidence and Puritan belief, uncertainties were inevitable, as the trial records themselves testify.[43]

In his 1697–1700 revisions, Mather used the *Magnalia* to vindicate his judgment about the action of spirit forces in the mortal world. Although "Sadducismus Debellatus" is in large part a defense of his views about demons and witches, it is introduced into the *Magnalia* with related materials that radically alter the fearful judgments that pervaded his writings up to 1693. These materials were "A Token for the Children" (*M*, 2:480–86), which was placed right after "Sadducismus Debellatus," and the Thirteenth Example (*M*, 2:470–71), which was placed just before. Literally, "Sadducismus Debellatus" is surrounded by angels.

The Thirteenth Example shifts from the dark wonders taken up in the previous twelve examples to introduce the subject of good angels "*continually . . . fly*[*ing*] about in our defiled atmosphere, to minister for the good of them that are to be the 'heirs of salvation'" (*M*, 2:470). The passage anticipates the angelic stories in "A Token for the Children," which Mather presents as salvific ministers to a troubled community. We know that "Sadducismus Debellatus" and "A Token for the Children" were added no earlier than late 1797, but we can see that the Thirteenth Example must have been a late addition as well. The section quotes from the diary of John Bailey (1643–1697), a document that Mather could not have seen until after Bailey's death (late 1697). The Thirteenth Example and "A Token for the Children" reflect his effort to moderate the confident ferocity of his 1688–1693 writings about witches and demons.[44]

Mather's editorial hand is even more aggressively at work within "Sadducismus Debellatus," the appropriation of Hale's account of the trials.

Although *A Modest Enquiry* is quite a long book, Mather prints only a fifteen-page passage carefully chosen to corroborate Mather's key views about witchcraft.[45] Hale's text allowed Mather to support, however indirectly, the community's critical reflections on the witch trials he had so energetically promoted. It also allowed him to go on record opposing spectral evidence. Significantly, that move came in a series of annotations (*M*, 2:478–79) he added to his excerpt from Hale.

But Hale also helped Mather stand by his judgments of George Burroughs and the others executed for witchcraft. Like Mather, Hale himself believed that witchcraft was at work in the events of 1692–93. Like Mather, Hale also judged that demons could use a religious community's religious fears to deceive and damage itself. So Hale reflects that as "the number and quality of the persons accus'd" grew, the authorities ("those that were concern'd") "feared that Satan by his wiles had enwrapped innocent persons under the imputation" of witchcraft (*M*, 2:476). The passages Mather quotes from Hale all emphasize what Hale represents as the reasons for supposing the guilt of the executed.

But Hale's report is finally an expression of uncertainty about the judgments passed and of regret that innocent people were killed. Indeed, Hale argues that the fearful "errors and mistakes that have been in the year 1692" (*ME*, 167) have a long New England history. Because "a foundation [was] laid to lead into error those that came after [i. e., Hale and his generation]," Hale writes, "May we not say in this matter, as it is, Psal. 106:6. *We have sinned with our fathers?* And as, *Lam* 5:7. *Our fathers have sinned and are not, and we have born their iniquities?* And whether this be not one of the sins the Lord hath been many years contending with us for, is worthy our serious enquiry" (*ME*, 166). So Hale ends his book with extensive prayers for forgiveness on behalf of the community: "But such was the darkness of that day, the tortures and lamentations of the afflicted, and the power of former presidents [i.e., precedents], that we walked in the clouds, and could not see our way.... So that... in the day when [the Lord] shall visit, he will not visit this sin upon our land, but blot it out, and wash it away with the blood of Jesus Christ" (*ME*, 167–68).[46]

Mather includes none of that material in the *Magnalia*, because he wants to preserve the authority of the church's long-established religious institutions ("those that were concern'd"). He doesn't mention the "Day of Prayer and Fasting" (January 14, 1697) or the public recantation by the jurors. Because belief in spirit forces is for Mather fundamental to the community's life and "church order," the institutions charged with sustaining that belief have to be protected. In Hale's view, the first two generations of Puritans passed "downwards" to the third generation dangerous "presidents" about witches. But Mather's whole approach in the

Magnalia was to glorify the previous civil and ministerial generations and to cite case after case of pneumatic phenomena.

Hale's account, endorsed by Mather, reports that the trials were stopped by Governor Phips when "the number and quality of the persons accused" swelled alarmingly. The juries began to "fear . . . they had gone too far" (*M*, 2:476). In a later view, certainly our own, even to authorize such trials would be going too far. But that was not the view of Hale or Mather or their community. If Mather had ever thought the discovery of witches was so important that fatal misjudgments had to be accepted, after 1693 he saw the prudence of proceeding cautiously. Lest his caution be misunderstood, he ends his comments on Hale by pointing out that "[u]pon the whole, [Hale] spends whole chapters to prove that there yet is a witch" (*M*, 2:479).

But how does one recognize a witch? Mather closes "Sadducismus Debellatus" by quoting what he represents as Hale's definition of a witch: "a person 'that, having the free use of reason, doth knowingly and willingly seek and obtain of the devil, or any other god, besides the true God Jehovah, an *ability* to do or know strange things, or things which he cannot by his humane abilities arrive unto. This person is a witch'" (*M*, 2:479). But that is not verbatim Hale, who actually says that witches are persons "that being brought up under the means of the knowledge of the true God, yet being in their right mind, or free use of their reason, do knowingly & willingly depart from the true God, so as to devote themselves unto, and seek for their help from another God, or the Devil, as did the Devils Priests, and Prophets of old that were Magicians" (*ME*, 128).

The differences between these two passages are significant. First, that the two men would have different definitions only shows that a consensual definition would be difficult, if not impossible. Indeed, the different definitions underscore the fundamental problem of the witch trials themselves. Beyond that, what do we make of Mather's misquotation? A generous reading might say that Mather was simply trying to clarify Hale. Besides, quoting Hale objectifies the judgment being offered on this crucial matter. That move returns "Sadducismus Debellatus" from Mather writing in propria persona to its rhetoric of quotation.

Here is the key phrasal difference: "an ability to do or know strange things, or things which he cannot by his humane abilities arrive unto." Perhaps Hale avoids that kind of formulation because he saw that the trial courts wandered into deadly error by judging that they could "know strange things . . . by . . . humane abilities." Mather, however, is convinced that the judges are able to judge correctly because their institutions were planted by God and full of grace, as books 2–5 attest. For Hale, that institutional history is also a history of human self-deceptions about witches and demons, if not about other matters as well. For Mather, the deceptions are not institutional, the iniquities of the fathers; they are counterinstitutional seditions and apostasies. The *Magnalia*'s books of the governors and the divines (books 2 and 3) do not tell of iniquities, the history of Harvard (book 3) is a glory road, and book 5 is a decisive manifesto. Even "godly" persons are excluded from the faithful of book 3 if they are judged to have disrupted "church order."

But while the *Magnalia* preserves the distinction between the faithful and the fallen in its very structure, its tales introduce complications. For Mather, the Americans are, as they were for nearly all the colonials, Canaanites and hence enemies of God ordained for extermination, according to scripture. Because Dustan and Swarton are for Mather virtually antitypes of Jael, their narratives are uncomplicated tales of heroic endeavor. Yet *history*, Mather's focus, has inevitably drawn out the complications of Swarton and Duston's fearful tales, and Mather's own fearful tale-tellings have been a great aid to that re-memory. A larger history than Mather's broods over these texts, telling us to trust the tale's whole truth as we try to close with the teller's particular intentional truth. We negotiate this double-edged reading because Mather's intentions are so perfectly declared that they throw into relief everything their purpose-driven views are determined to cast out.

This generic character of Mather's prose explains why his definition of a witch, and not Hale's, speaks most clearly to the truth of the trials and their threat to the community. To the best of their abilities, the jurors sought knowledge of the invisible world and then took action on behalf of the community. Hale's argument is that the court had "gone too far" because an unexpected number of persons—and, most important, an unexpected class of persons—were being brought to judgment. But in defining a witch, Mather touches on a more insidious and fundamental problem than the crude one of too many executions. The jurors had gone too far because the community had gone too far—Mather had gone too far—in assuming a human "ability to do or know strange things" and in establishing a political instrument for executing that presumed power.

This reading takes Mather, so to speak, at his word. Did he actually *intend* to suggest that the community was unknowingly bedeviled? He did not say that explicitly and certainly never would have. But of Satan's power he had no doubt, so he gave a fearful inflection to Hale's afflicted and movingly helpless account. That inflection echoes the tell-tale heart of the *Magnalia*'s history and of Mather himself. He took a great interest—perhaps that would be, as such, an inordinate interest—in angels and devils and, by his own accounts, carried out serious investigations into apparent spirit-world phenomena. He believed in and had personal experience of "strange things" and intervened to do something about them, as we know best from his own stories of Margaret Rule and the Goodwin family. Mather's entire history, education, and experience led him into temptations that he himself knew were temptations.

So when Calef argues that Mather had gone astray because of his "prejudice of education,"[47] his remark brings a profound insight into Mather, the "church order" of the community, and the trials themselves. The *Magnalia* is not a history of New England but an *ecclesiastical history* of the region. All the secular struggles and dangers are intelligible within Mather's religious frame of reference: "But of all History it must be confessed, that the palm is to be given unto Church History.... the History of the people whom the Son of God hath redeemed . . . in expectation of a Kingdom, whereto they shall be in another and a better World advanced" (*M*, 1:28). But before the coming of that "better World," Mather and his community lived in a world whose prince was Satan and whose rule was sanctioned by God himself. It was the same world that they left behind and then brought over from Europe and that they found waiting for them—even *promised* to them—to settle.[48] The one world they did *not* discover when they came was the new world of the indigenous people living there. But because of the "prejudice of education" Mather lays out in *Magnalia*, especially in books 2–5, "we walked in the clouds, and could not see our way."

So while it seems to me shrewd and just to call "Mather's ever present narrative voice—learned, facetious, emphatic, at once intimate and grand," it also seems a serious failure of judgment to call it "showman-like, as if his history were some banquet and he the master of ceremonies."[49] Even in its most academic or facetious moments, which are many, Mather's prose is a work of difficulty and temptation. Its predicament is fairly defined in Mather's biography of the man who more than any other was the type to his antitype, the "rich scholar" and "*walking library*" John Cotton (*M*, 1:254 and 273). In writing his life, Mather singles out Cotton's "vain persuasion" that brought him to his first, and thoroughly characteristic, crisis: "that, if he became a *godly* man, 'twould spoil him for being a *learned* one" (*M*, 1:255). Mather's learned life was the field on which his godly life was fought. It was a field on which, by definition or by fate, he could not possibly triumph.

The *Magnalia* is the representation of a society that lives in fear and trembling of its circumstances and of itself as the muddled—sometimes even the secret—agent of those forces. And Mather is that Puritan society's Everyman. The tales and the telling of the tales are rich because they are all, as he insists, greater than their compiler and teller, who becomes thereby the struggling and bewildered hero of his own time. Composing and organizing the *Magnalia* was itself an event that reflects the occasional forces Mather had to deal with. It is not a well-wrought work—it is a *relentless* work. It was cobbled together over time—eight years—from pieces that forced themselves to attention and came in randomly. Its composition history is a revision history. However, coming as great blocks of finished prose, the new content creates even greater "semantic interferences" than those spun off by Mather's elaborate quotations and allusions.

Because nearly all of these materials—the sermons are exemplary—possess their own formal integrity, they are extravagant in relation to the *Magnalia* as a whole. Polemically focused on specific persons, circumstances, or events, they make two simultaneous declarations: that if Mather's engagements are rich and intense, their negative spaces are equally so. Consequently, while Mather's prose is always trying to say exactly what he means—his prose is decisive and intentional—it is always poised to say more than it means. But its excess is not aesthetic in a Romantic sense. It does not emerge from untapped symbolic resources, but from its collision with the reality it insists upon engaging. So might the *Magnalia* be called "a great work of imagination." Like Ahab hurling himself and the *Pequod* against Moby-Dick, Mather and the *Magnalia* hurl themselves against an invincible enemy, the prince of this world and his satanic forces. That's why "failure stalks in every word" and literary move the *Magnalia* makes.[50] That's also why it strikes one as at once, like Ahab, so piteous, so terrible, and so stupendous.

INTERCHAPTER 1

COVENANT CHAIN TREATY-MAKING AND FRANKLIN'S TREATY FOLIOS

As the 1621 treaty between the Plymouth Colony and the Wampanoag Confederacy shows, treaty-making was a conglomerate and volatile event. The Native conventions that organized the events persisted throughout the eighteenth century, though they began to change when the Revolution erupted, as the disgraceful Treaty of Fort Pitt (1778) foretold.[1] With the founding of the United States, the treaties the Americans made with the former English colonists were declared void.

The most celebrated colonial records of Indian treaty-making are the set of handsome folios that Benjamin Franklin printed between 1736 and 1761.[2] They all follow a carefully planned bibliographical design, like this, the title page of the 1742 *Treaty held with the Indians of the Six Nations, at Philadelphia, in July, 1742* (see fig. 6).

Keying on the fine spacings and well-molded type, Constance Rourke judged that the designs "magnificently expressed the occasion[s] ... with full dignity and an inherent drama." The folios, she went on to say, were fit reflections of an "immemorial" history.[3]

But the folios were far from accurate reflections of the treaties' immediate history and occasions. Rourke was reading the folios, not the treaties, and the folios drastically reconfigure the treaty-making into an "immemorial"—that is to say, Western European colonial—Enlightenment event. Far from reaching beyond memory or tradition, however, these treaties were deeply invested in preserving both. So in reading the beautifully attenuated folio records, we do well to recall James Merrell's extraordinary description of the physical scene of the treaty made at Easton in 1756. Merrell's tour-de-force reconstruction of the event reminds us that treaty-makings, not least the Covenant Chain treaties, were messy and turbulent affairs, as difficult to arrange as to manage.

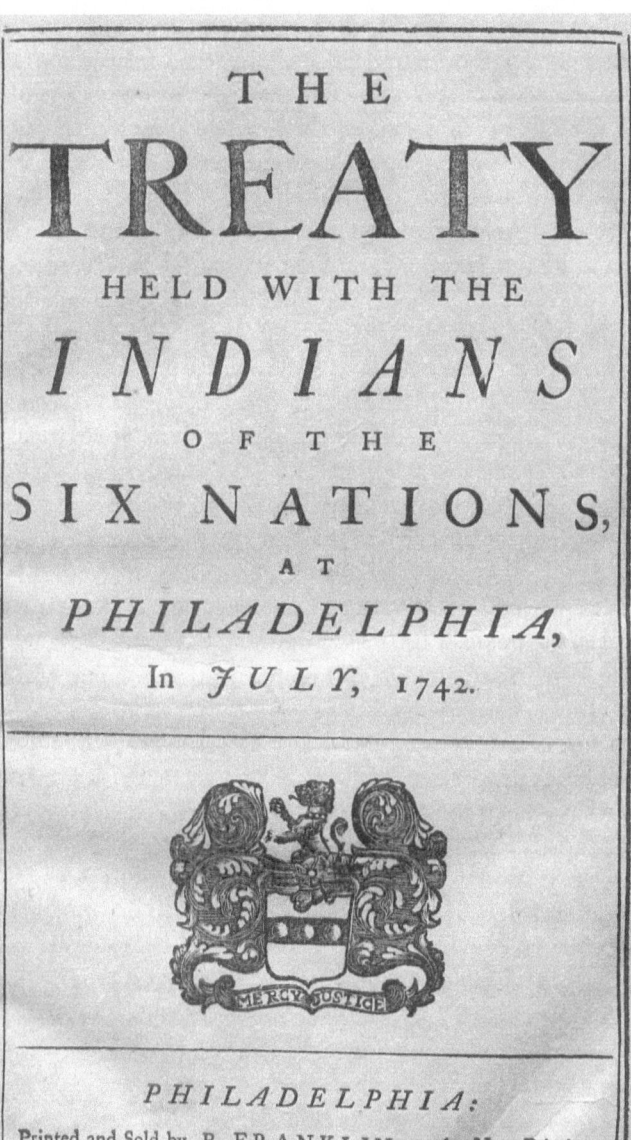

FIGURE 6. Title page of Benjamin Franklin's folio printing of *The Treaty Held with the Indians of the Six Nations, at Philadelphia, in July, 1742*. Photograph: American Philosophical Society.

The first thing to strike any visitor at a treaty site was the human carnival there. The sheer number of people packed into the houses, taverns, council-chambers, and streets beggared belief.... The council was a special occasion that tempted many Pennsylvanians to drop what they were doing and take a look.... A similar curiosity enticed... Indians to a treaty... who, despite the fear of disease, wanted to see the sights for themselves.... The treaty ground was a visual feast. Colonists ranged in appearance from the powdered wig and laced cuffs of a governor or councilor to the moccasins and leggings of a fur trader, from the sober garb of Quakers to the work clothes of farmers and tradesmen [and] the colors of provincial troops and the redcoats of British regulars.... Even if many natives seemed, to colonists, "poorly dressed" in ragged matchcoats or dirty leggings, they still cut imposing figures with their scalp locks, body tattoos, and facial paint. This treat for the eye was accompanied by an assault on the ear... the din of a colonial street.... To these sounds a congress added the song of natives announcing their arrival, the rattle of wampum they wore around neck and arm, the clank of the men's silver gorgets, the tinkle of the bells and thimbles women wore on their ankles—and sometimes, deep into the night, the thump of a drum beneath the sharp cries of dancers.[4]

As Merrell's prose suggests, Franklin's stately folios are imperfect mirrors of what actually took place. As such, they are also historical (textual) events of great consequence. Franklin wanted his arresting bibliographical designs to advertise the significance of the treaties for colonial and European audiences. Indeed, the folios' designs call attention to the challenging character of the exchanges. While these documents are quasi-official records of political agreements, they reflect the treaty-making through a dark glass.[5] Being at once notably artful and notably public works—far more artful and public than any of the other surviving treaty documents—the folios actually foreground their intentional character: to shape the course of events to colonial rather than native perspectives. But for all their artfulness, the folios have not often drawn the attention of literary scholars.[6]

Two specifically literary problems complicate the declarative transparency that the folios want to project. One relates to the uncertain status of the colonial documentary record, the other to the radically abbreviated, and often only partially understood, multimedia expressive forms of native discourse.

As to that first problem: despite their fame, we know precious little about the editorial emergence of the folios. Consequently, as Merrell remarked in his essay on the 1756 treaty at Easton, "a definitive account of what passed at Easton is a will-o'-the-wisp," a comment that might be applied to all of the treaties.[7] We don't have printer's copy for any of the folios and don't know which source documents stood behind the printer's copy. The texts of ten of the Franklin folios are certified with closing secretarial testimony, but even in those cases we cannot know how the final printed copy was constructed nor even by whom, though the Pennsylvania Council secretaries and Franklin both had a hand in it. A provincial secretary was present at the treaties to record what happened, and it is apparent from various details—the lists of names, the gifts, and the time-stamping—that he strove to set down a factual record. But we know, in fact and a priori, that there were lapses.[8] Besides, and most important, the folios put in print only a fraction of what transpired.

The surviving records show that the treaty events spawned a wide range of views about what took place, and they also sometimes suggest, or even positively expose, different prepossessions (whether purposeful or inadvertent is not always clear). As to the sign system executed by the Indian parties to the events—a subject that Merrell does not pertinently address—the folios and other colonial documents demonstrate that a multimedia system was operating, and scholars have long struggled to illuminate how it worked.[9] But we don't have even the wampum record for the thirteen treaties represented in Franklin's folios, much less adequate accounts of the expressive ceremonial actions that organized the numerous specific treaties and the thousands of other interpersonal exchanges that involved wampum. The truth is that we continue to have virtually no understanding of the *particular* expressive significance of the Indians acts of wampum exchange that took place under the particular circumstances that defined the exchanges. Unlike the Western written treaty record, the wampum record—the record that gave the Indian point of view—is all but completely shattered. The scholarly accounts that attempt to explicate that record are all, without exception, more or less generalized—which is to say, variously translated into Western frames of reference.[10]

Little wonder, then, that these celebrated works of Franklin's art scarcely appear in the American cultural canon or command the regular attention of literary scholars. Certain Indian speeches made during the negotiations are culled from the folios and set aside as objets d'art because we have a ready-to-hand subgenre of Native American rhetoric for accommodating such expressive forms; Canasatego's opening address to the 1744 Lancaster assembly has become a regular example. But the explanatory merits of such interpretive moves come at a notable cost, for they distract us from the folios themselves, and not least from understanding how those documents shape the presence and readability of native and non-native agencies and meanings.[11] The interpretive difficulties we have with the treaties and the folios reflect contradictions and disfunctions that were in play from the start.

Generic Form and Structure

To explicate the Franklin folios' interpretations of the treaties, we want to know how they operate as public works of culture. That means getting a reasonable grasp of their formal (generic) functions and structures, on one hand, and the social contexts that they feed and feed upon. Reading specific features of a particular folio—moments of semantic, thematic, or bibliographic expression—hangs upon those higher order semiotic operators.

Let's start by recalling a common misunderstanding. Though regularly called the "Franklin treaties," the folios are not the treaties, nor are they even official colonial records of the treaties.[12] Rather, they are the most well-known and publicly available accounts of the thirteen treaties Franklin chose to print and distribute to friends and other interested parties in England and America. The treaties themselves were public events that involved many people, sometimes hundreds and even thousands, and they carried over many days, weeks, or months.

Highly ceremonial and performative affairs, the treaties recorded by Franklin were also serial rather than one-off events. Each treaty picked up on matters that had been engaged in earlier treaties, and it was understood that they all had a prospective focus as well.[13] Briefly, the treaties required constant renewal and extension, for "[i]n the Iroquoian view the alliance was naturally in a state of constant deterioration and in need of attention."[14] Understanding one of the folios entails considering as well its place in the "chain" of treaties that it was extending. We also want to bear in mind that Franklin did not print all the treaties that were agreed between 1736 and 1761.

Equally important to understand is the relation of the formal structure of the folios to the formal structure of the treaties. A Franklin folio is a colonial record of an event whose organization and ceremonial protocols were fundamentally Native American in origin and character. More clearly than most colonial records of treaty-making, the folios reflect negotiations in which the Iroquois Confederacy was the dominant native player. Iroquois ascendancy came about partly because of their military power, but even more because of their political influence, which grew out of their two-row wampum belt ceremonials. These were recognized and modified by the nations of the Eastern seaboard and the *pays d'en haut*, and they dominated treaty-making in North America from the late 1670s until the end of the Seven Years' War (1763).[15] "Based on coexistence of power in a context of respect for the autonomy and distinctive nature of each partner,"[16] these "Edge of the Woods" ceremonial negotiations governed the Confederacy's political relations with New France, the different English colonies, and a broad range of indigenous peoples. So far as the English colonies were involved, these Covenant Chain treaties saw the emergence of the Middle Colonies, and in particular Pennsylvania, as the pivotal agent.

Highly flexible, the Iroquois model could be adapted to "changes of situations, issues, and time [over] the span of historical actuality."[17] Eventually the Iroquois formulary would begin to be "modified by the influence of Europeans."[18] This began in 1677 when the first of the Covenant Chain treaties were worked out. William Penn then arrived to put his decisive mark on the treaty-making.

While the Franklin folios do reflect Penn's approach to Covenant Chain treaty-making, the fundamental model was Iroquoian—a sophisticated dilation of widespread native gift-exchange peace-and-friendship ceremonials. Although the Massasoit/Plymouth treaty of 1621 does not reflect some of the most distinctive features of Iroquois *kaswentha* treatying, it does register a key element of all Native American treaty-making: ritualized Maussian gift exchange. As we have seen, the 1621 treaty came about through elaborate native gift ceremonials that extended over many months both before and after the treaty was recorded in a colonial document. And while it does not specifically reference the condolence ritual—*kaswentha*—so central to the Iroquois League's ceremonials, mourning for the deaths and violence suffered by the different parties stood behind the 1621 event and shaped its purposes.

The colonial experience in Virginia from the founding in 1609 is also pertinent to recall. In this case the evidence takes a negative form. The Virginians plunged almost immediately into their decades-long wars with the Powhatan Confederacy (1610–46) exactly because, unlike the Plymouth colonists, they refused to accommodate to native gift-exchange ceremonies and expectations.[19] Violence in New England was delayed for a few years, but the outbreak of the Pequot War (1634–38) and its even more devastating sequel, the 1675–76 Narragansett War, were a direct consequence of the failure of the Puritan colonies to keep up the original peace-and-friendship treaty-making that had made the colonial settlement of New England possible.

The Franklin folios reflect some of the basic elements of Covenant Chain treaty-making. While each folio has a distinctive textual integrity, taken together they make up a larger set that exposes the connections each has with the other documents and events. In addition to the interconnections within the group of thirteen, the set itself operates within the larger context of Covenant Chain treaty-making (and implicitly the even larger context, reaching back to the earliest period of colonial settlement). Considered strictly as elements within a referential discourse field, characters—individual persons and collective agents—come and go and come again, and certain places—Albany, Philadelphia, Lancaster, Easton, Onondaga—and certain events prove to be crucial points in the unfolding action: Penn's original treaty-making in the 1680s–90s, the summative Treaty of 1701, and, more darkly, the Walking Purchase fraud (1737).[20]

The folios' visual design is arresting: a lavish format, generous leading, large Caslon types with a complex and dramatic interplay of roman and italic fonts, and page layouts that draw distinctions between—and focus attention upon—particular textual elements. Standardized across all the folios, even after David Hall took over the presswork in 1748, the bibliographical format reinforces the continuity of the networked treaties. The only significant alteration came in 1756, when the heading of each folio changed from "Treaty" to "Minutes"—whether at Franklin's direction or not we don't know.

The folios also have a rhetorical shape that seems a fair, if also massively abbreviated, reflection of the regular treaty protocols and ceremonies. Framed within elaborate opening and closing ceremonies, the heart of treaty-making was the condolence ceremony and gift exchange. When William Fenton remarked that "[t]he proper way is reciprocal action,"[21] he located a central object of the ritual form of the engagement, not least the *kaswentha* ceremony. Because treaty-making laid primary stress on preserving continuity between the past and the future, memory and faithful promise were dominant concerns.

Treaty-making moved at a snail's pace at every stage, a fact that drove many English participants to distraction. Specific and pragmatic results were held in view—"fixing boundaries, land cessions, and formal alliances for peace and war"—but fundamentally *kaswentha*'s object was "extending the Chain" itself, because the success of the pragmatic goals depended on faithful and credible commitment.[22] Hence the repeated expressions of brotherhood by all the parties and, even more, the recurrent acts of ceremonial reciprocity (wampum and gift exchange).

But while the folios do reflect important treaty matters, they radically abbreviate their ceremonial character in order to emphasize what the colonials saw as the important practical issues. Even the gift exchanges in the folios look like economic rather than social transactions—which is in fact what they were for the colonists, though not for the Americans. Land cessions are regularly called "purchases," even though land transfer in a native economy did not involve "sale" or "purchase." And while the records, including the folios, show that the Indians came to understand what land cession meant for the colonists when set down in "pen and ink," and even came to accommodate to that view, they also show that the Indians did not relinquish their view of the land or of the significance of the transactions.[23] The Indians never sold their lands simply because, in their most basic economic conception, land could not be sold or alienated. No sachem or king or nation possessed such power, though the crowns of Europe, and eventually the American republic, could and did claim it through a claim of sovereignty. But when the earth itself was ultimate ground and sovereign source, as it was for the first people, treaty-authorized land cessions were not "sales" but "releases" of authority and administrative control from one power to another. To the European mind that meant a transfer of sovereignty; to the Native American, a willing transfer of political responsibility to an alliance partner.

The colonial treaty documents of the seventeenth and eighteenth centuries show that the native and non-native parties, despite their basically different views about land, were able to treat of it so long as shared usufruct prevailed. When land cessions were arranged, native use rights—hunting, farming, fishing, trapping—were understood, and often explicitly stated, to be reserved. Conflicts never ceased to arise, because of the differences between colonial and native economies, but the treaties themselves were engaged to mitigate those differences through forged alliances of peace and solidarity.[24] So long as a social equality was recognized and preserved between the parties' different *habitus*, it did not matter—in the native view—who was the administrative authority. Native groups would even choose to depart to new regions if they judged a move would preserve the *habitus* of their people within the shifting intersocial circumstances. After the founding of the republic, choosing was no longer an option.

In the folio perspective, native treaty-making appears basically tripartite, consisting of a prologue where the place, date, and occasion for treatying is specified, the cast of characters is named and identified, the social and political context—both immediate and prevenient—is sketched, and basic topics or treaty "Articles" are proposed. In the treatying, the condolence ceremony climaxes the opening events, but—significantly—the folios have few resources to give it adequate representation. But its importance cannot be overstated, and in one of the folios—for the 1753 Treaty at Carlisle—its significance, if not its eventual details, is unmistakable. Franklin, who was a party at the event, made certain that the folio he printed would reflect that significance.[25] But often the white reports either mention the ceremony in the most perfunctory way or don't note it at all. It's likely that in some cases—the 1621 Plymouth treaty, for instance—the colonials may have been unaware that it was occurring.

After the folio's opening section comes a body of texts that explain and examine the problems raised by the initial set of articles, agents, and circumstances. These lead to the concluding section where agreements are specified along with any material exchanges ("presents") or deeds of exchange and where unresolved issues are also made explicit, thus pointing toward the expectation of further treatying. Dialogic exchange characterizes all three phases of both the treaty and its documentary representation, and each phase of the treatying, which can be relatively brief or greatly extended, is place- and date-stamped in the folios. All three sections of the folios also feature more or less detailed commentaries and prose summaries of declarations that are not represented verbatim. These particular texts often illuminate how the action is being shaped and interpreted in the folio.

But all the folios have one crucial debility. Because the treaty protocols were Native American, key aspects of the treaty were communicated through dance, singing, ceremonial action, and details of costume and ornamental or symbolic expression. All of these elements go largely unrecorded in Franklin's folios. Thus, ritualized events that took many hours or all day, are redacted in the folios to abstract textuality. The folios' truncated presentation of *kaswentha* ceremonies is one of their most serious deficiencies, but also sorely missed are more detailed accounts of the wampum presentations, which were the chief native means for recording and executing the treaties: native and colonial speakers would address each other as they presented and exchanged strings or belts of wampum.[26]

Each gift of wampum comprised an expressive text whose meaning was specified by the individual, who handles and then hands off the wampum. But the precise significance remains obscure because few of the specific wampum records, and none of the oral exchanges, survive. At the outset of the 1761 council held at Easton, for example, the Seneca spokesman, George, presents four strings and four belts of wampum to Pennsylvania Governor James Hamilton. All except the last two strings are clearly given as part of a condolence ceremony. More than that we cannot say, however, even though we can be certain that George's wampum presentation is saying a great deal more: "*A black Belt of eight Rows, streaked with White . . . A white Belt of seven Rows, with four black Streaks . . . A white Belt of five Rows, with three black Bars*" (*Indian Treaties*, 4/248).

These and the other wampum come with George's commentaries. But the folios elucidate the meaning of the wampum presentation only in the most general terms. What, one wonders, dictates the sequence of George's action? Or consider that while these wampum ceremonials and associated comments are directed by one specific party to another, they are to be heard and considered by everyone present: in this 1761 case, the Pennsylvania delegation, representatives of four Iroquois and five other nations along with an assembly of "*about Four Hundred in Number, which encreased afterwards to near Five Hundred*" (*Indian Treaties*, 3/247)—whether native or English or both the folios do not say. Elliptical representation is recurrent and typical of the folios. "We present you with a belt of wampum," Canasatego tells the Maryland deputation at the 1744 Treaty, to which the folio simply adds: "*Which was received with the usual Ceremony*" (*Indian Treaties*, 37/77).

Close Reading: The Treaty and Folio of 1736

The first of Franklin's folios—*A Treaty of Friendship Held with the Chiefs of the Six Nations, at Philadelphia, in September and October, 1736*—is worth careful study because of its position in the sequence, because it is relatively brief and its form relatively uncomplicated, and not least because it introduces most of the key topics and interpretive issues. Its tripartite structure is clear: the prologue (pp. 1–5), the body and central negotiation (pp. 5–13), and the closing ceremonies and exchanges (p. 14).[27] These textual units correspond to events that took place on September 27–October 1, October 2–13, and October 14.

Most treaty negotiations, including the treaties represented by the Franklin folios, were polyglot affairs. The parties addressed each other in their own languages, which were then relayed in translation by the interpreter. For most of these Pennsylvania treaties that interpreter was Conrad Weiser, the Palatine German who had lived among and was adopted into the Mohawk nation and in 1731 had moved from New York to eastern Pennsylvania and become intimate with James Logan, the Council president and chief colonial agent for the Proprietors, the sons of William Penn. The 1736 folio reveals, however, that the colonial spokesmen, Logan and Thomas Penn, did not in fact address the assembly: Weiser delivered everything the English had to say in the public ceremonies in one or another Iroquoian dialect. Except at a series of private negotiations between the Iroquois and the colonial authorities (between October 2 and October 12), the only English heard at the treaty-making ceremonies came when Iroquois addresses to the colonials were translated into English by Weiser. What this means is that Iroquoian speech in this 1736 treaty dominated the public treaty exchanges to a marked degree.

The move was a policy decision taken by the Pennsylvania authorities at "the Interpreter's [i.e., Weiser's] Advice" (*A Treaty of Friendship*, 4). It created a setting where native protocols—a specifically *kaswentha* gift-exchange ceremonial—would be conspicuous and Indian authority would appear paramount. Weiser's advice laid a mise-en-scène over the proceedings, staging a kind of play within the drama of Indian treaty-making. All of the public forms of the treaty-making would be native. But operating within those forms were colonial translations that achieved their final expression in Franklin's printed folio. The intermediation procedure Weiser designed for these treaties gained him enormous respect from the Indians, as all the treaties show. But it also left the colonials free to misrepresent and misunderstand—sometimes deliberately, sometimes inadvertently—what was actually taking place so far as the Indians understood the public events. Writing of Canasatego's famous speech at the 1736 conference, Bruce E. Johansen underscores how "pen and ink witchcraft," by chance or by choice, came about: "What we have [in the 1736 folio] is Franklin's typescript of Canassatego's words as translated by Conrad Weiser, reduced to writing by the secretary of the conference, Richard Peters."[28]

The great significance of Weiser's plan becomes clear when we expose the context of the treaty. The Pennsylvania colonists convened the 1736 meeting "to confirm the Treaty" (*A Treaty of Friendship*, 3) of 1732, where the proprietor and Logan had laid the groundwork for completing the shift of Covenant Chain treatying from New York to Pennsylvania (in the ceremonial terms of both treaties, moving the Council fire from Albany to Philadelphia). At the 1732 treaty Weiser was again the interpreter advising Penn and Logan on how to proceed. The immediate common goal was to establish the Iroquois League and the Pennsylvania colony as the agents that would coordinate native and non-native relations in the region. Achieving that goal meant that the League would cease pursuing alliances with the French and would work to separate non-League and allied nations, especially the Shawnees and Ohio Delawares, from their French connections.

The treaties of 1732 and 1736 were coordinated by Thomas Penn and his agents, and the 1736 folio shows both parties explicitly recalling the earlier treaty. Equally notable is that both treaty documents invoked William Penn's original treaty-making of 1682/83–1701 with the Delaware and other regional nations. Although the Iroquois were not a party to the Penn negotiations that culminated in the famous Treaty of 1701, they had since confirmed their native hegemony in the region, the Delawares themselves having become Iroquois tributaries.

The continuity between 1682 and 1736 is marked when the English documents echo the native language that Penn had recorded in his 1683 *Letter from William Penn . . . to the committee of the Free society of traders . . .*: "that great Promises past between us of Kindness and good Neighbourhood, and that the Indians and English must live in Love, as long as the Sun gave light."[29] Thus in 1736 the Seneca speaker Kanickhungo declares that "we and you should be as one Heart, one Mind, and one Body, thus becoming one People... between our Children and your Children, to all succeeding Generations" (*A Treaty of Friendship*, 7). Replying in kind, Thomas Penn declares that by "the Treaty held here with your Chiefs, we confirmed all our former Treaties with you... and made ourselves and you one Body and one People... for our Children and Children's Children, to all Generations, as long as the Sun, Moon, and Earth, endure" (*A Treaty of Friendship*, 10).

But in two other respects the difference between the record of the 1732 treaty and the 1736 Franklin folio is startling.[30] Speaking for Penn, Weiser opened the 1736 discussions with a condolence ceremony (*"you must... put away all Grief and Uneasiness, and brighten your Eyes, that we may see and be chearful with each other"*; A Treaty of Friendship,). If a condolence ceremony opened the 1732 assembly, the official treaty record does not show it, even though *kaswentha* had been the framework for treaty-making with the League from the earliest Iroquoian treaty record that we have, that is, the 1645 Treaty of Trois-Rivières between the Iroquois Confederacy and New France.[31] The English opened the Treaty of 1736 by "confirming" 1732 and the entire line of Penn treaties in a remarkable way. Ventriloquizing Thomas Penn in native speech, Weiser declared that Iroquois *kaswentha* was the organizing structure of native and colonial relations. In 1736 at Philadelphia the Indians watched a colonial power make a conscious and public demonstration of its allegiance to the Iroquois system.[32]

Both the 1732 and the 1736 treaties are primarily concerned with forging an alliance of friendship based in *kaswentha*. The English want this in order to blunt French influence with the Indians, the Pennsylvania authorities want it in order to establish a special position for themselves among native people and the other colonies, and the Iroquois want it in order to make themselves the dominant native power in a vast region extending from Canada to Carolina and from the seaboard to the Ohio country and the *pays d'en haut*. In 1732 no land disputes were raised, and no land formed part of the gift exchanges, which were entirely ceremonial and symbolic.

In 1736, however, a gift exchange takes place involving a "Delivery of Presents" to the Indians in exchange for "Releas[ing] to [the Proprietor] all the Lands lying between the Mouth of *Sasquehannah* and *Kekachtaninius* Hills [i.e., the Blue Hills or Endless Mountains]" (*A Treaty of Friendship*, 9). Though the folio calls this a "Purchase," which is how it would be treated by the English, it is also a gift and would have been seen as such by the Indians. By it the League was declaring that the released land would pass from native to colonial administrative authority and that the League had the authority to make the release. Such a gift was highly appropriate to a treaty occasion of mutual friendship organized in relation to Iroquoian *kaswentha*.

Two passages in the folio underscore the mutual exchange of authority that the treaty was enacting and that both parties were participating in. The first comes at the outset, when Thomas Penn, speaking through Weiser in one or another Iroquoian dialect, says: *"you shall shelter yourselves under our Covering... for you are our Brethren"* (*A Treaty of Friendship*, 4). This is the third of the opening "Articles" of friendship that Penn gifts to the Iroquois "with three small Strings of *Wampum*."[33] Reciprocating, the Indians "expressed their satisfaction [by] delivering a String [of wampum] as each Article was spoke to." But as to the third Article "they said, *They could not receive and treat us as we did them, they are now with us, and give themselves to us, and depend on our Protection*" (*A Treaty of Friendship*, 4).

The reply, even in Franklin's English transliteration, exposes the remarkable diplomatic acuity of the speaker (presumably Kanickhungo, though it may have been Hetaquantegechty). It references the fact that the Iroquois delegation had left New York and come to fasten the Chain to the Pennsylvanians at Philadelphia. The move underscores the responsibility that Pennsylvania, now in alliance, owes to their Indian "Brethren." Pennsylvania would not be able to take up its responsibility until it explicitly renewed the gift exchange that William Penn had established thirty years before. That first *kaswentha* alliance was a recurrent point of reference in both 1732 and 1736. Having responsibility for maintaining the peaceful coexistence of Indians and settlers within "all the Lands lying between the Mouth of *Sasquehannah* and *Kekachtaninius* Hills," Pennsylvania—"Brother Onas," in his native incarnation[34]—would have received a gift that is designed, as we might now say, to keep on giving.

The other significant passages come at the close of the treaty. After reconfirming the alliance "*through all Generations ... as long as the Earth endures*" (*A Treaty of Friendship*, 13), the native speaker (unnamed) calls attention to "*the Sale of our* [i.e., English] *Goods* (*A Treaty of Friendship*, 13). Reporting the speech in a third-person English syntax, the folio describes the ethos that underlies the native approach to treaty-making and gift exchange: "*That amongst them there is never any Victuals sold, the Indians give to each other freely what they can spare; but if they come amongst our People, they can have none without paying; they admire that we should take Money on this score*" (*A Treaty of Friendship*, 13). This narrative report uses the word "admire" in its original English sense, signaling how strange the English mercantile spirit appears in the view of the natives. That the colonials registered this judgment is clear from Weiser's reply, the last speech reported in the folio. After "confirm[ing] all these Articles to be kept ... by our Children and their Children to all Generations," Weiser responds directly to what the Indian speaker had said, making a careful declaration of the commercial *ethos* that underpins English treaty exchanges: "all the white People, tho' they live together as Brethren, have each nevertheless distinct Properties and Interests, and none of us can demand from another Victuals or anything of the Kind without Payment. . . . all Victuals cost money" (*A Treaty of Friendship*, 14). The 1736 treatying ends with that fundamental antinomy left unresolved. Not only will it remain unresolved through all the succeeding treaties, but its true profundity will assume increasing consequence as fraught land issues become what in fact they always were in colonial treatying between the Indians and the British, a paramount treaty subject and problem.

That dark future comes briefly into view at the end of the 1736 treaty when Weiser, speaking for Brother Onas (Pennsylvania), refers to "the Claim [the Iroquois] make on the Lands of *Maryland* and *Virginia*" (*A Treaty of Friendship*, 14). The League had made this claim and was asking Pennsylvania to raise it on their behalf with the Crown and the affected colonies. Not until 1744 would Pennsylvania succeed in bringing Maryland and Virginia to treat about the unauthorized frontier settlements that were at the heart of the Iroquois claim, and by that time the Walking Purchase fraud (1737) perpetrated by the Proprietors had further exacerbated the land disputes, and King George's War (1744–48) was looming.

Close Reading: The Treaty and Folio of 1742

The record of treaty-making in Franklin's 1742 folio is more chaotic, even in a sense hysterical, than 1736, a fact underscored by the absence of a record of the condolence ceremony. Because the colonists' paramount concern was the "daily expectation of a *French* war," they called the meeting to "discover what Dependence we might have . . . in case [Iroquois] Aid should be wanted" (*Indian Treaties*, 6/20). For its part, the League's focus is the still unaddressed land claims against Maryland and Virginia frontier settlers, as will become apparent in Canasatego's opening treaty speech. But in the weeklong runup to the treatying (June 30–July 6: *Indian Treaties*, 1–9/15–23), that issue is not so much as mentioned. The prelude to the treaty-making appears instead as a wrangle of recriminations and cautious assurances on both sides: lapses in gift giving, border bloodshed, "loose Sales of Land" by unauthorized parties. Lest the circumstances damage their chief aim, the Pennsylvanians lay out "an handsome Dinner." Elaborate expressions of Pennsylvania's commitment to "the strictest League of Amity and Friendship with you" (*Indian Treaties*, 7/21) are a major part of the treaty preparations.

This Franklin folio is famous for printing two speeches by the Onondaga chief Canasatego. The first marks a pivotal event in the treaty-making proper (July 6–10: *Indian Treaties*, 12–20/26–34) while the second comes "at the Conclusion of [the] Treaty" and after its "Publick Business" was finished, which happened on July 10 (*Indian Treaties*, 20/34). The parties then broke for a day (July 11) and returned on July 12 to make their closing remarks. It was then that Canasatego delivered his notorious second speech. A close reading of what he said in those two speeches—a close reading of the folio document as well as the speeches' enabling context—is revealing. The second speech in particular does not mean precisely what scholars (for the most part, historians) have concluded. The difference is significant.

In his first speech (July 7: *Indian Treaties*, 12–13/26–27), Canasatego addressed "the Governor and Council" of Pennsylvania in strong terms on the issue of the Iroquois land claims (in this case briefly including the claims by "our Cousins the *Delawares*" [*Indian Treaties*, 13/27] over the Walking Purchase fraud). But his key—indeed, his burning—concern was that Pennsylvania had "not done anything" to press Maryland and Virginia on the issues raised in 1736: "That Country belongs to us, in right of Conquest; we having bought it with our blood" (*Indian Treaties*, 13/27) Canasatego demanded that the southern colonials be brought to treat about the Iroquois claims, adding that if they refused "we are able to do ourselves Justice, and we will do it, by going to take payment ourselves" (*Indian Treaties*, 13/27). He then closed with "a Present of Skins" and placating words "in Testimony of our Regard."

Canasatego's threat to use force registered. The next day, July 8, the colonial Council ordered that the southern colonies be summoned, and on July 10 a letter was drafted "to be dispatch'd tomorrow morning" (*Indian Treaties*, 18/32).[35] The treatying that continued through July 9 included more ceremonial feasting as well as Canasatego's assurance that certain native acts of violence would be dealt with in order to "aid [our] Brethren the white People in obtaining Justice" (*Indian Treaties*, 16/30). Governor Thomas Penn then let "the Chiefs of the *Six Nations*" know that such justice would not be realized until "your Cousins, a Branch of the *Delawares*," were "remove[d] from the Lands in the Forks of *Delaware*, and not give any further Disturbance to the Persons who are now in Possession" (*Indian Treaties*, 18/32). The governor was recalling the Walking Purchase of 1737 and rejecting the (truthful) Delaware charge that it was executed through fraud and deceit. He strongly protested that the "Delawares from the Forks" had "the Insolence" to continue pressing their land claims with various colonial authorities (*Indian Treaties*, 17/31). The governor was addressing the League directly, but representatives from the "Insolent" eastern Delawares were present and were meant to hear. They had come to the conference under the League's auspices.

On July 10 the treaty articles were specified, the alliance was renewed between "good Friends," and gifts "from the Governor, the Council, the Assembly, and all the People of *Pennsylvania*" were received by the League with "solemn Thanks" (*Indian Treaties*, 20/34). Having "no more to say as to Publick Business," the negotiations ended, and the parties took a day of rest before returning on July 12 for the concluding ceremonies. Both seemed to have gained their principal goals: the League would have its land claims addressed at a treaty soon to be convened (1744), and Pennsylvania was assured that the Covenant Chain would hold if war broke out with New France, as indeed it soon would.

But Canasatego had a good deal more to say. His second speech (*Indian Treaties*, 20–23/34–37) falls into three distinct parts. In the first he addressed the colonials directly and declared that, having given "a long and full Examination" to "the several Writings" that bore upon the Delaware land claims over the Walking Purchase, he announced that "We see with our own Eyes, that they [the Delaware "Cousins"] ... are altogether in the wrong" (*Indian Treaties*, 21/35). He then turned to the listening Delawares and sternly berated them as "women," with no right to treat about land with the colonials. His final words to the League's "Cousins" are remarkable: "We have some other Business to transact with our Brethren"—that is, with the colonials. Turning then to the Delawares, he ordered them expelled: "depart the Council," he declared, "and consider what has been said to you" (*Indian Treaties*, 22/36). Presumably the Delawares did leave as they were so summarily told by their "Uncles." Here Canasatego's "brothers" were not the Delawares, they were the white colonials Onas, Corlear (New York), Assaragoa (Virginia), and Tocarry-Hogan (Maryland).

In speaking this way Canasatego had a double purpose: to make a dramatic show of the League's power and authority and to bind Pennsylvania to fulfill the promise they had made in 1736 to deal with the League's southern land claims.[36] The Delawares were not League members, were perhaps not even what the League spokesman (was it in fact Canasatego?) called them: "[t]ributaries" (*Indian Treaties*, 8/22). The League and Canasatego may have come to the conclusion that the Delawares were fighting a lost cause, that the eastern Pennsylvania region was now completely overrun with white settlement. Weiser himself had settled the region in 1731 with a large contingent of Palatines from New York.

Whatever Canasatego and the League concluded from those "several Writings" (land transactions) presented by their white "Brethren," we now know that the documents were, as the Delawares had always insisted, fraudulent. That Canasatego should have so decisively accepted the paper testimony is more than a little odd, since colonial deeds were widely regarded as "pen and ink witchcraft" by native people.[37] Even accepting the Iroquois assertion that "we conquered you [and] made Women of you" (*Indian Treaties*, 21/35), no one is sure when such a Delaware dependency on the League took place. Not that the date would greatly matter in this case, since the Delaware and other regional tribes, as Canasatego would not have forgotten, had on their own behalf been making land cessions with William Penn from the earliest days of the colony.[38] Indeed, subsequent treaties show that the League would reverse itself and support the Delawares' land claims in eastern Pennsylvania, forcing the governor in 1761 to reopen the Delawares' land claim with the Crown authorities.[39]

As for declaring the Delawares "Women": if the League could cast them in that institutional role in 1742, the Delawares could choose to cast it off, as Canasatego well knew, since Native American *habitus* recognized all nations as free agents. Indeed, the folios' lists of native participants in the treaties between 1736 and 1756 discloses the interesting fact that the Mohawks, one of the most powerful of the League nations, refused to be party to the League's negotiations. So unhappy had the Mohawks become with the League's Pennsylvania "Brethren" that in 1753 they renounced the Covenant Chain altogether.[40] As for the Delawares, in 1755 they turned into warring "women," attacking Pennsylvania settlements, and from 1756 to 1762 they were perhaps the chief independent agent in the treatying that continued with Penn's colony.[41]

Whatever else we can say about Canasatego's speech, then, its meaning is by no means transparent. If parsed in its discursive contexts—both native and non-native—its anomalies are striking. More was being said here than meets the casual eye, an impression reinforced by a passage I have not seen discussed. It comes at the end when, as Canasatego remarks, "all we have to say about Publick Business, is now over" (*Indian Treaties*, 23/37). The passage has the form of a complacent salute accompanied by a farewell gift: "When we first came to your [colonial] Houses, we found them clean and in Order: But we have staid so long as to dirty them.... And therefore, as we cannot but have been disagreeable to you..., we present you with some Skins to make your Houses clean" (*Indian Treaties*, 23/37). This is a disorienting way of calling attention to "our different Way of Living from the white People," since it strips away the high-minded cultural rhetoric that the folio translations try to maintain. "Disagreeable" is itself a polite way of expressing the disgust most colonials felt about the native "Way of Living." Indeed, how *would* a gift of animal skins "make your Houses clean"? Symbolically? The speech brings into disturbing question the entire ritual fabric of peace, friendship, and brotherhood.

That the speech involves a complex irony is underscored when Canasatego proceeds to request that Weiser, "[a] member of our Council as well as yours," should get a special reward for his services: "When we adopted him, we divided him into Two: One we kept for our selves, one we left for you. He has had a great deal of Trouble with us ... and dirty'd his Cloathes by being among us, so that he is become as nasty as an *Indian*" (*Indian Treaties*, 23/37). Weiser's ambiguous cultural identity indexes this unstable reflection on *kaswentha* gift exchange. A deep truth is leaking out of Canasatego's knowing words: that the English are estranged from their treaty partners at a dangerously primitive level. Who seems more disgusting here, nasty Indians or dainty colonials? A dubious rhetoric undermines both the authority of the passage (who is responsible for, who authorized, who is expressing these words?) and its ironic target (native people? nonnative? the treaty-making they pursue? perhaps the readers of the folio?). The treaty folio leaves these questions hanging fire.

Close Reading: The Treaty and Folio of 1756

After the Walking Purchase, "land hungry settlers and squatters"— the phrase is ubiquitous in contemporary and subsequent historical accounts—turned Pennsylvania into an increasingly dangerous territory for everyone. Forbidden in 1742 by their Iroquois "Uncles" to make war or treat for stolen or disputed land, the Delawares of both Ohio and eastern Pennsylvania were finally driven to act on their own behalf, as the Iroquois had threatened in 1742 to do against Maryland and Virginia. They struck various settlements in 1754–55, provoking Pennsylvania first to declare war and then to seek a treaty accommodation. This was the occasion for the Treaty of 1756 at Easton, where the Delaware sachem Teedyuscung emerged to take up the cause of the betrayed Delawares.

Asked by the Pennsylvanians why the Delawares had struck the settlements, Teedyuscung replied that it was because the colonials "have settled or wrought this Land, so as to coop us up as in a pen" (*Indian Treaties*, 22/156). "This very ground under me," he went on, " (striking it with his Foot) was my Land and Inheritance, and is taken from me by Fraud; when I say this Ground, I mean all the Land lying between the *Tohiccon Creek* and *Wyoming, on the River Sasquehannah*" (*Indian Treaties*, 23/157). Twenty years gone and the Walking Purchase fraud was not forgotten by the "insolent" Delawares. Even the League, which had handled their "Cousins" so disgracefully at the Treaty of 1742, was now taking a very different line, as Teedyuscung told the colonials when he gave them a belt of wampum on the second day (July 29) of the 1756 conference proper.

The Belt [he said] was sent him by the *Six Nations* and he accepted it: You see ... a Square in the Middle, meaning the Lands of the Indians, and at one End the Figure of a Man, indicating the *English*; and at the other End, another, meaning the *French*; our Uncles told us, that both these coveted our Lands; but let us join together to defend our Lands against both, you shall be Partakers with us of our Lands. (*Indian Treaties*, 11/145)

The wars between France and England that began to climax in 1744 had driven the English colonies, the Crown, and the Iroquois League to retreat from what the English thought had been settled at the treaties of 1742 and 1744. Because the English felt secure Indian alliances were imperative in the struggle with France, the problem of the Delawares, who had never renounced their land claims, had to be addressed. So the Crown and the Pennsylvanians turned not to the League but to the Delaware sachem Teedyuscung, requesting that he summon a large delegation of regional Indians to the treaty at Easton—the center of the Walking Purchase swindle—in a series of treaties of 1756, 1757, 1758, and 1761.[42]

William Penn had set a model for treaty-making between 1681 and 1701. That is to say, he recognized and accepted the Iroquois *kaswentha* model as the framework within which to seek land releases. Peace and friendship were to be the alpha and omega of the meetings, with land release coming as Maussian gift exchanges ("presents" and "purchases"). These were the predicate of the *kaswentha* protocols, the performative testimony that friendship and brotherhood were actually being practiced. Penn's original policy was believed and thereafter revered by the native peoples, and the colony's later governors and proprietors invoked his example repeatedly in their treaty discussions. But the Walking Purchase fraud struck at the heart of *kaswentha* gift exchange, exposing to the Americans that their colonial partners were unreliable, perhaps even dishonest.

So beginning in 1756 Teedyuscung put the Walking Purchase at the center of the treaty discussions. But his move was meant to raise even more consequential matters than that particular land swindle. It suggested that colonial declarations of brotherhood "as long as the Sun, Moon, and Earth, endure" might be untrustworthy. But *kaswentha* was fairly grounded in mutual candor and honesty.[43] Perhaps even more significant, the land swindle also exposed the fearful difference between the colonial attitude to alienable land and the native belief in the sovereign Earth. "The Land is the Cause of our Differences," Teedyuscung averred during the treatying, "that is, our being unhappily turned out of the Land" (*Indian Treaties*, 9/197).[44]

Referring explicitly to the Walking Purchase fraud, he insisted on "Satisfaction for these lands" that were unjustly seized for colonial settlement, and went on to speak of "settl[ing] at *Wyoming*" with "certain Boundaries fixed between you and us; and a certain Tract of Land fixed . . . [for] the Use of our Children for ever" (*Indian Treaties*, 9–10/197–98). He recurred to the issue of "the Earth" in his 1757, 1758, and 1761 speeches, and his remarks express a profundity that would echo throughout American history, literature, and culture. Teedyuscung was framing his concern less in relation to violated land rights than to a fear that he might "wrong my Posterity" of "a Home for ever" (*Indian Treaties*, 20/232) and betray "my Children and Grandchildren" [from living] there as long as the World lasts" (*Indian Treaties*, 7/257).

"The Reason of this great Cloud of Mischief that has been past," he told Governor William Denny, "is, that our . . . Forefathers . . . never looked forward for their Children: They only had a view of this that decays . . . the Things on the Earth, that are soon gone . . . (*Indian Treaties*, 6/194). "The Earth" itself, not "the Things" on it, had to be kept in focus, along with the legacy of the Earth that natives and non-natives alike were to pass on to their children and grandchildren forever. It was the deep historical perspective of the transhuman earth, not of European law, that Teedyuscung was endorsing. What was the legacy to be, native "Earth" or neo-European "Property"?

In his initial reply, Governor Denny dismissed Teedyuscung's view that "the Land was . . . the Cause of our first Differences." Indeed, he airily insisted that "[h]owever we may differ about Matters of Property, these are trifling Considerations, compared to the important Affair of uniting together" (*Indian Treaties*, 11/199). In Denny's mind, the war had created a firm alliance that was as crucial for the Indians as for the English. "Matters of Property" seemed trifling in the context of what was for Denny the immediate emergency, the struggle with France. But in another and larger context, matters of property were and had always been—certainly for the English—the most imperative, if not precisely life and death, concerns. And as for Teedyuscung, this matter of property that threatened a people's entire *habitus* and spiritual life had reached a real crisis by the 1750s. After all. if land was seen by Governor Denny as a matter of property—a trifling matter—to Teedyuscung it was a matter of existential subsistence.

The Seven Years' War would end many lives but in no sense put the European mercantile *habitus* or European "Posterity," French or English or colonial, in danger. Indeed, the Seven Years' War and the American Revolution itself, shortly to follow, might well be judged trifling by comparison with the peril facing Native American civilizations and, as we are today growing to suspect, the earth itself as Teedyuscung conceived it. Set in historical horizons beyond Denny's July 1757 perspective, beyond even

Teedyuscung's specifically Delaware and native perspective, Denny's call for "uniting together" in brotherhood—the very heart of *kaswentha*—radiates meanings that would only come to the fore in the afterlife of Denny's and Teedyuscung's place and time.

Teedyuscung's admonitory words about native land disclose an economic and ethical horizon that for him and his people is unconditional religious ground. If Denny's progressive ideology recognizes—perhaps even vaguely remembers—the truth to which Teedyuscung is pledging allegiance, the folio treaty text shows that he has decisively put it out of his mind. Denny's Anglo-American posterity would make much of that clash of worldviews. A host of later perspectives will trade upon both the yet-to-be realized forethought lurking in Teedyuscung's view (land as the earth) and Denny's just-in-time pragmatism (land as exploitable property).

The treaties stage and the folios represent this primordial American contradiction, which comes starkly to the fore in the late treaties at Easton. At that point the significance of the bibliographical style of the folios becomes particularly apparent. The treaties record how the English colonials who treated land as property struggled with native civilizations that treated land as the earth. More remarkably, they show how the English were driven by circumstance to accept and accommodate the native treaty protocols. These were all fundamentally alien to the European *habitus* of the colonies. But for the Americans, the primary facts, and acts, of social intercourse assumed the sovereignty of the earth (rather than those who occupied it), a subsistence economics (rather than capital development), and gift giving (rather than mercantile exchange) as the primary acts of social intercourse. Most remarkable of all, when the Franklin folios transmediated the treaties into factual and declarative texts, the very artfulness of the interface would make the tensions and disfunctions dismally clear.

The folios' declared intentions were on a collision course with their disjointed factual particulars. That collision gives their face values more value than if we only read them as finished documentary records. Nor does it matter how authorization frames any particular passage (whether as verbatim quotation, in a factual list, or through an expository passage). All come to operate within the implicate order of declarative discourse, which understands, so to speak, how to extrapolate meanings out of the logic of its immediate textual condition. Bibliographically typified, the folios' impersonal rhetoric elevates their liberal address, introducing rhetorical formalities into a real-world context far more rich and strange, perhaps, than any (necessarily less complex) textual continuum. The folios demonstrate how a culture's carefully organized archival records turn into a kind of vox populi through which its once and future voices will only ever half perceive what in the first instance they only ever half created.

Reading Early American Literature: The Model of the Indian Treaties

Though the settlers did not understand it at the time, the treaty-making at Plymouth began when the diplomatic envoy Samoset entered their encampment and bid them, in English, "Welcome" to Massasoit's country. Within a few weeks Massasoit would sign the document that assured the English of his long-term goodwill. Massasoit's treaty-making would continue for the next eight months, culminating in what subsequent white records would call "the first Thanksgiving." The two surviving treaty documents were schematic English translations of events that had been elaborately orchestrated by Massasoit.

Now consider again the 1736 treaty-making at Philadelphia and Franklin's folio record. While the native ceremonial forms continue to organize the events, significant differences have emerged. Here the hosts, the Pennsylvania colonials, do not project Massasoit's magisterial authority but serve as a kind of committee who have engaged to renew the treaties and respect their ritual formalities. Weiser's "Advice" to the Pennsylvania authorities—that he mediate all the exchanges so that the actual treatying would be grounded in native languages—was a shrewd diplomatic move. It affirmed the treaty-making rules and ritual formalities as American rather than colonial. This necessarily marked the folios' accounts not only as translations, but as translations that couldn't even begin to develop equivalent representations of the multimediated events. All the folios' careful typographical designs mark each of the events as having been satisfyingly completed. But the objective truth is that as the treaty-making proceeded, the tensions and contradictions only grew more difficult and unresolved—really, as we can now see so clearly, unresolvable.

Distrust would figure prominently through these treaty-makings because the Penns' Walking Purchase swindle, which took place less than a year after the 1736 treaty council, did not brighten the Covenant Chain; rather, it rekindled long-standing native suspicions. In the wake of the debacles of the 1670s in New England and Virginia—the Narragansett War and Bacon's Rebellion—William Penn had been careful to establish trust and fair dealing as the hallmarks of Pennsylvania treaty-making.[45] The success of his efforts brought considerable stability to the region and soon gained virtually mythic status for Penn and his colony, which would remain largely free of large-scale violence for forty years.[46] But the Walking Purchase itself would assume its own mythic status because of the damage it did to that carefully nurtured but ultimately fragile structure of peace and friendship.[47] King George's War would slowly but surely make its way from the *pays d'en haut* into Pennsylvania.[48]

When the Delaware protest at the fraud made no headway with the Pennsylvania authorities, the nation appealed to the League, their "Uncle," to defend their claim. The League reconvened the parties at Philadelphia in 1742 partly in order to take up the case, although assessing its justice was far from the League's principal object. Readers of the treaty record have made much of the fact that Canasatego rebuffed the Delaware claim and called them "women." But in the effort to gloss the native political meaning of that arresting English word, readers have been distracted from what is truly startling about Canasatego's second speech: his affirmation of the authority of the colonial records against the oral testimony of the Delaware, who were in a tributary relation to the League.[49]

The speech argued that the League's true brotherhood was with the colonial powers, not with the weakened but once formidable Leni Lenape (Delaware) nation. The League was quite prepared in 1742 to sanction the Walking Purchase fraud in order to establish its position with the colonies as the dominant native regional power. Canasatego's second speech denouncing the Delaware was as aggressive as his first, in which he pressed the League's claims to disputed lands in Maryland and Virginia and demanded that the League's colonial partners address the matter. He was proposing a quid pro quo arrangement between the League and Pennsylvania that would firmly establish the League's authority in the Covenant Chain treaty-making that the Delaware had initiated with William Penn.

But the political tensions on the ground were such that none of the parties, even when they purposed to work in concert, were able to keep control of the events. The colonies were at odds with each other, and so were the two European and the multiple American nations, and the frontier was a perilous locale where different groups of colonial squatters fought with both the natives and their own Crown authorities, as Canasatego's first speech in 1742 pointed out. Although King George's War was fought far from Pennsylvania, it forecast the violence that would soon engulf the entire region. As events spun increasingly out of the control of the treaty-making efforts, the League would eventually reverse its judgment about the Walking Purchase fraud. When in 1753 the powerful Mohawks renounced Covenant Chain treaty-making altogether, the true state of the volatile situation was fully exposed.

That course of events provides a truthful gloss on the studied composure that the Franklin folios mean to project. Native treaty-making from the beginning was an instrument to prevent war and mitigate violence, and both the content and the interface of the folios pledge allegiance to that legacy. While the first two folios reflect what had been accomplished between 1701 and 1737, the next five—from 1744 through 1755—give a dramatic picture of things falling apart. The return of the Delaware to treaty-making in the mid-1750s speaks volumes about the unstable political situation and supplies the real-world context that was driving Teedyuscung's dark reflections. "Our Country [is] covered with our own Blood (we mean yours and ours)," the Shawnee chief Paxinosa told the 1756 assembly at Easton, and "evil Spirits reign" across the land (*Indian Treaties*, 4/138). As practical instruments aimed at promoting peace and social order, the final six Franklin folios, from 1756 to 1762, are little more than whited sepulchers for all the parties directly involved—the Crown, the colonies, and the native Americans.

But that very quality underscores the great significance of all the Franklin folios as foundational documents of American literature. They lay bare the piteous truth of a history they had committed themselves not just to record, but to establish.

Because of the theatrical character of oral treaty-making, we are not amiss to read their records—in this case, the Franklin folios—as I have tried to read them here: as "memorial reconstructions" of the original scenes in which the colonists were among the principals.[50] If the folios could speak they might have channeled Virgil's famous words to Dido when he began telling of his part in the Trojan War: "ipse miserrima vidi / et quorum pars magna fui" (I myself both witnessed and played no small part in these dreadful events: *Aeneid* 2.5–6). The documents have to be read with a scrupulous philological eye partly because they are slanted and belated, but even more because they record events that were played out in the theater of brutal realities. Because the folios are an aesthetic hall of mirrors, they project representations where more is being meant and said than the folios intended to mean or say. That's why their poetry, as a poet would say of another literature of violence, is in the pity.

PART II

Secular Enlightenment: The Importance of Failure

CHAPTER EIGHT

Franklin's *Autobiography*: Composition as Explanation

Benjamin Franklin is such a gifted stylist that one easily forgets how topical and purpose-driven is virtually everything he wrote. Some are put off by his carefully managed prose, and especially by one of its key features: the projection of the myth of himself as candid, modest, and committed to benevolent social projects. Like Cotton Mather, Franklin wrote to make things happen that he thought should happen in the actual world, and his public persona was a device to forward his projects. It is a persona with many faces because the circumstances that called out and shaped his interventions were so numerous and so different. Choosing to meet that great force of objective circumstance, his literary works lay themselves open to judgment by objective conditions.[1]

In that connection, consider again Franklin's treaty folios—the culminant achievement of his career as a printer, publisher, and media entrepreneur. They clearly demonstrate how shrewdly he worked to make himself a public figure of consequence. The design was first used to print the Treaty of 1736 at Philadelphia, which he correctly judged a momentous event in Pennsylvania colonial history. It signaled the shift of the Covenant Chain council fire from New York to Pennsylvania. Thomas Penn moved from England to Philadelphia in 1731 to make his colony the focal agent for the Crown's North American empire. After beginning negotiations with the Iroquois League at the Treaty of 1732, the 1736 treaty settled Pennsylvania as the regular treaty-making host for negotiating military, political, and commercial affairs among a conglomerate of colonies and Indian nations.

Franklin followed these events closely, and in 1736, as printer for the colony, he published the treaty minutes in a spectacular format to signal the importance of the event. But it also signaled that Franklin and Philadelphia were important agents in European imperial affairs—a key message being carried by all his subsequent folios. As he later wrote in his *Autobiography*, at that point "I began ... to turn my thoughts a little to public affairs" (*Writings*, 1404).[2] Silence Dogood, Poor Richard, and his other masks began to recede as important expressive devices for him.

The world represented in the folios was seen very differently by Thomas Penn, whose treaty-making had inspired Franklin to create the folios in the first place. Indeed, the folio project set Penn and Franklin on the famous collision course that would carry on into the 1760s. In a practical sense Penn found the folios helpful for ordering his administrative affairs with all the parties: "particularly fortunate and useful" documents, as he told his secretary, Richard Peters.[3] But as he went on to write, Penn seriously disapproved of their lavish format. "Franklin judged very ill to print them in a folio," he wrote, because the design "makes them [the treaties] look larger than they are." Penn did not want undue attention paid to the land schemes that brought him to Philadelphia in 1731. Since 1734 he and his land agent, James Logan, had been laying plans for the notorious 1737 Walking Purchase, the event that perhaps more than any other would destabilize England's relations with the colonies and the Indian nations.

But Franklin wanted those records to look impressive because he grasped the great significance of treaty-making in the American theater of European imperial competition. They made up a history of the use and disposition of American land by many different native and colonial parties. More important, written treaties of record set down a view of the history that was meant to shape and drive it to colonial purposes. Making certain that all the folios would be widely distributed in the colonies and especially in England throughout the volatile 1740s and 1750s, Franklin showed himself knowledgeable about Crown public affairs as well as a key colonial promoter of England's North American empire. He was one of the Pennsylvania Assembly's negotiating agents at the 1753 Treaty of Carlisle; he was a chief delegate at the 1754 Albany Congress, where he presented his Plan of Union; and in 1756 he was appointed by the Crown to the commission inquiring into "The Causes of the Alienation of the Delawares and Shawanese from the British Interest" during the critical Seven Years' War.[4] By the time he left for England in 1757, he had made himself a public figure of importance not only throughout the colonies but in England and Europe. No American colonist had ever gained such international stature.

Whatever its scale, virtually all of Franklin's literary work has immediate and topical focus. Even the playful works are "practical letters." While that is also true of the *Autobiography*, its audience—and hence the practical leverage it seeks—is less immediate than foreseen, like the very differently foreseen audience Whitman summoned in "Crossing Brooklyn

Ferry." In that respect the *Autobiography* sets a touchstone for how we and others who are part of Franklin's foreseen audience read him.

Has there ever been an American work more clearly marked by its publication and reception history? Indeed, at a key moment in the *Autobiography*—the opening of part 2—Franklin made his readers an explicit, determining presence in the composition process itself. Those readers—Abel James and Benjamin Vaughan—saw the work as an exemplary Enlightenment life "in the American Grain." In that respect both read it in the very spirit in which the author wrote it.

Or more exactly, in the spirit of 1771, when Franklin began its composition. The point is important because the *Autobiography* was composed in parts at three significantly different moments in his life—1771, 1784, and 1788–89. As we know from the outline he sketched in 1771 when he finished part 1, the work "was planned as a whole when [he] began composing it."[5] In 1771 it was addressed to his son William and was presented as a story of successes lifted from adversities thanks to divine Providence, on one hand, and personal enterprise and benevolence on the other. The incarnation of Franklin's best hopes and dreams, William in 1771 was the child of his promised land. Thanks in great part to his father, he became a figure of consequence in imperial Britain. But even as the most important years of Franklin's public life were about to happen, his secular morality tale was being pressed by unforeseeable events. When he resumed the *Autobiography* in 1784 and again in 1788–89, the spirit that launched its composition in 1771—his dream of the British Empire and colonial America's place in that dream—was long gone.

Also long gone was another dream that he first passed along to his son William and then had gifted back to him by his son. We now name it Vandalia, a vast territorial version of the American Dream that Franklin began to imagine when he got involved in colonial treaty-making in Philadelphia and turned out the treaty folios. Treaty-making would fail, Vandalia would fail, and Franklin would suffer a dire personal loss—all at exactly the time the United States was being born.

Untold stories grow up with the stories Franklin told in the *Autobiography*, like tares among the wheat, because the *Autobiography* is a doubled narrative. One gives the incomplete story of Franklin's life up to 1758. The other is the story of how he shaped that life in the record he made of it. But it is an odd record, because the three parts are so discontinuous. Though "planned as a whole" when Franklin began it, it was shocked and changed by events. But it wasn't abandoned. To see it as a whole and on its own terms, we have to see how and why it changed. Because Franklin deliberately made the *Autobiography*'s composition history a key index to his life history, the relationship between those two histories is important both as Franklin saw the relationship and as it might otherwise be seen. So let's begin by recovering the relevant facts of those two interconnected histories.

A span of almost twenty years separates the first act of composition from the third and last. Part 1 was written in the summer of 1771 in England, part 2 in the summer of 1784 in Passy, France, and part 3/4 at different times in 1788–89 in Philadelphia. We shall have to look more closely at those places and dates to see their bearing on Franklin's work. A fractured and fracturing public history is echoed in the *Autobiography*, though the story of Franklin's public life never gets beyond 1758. Although those substantive echoes are often muted and distant, they come through clearly in the work's odd formal arrangement.

Part 1 and part 3/4 are an explicitly continuous chronological unit: part 1 ends in 1731 with the founding of the Philadelphia subscription library, and part 3/4 takes off from that point, carrying the story forward to the beginning of Franklin's first mission to England in 1758. Part 2 is notably different. Opening with the James and Vaughan letters from the early 1780s, it is immediately dislocated from the chronology of part 1. Franklin briefly recalls the subscription library and his intellectual life in Philadelphia but then pivots into the section's main event: the self-contained moral/philosophical tale of his "bold and arduous Project of arriving at moral Perfection" (*Writings*, 1383). Unlike "The Way to Wealth" and Franklin's other fictional tales of that kind, part 2 of the *Autobiography* is drawn from his own life, though some of the tale is not literally true, and much of consequence is left out. The verity of its details is a secondary consideration, however, for the story is there to make an argument about Franklin's life, which in the *Autobiography* is less a chronicle than an exemplum. But the absent matters are far from secondary. As for part 2, if it were removed the chronology of Franklin's work would be undisturbed. But the significance of the *Autobiography* would be radically different. Indeed, part 2 of the work is its heart and soul.

I

To see how that is so, let's look at each part separately. The *Autobiography* opens under signs that mark its literary character and circumstances: "Part One. / Twyford, at the Bishop of St. Asaph's 1771. / Dear Son" (*Writings*, 1307). He is " sit[ting] down to write... the Circumstances of [his] life" as a letter to William. The date and the place of writing are important as both men would understand, though we shall have to decode them. Franklin quickly turns to the writing itself and his idea of it—specifically, his determination to seize "the Advantage Authors have in a second Edition to correct some Faults of the first" (*Writings*, 1307). Correction in this case came with what Franklin records in part 1 as his life's "errata." Though he doesn't say that he will change the record or expunge anything, he will in fact do just that.

Part 1 tells us that the *Autobiography* is to be an edifying tale of Franklin's progress from "Poverty and Obscurity . . . to a State of Affluence and some Degree of Reputation in the World, and . . . a considerable share of Felicity" (*Writings*, 1307). Indeed, to strive seriously for perfection is perhaps to invite or—worse yet—even to tempt a falling short.

If Franklin cast his early moral life as a printer's lesson in achieving a "tolerable" moral character, the idea of perfection looms over part 1's account of the "dangerous Time of Youth and [its] hazardous Situations" (*Writings*, 1360). "Some degree of Reputation" and "considerable share of Felicity" recognize conditions where errata will prevail and where moral perfection must be a strait gate. His errata do not involve any "willful gross immorality or injustice," he insists, but simply "my youth, inexperience, and the knavery of others." So in this "dangerous Time of Youth" he was kept uncorrupted" by "the kind hand of Providence, or some guardian Angel, or accidental favourable Circumstances and Situations, or all together" (*Writings*, 1360).[6]

Set in the larger context of Franklin's life, the passage is notably insinuating. Part 1, after all, says nothing about what was surely the most significant erratum in Franklin's early life: that he fathered an illegitimate child, William. Here Franklin may be both alluding to it and trying to mitigate the offense by suggesting it wasn't "willful." Being so invested in launching his son on the successful public career William had achieved by 1771, when Franklin wrote this passage, he would have shrunk from writing anything that could damage the figure William was cutting in both England and the colonies.

Part 1 climaxes by recording two impressive events. In the autumn of 1727 Franklin directed the formation "of my ingenious Acquaintance into a Club for mutual Improvement" (*Writings*, 1361). His career as a writer and printer helped him gain this ingenious acquaintance and then set up its formal constitution as the Junto (also known as the Leather Apron Club). That event led directly to the creation in 1731 of Franklin's "first Project of a public Nature . . . a Subscription Library" (*Writings*, 1372). Part 1 then closed with a forecast that will be echoed in the prologue to part 3/4. The subscription library was the very exponent of Franklin's commitment to education and enlightenment: "These libraries have improved the general conversation of the Americans, made the common tradesmen and farmers as intelligent as most gentlemen from other countries, and perhaps have contributed in some degree to the stand so generally made throughout the colonies in defense of their privileges" (*Writings*, 1372). When Franklin sums up the library as "a great thing itself, & continually increasing" (*Writings*, 1372), he is also summing up the central argument of part 1: that his life up to 1731 had achieved a condition of hopeful aspiration. Part 1 is a sanguine narrative of errors and difficulties surmounted and various benevolent projects set running.

Thus does the *Autobiography* mirror Franklin's assessment of his life as it stood in 1771. Though his mission to England was public service on a scale he had not yet experienced, he had been long training in it from his home base in Philadelphia. By 1757 he had become a figure of consequence throughout the colonies and, because of his scientific work, even abroad. He was coming to England as a colonial patriot filled with admiration for British political ideas and ideals—republican liberty, personal freedom, the rule of law—and especially for the British Empire.[7] The most significant political event of his work before this diplomatic mission had been his Albany Plan for extending the British Empire by reorganizing the power and resources of the colonies. Franklin took a dim view of Indians and their lifeways, but the organization of the Iroquois League had inspired him with a model of cooperative political action that he thought would prove useful both to the separate colonies, often at odds with each other, and to the Empire they were part of. But even though his plan was rejected in 1754 by the colonies as well as by Whitehall and the Crown, Franklin never ceased to believe it would enhance the power and glory of the Empire as well as her most glorious—her North American—colonies.

He also left Philadelphia on good terms with the newly appointed Governor Denny and was sanguine that he could succeed with his mission to the proprietors. He believed that because the struggle between France and England threatened the North American colonies, the jewel of the British empire. The Pennsylvania proprietors, he thought, would recognize their duty to help fund the war.[8] An avid imperialist, Franklin supported the war and the taxes needed to prosecute it. As early as 1735 he was in favor of taxes that were "proportion'd to Property"—a formula that would have hit the Pennsylvania proprietors hard, as the sons of William Penn well understood.[9]

By 1762, however, his mission with the proprietors had essentially failed. Yet that failure was countered by a notable success that showed how influential he had become with the Crown and key members of Parliament. In 1762 William was appointed Crown governor of the New Jersey colony. It was a brilliant and unexpected appointment and catapulted William into some of the most significant Crown plans for settling its colonial and Indian affairs in America. With the establishment of the Crown's Proclamation Line of 1763, those plans created serious divisions in the colonies and eventually precipitated the rebellion of two-thirds of England's colonies as well as civil war within the colonies. It was an outcome that both father and son deplored and had worked hard to prevent.[10]

After nine years at home (1762–71), Franklin returned to London as the colonial agent for Pennsylvania, Massachusetts, Georgia, and New Jersey. Despite increasing tensions between the colonies and London, Franklin and William expected the differences would be reconciled. At that point both were heavily and personally invested in the expansion of Britain's American empire. Father and son were also much admired in England, though Franklin's forthright defense of colonial grievances soon involved him in controversy. But the Hutchinson Affair was still two years off.[11] Being on particularly intimate terms with William Shipley, the bishop of St. Asaph, and his family, he accepted an invitation to a summer sojourn at Twyford, England, where he set down the confident prospect of a happy life that is the subject of part 1.

II

Part 2 and the eventual context that shaped it are very different. "The Affairs of the Revolution" interrupted the *Autobiography*'s composition, Franklin wrote at the outset of part 2 (*Writings*, 1372). That was Franklin's public shorthand for how deeply the hiatus of 1771–84 had unsettled his life. Part 1 was begun in England with deliberation. In 1784 he was in France serving as the Continental Congress's commissioner and had no thought of the *Autobiography* he started thirteen years before. He only resumed it "in compliance with the Advice contain'd in [two] Letters" he unexpectedly received from persons who read part 1 and wrote to encourage him to continue his uplifting project (*Writings*, 1372). One was from the Philadelphia Quaker merchant Abel James, the other from the British diplomat Benjamin Vaughan.

In part 2 Franklin's first audience, William, has been succeeded, indeed supplanted, by a second audience chosen not by the author but by chance or fate. "There fell into my Hands," James wrote Franklin, "about 23 Sheets in thy own hand-writing containing an Account of the Parentage and Life of thyself, directed to thy Son ending in the Year 1730" (*Writings*, 1373).[12] With a larger audience now drawn into the work, the *Autobiography* was becoming yet more explicitly not just a story of Franklin's life in time, but a story of when and where the record was made and how it was being received. William's reaction to what his father began as a personal letter to him never comes into the *Autobiography*, though other records, as we shall see, fill in that blank.

After quoting the James and Vaughan letters and making a brief link to the subscription library mentioned in Part 1, Franklin launched into part 2's central subject, the project of moral perfection (*Writings*, 1383). The story would move through two stages of failure. The first was the failure of the perfection project, the second the failure of his plan to write his Book of Virtue. In this progress part 2 unfolded a critical commentary on the keynote of part 1, the tale of his errata, of being improved by failure and error.

The perfection project failed because the tests of lived experience—whether from God, angels, or circumstance—taught him that he should have striven for virtue, not perfection; the two are very different. As unattainable as perfection, virtue operates in the quotidian order, where it is always being gained and lost (and then perhaps also lost and gained).

To call moral failures "errata," as he does in part 1—for *a printer* to call them such—suggests more than a set of amendable errors. Books are for readers, and readers have elementary expectations. Meeting those expectations, as objective in their own way as perfection, might well be perhaps even more difficult, for one's acquaintances (or one's monitors) would be as fallible as oneself. Consider, too, that while every new edition—it is the fundamental law of textuality—will change what has come before, each inevitably brings its own (at first unrecognized) problems.

Part 2 of the *Autobiography* thus ran with the practical and moral preoccupations of part 1. As it proceeded—as the project's difficulties grew increasingly clear—it succumbed to its own investigations. Its scrupulous examination of moral dangers slowly exposed "errata" as an inadequate, even a ridiculous, term for human faults. Problems multiplied as Franklin augmented his list of necessary virtues. His initial set of twelve grew to thirteen when a Quaker pointed out that he lacked humility. But the new imperative—"Imitate Jesus and Socrates"—seemed extravagant and overweening (*Writings*, 1385). Is humility worth state execution?

The addition propelled him to further presumptions. To secure a "*Habitude*" of perfection he conceives the need for "*Silence*," "RESOLUTION," "*Frugality*," "*Industry*," "*Sincerity*," "*Justice*,: and most imperative, "*Order*" and a "METHOD" to secure it. He begins to tabulate his quest in a "little Book" with elaborate accounting devices that will promote strict daily and weekly attention. He reads assiduously in moral authors—Cato, Cicero, Solomon—and annotates his "Tables of Examination" with prayers to God and snatches of moral poetry. The "Precept of Order" becomes so demanding that the project begins to break down under the pressure of its insignificant but "vex[ing]" details ("Places for Things, Papers, etc."). The perfection scheme is making war on the scheme itself, with Franklin losing his grip on the eleventh of the original set of virtues: "TRANQUILITY ... Be not disturbed at trifles." Sorely "vex'd," Franklin admits that he "was almost ready to give up the Attempt, and content myself with a faulty Character" (*Writings*, 1385–90).

A timely utterance brought relief to Franklin via another moral tale about a man who wanted his ax sharpened so that "the whole of its Surface [should be] bright as the Edge." Finding a perfectly clean ax-head difficult and ultimately unnecessary in point of usefulness, Franklin decides that "*I think I like a speckled axe best.*" The story lets him draw the moral that "a benevolent man should allow a few Faults in himself, to keep his friends in Countenance" (*Writings*, 1390).

That notably crafted remark deserves our attention. Franklin is defining "a benevolent man," a person who promotes the good of others, as one who can accept ("allow") his own faults—but only "a few faults," perhaps five in twenty-five years—in order to ensure that others won't be discomposed by his image of perfection. It would be unfriendly to project such a view of himself—a reproach on others, putting them out of countenance for having their own imperfections reflected back from Franklin's bright, unspeckled surface. As he pointed out earlier in the story of the founding of the public subscription library—in the introductory section of part 2—benevolent projects should be managed "as a scheme of a *number of friends*" lest the special "merit" of one person provoke the "envy" of others.[13] Implicit here is Franklin's keen awareness of human frailty. "Men are so wicked as we now see them,"[14] he wrote to an unnamed correspondent in 1757. The comment recalls a proverb from *Poor Richard Improved* for 1753: "*He that best understands the World, least likes it.*" Critical self-reflection had launched his perfection project, but it did not begin to succeed until he wrote up (in the summer of 1784) its collapse (in 1731) under the blind weight of a finical method and an obsession with regularized order.

So as Franklin advanced his story, a new bibliographical project emerged, "my BOOK the ART of *Virtue*," conceived to show "the *Means* and *Manner* of obtaining [Virtue]" (*Writings*, 1392). But writing that book turned out an "Intention" that he "never fulfilled." It was thwarted by "the necessary and close attention to Private ... and Public Business" that occupied so much of Franklin's life. The circumstantial order of the world— "an unforeseen Succession of Employs"—overwhelmed his book project (*Writings*, 1392).

What was fulfilled was his account of the failure of both the perfection project and the book project. The failures revealed Franklin to himself: not only that he was "incorrigible with respect to *Order*" but that he was yet more seriously fallible (*Writings*, 1391). That climactic revelation comes in the final paragraph of part 2, which closes by confessing a grievous and ineradicable fault: Satan's sin, ambition and pride: "There is, perhaps, no one of our natural passions so hard to subdue as *Pride*. Disguise it, struggle with it, beat it down, stifle it, mortify it as much as one pleases, it is still alive, and will every now and then peep out and show itself; you will see it, perhaps, often in this History; for, even if I could conceive that I had compleatly overcome it, I should probably be proud of my Humility" (*Writings*, 1393–94). Those are singularly nuanced remarks. Partly they ask us to see his humility as a function of his deathless pride. Though it may only surface "every now and then," in fact it is pervasive. It might be "see[n] ... often in this History" were it not for his serious pursuit of virtue. His practice of humility throws his pride into regular eclipse. So does the intention to virtue have certain equivocal consequences.

According to part 2 of the *Autobiography*, virtue and even the appearance of virtue are dangerous and deceptive for anyone choosing to pursue benevolent action, both private and public. The step-by-step account of Franklin's shortfall of perfection initially turned out to be a perverse kind of success story because it left Franklin with an achievable view of virtue ("speckled"). But the success proved anticlimactic in the narrative because achievable virtue brought with it the revelation of existential vice of the most serious kind. Pride is the indexical sign of the condition of insurmountable evil, and humility is the condition that makes it both knowable and, worse (as the Puritans never tired of reminding themselves), knowingly unavoidable. At the end of part 2 we and Franklin are far beyond imagining ethical and political problems in terms of errata.

Although part 2 concludes at that point, what he wrote for the *Autobiography* in 1784 was not finished. He added a paragraph to the outline he had written in 1771: "Hutchinson's Letters. Temple. Suit in Chancery, Abuse before the Privy Council. Lord Hillsborough's Character and Conduct. Lord Dartmouth. Negociation to prevent the War. Return to America. Bishop of St. Asaph. Congress, Assembly. Committee of Safety. Chevaux de Frize. Sent to Boston, to the Camp. To Canada. to Lord Howe. To France, Treaty, &c."[15] This is a schematic picture of events that fell out in 1772–83, with the "&c." pointing beyond the 1783 Treaty of Paris. The entries show that Franklin intended to give his view of the notorious Hutchinson Affair, the collapse of his efforts to prevent a break with England, his involvement in the war theater, and his mission to secure the support of France. But the outline is most important for an entry it didn't include and, in that omission, for another that had been left out of the previous outline. Each involved private schemes and public dreams that Franklin had long cherished. They were closely related. One had to do with his son William, whom Franklin brought to England in 1758 to prepare him to become a major player in British imperial adventure. The other was Vandalia, the colonial project William and his father worked at with a company of land speculators. When Franklin returned to Pennsylvania in 1775, his hopes to save England's North American empire—though not his son's hopes for it—were essentially dead. But both men were still actively promoting Benjamin's long-cherished dream of a great imperial colony—a Crown proprietary colony, no less—in the native lands of America.[16]

The Vandalia scheme was fatally crippled when war broke out, though it would linger on for a few more years. But a far worse consequence followed the outbreak of the war in April 1775. William kept his pledge of allegiance to the Crown. From September 1, 1775 to August 16, 1784 Franklin cut off all contact with his son.[17] Though urged by friends to help William after war broke out, Franklin refused. William would be imprisoned for a year in the notorious Litchfield jail and his wife Elizabeth would suffer a breakdown and die. Franklin did not intervene and offered no help.

After the war, William sought "a Renewal of our former affectionate Intercourse" with a touching letter to his "Dear and Honoured Father" on July 22, 1784. It offered a kind of private condolence ceremony in which both men could grieve for the anguish and loss each had suffered. In 1753 Franklin had experienced at first hand, and recorded in unusual detail, the importance of the condolence ceremony in the Indian treaty-making he had recorded in his famous folios. But if he admired the political organization of the Iroquois League, he was untouched by its ceremonial heart, *kaswentha*. His hurt had become so inwardly rooted that he had no access to what his son's letter briefly recalled: "the cruel Sufferings, scandalous Neglects, and Ill-treatment which we poor unfortunate Loyalists have in general experienced." So instead of exchanging sorrow and compassion with his son, Franklin could manage only an aggrieved reply.

> [N]othing has ever hurt me so much and affected me with such keen Sensations, as to find myself deserted in my old Age by my only Son; and not only deserted, but to find him taking up Arms against me, in a Cause wherein my good Fame, Fortune and Life were all at Stake. You conceived, you say, that your Duty to your King and Regard for your Country requir'd this. I ought not to blame you for differing in Sentiment with me in Public Affairs. We are Men, all subject to Errors. Our Opinions are not in our Power; they are form'd and govern'd much by Circumstances that are often as inexplicable as they are irresistible. Your Situation was such that few would have censured your remaining Neuter, tho' *there are Natural Duties Which precede political Ones, and cannot be extinguish'd by them.* This is a disagreable Subject. I drop it.

And we will endeavour as you propose mutually to forget what has happened relating to it, as well as we can. (August 16, 1784)[18]

"*Natural Duties*" had become a one-way street for Franklin. Though political differences did not fracture his friendships with other British loyalists, his affection for William was "*extinguish'd*" forever by their different political commitments. William's July letter had "propose[d] mutually to forget" all that dreadful history, but Franklin could not. His son's unstinting love perhaps even magnified Franklin's affliction, for unforgiving pain wrote the cruel words he left William in his "Last Will and Testament": "The part he acted against me in the late war, which is of public notoriety, will account for my leaving him no more of an estate he endeavoured to deprive me of."[19]

Like many last words, these recall more than matters of public notoriety. The passage is crossed with Franklin's distressed memory of the elaborate project on which he and William had been closely cooperating for the ten years before their 1775 breach. William not only never worked to deprive his father of an estate, from 1766 he had brought Franklin into a land speculation scheme that, if successful, would have created colossal fortunes for both.

This was Vandalia, one of the most sordid enterprises of the late colonial period. Yet it began very differently, in the benevolent imperial dreams that had dominated Franklin's imagination at least since 1754, when he initially formulated his *Plan for Settling Two Western Colonies*.[20] What he envisioned was a rich "settlement" beyond the Appalachians (for "the nobility and gentry of Britain [and] with such Americans as shall join them") that would promote "the general good of the British empire." Some months later "one Mr. Hazard" read the *Plan*, Franklin told Peter Collinson, and, fired with enthusiasm, wrote up one of his own in which he would "become a Proprietor like Mr. Penn [and] make a strong English Settlement." "I wish to see it done," Franklin wrote, but thought Hazard not the person to drive the project.[21] Then a year later he sent an ecstatic letter to George Whitefield wishing "that you and I were jointly employ'd by the Crown to settle a Colony on the Ohio."

> What a glorious Thing it would be, to settle in that fine Country a large Strong Body of Religious and Industrious People! What a Security to the other Colonies; and Advantage to Britain, by Increasing her People, Territory, Strength and Commerce. Might it not greatly facilitate the Introduction of pure Religion among the Heathen, if we could, by such a Colony, show them a better Sample of Christians

than they commonly see in our Indian Traders, the most vicious and abandoned Wretches of our Nation? (July 2, 1756)

Franklin's dream of this western colony arose from his view that "all the Country from St. Laurence to Missisipi [sic]" would be crucial for "the Foundations of the future Grandeur and Stability of the British Empire," as he wrote to Lord Kames (January 3, 1760), running through the "immense Increase ... of Commerce ... Power [and] influence round the whole Globe [to] awe the World!" Perhaps reading this effusive account, Franklin took a breath and moderated his prose, "for I see you begin to think my Notions extravagant, and look upon them as the Ravings of a mad Prophet."

These are exorbitant dreams. Not even Jefferson was more fired by trans-Appalachian imperial visions. Unlike Jefferson, however, as the letter to Whitefield shows, Franklin's dream was first dreamt in a thoroughly British mode. He never gave up that imperial model, but eventually—reluctantly—he gave up on Great Britain. The letter also suggests that "the idea of such a colony" as Franklin was imagining was important as an ethical undertaking. "In such an Enterprize," the letter to Whitefield goes on to say, "I could spend the Remainder of Life with Pleasure; and I firmly believe God would bless us with Success, if we undertook it with a sincere Regard to his Honour, the Service of our gracious King, and (which is the same thing) the Publick Good." That it would involve the appropriation of a vast tract of native American land was not a consideration for either William or his father.

So when the prospect of founding such a colony arose in 1766 as a practical possibility and was presented to him by his son, Franklin did not hesitate. But he should have, for, as Jack Sosin laconically remarks, the "land speculators" that Franklin and William were joining "were not the most scrupulous of men."[22] What drove them was not dreams of an enlightened imperial civilization but avarice. Unlike the often deplorable but fairly straightforward methods for appropriating native lands that had been practiced over the previous 150 years, however, this plan, because colonial circumstances had so radically changed with the end of the Seven Years' War, required an unusual degree of resolute deviousness. Briefly, the problem was the Proclamation Line of 1763, which forbade further encroachments on Indian lands by the established colonials until the Crown decided exactly how to manage its now greatly increased American enterprise. The Proclamation Line called an abrupt halt to a whole series of private land speculations by the colonials that had begun in the mid-1740s.

Some account of the scheme is relevant here because of how it reflects on the limits of Franklin's moral compass and his interest in a path toward wealth very different from the one promoted in Poor Richard's famous last words. The Franklins were joining a company formed in 1766 under the leadership of George Croghan, the Indian superintendent Sir William Johnson, and William Franklin. Because Johnson and William Franklin were colonial agents, their part in the scheme was kept secret. Their object was to persuade the British government to approve a land-development grant on the western frontier that in its initial conception amounted to some 1.4 million acres. Owing to their official positions, William Franklin (Governor of the New Jersey colony) and Sir William Johnson (Superintendent of Indian Affairs for the Northern District) were especially well, if also quite delicately, placed to forward the scheme. As in situ colonial supervisors, they could use their authority to drive the project, while Franklin, as a colonial lobbyist in London, could maneuver it through the government bureaucracy.

The governor and the superintendent saw an unusual opportunity to advance the project by manipulating the outcome of the Treaty of Fort Stanwix (1768), which Whitehall saw as the pivotal event in the series of Indian treaties it was pursuing to settle the frontier line from Canada to the Floridas. Franklin and Johnson prosecuted the treaty ostensibly on behalf of the interests of the British government. In fact, however, they were managing the events so as to make their private scheme appear not only congruent with British policy, but also as an opportunity the government would want to seize. This result is obvious from the map of Vandalia (see fig. 7). The Proclamation Line in the region of the Vandalia scheme ran along the Allegheny Mountains. In the 1768 treaty negotiations, however, the Crown representatives—Johnson and William Franklin—pressed for a line much farther to the west. It followed the course of the Ohio River from present-day Pittsburgh south to its confluence with the Kentucky River at Carrollton, sixty miles below Cincinnati. This meant that the Vandalia speculators could map out Vandalia as a new inland colony situated in a vast stretch of Indian territory west of Virginia.

When the treaty was signed, the company, now known as the Walpole Company, began moving to secure the grant and establish—indeed, vastly extend—its boundaries. Benjamin Franklin's role was to make the case for the enterprise in England, and he worked hard at his task. Prosecuted for nine more years, even after Franklin left England in 1775, it was always on the brink of a success that finally eluded the projectors.

During those years the initial speculation project changed into a proposal to establish a colony that would have been larger than New Hampshire, Vermont, Connecticut, and Rhode Island combined: not just a path but a highway to wealth. Paradoxically for Franklin, the project would also

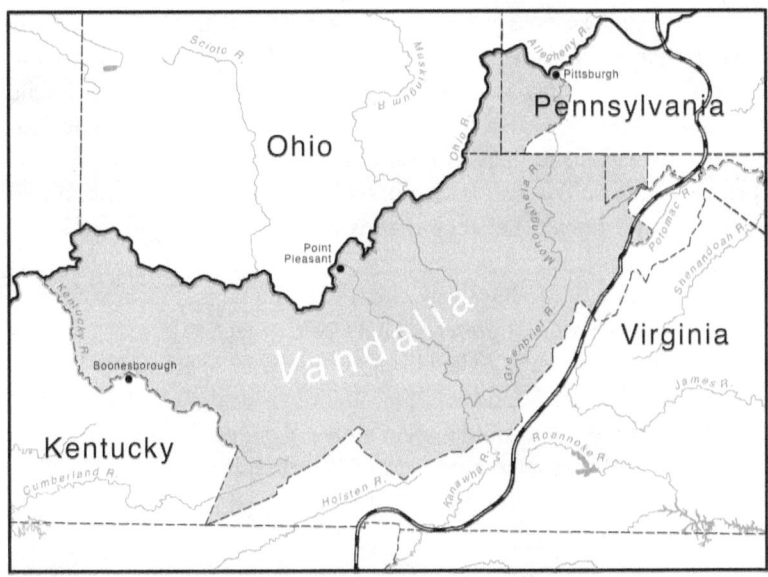

FIGURE 7. A schematic map of the proposed colony of Vandalia (1768), with its relation to the Proclamation Line (1763). Map by Lauren Nassef.

come to be reconceived as the kind of proprietary colony that Franklin had spent so many years trying to dismantle in Pennsylvania.

III

Part 2 of the *Autobiography* was written in 1784. At that point the war was over and, in the main event for the United States, successful. But the new nation was fearfully in debt, as Franklin, who took on the onerous job of dealing with it, knew all too well. Besides, the Articles of Confederation (1781) had quickly emerged as a serious national problem. They were rife with present and future state and federal conflicts that would have to be dealt with. And then, heaped on those difficulties was the remembrance of dark things past. As Franklin came to judge the failures of his 1731 Perfection Project and Book of Virtue, did he think of William and Vandalia as a revelation of investments in misconceived ideals? A late essay (1786) that he wrote for the bishop of St. Asaph's daughter Catherine Shipley, "The Art of procuring Pleasant Dreams" (*Writings*, 1118–22), suggests he did. It is an incisive commentary on the relation that pleasant dreams can have to fearful nightmares. It is also a prime example of the skeptical turn his mind took in the years between 1784, when he wrote part 2 of the *Autobiography*, and 1788–89, when he wrote part 3/4.

We've seen the essay's procedural method before, most dramatically in the narrative of the Perfection Project: accumulating and adding circumstances until they drag an original idea down to earth.[23] Here Franklin marches Shipley through a series of behavioral instructions, physical exercises, and various strategies to ward off "painful Dreams" and promote "pleasing Dreams." He elaborates the specific pieces of advice with different anecdotes, as when he recommends sleeping with an open window.

> It is recorded of Methusalem, who, being the longest liver may be supposed to have best preserved his Health, that he slept always in the open air; for when he had lived 500 years, an Angel said to him, Arise, Methusalem, and build thee an house for thou shall live yet 500 years longer: But Methusalem answer'd and said, If I am to live but 500 years longer, it is not worth while to build me an house; I will sleep in the air as I have been us'd to do.

Or when he recommends moderate eating before bedtime: "Nothing more common in the newspapers than instances of people, who, after eating a hearty supper, are found dead a bed in the morning" (*Writings*, 1119).

Franklin closes with a general reflection that "when the Body is uneasy . . . disagreeable Ideas of various kinds will in sleep be the natural Consequences." Then after citing six "Remedies preventive and curative" to ward off ideas that feed bad dreams, Franklin turns the table on the entire composition with "a Case in which the most punctual Observance of them all will be totally fruitless." Like Father William's 1758 warning against too great a dependence on Industry, Frugality, and Prudence, the essay pivots upon itself at the end:

> I need not mention this case to you my dear friend; but my account of the art would be imperfect without it. The case is,
> When the person who desires to have pleasant dreams, has not taken care to preserve, what is necessary above all things, A GOOD CONSCIENCE. (*Writings*, 1122)

On its face that move takes one up short. It is especially startling because Franklin at the outset had told Shipley about his own "nightmares and horrors inexpressible": "we fall from precipices, are assaulted by wild beasts, murderers, or demons, and we experience at times every variety of distress" (*Writings*, 1118–19). So this happiest of men, blessed by God and good fortune, has not always "taken care to preserve a good conscience." Nightmares perhaps come to surveille pleasant daytime dreams and to spur the commitment to an awakened conscience.

Or consider his speech on September 17, 1787, the last day of the Constitutional Convention (*Writings*, 1139–41). Of Franklin's many literary works, perhaps none is more celebrated. He wrote it because, although the deliberations were complete and the document drawn up, it was far from universally approved. The possibility that it would be sent to the states for ratification without the endorsement of all the delegates was considered likely, and in fact that is exactly what transpired. Because Franklin himself had serious reservations about the final work, the most he would say in favor of its compromises was that "I consent . . . to this Constitution because I expect no better, and because I am not sure that it is not the best" (*Writings*, 1140).

Acknowledging its weaknesses, however, Franklin urged the importance of a show of "real or apparent Unanimity" of approval by the delegates, who, he remarked, should "doubt a little of [their] own Infallibility" about what was right or wrong with "this instrument" (*Writings*, 1141). A public declaration of unity was crucial, he argued, since only a concerted effort could focus "our future Thoughts and Endeavours" on the greatest difficulty of all: "having it well administred." Underlying this argument is Franklin's long-standing skeptical judgment about the complex problem of achieving social improvement and political success: "[W]hen you assemble a Number of Men to have the Advantage of their joint Wisdom, you inevitably assemble with those Men all their Prejudices, their Passions, their Errors of Opinion, their local Interests, and their selfish Views" (*Writings*, 1140). There is Franklin's considered view of the Convention and of the much-revered instrument that assembly was able to forge, the Constitution of the United States of America. That it was and still is a fearful document is not often enough acknowledged. All of the original ten Amendments, added in 1788–89 when some of those fears were loudly declared, were born of fearful apprehensions, though perhaps only the Second Amendment clearly exposed the reciprocity between fear and violence.[24]

When Franklin resumed writing his *Autobiography* in the summer of 1788, the Convention and the Constitution were still much on his mind, as the prefatory section of part 3/4 makes clear. Both were closely connected to the "great and extensive project," mentioned toward the end of part 2, that "an unforeseen succession of employs prevented my attending to." As the different states were considering whether or not to ratify the Constitution, Franklin set that project at the front of the *Autobiography*'s new installment he was writing in Philadelphia.

Part 3/4 made a return to where Franklin had left his chronicle in 1771. The bulk of the final part is a narrative of the many successes that he had ventured between 1731 and 1757 (as he had listed them in the outline he sketched after he finished part 1). But before he laid out that parade of achievements, Franklin set down a new version of his "*great & extensive*" project for human betterment. Modified by the critical analysis he produced in part 2, the revised scheme shifted the focus from a personal to a social endeavor. Part 3/4 put front and center the codependence of the two culminant events of part 1, the Junto and the library.

Having the Convention's struggles and compromises with state-sponsored slavery fresh in his mind, Franklin was trying to move back to the future. Nearly sixty years before he had written up what he judged a useful sketch of his project, the "Observations on my Reading History, in Library, May 19th, 1731." He now recovered that document and placed it at the head of this last part the *Autobiography*. It is a proposal for "an united Party for Virtue [formed of] the Virtuous and good Men of all Nations into a regular Body, to be govern'd by suitable good and wise Rules, which good and wise Men may probably be more unanimous in their Obedience to, than common People are to common Laws" (*Writings*, 1395). Recovered in 1788, Franklin's Junto proposal of 1731 has not only been ramped up onto a global scale; it becomes a commentary on the recent Convention and Constitution and the "future Thoughts and Endeavours" (*Writings*, 1141) that the new nation must deal with. Founded by those fallible mortals Franklin spoke about in his final Convention speech, these new men must keep clearly in mind their permanent character and social condition as they enter upon "the great Affairs of the World," with its "Wars, Revolutions, &c." (*Writings*, 1395). Those affairs "are carried on and effected by Parties," for which it is true

> [t]hat the View of these Parties is their present general Interest, or what they take to be such.—
>
> [t]hat the different Views of these different Parties, occasion all Confusion.
>
> [t]hat while a Party is carrying on a general Design, each Man has his particular private Interest in View.
>
> [t]hat as soon as a Party has gain'd its general Point, each Member becomes Intent upon his particular Interest, which thwarting others, breaks that Party into Divisions, and occasions more Confusion.
> (*Writings*, 1395)

To gloss this passage as it falls into the last part of the *Autobiography*, we might reasonably turn to a later master of the wisdom of nonsense: "We think so then [in 1731] and we thought so still [in 1788]."[25]

Against the inertia of such forces Franklin proposes a "Sect" assembled from a core of "ingenuous well-disposed Youths" (*Writings*, 1396). Until its numbers should "become considerable," it should be a secret society "to prevent Solicitations for the Admission of improper Persons."

> Members should engage to afford their Advice Assistance and Support to each other in promoting one another's Interest, Business and Advancement in Life . . . [and] for Distinction, we should be call'd the Society of the *Free and Easy*; Free, as being by the general Practice and Habit of the Virtues, free from the Dominion of Vice, and particularly by the Practice of Industry and Frugality, free from Debt, which exposes a Man to Confinement and a Species of Slavery to his Creditors. (*Writings*, 1396)[26]

"Multifarious Occupations public and private" kept Franklin from pursuing this project until, at the age of eighty-two, "I have no longer Strength or Activity left sufficient for such an Enterprize" (*Writings*, 1397). But the project, he insists, was and still is "[a] practicable Scheme," so he concludes with the thought "that one Man of tolerable Abilities may work great Changes, and accomplish great Affairs among Mankind, if he first forms a good Plan, and, cutting off all Amusements or other Employments that would divert his Attention, makes the Execution of that same Plan his sole Study and Business" (*Writings*, 1397).

That might be a fair—it is certainly a generous—assessment of the one man who wrote it, but no one, least of all Franklin, could think that it was complete or candid. He had long since understood that "one Man" could do little without a Junto, just as he had long since realized that "[m]en are so wicked as we now see them," so that a Junto itself might bring its own devils, especially if it were formed secretly. Had he forgotten, or was he deliberately ignoring, what he had written in 1784 about the dominion of that mastering vice pride, or what he said only the year before in his speech of June 2, 1787 to the delegates at the Convention about the "two Passions" that most influence men's actions?

> There are two Passions which have a powerful Influence in the Affairs of Men. These are *Ambition* and *Avarice*; the Love of Power, and the Love of Money. Separately each of these has great Force in prompting Men to Action; but when united in View of the same Object, they have in many Minds the most violent Effect. Place before the Eyes of such Men a [Post] of *Honor* that shall at the same time be a Place of *Profit*, and they will move Heaven and Earth to obtain it.[27]

Given the shameful Vandalia scheme, the passage has a shocking relevance for Franklin personally, and perhaps an even more shocking one for Americans who might read it after 2016.

Franklin spoke well to speak this way at the Convention, but in his *Autobiography* a year later he shifted back to pleasant dreams. Is it just a later American usage that makes one uneasy at a "Society of the Free and Easy"? Or at the idea of "ingenuous and well-disposed Youth"? Or at the apparent contradiction between men of free and easy virtue driving a scheme for a rigorously purpose-driven life? And why, after all, isn't Franklin proposing a "Society of the Speckled Axe"?

I pose these questions because I think we can't tell exactly what Franklin means as he launches this new section of the *Autobiography*. It has much in common with the fantastical flight Crèvecoeur imagines in Letter XII of *Letters from an American Farmer*. Franklin's essays regularly proceed by provoking readers—including himself—to rethink what they set about trying to think about. Part 2 of the *Autobiography*, as we've seen, was just such a work, making a final turn upon itself that is a recognizable technique of his satirical polemics.

After the Treaty of Paris (1783), Franklin's writings became notably provocative on the subject of the new United States. The paired 1784 essays "Information to those who would remove to America" and "Remarks Concerning the Savages of North America" are a dialogue between a hopeful vision of the "Mediocrity" of American culture and a manifest satire on the nation's "parochialism and hypocrisy."[28] That same year he wrote a satire on the formation of the Society of the Cincinnati and what it reflected about the ethos of the emerging country.[29] His final admonitory speech to the Constitutional Convention was a warning, and while he never itemized what he judged to be the "errors" of the final document, we can be certain he deeply disapproved of at least one (notorious) part: Article 1, Section 2. We know this not because of anything reported out of the convention but because of his efforts following the convention to promote abolition. He became president of the Pennsylvania Abolition Society, lobbied against slavery and its American legalization, and early in 1790 presented an abolition petition before the Senate and House of Representatives. His action caused an uproar among representatives of the slave interest, and when James Jackson of Georgia spoke aggressively against the petition, he responded in the *Federal Gazette* (March 23, 1790) with his sly "Sidi Mehemet" satiric hoax (*Writings*, 1157–60).

Yet facing all that is the great and extensive project of the Society of the Free and Easy. If it seems a utopian folly, perhaps even a dangerous folly and, besides, textually self-contradictory, no reader has thought to insist on that view, and to this point few even entertain it. Yet the idea of the practicality of a fantastic, even a preposterous, dream is decidedly provoking. When Father Abraham's speech in the 1758 almanac sets Prudence against Folly, he is clearly Franklin's spokesman. But when Franklin dismantles Franklin in the 1784 installment of the *Autobiography*, the document is undermining its own intentional authority and putting its arguments at serious risk. And when we arrive at the 1788 installment, with the narrative hanging fire, Franklin has left us entirely to our own resources. Which may be, for us at any rate, the point.

Seen that way, Franklin's work has recalibrated the relation between what we might take it to mean and what Franklin might have meant it to mean. Initial authorial uncertainties anticipate, probably solicit, meanings—practical applications—from even more uncertain and circumstantial contexts present and to come. What is at stake is not the usable past, but a usable future. In that connection we might recall Franklin's celebrated reply to Mrs. Powel as he was leaving the convention hall on September 17. According to the diary of Dr. James McHenry of Maryland, "A lady asked Dr. Franklin Well Doctor what have we got a republic or a monarchy. A republic replied the Doctor if you can keep it."[30] But the question is not *if* it will be kept, but *how* it will be carried on. As ancient and contemporary history testifies, republicans can be—and it has long been argued, are among the most *likely* to be—thoroughly depraved.

CHAPTER NINE

The Education of Thomas Jefferson

Franklin's anxieties about the future of the United States follow from his lifelong judgment about the fallibility of human beings: "Men are so wicked as we now see them." But his commitment to the power of "benevolence" made him judge himself less sternly. Franklin makes mistakes but we are not to think of him as wicked. So he drew a veil over events that might have called out more severe judgments.

Jefferson's *Notes on the State of Virginia* adopted a more exacting line.[1] This is especially apparent when *Notes* took up its two most problematic topics: the condition of Blacks and of Native Americans. In each case, they were dire topics—the original sins of white America, as they would come to be called. What he wrote on these matters highlights what I judge the great strength of *Notes* as a whole: Jefferson's struggle for candor, thoroughness, and sincerity. Precisely his *struggle*—quite as impressive as John Winthrop's or Cotton Mather's—for when he took up both subjects his purpose was to lay out the shifts that his thinking forced him to take.

Addressed initially to a French *philosophe*, the French diplomat François Barbé-Marbois, Jefferson saw *Notes* as an educational primer, thinking he might give it "to each of the students of W[illiam and] M[ary] C[ollege]" and other "friends" committed to the advancement of learning.[2] He saw the book, not without reason, as an example of an inquiring mind in action—a work meaning to teach not by precept but by example. The work's judgments were laid down for assessment and further judgment. As a consequence, the *Notes* would expose Jefferson in ways that Franklin would never do so directly.

Although Mitchell Breitwieser has drawn important comparisons between Franklin and Cotton Mather, in point of temperament it is perhaps Jefferson who is closest to Mather, and the *Notes* closest to the *Magnalia*. Consider the difference between Franklin's skeptical views in 1788–90 and the climactic passage in *Notes* at Query XVII. Pleading against any establishment of religion in the new United States and the need for "free inquiry," Jefferson holds out the success of "[o]ur sister states of Pennsylvania and New York": "They have made the happy discovery, that the way to silence religious disputes, is to take no notice of them." So, he argued, "[l]et us too give this experiment fair play." But as he pressed the idea of this "happy" social condition, his mind turned to question the reliability of "the spirit of the people" or any form of "government," and from that to consider a yet more ominous thought: "Besides, the spirit of the times may alter, *will alter*" (my italics).

> Our rulers will become corrupt, our people careless. A single zealot may commence persecutor, and better men be his victims. It can never be too often repeated, that the time for fixing every essential right on a legal basis is while our rulers are honest, and ourselves united. From the conclusion of this war we shall be going down hill. It will not then be necessary to resort every moment to the people for support. They will be forgotten, therefore, and their rights disregarded. They will forget themselves, but in the sole faculty of making money, and will never think of uniting to effect a due respect for their rights. The shackles, therefore, which shall not be knocked off at the conclusion of this war, will remain on us long, will be made heavier and heavier, till our rights shall revive or expire in a convulsion. (Jefferson, *Notes*, ed. Shuffleton, 167)

That is Jefferson's secular version of Mather's Puritan emergency. For all the difference between Mather's baroque prose and Jefferson's plain style, both men's work is austere and determinate. No nonsense, none of the language games that Franklin cherished and played so well. Of course Franklin can be straightforward when practical conditions make it necessary, and Mather is not without his wry humor. Still, for Jefferson and Mather, writing is always a serious business.

As is by now widely recognized, Jefferson's *Notes* is a machine for raising questions and promoting intellectual dialogue with himself and his readers. Born from a set of questions that were put to him by someone else, it turned out to be a dramatic public display of what Matthew Arnold called the dialogue of the mind with itself and, consequently, a model and invitation for reader response. His rhetorical posture is, like Franklin's, provocative, but Franklin's rhetoric is very different, as part 2 of the *Autobiography* shows most clearly. Part 2 told a dramatic story of Franklin discovering the limits of his benevolent projections. It is in that respect a "critical" account. But the account is complete and the lesson delivered, even if it is a lesson that has to be repeatedly relearned. By contrast, Jefferson's declarative address delivered a drama of critical thinking that began and stayed to the end in medias res. If Franklin's *Autobiography* calls up Whitman's *Song of Myself*, Jefferson's *Notes* might be judged his Notes toward a Supreme Fiction.

I

Notes is not a story, but a set of reflections on a set of topics that Jefferson did not himself propose or expect, and the set has no narrative, argumentative, or conceptual order (though there are embedded narratives, arguments, and conceptual representations). That lack of supervening structure licenses the work's arresting intellectual character: every moment of the commentary opens up a fresh intellectual event, and those events then lay themselves open to further expansion, revision, and the danger of errors that might be more than mere errata.

Jefferson's declarative posture puts his readers in a privileged position. What is being averred is at every point laid open to review, dispute, and development. So do the *Notes* educate one to read all of his work in an inquiring spirit, even a topical polemic such as the Declaration of Independence. For instance, when Jefferson in the Declaration called the American nations "merciless savages" and George III a "tyrant," his words were true to the performative document that sent them forth—they are fighting words—but they are far from accurate or even adequate descriptors of either the Indians or the king. Indeed, "merciless savages" is an altogether unsatisfactory phrase for Jefferson's complex ideas about native Americans,[3] and not even the pressing occasion that called it forth justified its use there. In the *Notes* they are only sometimes "savages," and they are not "merciless."

The rationale for the *Notes* turns away from that immoderate phrase in the Declaration, inviting us to speak truth to its truth. It was the same truth-telling rationale that led Benjamin Banneker to write Jefferson his letter of August 19, 1791 calling him out on certain dreadful public policies he and his colleagues had recently codified in the Constitution. Appealing to Jefferson's moral "sensibility" and his intellectual "candor and generosity," Banneker asked Jefferson to consider that while he made himself a champion of mankind's "equal . . . and unalienable rights," he also found himself "at the Same time . . . guilty of that most criminal act ['Slavery'], which you professedly detested in others" (Jefferson, *Notes*, ed. Shuffleton, 273).

Everything about the *Notes* tells us that Banneker wasn't wrong to expect a sympathetic hearing from Jefferson. Consider, for instance, Jefferson's comparative discussion of government in Query XI ("Aborigines"). Leaving aside the broad generalization, it seems a simple factual error to refer to "so many little societies [without] any shadow of government" (Query XI, in Jefferson, *Notes*, ed. Shuffleton, 98). Indian social and governmental systems had long been recognized and studied by the invading Europeans, as Jefferson knew. But the context shows that he is thinking about the differences between indigenous and European governmental organizations.

In the first edition (Paris, 1785) Jefferson closes the opening paragraph of Query XI thus: "Very possibly there may have been antiently three different stocks, each of which, multiplying in a long course of time, had separated into so many little societies, the principles of their government being so weak as to give this liberty to all its members." When Jefferson expanded this in 1787, the "weak" government of 1785 became in 1787 a mélange of "little societies" with no "laws [nor] any shadow of government." What is happening here? Why is Jefferson revising his argument? What he wrote in 1785 would have been as ignorant as what he wrote in 1787, but it would have at least been more accurate.

Let it be said that being ignorant was always primarily an opportunity rather than a problem for Jefferson, as this revision shows and tells. Let it also be said that there is more ignorance throughout the *Notes*, more significant ignorance as we shall see, than Jefferson either acknowledges or recognizes. How to assess it is a problem that *Notes* itself raises. At this point suffice it to say that the actualities Jefferson's work was determined to engage are constantly glossing the *Notes*, forcing them to important revelations they had not anticipated.

Between 1785 and 1787 Jefferson is rethinking his positions, and it seems that the Constitutional Convention is weighing on Jefferson's mind. The change from "weak" government to "[no] shadow of government" wasn't the only 1787 revision to the original paragraph. Extending the paragraph's discussion of Indian languages by some 170 words, Jefferson speculated about "whether no law, as among the savage Americans, or too much law, as among the civilized Europeans, submits man to the greatest evil." Being strongly prejudiced toward his white reading of red America, he judges that for someone like himself "who has seen both conditions," the decision would favor Indian lawlessness. He then closes the new paragraph with a pair of arresting reflections: "It will be said, that great societies cannot exist without government. The Savages therefore break [their governments] into small ones" (Jefferson, *Notes*, ed. Shuffleton, 99).

Elegant to a high degree, the extended passage recalls nothing so much as Montaigne rewriting the *Essais*. Here the American democrat uses a (false) fact about the "the savage Americans" to make a critical reflection on "civilized European" government. No "shadow" of such an "evil" European government hangs over Jefferson's "Aborigines," but it is exactly the European shadow that concerns Jefferson. Implicit in the new commentary is the unmentioned Jeffersonian ideal of states' rights and localized government, which he sees reflected in the "many little societies" of "the savage Americans." And then out of that comparison rises the problem of the government of the Unites States, whose structure is so heavily in debt to European law and is organized on European models. All of the fraught controversies about how to constitute the laws of the emerging republic are lurking in this paragraph.

So well managed is Jefferson's prose, so studied the revision, that one can hardly doubt he intended to provoke his readers with such difficult and pressing political questions. *Notes* is an important educational document and was explicitly conceived as such. The chief index of that educational argument is shown in the famous set of additions and revisions that *Notes* accumulated from its initial composition in 1781, through its several printed forms (in English and French), to its final, open-ended condition: Jefferson's unique copy with the further notes, revisions, and additions that he planned to incorporate into a final edition.[4] That he never managed to carry out his plan—though he certainly had the time and leisure—has perhaps been the appropriate and even blessed outcome. Because *Notes* was a work committed to telling the truth, it had constantly to face the limitations and untruths that its own commitments summoned from the real world, that implacable reader whom Jefferson kept trying and failing to satisfy.

Two later passages in Query XI are notable in this connection. Commenting on how "the lands of this country" were acquired by the colonists, Jefferson remarks that "it is not so general a truth as is supposed" that the land was taken from the Indians by force: "I find in our historians and records, repeated proofs of purchase" in the "lower country," that is, in the eastern regions of Virginia. In his manuscript Jefferson glossed the passage with a note: "[I]t is true that these purchases were sometimes made with the price in one hand and the sword in the other." Later he deleted that gloss, though it certainly told an important truth, as recent editors have observed. Perhaps Jefferson rejected the note because of his next sentence, which he did not gloss: "The upper country [i.e., western Virginia] we know has been acquired altogether by purchases made in the most unexceptionable forms." But if the forms were unexceptionable documents of purchase, the sentence gives an "altogether" mystified account of how the Indians were dispossessed of their lands. Jefferson makes no reference to the regular practices of fraud and deceit involved in such transactions; more blindly, he ignores altogether that both "price" and "sword" were instruments of dispossession throughout the western lands that Virginia claimed, surveyed, and eventually even presumed the right to relinquish to the federal government—"more blindly" because Jefferson made no secret, at least among his white countrymen, that he himself supported and drove a policy of dispossession through economic coercion and the threat of force.[5]

Jefferson's words are not exactly disingenuous. He is telling the truth but, to adapt a famous remark by Emily Dickinson, telling it according to the slant of preconceptions he is aware of. But because preconceptions are a priori limiting and limited, they always set declarative records in a further range of truth telling. Sometimes we see Jefferson seeing and then pursuing further truths, as he did in his extended reflections on native government. This happens repeatedly in *Notes*, not least of all in Query VI, whose text and manuscript annotations are filled with Jefferson's fascinated speculations about the American "Aborigines." But while he could boast, with some justification, to having "seen both [European and Aboriginal] conditions," he was in many respects deeply ignorant of the latter. His comments in Query VI on the "barbarous" position of women in native societies—even more mistaken than what he wrote about native government—reflect just how little he understood native society and politics. Jefferson judged that because "force is law" in the Indian world— itself a serious mistake—"the stronger sex . . . imposes on the weaker." From that follows a remarkable generalization: "It is civilization alone which replaces women in the enjoyment of their natural equality" (Jefferson, *Notes*, ed. Shuffleton, 64).

Civilized Europe, colonial America, and the future United States, like Jefferson, entertained an interpretation of women's "natural equality" that was indeed quite different from the view the Iroquois League took on the position of women. Charles Johnston's succinct account of their duties and powers in the League is now, at any rate, common knowledge: "The government established by the clans was firmly controlled by the women, who enjoyed the right to select and even depose chiefs, and had competence in such matters as land allotment, supervision of field labour, supervision of the treasury, the ordering of features, and the settlement of disputes."[6] Jefferson's respect for knowledge was such that, even in the case of his racist views, he imagined that "further observation" and study might show that his judgments were mistaken (Query XIV, in Jefferson, *Notes*, ed. Shuffleton, 149). His science convinced him that Indian reports of the existence of the mammoth were correct because "[s]uch is the oeconomy of nature, that no instance can be produced of her having permitted any one race of her animals to become extinct" (Query VI, in Jefferson, *Notes*, ed. Shuffleton, 55). His respect for scientific inquiry was such that, had he lived even a bit longer, he would have retreated from that judgment.

The deepest problem with Jefferson's science was not the poverty of his information but the prejudices of his mind and education. Sometimes these erupt into his own fearful view, as in Query XIV, when he foresees "convulsions which will probably never end but in the extermination of the one or the other race [of whites and Blacks]" (Jefferson, *Notes*, ed. Shuffleton, 145). Or in the profoundly dismal conclusion of Query XVII, when he observes that "[f]rom the conclusion of this war [the Revolutionary War] we shall be going down hill" (Jefferson, *Notes*, ed. Shuffleton, 167), because "the spirit of the people [is not] an infallible, a permanent reliance." Like all his enlightened contemporaries and precursors, he read the history of republican government as a cautionary tale. He knew that the republican venture of the United States was a noble and brave but also a perilous undertaking. So while we are moved by such passages as the conclusion of Query XVI, perhaps even more moving are those where we watch the *Notes* being led along—overwritten, as it were—by an invisible hand. This happens quite dramatically in the most celebrated section of Query XI: the extended account of excavating the native "[b]arrows... found all over this country" (Jefferson, *Notes*, ed. Shuffleton, 104).

Jefferson's empirical speculations are on full display in a passage regularly praised as an early example of meticulous archaeological fieldwork. It is also the pivot of a well-made narrative of the trials of the research scientist seeking knowledge of human history.[7] The story opens with Jefferson's comment that "I know of no such thing existing as an Indian monument" (Jefferson, *Notes*, ed. Shuffleton, 103), meaning that the North American landscape does not have the majestic ruins that elsewhere, not least in the European world, testify to the presence of once-imposing civilizations. The barrows—"repositories of the dead" (Jefferson, *Notes*, ed. Shuffleton, 104)—are all that previous Indian generations have left behind. After surveying the received explanations of what occasioned their construction, including "a tradition said to be handed down from the Aboriginal Indians," Jefferson decides to "satisfy myself" by excavating "one... in my neighborhood."

It turns out to be a vast repository of skeletal remains—he conjectures "there might have been a thousand skeletons" (Jefferson, *Notes*, ed. Shuffleton, 106)—that seemed "lying in the utmost confusion" (Jefferson, *Notes*, ed. Shuffleton, 104). After making a deeper "perpendicular cut through the body of the barrow" (Jefferson, *Notes*, ed. Shuffleton, 105), he discovered that the bones were arranged in "strata." But the disorder of the place is his dominant impression, for the different strata appeared to have "no correspondence with" the other levels in the barrow. Jefferson is especially arrested by the prominence of children's remains, and though he doesn't say why, the detail is full of mournful affect. His examinations are very close, handling all kinds of different skeletal parts, and the plangent affect is especially strong when he observes in the simplest declarative prose: "The sculls were so tender that they generally fell to pieces on being touched" (Jefferson, *Notes*, ed. Shuffleton, 105).

Following the account of the excavation Jefferson recalls an event he witnessed when he was a boy ("about thirty years ago"; Jefferson, *Notes*, ed. Shuffleton, 106). A party of Indians "passing through the country where this barrow is, went through the woods directly to it, without any instructions of enquiry, and having staid about it some time, with expressions which were construed to be those of sorrow, they returned to the high road, which they had left about half a dozen miles to pay this visit, and pursued their journey" (Jefferson, *Notes*, ed. Shuffleton, 106). Jefferson presents the episode as a symbol of cultural dislocation, a meaning reinforced by the rest of the paragraph where he briefly mentions other mounds "in other parts of the country" that are also disappearing either through excavations like Jefferson's, simple plundering, or through being "put under [agricultural] cultivation" (Jefferson, *Notes*, ed. Shuffleton, 106–7).

Charles Thomson's annotation to the passage, which Jefferson solicited for Appendix 1 of the *Notes*, makes an illuminating response to Jefferson's narrative: "[I]t is customary when [the Indians] die at a distance from home, to bury them, and afterwards to come and take up the bones, and carry them home" (Jefferson, *Notes*, ed. Shuffleton, 215–16). He underscores what Jefferson's tale is suggesting: that the disappearing mounds populate what was once the homeland of that Indian party Jefferson watched when he was about ten years old, and that the Indians have come from far away and, though long dispossessed, preserved a perfect memory of their homeland and their people.

Jefferson here was writing a lamentable tale of the Vanishing American, but its purport was to underwrite a different tale of lamentable loss. Following the excavation tale, he reflects on the passing of various aboriginal "inhabitants" from all over the world. These passings present a great problem for Jefferson's enlightened philosophic quest for the knowledge of human origins: "It is to be lamented then, very much to be lamented, that we have suffered so many of the Indian tribes already to extinguish, without our having previously collected and deposited in the records of literature, the general rudiments at least of the languages they spoke" (Jefferson, *Notes*, ed. Shuffleton, 107). Jefferson's own living history makes such a passage difficult to read without an almost insupportable sadness.

Terrible realities burn through the awkward syntax of "we have suffered so many of the Indian tribes already to extinguish," and, especially given the excavation story, through "without our having previously collected and deposited in the records of literature." Had Jefferson thought more deeply about the dreadful logic of that particular remark, would he have revised it?

A pious reading of *Notes* would say, has often said, "yes." He was devoted to honest rational inquiry, and *Notes* makes his Enlightenment faith a regular devotional practice. That faith is perhaps nowhere more apparent than in Appendix 4, which he added to *Notes* in 1800: the extensive reconsideration of what Jefferson had set down in Query VI, "Relative to the Murder of Logan's Family," in 1774 and the famous speech attributed to Logan. As to the identity of the murderers, Jefferson lays out as much objective evidence as he can find and leaves a resolution of the question to further "inquiry." On that matter he is open to correction, and historians since have pretty much decided that Michael Cresap was not in fact responsible.

But in reconsidering Logan's speech Jefferson faced a more vexing problem. In 1797 Luther Martin publicly charged Jefferson with forging the speech because he judged that Jefferson offered it to counter the Comte de Buffon's "unfounded and degrading" view of the degenerate condition of America. The speech was a fiction invented to "prov[e] that the man of America was equal in body and mind, to the man of Europe" (Jefferson, *Notes*, ed. Shuffleton, 237). In defending the speech—more specifically, in defending his use of the speech—Jefferson appeals to its provenance as proof that it was no invention of his. Beyond that and even more remarkably, the transmission history becomes for Jefferson simply further proof of his argument against Buffon: "But wherefore the forgery; whether Logan's or mine, it would still have been American. I should indeed consult my own fame if the suggestion, that this speech is mine, were suffered to be believed. He would have a just right to be proud who could with truth claim that composition. But it is none of mine; and I yield it to whom it is due" (Jefferson, *Notes*, ed. Shuffleton, 237). For Jefferson, it is sufficient to point out that the speech is "American" and, as such, a glorious tribute "to the Man of America, both aboriginal and emigrant." But suppose he were shown the philological evidence, which we now have, that the speech is indeed a forgery.[8] That evidence shows why "[w]herefore forgery" is such a pertinent question and hence why it is even more pertinent that Jefferson could not, given his rhetorical purposes, see it. If the evidence were handed to him, how would be respond?

I don't pose that question because I imagine it has an answer, but because it can help us see the true depth of *Notes*' intellectual candor. Its

Enlightenment piety seems to me more profoundly troubled than our own enlightened views of *Notes*—positive or critical—often recognize. Though *Notes* shrinks from saying so explicitly, its presiding deity is a *jus absconditus*. That deity's fled presence haunts Jefferson's account of the barrow excavation, the Logan materials, and—in an especially striking way—his reflections on American slavery and white racism in Queries XIV and XVIII.

Jefferson did not need Benjamin Banneker to remind him that his life gave the lie to what he had proclaimed in the Declaration of Independence: the "true and invaluable doctrine... 'that all men are created equal.'" Like everything he wrote on the subject of race, *Notes* is tormented by the contradiction between his Enlightenment convictions and what Banneker's letter describes very simply as Jefferson's "narrow prejudices." That contradiction is exactly the subject of his arresting discussion in Query XIV—rambling and convoluted as it is—of American racism (Jefferson, *Notes*, ed. Shuffleton, 144–51). Launched out of Jefferson's account of the "Laws" of Virginia and his 1779 "Report" to the Virginia Assembly for revising those laws, the commentary shows that if those prejudices are narrow, their sources and character are anything but simple. Indeed, Jefferson does not conceal his perplexities: "The opinion"—*his* opinion—"that [Blacks] are inferior in the faculties of reason and imagination, must be hazarded with great diffidence" (Jefferson, *Notes*, ed. Shuffleton, 150).

But the discussion is not an inquiry into the evidence for and against that hazardous if widespread opinion. Rather, it is an effort to show that "their inferiority is not the effect merely of their condition of life." "No body wishes more than I do," Jefferson wrote politely to Banneker, to be convinced that "the appearance of want in them is owing merely to the degraded condition of their existence" (Jefferson, *Notes*, ed. Shuffleton, 274). From that wish he can imagine the possibility of "a good system" of education "for raising their condition both of their body & of mind to what it ought to be, as fast as the imbecility of their present condition... will admit." But whereas Jefferson holds out the prospect of educating "uncultivated" Indians to "a level with whites," he doubts this possibility for Blacks, whose "imbecility" seems to him a natural condition.[9]

The view is bewildered because of the racist argument that pervades Query XIV about the "improvement of... body and mind" that Blacks gain when they mix with white people: "The improvement of the blacks in body and mind, in the first instance of their mixture with the whites, has been observed by every one, *and proves that their inferiority is not the effect merely of their condition of life*" (Jefferson, *Notes*, ed. Shuffleton, 148; my italics). He offers Query XIV's lengthy comparison between slavery in the ancient world and American slavery to argue, first, that American slavery is far more humane than the Roman system; and second, that because Roman slaves "were of the race of whites" and American slaves are Black, Roman slaves' famed excellence in the arts and sciences proves that "it is not [the American slaves'] condition, then, but nature" that explains their "inferiority" (Jefferson, *Notes*, ed. Shuffleton, 148 and 149).

But "the first instance of their mixture" was not on the plantations, fearful as they often were. It was on the slave ships of the Middle Passage from Africa to America, whose conditions were so shocking and inhuman as to make the idea of the "white" civilization that ran them a contradiction in terms. The records of the Middle Passage are among the most eloquent testimonies we have of what Walter Benjamin called "documents of barbarism."

The ground of these blind and torturous speculations emerges at the climax of Query XIV's long discussion of American slavery. Taking up, at last directly, the issue of "the emancipation of these people," Jefferson's "deep rooted" fear of race mixing, announced briefly at the opening of the discussion, now closes it down.

> Will not a lover of natural history then, one who views the gradations in all the races of animals with the eye of philosophy, excuse an effort to keep those in the department of man as distinct as nature has formed them? This unfortunate difference of colour, and perhaps of faculty, is a powerful obstacle to the emancipation of these people. Many of their advocates, while they wish to vindicate the liberty of human nature, are anxious also to preserve its dignity and beauty. Some of these, embarrassed by the question "What further is to be done with them?" join themselves in opposition with those who are actuated by sordid avarice only. Among the Romans emancipation required but one effort. The slave, when made free, might mix with, without staining the blood of his master. But with us a second is necessary, unknown to history. When freed, he is to be removed beyond the reach of mixture. (Jefferson, *Notes*, ed. Shuffleton, 151)

"Without staining the blood of his master": primitive racial fear makes common cause between cultivated libertarians like Jefferson and brutal slavers "actuated by sordid avarice." The story of Monticello—of Jefferson's commitment to truculent overseers like Gabriel Lilly, of Jefferson's secretive and intimate relations with Sally Hemings—seems a nearly perfect exponent of the gothic labyrinth of fear and desire in which he and his America were lost.[10]

While Query XIV does not cite those kinds of alarming chapters and verses, it fairly blazons their affects by commencing with the disturbing thought that America's racist condition "will divide us into parties, and produce convulsions which will probably never end but in the extermination of one or the other race." That ghastly, not to say apocalyptic, vision hovers over Query XIV "(Laws") and then receives full expression in Query XVIII ("Manners").

> [C]an the liberties of a nation be thought secure when we have removed their only firm basis, a conviction in the minds of the people that these liberties are of the gift of God? That they are not to be violated but with his wrath? Indeed I tremble for my country when I reflect that God is just: that his justice cannot sleep for ever.... (Jefferson, *Notes*, ed. Shuffleton, 169)

Shrinking from that terrorized prospect, Query XVIII closes with the "hope [that] the spirit of the master is abating" and that a "total emancipation" will come "with the consent of the masters, rather than by their extirpation." Here that hope assumes a uniquely forlorn expression because Jefferson has brought the degradation of the "masters"—his own degradation—to the center of attention. Whereas Query XIV saw both races threatened with "extermination," Query XVIII moves well past its moving and muddled candor. Query XVIII casts a cold eye on a society "nursed, educated, and daily exercised" in the degrading idea of mastery. Jefferson makes a devastating witness here because he speaks from an inner standing point.

> The man must be a prodigy who can retain his manners and morals undepraved by such circumstances. And with what execration should the statesman be loaded, who permitting one half the citizens thus to trample on the rights of the other, transforms those into despots, and these into enemies, destroys the morals of the one part, and the amor patriae of the other. For if a slave can have a country in this world, it must be any other in preference to that in which he is born to live and labour.... (Jefferson, *Notes*, ed. Shuffleton, 168)

The syntax of the series of parallels begins from a clear distinction between the trampling and the trampled but ends with its erasure. In the event of his prose, Jefferson's fear has licensed his transfiguration from statesman to citizen. There are no prodigies in this vision of America, only men, though some of the best (or the worst) may be more honest—as these shocking passages show—than most of us.

While they might seem very different, the terror of Query XVIII rhymes with Query XI's mournful report on the barrow excavation. The

Indians had mounds of records, but Jefferson, much as he wanted to, could not read them well, as he knew and as his tale was meant to remind us. The effort to engage the splendors and miseries of Enlightenment is the great overarching subject of all the *Notes*. But in pursuing that project the work places itself under the more powerful microscope of the reality it has summoned to attention.

Jefferson glossed his excavation tale with a striking annotation—a note showing that the mounds and the Indians reminded Jefferson of Homer and Herodotus and the "barrows . . . antiently prevalent" raised for the prodigious heroes of archaic Greece (Jefferson, *Notes*, ed. Shuffleton, 315). So the Indians in Jefferson's tale get "deposited in the records of literature"—both the living and the dead Indians—as specimens to be examined and collected. Yet even as Jefferson is thus murdering to dissect them, *Notes* exposes the living reality of their human world and, in that event, his own. More, it argues—not by precept or logic but by the demonstrative example of its own literary action—that the contours of the human world are always much larger than we are often able to imagine, and that even the distinction between a dead and a living world can be justly judged an intolerable—an inhuman—conception. The Mystery God himself, as in Query XVIII, may be summoned by a secular deist thinker when he is abandoned by the *jus absconditus*.

We might think that these kinds of passages in the *Notes*—they are prevalent—deliver us a debunked Jefferson. But to read them that way is, I think, an insidious secular temptation to keep up the myth of Enlightenment mastery. Jefferson seems most awakened from the sleep of reason when those Indians and slaves escape his mistaken death wish.

II

Benjamin Banneker's 1791 letter to Jefferson (Jefferson, *Notes*, ed. Shuffleton, 271–74), which pivots around the celebrated second sentence of the Declaration of Independence, gives no indication that he had read the *Notes*, though the gift of his almanac suggests the possibility. But Banneker was thinking most of the Declaration, because in 1791 the prospect held out by that bold venture was moving toward constitutional settlement. When final ratification was achieved in January, the Constitution institutionalized slavery in the apportionment clause (Article I, Section 2), the slave import limitation clause (Article I, Section 9 and the related Article V), and, perhaps most egregiously, in the fugitive slave clause (Article IV, Section 2).

Appealing to Jefferson's Enlightenment mind, the letter was a call for him to act—"to Lend your aid and assistance to our relief from those many distresses and numerous calamities to which we are reduced." Banneker wanted Jefferson to make an "active diffusion of your exertions" that might eventually "eradicate that train of absurd and false ideas and opinions which so generally prevails" (Jefferson, *Notes*, ed. Shuffleton, 271–72). Unlike Franklin in his last years, however, Jefferson did not lend his aid and assistance at a moment when his voice might have made a great difference. When his friend James Madison wrote up the articles of the Bill of Rights in the fall of 1791, just after the exchange of letters between Banneker and Jefferson, the question of slavery went entirely unaddressed.

Jefferson was unimpressed by Banneker's letter, which he thought revealed, as he told Joel Barlow, "a mind of very common stature" (Jefferson, *Notes*, ed. Shuffleton, 280). One of the most arresting qualities of Jefferson's correspondence is his eagerness for exchanges of ideas with others. But his polite reply let Banneker know that there was nothing more they had to say to each other. And yet the *Notes*' troubled reflections about race and slavery in colonial history and the new United States show how deeply he appreciated the practical importance of both questions. But he wasn't prepared to discuss them with as common a person as Banneker. With Condorcet or Madison or Barlow or Adams? Yes, and most of all with himself, as he does so candidly in the *Notes*. But as Arnold would soon observe, in "the dialogue of the mind with itself" one might only conclude that everything is to be endured and nothing is to be done, which was clearly Jefferson's conclusion. His correspondence is an extensive dialogue with many of the most enlightened minds of the West.

But if *Notes* is Jefferson's dialogue with his own mind, the alternative voices—including his own alternative voices—come to expose further, to himself and to us, an awareness of his limitations. Are the Native Americans he knew "savages," as he often calls them, or do their societies reveal political forms that cast a cold eye on England and Europe, as he lets us know he thinks? As one reads the *Notes* one comes clearly to see Jefferson's unsettled mind on what are—for him and still for us—seriously pressing questions. Well before the environmental crises that now envelop us, Marshall Sahlins understood why the Stone Age economics of native America is far from a dead letter.

The failures of *Notes*—of the Declaration, the Constitution, and the Bill of Rights—are the source and end of the test of their continuing life. That is the implicit argument made by Danielle Allen in *Our Declaration: A Reading of the Declaration of Independence as a Defense of Equality*.[11] Against customary readings that describe the Declaration's topical "sections," Allen proposes "to divide [it] into [the] actions" to which it lent its aggressive "aid and assistance." So she lays out the "four concrete steps" that Jefferson had taken: "declaring reasons [for 'the separation'], presenting facts to witnesses, declaring independence, and making pledges."[12] Her Declaration is a machine "to . . . make something happen" once again,[13] that is to say, in her and our now-time.

Although very much a formal—even an academic—reading of the Declaration, of its rhetoric and its logical structure, Allen's book echoes Jefferson's polemic as a call to action. So when she parses its "philosophical argument," she is far less concerned with the emergency of 1776 than with an emergency she locates in 2014.[14] She writes to lift the document out of its original historical context.

If on Mondays, Wednesdays, and Fridays I am caught up in Allen's view, Tuesdays, Thursdays, and Saturdays force me to remember the force of the Declaration's original circumstance (leaving me Sundays to pause and reconsider). Truth to tell, although Allen says that she "treads lightly on the historical side of the tale,"[15] *Our Declaration* knows a great deal about that history. She spends as much time presenting pertinent historical materials as she does explicating the Declaration's argument. She could hardly do otherwise. Like all works of practical letters, the Declaration is impinged by the historical realities, both past and present, that it deliberately engages, including the historical reality of the relation between the past and the present which is the key subject of her book, as it was the key focus of the Declaration. Because all practical works acquire their meanings by seizing the day, they are fated to an endless struggle of conflicting intentions. They have to engage the resistant realities—those of the present and those inevitably to come—that their bookish words were so bold as to brave, including the realities of their own commitments.

In place of Jefferson's blindnesses we might think we're called to substitute our insights—for instance, that he was a racist and supported American slavery. But those aren't our enlightened discoveries. Nothing Jefferson ever did or wrote suggests that he wasn't a racist or didn't support American slavery, and both he and Madison—they were far from alone—strongly endorsed Indian nullification and advanced seriously inadequate accounts of colonial settlement. We won't profit much from Jefferson's candid prosecution of these ideas and convictions if the example he set doesn't enlighten us about our present circumstances.

Like the other works I've tried to conscribe in this book, Jefferson's *Notes* strikes me as an archaic torso of Apollo struck Rainer Maria Rilke.[16] Face to face with a reality one can never know ("Wir kannten nicht sein"), one may be so blinded by its strong light that suddenly you realize "there is no place that doesn't see you" ("denn da ist keine Stelle, / die dich nicht sieht"). What follows on that recognition are declared by the last five words of Rilke's poem: "[Y]ou must change your life" ("Du musst dein Leben ändern"). Although Jefferson often urged that thought, he framed it within the poverty of his secular enlightenment, which ought to come, as with the similar view of the enlightenment of grace, with an important instructional direction: "Ever tried. Ever failed. No matter. Try again. Fail again. Fail better."

INTERCHAPTER 2

THE END OF *KASWENTHA*: A BRIEF HISTORY

> Robbers of the world, having by their universal plunder exhausted the land, they rifle the deep. If the enemy be rich, they are rapacious; if he be poor, they lust for dominion; neither the east nor the west has been able to satisfy them. Alone among men they covet with equal eagerness poverty and riches. To robbery, slaughter, plunder, they give the lying name of empire; they make a solitude and call it peace.
>
> Speech attributed to the Caledonian chief Calcagus (TACITUS, *Agricola*)

The American Revolution. Though it would be wrapped in pieties of Enlightenment, it was a war for colonial control of North American economic resources and, not only but not least, of the land resources that Indian nations had been using and managing for centuries. The Revolution did not commence in Boston in 1773 nor with the shot heard round the world at Lexington and Concord in 1775. As John Adams would later tell Hezekiah Niles, "the real Revolution" and the War for Independence were two entirely different affairs.[1] First came a revolution of hearts and minds among the disaffected populations of certain British colonies in North America. It took more than ten years to effect the necessary *"radical change in the principles, opinions, sentiments, and affections"* before the war that succeeded, when thirteen of England's twenty colonies struck out for independence.

Historians now estimate that while approximately one-third of the colonials wanted independence, one-third wanted to stay under British rule, and one-third were ambivalent and chose neither side. When war began it brought the colonists to a civil war that—like all civil wars—would turn the war for independence into a frequently brutal affair. Among contemporary records of the internecine violence none are more striking than Crèvecoeur's various documentary reports. The most celebrated is the final letter of *Letters from an American Farmer*, "Distresses of a Frontier-Man," but other pieces he wrote in the late 1770s are even more striking evidence of the civil war in the colonies because they are not shaped by the fictional framework of the *Letters*.[2]

Adams and later commentators date the Revolution from 1764–65, when Parliament passed the Sugar Act and the Stamp Act. Because the Seven Years' War had left Britain with significant financial debt, it judged that the colonies secured by the war should contribute to reducing it. Not only did England not see the new taxes as especially burdensome, it thought they were in certain respects financially beneficial to the colonies. But when Crown and Parliament authorities in England and the colonies began implementing the new laws, they met with colonial resistance. As early as mid-1765 Patrick Henry had induced the Virginia House of Burgesses to pass the Stamp Act Resolutions, which declared such laws should not be passed without the "consent" of the chartered colonies.[3]

But if the new taxes were opposed by many, the real problems had to do with land—especially trans-Appalachian land—and with Britain's moves to exercise greater control over the colonial economies. Private land company speculation from New Hampshire to the Carolinas had begun in earnest in the late 1740s, and the Virginians were among the most involved in it. So the problems that brought revolution and then war were laid in at the Paris peace conference in February 1763, when France ceded to England all of its North American territories east of the Mississippi River and induced Spain to cede Florida as well. Seven months later George III issued his Royal Proclamation, setting aside the lands west of the Appalachian chain as the Indian Reserve and forbidding private sale or settlement. Britain then hoped to seal the proclamation by controlling colonial expansion, a goal they thought was in sight after the Treaty of Fort Stanwix (1768).

But the Proclamation Line turned out to be both belated and unenforceable. Before the Paris treaty, land companies—the Ohio Company was perhaps the most famous—had been surveying and speculating in trans-Appalachian lands for at least fifteen years. The company had no rights to the lands, nor did its agents have or seek formal approval from native possessors. The Virginia House of Burgesses and many notable Virginians—George Washington, Thomas Lee, George Mason, Peyton Randolph, and Patrick Henry among them—were all active in these ventures, and they were determined to protect their financial interests.[4] When in 1763 the Crown gained those land rights at Paris—at least by the fiat that European powers had been proclaiming for almost three hundred years—the colonists looked for the Crown to legalize what they had been doing. But Britain had other plans. It wanted to pacify the frontier and manage colonial affairs, including the long-running and often bitter intercolonial disputes, through more direct control.

What Dorothy Jones named the "License for Empire" was issued through the colonial treaty-making that opened with two British/Native events, the Treaties of Augusta (1763) and Fort Niagara (1764), and closed with an all-American event, the Treaty of Greenville (1795).[5] After Paris, Whitehall was faced with implementing the Proclamation on native grounds. Parallel negotiations were quickly opened for both the Northern and Southern Districts of the British Indian Department under the direction of their respective superintendents, Sir William Johnson and Captain John Stuart. Although all—even the Treaty of Greenville—made peace and friendship an explicit feature of the treaty-making, *kaswentha* ceremonials were not followed in the Southern District, so far as we can judge from the documents. Of the southern colonies, only Virginia—and it reluctantly—had been drawn into eighteenth-century Covenant Chain treaty-making. This began soon after Bacon's Rebellion because Virginia was so deeply involved in land disputes with the northern colonies and the Iroquois League.

The Seven Years' War had two principal theaters, one in Europe and one in North America. When the conflicts ended in 1763 with the Treaty of Paris, neither the British colonials nor the native American nations were party to the events. That England would first settle its affairs with the European powers signals the Eurocentric focus that had organized the colonial view of law and diplomacy since the discovery of America. Turning its thoughts to the North American war theater, England had two primary objectives: to centralize administrative control of her twenty colonies and to pacify the frontier, where the American nations and the colonials were in continual, violent conflict. The Proclamation of 1763 and the Line it drew were the levers that set the policy in motion.

With France's power in America broken in 1763, Great Britain began a concerted effort to establish practical conditions for continuing relations of peace and friendship with the Native American nations. The plan was ambitious because it meant to include all the nations east of the Mississippi, north to Prince Rupert's Land, and south to East and West Florida, a diverse and numerous group of fiercely independent peoples, not least of all those allied to the Iroquois League. The plan was also simple. The Proclamation Line was England's public commitment to the American nations that it was determined to set a limit to colonial land claims and incursions.

Three closely related treaties were to ground England's new vision for its American operations: the Treaty of Augusta (October–November 1763), the Treaty of Fort Niagara (July–August 1764), and the culminating Treaty of Fort Stanwix (September–November 1768), already discussed.

The first was negotiated with the nations of the Southern District, the second with the Northern District peoples, after which came a series of negotiations with various Indian nations. All of these treaty-makings were to settle the western colonial boundaries from Canada to Florida. The culminating treaty event for the Southern District came at the Treaty of Hard Labor (October 1768), and for the Northern District at Fort Stanwix immediately afterward. As it happened, the lines established for the Southern District did not precisely match those established at Fort Stanwix, and new lines had to be drawn for the Southern District two years later at the Treaty of Lochaber.[6]

The Crown began its work in the Southern District, where John Stuart oversaw the sealing of the Treaty of Augusta on November 10.[7] But treaty-making at Augusta was delayed for a month—from October 1 to November 4—partly because the Cherokees and the Creeks were seriously at odds, partly because certain tribes disapproved the treaty location, and, despite the Proclamation delivered by the Crown, not least because all the natives had apprehensions that the colonists would be acting in bad faith ("Minutes," 156–78). On October 18 the governors sent a dispatch to the Indians that reciprocated their intention to "hold fast" the Covenant Chain of friendship. The dispatch assured the Indian nations that "our Friendship will last as long as the sun shall shine or the Waters flow and to convince you that our Talk is strait and that we do not talk with double Tongues" ("Minutes," 171). Contrary to "the evil news you [the Indians] have heard," the colonists and the Crown, they wrote, had no "intent[ion] to possess your lands." The dispatch specifically noted the "King's design" to negotiate treaties that would bring about a comprehensive land settlement between the colonies and the American nations. The king was "ordering all his Governors to act in concert as one Man and in inviting all the Nations bordering on these Colonies" to join in forging the grand scheme ("Minutes," 171). The governors were well aware that the Crown would move equivalent negotiations in the Northern Indian District when the Augusta treaty was completed. This would be the Niagara Treaty, signed a year later. They were also aware that the Crown would then consolidate the treaty-making in the Treaty of Fort Stanwix.

Some seven hundred Indians convened for the treaty-making at Augusta. Significantly, no condolence ceremonies were performed, or at least none was recorded. The treaty-making began instead with a speech by Governor James Wright of Georgia declaring the goodwill of all the English parties and remarking several times on the perfidy of the French, who are now, along with the Spanish, "removed beyond the River Mississippi that the Indians and White People [i.e., the English] may hereafter live in Peace and brotherly Friendship together" ("Minutes," 181).

Two comments by Wright are especially notable. "Do we not act like Friends & Brothers," he asked rhetorically, "when we declare that all past offences shall be buried in oblivion and forgiveness." The remark indirectly calls attention to the absence of the condolence ceremony, which would be the salient native protocol for such a declaration. The record does not amplify Wright's words; more notably still, the conference has no record that any of the Indians reciprocated his assurance, which ought to have been sealed with an exchange of wampum and elaborate ceremonials.

The second remark is on its face even more arresting. As he stressed the need for brotherly peace and friendship, Wright told the assembled natives that "[i]t will be your Faults [sic] if this does not happen for we are authorized by the Great King to give you the most substantial Proofs of our good intentions and desire to live like Brothers with you" ("Minutes," 181). Proof of the Crown's intentions, if not the colonists', was apparent, first, in the very convening of the conference, and then again at its close when "the Interpreters were ordered to inform the several Nations... that the Great King had sent them presents as a Mark of his Esteem" ("Minutes," 197). The proof of the colonists' good intentions, however, hung upon whether they would faithfully execute the will of the king and the treaty's practical set of political agreements "as long as the sun shall shine or the Waters flow."

After Wright's speech, the "Minutes" record the responses of the representatives of each of the Indian nations, at which point the first day of the conference ended (November 9). All the speakers expressed goodwill and specified various practical concerns, but none exhibit a trace of the high rhetoric that is such a remarkable feature of earlier Covenant Chain records. Each of the Native American speakers sealed the truth of his promises with strings of wampum beads—twelve are recorded. Though it is inconceivable that the colonists did not make reciprocal wampum exchanges, the "Minutes" mention none.

The second day, which closed the conference, included an elaborate reply by the governors to what the Indians had proposed and requested the day before. While a few specific concerns had to be sent to the king for his approval, broad agreement was reached, and the chief of each nation rose to give his public assent. The governors then successfully moved their treaty document. The four articles reiterated professions of friendship and mutual cooperation. The treaty specified that certain "Goods" would be given to the Indians and that disputes would be fairly adjudicated. Most important for the native nations, it promised that the Indians would keep their regular hunting and fishing rights in all the lands they were ceding to English control, and that colonists settling those lands were forbidden to encroach beyond the Proclamation Line, which was specified in the final article.

The treaty had a significant coda: a letter sent to the Earl of Egremont, the Crown's Secretary of State, informing him of the event. After explaining their initial difficulties in convening the parties, the governors wrote that they were generally pleased with the results. But they pointed out that because hostile relations prevailed between the Creeks, the Choctaws, and the Cherokees, territorial peace remained uncertain. And then there was the problem with the notorious frontier "traders," who were as dangerous as or even more so along the western piedmont than those recurrently emergent bands such as Bacon's marauders a century earlier or, more recently, the Paxton Boys. Anarchic elements, the governors told Egremont, would not be "gratified with" the new arrangements ("Minutes," 205), and those dangers underscored a larger concern the colonial authorities had with their situation and resources: "[W]e beg leave to observe to your Lordship on this Head... that the general Promise of Goods which we have made by the Kings orders to the respective Indians requires such a performance as it is impossible circumstanced as we are to be answerable for we have no coercive Power over Traders" ("Minutes," 205). Might Parliament and the Crown be creating conditions such that the entire treaty system, so carefully built for almost a hundred years, would prove impossible to sustain?

The question did not seriously concern the London authorities at that point. Augusta completed, they turned to Sir William Johnson and the Northern District, where the conditions, while even more complicated and dangerous in certain respects, were helped by the authority of the Iroquois League. Negotiations for the Niagara Treaty carried over many months, from March to November 1764, before it was finally sealed in early November. The period saw a series of conferences with different Indian nations and groups, all convened under Iroquois *kaswentha* protocols with elaborate ceremonial events, exchanges of wampum, and most important of all, mutual condolence ceremonies.[8]

After Superintendent Stuart oversaw the culmination of the Augusta negotiations at the Treaty of Hard Labor, the Treaty of Fort Stanwix was to be the final step in executing British colonial plans.[9] It was not the last of the great Covenant Chain treaties—that would be the Treaty of Sandusky (1783), to be discussed shortly—but it was the last to be implemented. The treaty-making was a massive affair conducted by Superintendent Johnson and involving, on one hand, more than three thousand Indians from the Iroquois League, the nations of the trans-Appalachian Indian Reserve (so named by the Crown), and numerous "dependent" tribes;

and, on the other, the Crown authorities of New Jersey, Pennsylvania, and Virginia, "[w]ith sundry Gents: from different Colonies." It was convened to make a definitive "settlement of the Boundary Line between the Colonies and Indians, pursuant to His Majesty's orders" (*Treaty*, 111).[10] It was conducted throughout according to standard *kaswentha* protocols.

The gravity of the treaty-making was underscored in the first four days of the event (October 24–27), which were entirely given over to condolence ceremonies and speeches by the key native authorities reiterating their commitment to the one hundred years of Covenant Chain treatying. Then, on October 28, an unnamed sachem—he was an "Onondaga speaker" from the Iroquois League (*Treaty*, 129)—rose to focus the central issue. "We have been deliberating on what you said concerning a Line between the English and us," he told the colonials, "& we are sensible it would be for our mutual advantage if it were not transgressed, but dayly experience teaches us that we cannot have any great dependance on the white People, and that they will forget their agreements for the sake of our Lands" (*Treaty*, 120). Because the colonials, speaking for the Crown and the Proclamation of 1763, gave their solemn promise that these fears were without merit, he declared "that we are willing to beleive [*sic*] more favorably in this case."

Superintendent Johnson then made an extensive reply with assurances that the Line was greatly to the advantage of the nations. When the sachem answered that the Indians would deliberate on the map Johnson had introduced, the meeting adjourned. Negotiations broke off for two days, a hiatus that worried the colonists. When they resumed on October 30 the Indian spokesman—still unnamed—laid out a line of division that was far from the one proposed to them. Governor Franklin then rose and "in a long and warm speech to the Cheifs shewed them that the Line was not proposed to injure them, but that for a handsome consideration it was intended to obtain a Cession of as much Land as would give the people Room on the Frontiers" (*Treaty*, 123). But the Indians were not persuaded, and negotiations ceased for another day and a half as both parties reconsidered their positions.

As we have seen, Franklin's "long and warm speech" involved seriously consequential matters that the surviving treaty documents did not make explicit. Although the treaty-making at Fort Stanwix, on its face, involves a dialogue between the Crown and the relevant American nations—between Crown policy and Indian commitments—the southern nations, especially the Cherokees, were not party to the events. Whitehall was presuming that the Augusta and Hard Labor negotiations would be reconciled with what was taking place at Niagara and Fort Stanwix, but that assumption (or hope) proved seriously mistaken. Even more damaging, however, was that the Franklin party's special interests were secretly driving the Fort Stanwix negotiations, which affected their Vandalia plans, to the west of Virginia.

On November 1 the parties again came together, and the speaker for the nations, still unnamed, gave a long and diplomatic speech in which he laid out the "final resolution" (*Treaty*, 127) the nations had made about the mapped territories. In prefacing his description of "the Line we have marked upon your Map," he declared that the alternate line the Indians had drawn was to "be considered as final." He then added that "as we have made so large a cession" of land, certain conditions were essential.

> We do now on this on behalf and in the name of all our Warriors of every Nation, condition that all our Warriors shall have the liberty of hunting throughout the Country as they have no other means of subsistance and as your people have not the same occasions or inclinations—That the White people be restricted from hunting on our side of the Line to prevent contensions between us.

He then sealed the nations' proposals with "A Belt" of wampum and went on to reiterate their long-standing Covenant Chain commitments. The day closed with Sir William's assurance that he would respond to the Indians' demands the next day. Note here the American speaker's insistence that the land cession does not involve relinquishing land use in the customary native subsistence economy. Despite the massive increase of land cessions that had been taking place since the late seventeenth century, the Indian view of "land sale" remained radically different from that of whites.[11]

Johnson reconvened the parties and declared that the colonial authorities accepted the Indian proposals. At that point the final treaty-making ceremonials began. They ran for three days and included a further condolence ceremony performed "by the Onondaga speaker" (*Treaty*, 129). They closed with a series of carefully delivered formal speeches by all the principal negotiating parties.

An especially important feature of this treaty comes to attention when we set it beside the treaty of Augusta. The event at Fort Stanwix suggests that Covenant Chain treaty-making was alive and well and that its performative model might have benefited the Augusta proceedings. But the practical truth is that southern treaty-making had never completely adopted the Covenant Chain, least of all its *kaswentha* protocols. Differing land claims had made the Cherokee and the Iroquois League implacable enemies. The fact that the Iroquois League played such a prominent part in this treaty helps to explain why the most powerful southern tribes repudiated it. But

Superintendent Johnson had a long and close relationship with the League, and both parties exploited that relation to drive it home.

The 1763 Treaty of Paris had set England on a North American path that the colonies—at least thirteen of the colonies—found increasingly troubling. But from the English point of view, the Fort Stanwix treaty was so successful that it licensed the Crown's next decisive move, the Quebec Act (1774). For those thirteen colonies, this would be the most intolerable of all the Intolerable Acts. It gave freedom of religious worship to Catholics, it allowed French law to operate in private affairs, and—worst of all—it vastly extended the territory of the province of Quebec to include what the French called the *pays d'en haut*—the Indian Reserve of the Ohio Country, where extralegal squatting and land speculation had been carried on since the 1740s, as the American nations all complained about in the treaty-making of those years.

War broke out two years after the Quebec Act, and with the war came the collapse of the long-established system of peace-and-friendship treaty-making. The civil war among the colonists was matched by a similar fracture of the Iroquois League. The Oneida and most of the Tuscaroras broke with the League (and the Treaty of Fort Stanwix) and sided with the patriot colonials, who now began to press for their own treaties with the Indians. The most important—not to say notorious—of these was the first formal treaty made between the United States and an Indian nation. This was the Treaty of Fort Pitt (September 1778), negotiated with White Eyes and the Ohio Delawares, who had been a dependent tributary of the League since the end of the seventeenth century.[12] It was a mutual defense treaty with some stipulations for gifts, trade arrangements, and Delaware help for the American states in their war with England.

The surviving documentation for the Fort Pitt treaty records six brief articles and no condolence or other ceremonial exchanges. In their place is the schematic statement of Article I: "That all offences or acts of hostilities by one, or either of the contracting parties against the other, be mutually forgiven, and buried in the depth of oblivion, never more to be had in remembrance." But the offenses and hostilities that set the context for the treaty—indeed, for all North American treaty-making, but especially at this violent moment—required more than weak pen-and-ink magic if the partnership hoped to endure, in the standard native formula, "so long as the sun and moon shall last."

The Delawares entered the treaty hoping it would restore their former autonomy. That goal was recorded in the promise held out in the treaty's final article: "And it is further agreed on between the contracting parties should it for the future be found conducive for the mutual interest of both parties to invite any other tribes who have been friends to the interest of the United States, to join the present confederation, and to form a state whereof the Delaware nation shall be the head, and have a representation in Congress" (*Treaty*, 5). The Delaware ought perhaps to have paused at the words "found conducive for the mutual interest of both parties," and even more at the caveat that immediately followed: "Provided, nothing contained in this article to be considered as conclusive until it meets with the approbation of Congress." The Delaware would soon judge that the patriot states had treated in bad faith, having no intention to give republican representation to the "merciless indian savages" Jefferson named in the Declaration of Independence. Within a year the Delaware were once again allied with the British and the League.

The failed treaty was part of the emerging states' broad effort—constantly resisted by the British—to bring the nations in the Crown's Indian Reserve to their side. It called forward to another failed treaty, in this case one made by the British that was seriously meant to be honored: the Treaty of Sandusky (concluded in early September 1783) between the Crown and a large company of Indian nations.[13] The treaty-making was negotiated through the Governor General of the loyalist province of Quebec, Sir Frederick Haldimand, and through the great Mohawk chief Joseph Brant and the Iroquois League. Initially conceived in the first years of England's war with the rebelling colonies, it was seen as the climax of the Crown's 1763 Proclamation as it had been advanced by the 1768 Treaty of Fort Stanwix and the Quebec Act of 1774.

In the immediate run-up to the Sandusky treaty, which stretched from early May to late August, the British had to deal with one of the chief agents of the rebelling colonies' Indian policy, Ephraim Douglas, whom the British regarded as thoroughly treacherous.[14] Writing in early July to two colleagues involved in the Sandusky negotiations, General Allan Maclean enclosed and annotated a letter he had received from Douglas.

> I . . . am glad you have sent to bring him in to Detroit, for we really cannot be too much on our guard against these designing knaves, for I do not believe the world ever produced a more deceitful or dangerous set of men than the Americans: and now they are become such Arch-Politicians by eight years practice, that were old Matchioavell [Machiavelli] alive, he might go to school to the Americans to learn Politics more crooked than his own; we therefore cannot be too cautious. (Haldimand Papers, *Historical Collections*, 20:139)

The Quebec authorities, including Maclean, had received news early in 1783 that a "preliminary" peace agreement between the Crown and the United States had been reached in Paris in late 1782. Maclean's letter records his vexation not so much with the news but with how to handle the "deceitful" American States as a peace agreement was being negotiated. Haldimand shared Maclean's view, as correspondence at the time shows (Haldimand Papers, *Historical Collections*, 20:168).

Two matters are relevant for understanding why these British authorities in Quebec in 1783 kept pursuing a treaty designed to secure the Proclamation Line. First of all, while the British forces had been defeated in the territories of the thirteen rebel colonies, they had won the war in the loyal territories. Indeed, after the failed 1775–76 campaign against the loyal Canadian colonies, the American states effectively ceded the northern theater to British control. From 1777 forward the Crown plan to secure the Indian Reserve in the northern areas of trans-Appalachia remained a live commitment.

Second, Haldimand had been working assiduously since the early years of the war to lay the groundwork for the Sandusky Treaty with the Indians of the *pays d'en haut*. The extended 1783 Sandusky treaty-making was the finale of four years of treaty work between Haldimand and a wide array of Indian nations: besides the League nations and their dependents, these included "the Hurons, Delawares, Shawanese, Mingoes, Ottawas, Chippeweys. Poutteawatamies, Creeks & Cherokees," as well as the Wyandots, led by Sindatton.[15] Sandusky was to complete a series of at least twenty-five conferences and preliminary treaties that were being negotiated between June 1778 and June 1782 (Haldimand Papers, *Historical Collections*, 20:133–35).

Ironically, the actual treaty took place on September 2–8—that is to say, exactly as the Paris treaty was being concluded (September 3), which of course could not have been known in the Ohio country. It followed the classic form of Covenant Chain treaty-making, complete with condolence ceremony, a dialogue of speeches by the representative parties, elaborate wampum exchanges, and reciprocal declarations of peace and friendship. Perhaps most significant, it did not include any written set of treaty articles, a formality that the Indians always regarded with suspicion but that the British and Anglo-Americans, thinking in European legal terms, favored and normally succeeded in pressing.

From the Indian point of view, the absence of such articles would have been a strong sign that the Canadians were acting not only in good faith but on Indian terms—an assurance of the greatest importance under the circumstances. The oral and performative character of the native treaty-making carried the crucial expectation that permanent "friendship" would be continually renewed in face-to-face intercourse. In that context, what did the events at Paris portend for the Sandusky treaty? "Forging a treaty" with the native people, we want to recall, "did not constitute . . . a temporary alliance . . . producing a static document but rather [involved] a set of discussions creating a dynamic and organic kinship between treaty partners. . . . Maintaining the relationship was the central goal."[16]

Alex McKee, the British Deputy for Indian Affairs, made it clear in his opening speech that this was the British goal. Since learning of the "preliminary" treaty in Paris, Haldimand and his people had persuaded their Indian allies to cease all hostile acts against the rebels and their Indian allies. McKee's speech assured the nations that, whatever took place in Paris, the British were committed to the promises made in 1763 and then confirmed, as they believed, at Fort Stanwix in 1768.

> you are not to believe, or even think that by the Line which has been described, it was meant to deprive you of an extent of country, of which the right of Soil belongs to, and is in yourselves as Sole Proprietors, as far as the boundary Line agreed upon and Established in the most Solemn and public manner in the presence and with the consent of the Governors and Commissioners deputed by the different Colonies for that purpose: by your late worthy Friend Sir Wm. Johnson in the year 1768, at Fort Stanwix. (Haldimand Papers, *Historical Collections*, 20:177)

Joseph Brant then rose to affirm the nations' reciprocal commitment to the British, stating, "Altho' the force of the Americans appeared to be more powerful than that of the King, yet it did not deter us" from "[adhering] to our former engagements of Fidelity to the King of Great Britain." He concluded his speech "with a Large Belt" of wampum and his declaration that "let there be Peace or War, it shall never disunite us" (Haldimand Papers, *Historical Collections*, 20:179). After "Speeches by several of the non-League nations" affirmed their fidelity, the Delaware chief Dyonquat raised a serious concern. Although satisfied that "the Boundary Line was fixed," he informed the company "that the Virginians are already encroaching upon our Lands," and unless they are stopped their acts "will destroy the good work of Peace which we are endeavouring to promote" (Haldimand Papers, *Historical Collections*, 20:181).

Although Brant and McKee responded that they intended "to deal with" the encroachments (Haldimand Papers, *Historical Collections*, 20:182–83), Dyonquat had exposed the grave flaw in the entire proceedings. McKee's initial speech had assured the company that they should not "harbour an idea that the United States will act so unjustly or impolitically as to endeavour to deprive you of any part of your country under the pretext of having conquered it" (Haldimand Papers, *Historical Collections*, 20:177). But Haldimand and the Canadians had no doubt that the American states, victorious in the war, would deal harshly with the Loyalists and their native allies and press on with their aggressive land policies, as in fact they did.

So certain was Haldimand of his commitment, and so determined was he to fulfill his part in the Crown promise announced in 1763, that he spent the next year working to secure living arrangements in the Canadian provinces for the Indians and the Crown's loyalist soldiers. The most remarkable of these efforts came in October 1784, when, consciously echoing George III's Proclamation of 1763, he issued the Haldimand Proclamation, which made a land gift to the Iroquois League of 955,000 acres along the Grand River in what is now southwestern Ontario.[17] It was Haldimand's personal effort to uphold his and the Crown's honor as Euro-American law and diplomacy began its final turn away from what might be judged its most exceptional American opportunity.

The United States completed that turn after the Western Confederacy of Indian nations lost its struggle to maintain control of its lands in what the British had declared in 1763 as the Indian Reserve. Following the decisive Battle of Fallen Timbers (August 1794), the Treaty of Greenville was concluded between the United States Army—the agent and indeed the exponent of United States authority—and the representatives of fourteen American nations.[18] The treaty set the model—declarative and imposed—for all subsequent treaties made by the United States with Native Americans.

But it was a pale and, for both parties, a poisoned reflection of *kaswentha* treaty-making: that is, Maussian prestation driving "the suppression of Warre neither through the victory of one nor by the submission of all, but in a *mutual surrender*" executed through condolence ceremonies and gift exchanges. Because at Greenville only one party was delivered to mourning and only one—the other party—privileged to gifting, the result was not win/win but lose/lose. "The haunting of America" was decisively deepened when the white loss was entered in its win column as a capital gain. The word "Brothers," once a standard treaty formula, never appears in the treaty, and Article VII, which gifted to the Indians their usufruct *habitus*, made the true situation explicit: "the liberty to hunt within the territory and lands . . . now ceded to the United States . . . without hindrance or molestation." Worse yet, it was a gift that foreclosed a gifting return. Indeed, it was not a gift at all but a privilege granted, and as such it came with the next sentence's notable caveat: "so long as they demean themselves peaceably, and offer no injury to the people of the United States" (*Treaty*, 58). One recalls another missing *kaswentha* formula: "so long as the mountains & Rivers & the sun & moon shall endure."[19] One also recalls—this time by future perfect memory—how mistaken was the promise of Article I: that "peace is hereby established, and shall be perpetual; and a friendly intercourse shall take place between the said United States and Indian tribes" (*Treaty*, 54). *Ubi solitudinem faciunt, pacem appellant.*

PART III
Truth and Method

CHAPTER TEN

The *Arbella* Sermon: A Case Study

The hardest thing of all is to see what is really there.
J. A. BAKER, *The Peregrine*

As we approach the two-hundred-year anniversary of the discovery of this famous document, it is time to face up to its legend. This is important because the work occupies such a fundamental place in American memory. Perhaps even more urgent is what we have to learn, or relearn, about the relation between cultural truth and the ways we seek for it, and about the responsibility that scholars have to the community at large to preserve a clear view of and commitment to both.

"A Modell of Christian Charity" gave a local habitation—the Bay Colony settlement of New England—and a name—John Winthrop—to one of the foundational statements of the American ethos. Its argument climaxes in a bravura expression that remains resonant to this day: "Wee shall be as a Citty upon a Hill, the eies of all people are uppon us."[1] The Virginia and Plymouth plantations were founded well before Winthrop brought his fleet of ships and some one thousand settlers to what would become the Massachusetts Bay colony, and both the earlier colonies produced founding documents of great importance. But since George Folsom and James Savage introduced it to the public in 1838,[2] no early colonial text has been more influential than this work (see fig. 8), which, by its own account, was "Written / On Boarde ye Arrabella! / On ye Atlantick Ocean! By the Honr^ble John Winthrop. Esqr. / In His passage. (wth ye great / Company of Religious people of wch Xtian Tribes / he was ye Brave Leader & famous Govr!) from y^e Island of Great Brittaine, / to New-England in y^e North America. / Anno 1630."

That headnote describes the objective status of the document, naming its author, its date, its occasion, and its genre. In addition, it offers an

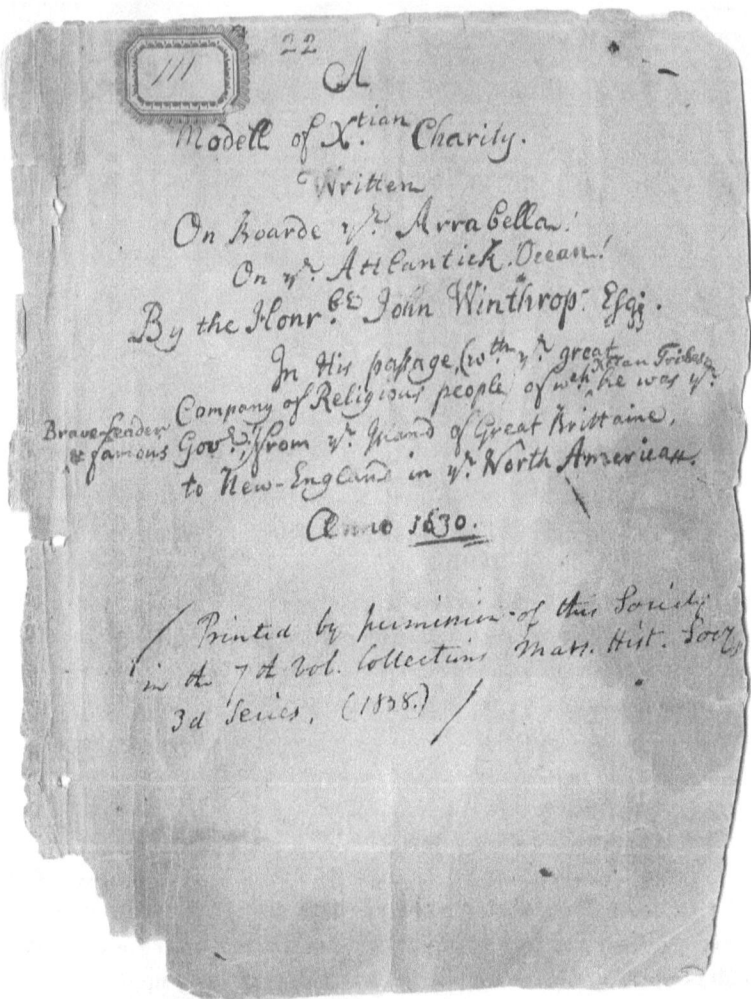

FIGURE 8. John Winthrop (attrib., 1630), "A modell of [Chris]tian charity" (late seventeenth century?). MS 2854, cover page. Photograph: Collection of the New-York Historical Society.

implicit interpretation that the event being recorded was a glorious one. Two of the interlinear insertions—"Xtian Tribes" and "Brave Leader & famous"—underscore the headnote's interpretive view. That view is reemphasized, surely if also sparely, by its exclamation points, which to date have gone unnoticed in any editorial or critical commentary, and which are publicly recorded only in the New-York Historical Society's online facsimile. But as we shall see, the entire headnote has still not been examined with the care it requires. The number "22" at the top, as we shall see, is important.³

Since 1838 that textual account and the facts it alleges have passed as settled truth. Largely until the early 1990s no one thought to reflect on the problematic character of its documentary status. And so a rich set of critical commentary arose—and persists still—that gets reified through numerous school and scholarly editions. Yet none of this scholarship accurately reflects the truth of the document, which is at once very simple and very difficult. Crucially, that truth is a function not only of what we know or think we know about the document, but of what we know (or don't know) that we don't know about it.⁴

Those inconvenient truths began to be seriously addressed only in 1991 when Hugh J. Dawson pointed out that the headnote was not written by the scrivener who copied the body of the text.⁵ Before Dawson, scholars believed that the entire document was "apparently contemporary" with the founding years of Massachusetts Bay.⁶ Inquiring more closely, Dawson called on the expertise of paleographers familiar with the production of early colonial texts. The watermarks and other textual evidence place the body of the scrivener's text in the seventeenth century, probably but not certainly early. As for the headnote, it clearly postdates the scrivener's text and the lifetime of John Winthrop. Because it casts such a retrospective glory around the enterprise of 1630, it reads like a third-generation Puritan text and might well be even later. Its antiquated orthography was conventional well into the eighteenth century.⁷ One correction in the body of the text is definitely late—the change from the original word "Massachusetts" to "New England" on page 39 of the manuscript.⁸ The correction may reflect the 1686 Crown move to undo the Massachusetts Bay Colony by incorporating it in the newly created "Dominion of New England."

Dawson's inquiry produced a further significant revelation about the document. He showed that if Winthrop delivered a "Christian Charity" sermon, the "famous Governor" must have done it, as the manuscript text declares, "heere in England."⁹ Unfortunately, that crucial phrase in the manuscript did not make it into the (first) 1838 Massachusetts Historical Society printing.¹⁰ Although, as Dawson pointed out, the mistake was corrected in some later reprintings, the error is to this day disseminated in most of the widely available reprintings.¹¹ Noting it, Dawson argued that the sermon must have been written before the *Arbella* and the rest of the fleet sailed.

The plain textual evidence ("heere in England") is corroborated by all of the pertinent contextual evidence. As Dawson wrote, the Winthrop *Journal*'s meticulous account of the emigration "makes no mention of the discourse."[12] Nor do Winthrop's other autograph papers and associated documents from the time, which are extensive. The surviving manuscript copy was kept among Winthrop's papers. We know that Winthrop had a copy, perhaps the autograph, from the founding years of the colony: in 1642 or soon thereafter, Henry Jacie (1603–1663) asked the governor's son John to send it to him. In any case, delivering a lay sermon would have been unusual for the governor. We know for certain that during his lifetime he delivered one lay sermon: at Ipswich in 1634, an event he mentions in his *Journal*. Non-separating Congregationalists, which is what Winthrop was, delivered lay sermons only under special conditions—typically if a minister were unavailable, which was not the case on the *Arbella* but which was the case at Ipswich.[13]

Neither is such a sermon noticed by any of the other emigrants, whether they sailed on the *Arbella* or on one of the other ships. Was it perhaps delivered before the fleet sailed? The distinguished Winthrop scholar Francis Bremer believes it was, but no such event is mentioned by anyone who participated in the momentous undertaking.[14] By sharp contrast, John Cotton's farewell sermon *Gods Promise to His Plantation* (1630), delivered at Southampton, was printed, commented on, and broadcast widely.

As Dawson remarks, the secretary copy might indicate that it was intended for manuscript circulation rather than print. But no manuscript copies are extant, and the work seems to have been mentioned only twice in the seventeenth century, once by Jacie and then later by Roger Williams, though Dawson regarded the Williams reference as dubious.[15] From then until 1809, when the manuscript was donated to the New-York Historical Society, the work was invisible, and of course it did not come to public notice until 1838. What is most remarkable here is that Winthrop's papers were available to and used by two of the most consequential seventeenth-century Puritan historians, William Hubbard and Cotton Mather. If either they or, later, Ezra Stiles, who also worked with the Winthrop Papers, were aware of the manuscript, they would certainly have used it.[16] It could have escaped their notice because of the secretarial hand, but not if it had that arresting headnote.

Dawson's examination of the manuscript showed that a third hand, "perhaps [...] a scrivener's assistant,"[17] went back over the transcript to correct various errors. Twenty-two years later Abram Van Engen, keying off Dawson's work, made two further important discoveries about the secretarial document.[18] First, he showed that the reference text for its biblical citations was the Geneva Bible, not—as might be expected—the English King James Version.[19] Second, while the document shows various interesting lacunae and errors, it "has suffered a much more significant corruption: it has lost its beginning."[20] Van Engen argues that because "A Modell of Christian Charity" "does not match the usual form of a Puritan sermon,"[21] we should see it as a truncated sermon. That reasonable suggestion seems to mean, however, that the manuscript we have is a copy made from another now lost and similarly imperfect copy.[22]

So then the question arises: why (and when) would someone want such a fragment copied, and who would that be? Van Engen does not question Winthrop's authorship—indeed, he asserts it—but he doesn't try to explain what it might have been that Winthrop thought he was writing, if in fact he was the author of the copy from which our extant manuscript was made. These questions become even more provoking when we remember a crucial further fact that Van Engen brought to attention but then left undiscussed: that when Winthrop quoted scripture, his reference point was not the Geneva Bible but, as we would expect, the King James Version.[23] If Winthrop wrote the discourse on Christian charity, why was he quoting from the Geneva Bible?

Before considering these key questions further, let me close this part of the inquiry by clearing up some related factual matters that have a significant bearing on the disappearance of "Christian Charity" from public notice. The only certain reference to the work that we have before 1838 comes in an early letter from Henry Jacie to John Winthrop Jr.[24] Jacie was a dissenting minister who became leader of the semi-separatist Jacobites in 1837. He was close with the Winthrops and, staying in England after the 1630 emigration, worked on their behalf and kept them abreast of the ongoing religious and political struggles in England and Europe. Here is the pertinent section of his letter:

> Now Sir since your going to york, I have found H. Kingsburies letter (which I could not light on) the bookes he desired me to procure him were these 3. 1 A Treatise of Faith. (I suppose The Doctrine of Faith by Mr. Jo. Rogers would be as useful for him, and about the same price.) 2 Perkins Principles. 3. The sweet Posie for Gods Saints (2d a peece, the 1 about 18d.) He writ he would pay for them. We shal be further indebted to you if you can procure the Map, the Pattents Copie, the Model of Charity, (also what Oath is taken) Mr. Higgisons letter, and the Petition to our Ministers for praying for them, made at their going, which is in print. Which of these you can best, with your letter, give to Mr. Overton Stationer in Popes head Alley, my good friend, and receive money of him for them. (*The Winthrop Papers*, 3:188–89)

In printing Jacie's letter, the Winthrop Papers do not annotate its references. Had they done so, the date they assign to the letter, ca. 1634–35, would have been pushed forward.[25] It cannot be earlier than 1642, when *A sweet Posie for God's Saints* was published.

The significance of the change is difficult at this point to assess with certainty, but it is not at all difficult to recognize. By 1642 the Long Parliament had been convened, Bishop Laud impeached and imprisoned, Strafford tried and beheaded, and the King and Parliament were in open conflict. Second, the reference to "Mr. Overton Stationer in Popes head Alley" and the request to give those key emigration documents to Overton suggests an intention to get them printed (or in the case of the last, reprinted). Overton was either the fiery Puritan pamphleteer Richard Overton (fl. 1640–1664) or, more likely, his son John (d. 1713), who had recently set up a stationer's shop that went on to specialize in maps and operated well into the eighteenth century.[26] But in the 1640s it was publishing semi-separatist works.

The most provocative fact revealed through Jacie's letter, however, is the connection between *A sweet Posie* and the Overtons and what it suggests about Jacie's request for the emigration documents. The title page of *A sweet Posie* identifies its author simply as J. O. and then gives this imprint information: "printed by R. Cotes, for Benjamin Allen dwelling in Popes-head-Alley, 1642." Is the author of the book John Overton? Do the Overtons have anything to do with Cotes and Allen, who are operating in the closest proximity—a tiny street, still extant, just south of the Royal Exchange? And is Jacie asking for those colony documents because he has some plan in mind to have them printed? Was the plan aborted because of the tumultuous events unfolding in England?

As Jacie's letter indicates, one of those documents—*The Humble Request of His Majesties Loyall Subjects* (1630)—was prepared at Southampton just before the fleet sailed to the New World. It was left behind and printed in London shortly thereafter. The intention of *The Humble Request* was to make an open declaration that the emigrants were not separatists but loyal subjects who recognized Crown authority. In 1630 such a semi-separatist position was for many of the emigrants problematic—Plymouth was already a separatist colony—but by 1642 the dissenters still in England were openly seeking far greater control at the very center of English power. Printing "Christian Charity" and reprinting *The Humble Request* in 1642 or later would have been vigorously opposed by many, perhaps even most, Puritans in both New and Old England. And by 1660, when the documents might have been made public, their political significance for second-generation Puritans was long past. By 1838, however, the communitarian message of "Christian Charity" would have had real importance in Congregationalism's ideological struggles with Unitarianism and, even more, its Emersonian overflow.

I

Let's be candid here. What I've just proposed is a rationale for explaining why "Christian Charity" remained virtually unknown between 1630 and 1838. It's an interpretation extruded from certain facts, some of them not previously recognized. This rationale does not solve the problems raised by the "Christian Charity" manuscript, but it can help us see more clearly the shape and conditions of our ignorance. So it is a provocation to strive for greater understanding. As such, I also think it puts us in a position to appreciate and go further with the provocation that Dawson initiated in 1991 and expanded in his 1998 essay.

The later essay proceeds from a recognition of the importance of a particular passage in "Christian Charity": the reference to "the *Church of England*, from whence wee rise, our deare Mother." That is a notable remark for a dissenting work, and it is a view with which some—perhaps most, certainly many—in Winthrop's company would have had serious difficulties. It is not a view that Winthrop himself expressed before he set the embarkation plans going, as Dawson argued in 1998. But for Dawson, "Christian Charity" reflects how the colonial undertaking itself changed Winthrop's mind.[27] The work is directed at two audiences, he argues, the emigrants as well as those "who had committed themselves to Massachusetts but who were staying on in England."[28] Looking "to England as much as to America," "Christian Charity" enlarges its argument by making a "conservative reaffirmation of established ways. Rather than being an environment hospitable to the release of new initiatives, the 'Citty vpon a Hill' would be an extension of the metropolis."[29] "Christian Charity" was not calling into question the "legitimacy" of the established church.

In laying out that view of the matter, Dawson rightly points to John Cotton (1585–1652) and John White (1575–1648), and especially to the semi-separatist Henry Jacob (1563–1624), who in 1616 had founded in Southwark what is regarded as the first Congregational Church in England. These "Jacobites," as they were called, organized around a group of ordained Anglicans who had fallen out with the established church because of its corruptions. They were firmly Calvinist in theology and hence worked out of the Geneva Bible, but they were unusual—"semi-separatist"—in holding that the established church was legitimate despite its grievous lapses from sanctity. Jacob and his sect are relevant here because after his death, direction of the group was assumed by John Lathropp (1584/88–1653), and after Lathropp was imprisoned by Bishop William Laud and eventually expelled from England, leadership of the group passed in 1637 to another important semi-separatist, Henry Jacie.[30]

A basic pair of very specific questions needs to be pressed for this famous work: who wrote the headnote, and who commissioned the scrivener copy? We still do not have answers to those questions. Their critical pertinence for understanding "A Modell of Christian Charity" is scarcely appreciated even today, and until Dawson's and Van Engen's work, they were hardly raised. Dawson in particular comes close to asking them directly. But he stops short even in 1998, when his doubts about the document's authorship had intensified.[31]

Let's look again at the work's documentary problems, starting with the contradiction between what is asserted by the headnote's "Written / On Boarde the Arrabella! / On the Attlantick ! Ocean!" and what is declared by the scrivener's "heere in England." Dawson reads "heere in England" as evidence about an historical event that happened in 1630. Assuming, reasonably, that the scrivener's text is telling the truth about itself ("heere in England"), Dawson argues that the headnote is mistaken, that the sermon wasn't "Written ... On Boarde the Arrabella ... On the Attlantick ... Ocean." But the textual situation here reveals something far more disturbing about the headnote. Assuming, again reasonably, that the headnote isn't simply lying, we have to wonder how it arrived at that judgment, and, more pertinently, *who* made the judgment. The headnote presents itself as a factual account of the scrivener's text, but it happens that its facts are wrong. When we realize that truth, that fact, about the headnote, we want to know what it means. It would help if we knew who penned the headnote or even when.

So before worrying about if, when, or where a sermon was delivered in 1630, and by whom, we have to know much more than we now know about the New-York Historical Society manuscript. The problematic headnote is a good place to start. Its author's interpretive designs, as we've seen, are clearly marked by the exclamation points and the interlinear insertions "Xtian Tribes" and "Brave Leader & famous." But let's look further.

We begin by trying for a clearer picture of the provenance of the manuscript, which was donated to the New-York Historical Society in 1809 by Francis Bayard Winthrop (1740–1817) along with a collection of early colonial printed documents (see fig. 9). "A Modell" was the only manuscript in the donation and was listed last—numbered "22"—in the donation list:[32]

Note the title given here to the document: "A Modell of Christian Charity written on Board the Ship Arrabella by John Winthrop ...." The congruences with the manuscript headnote—the first ten words, the spelling "Arrabella," and the final ellipsis—show that Winthrop's donation list echoes the manuscript text. But equally remarkable are the divergences between the two: the extra word "Ship" and the absence of the headnote line "On the Attlantick! Ocean!"

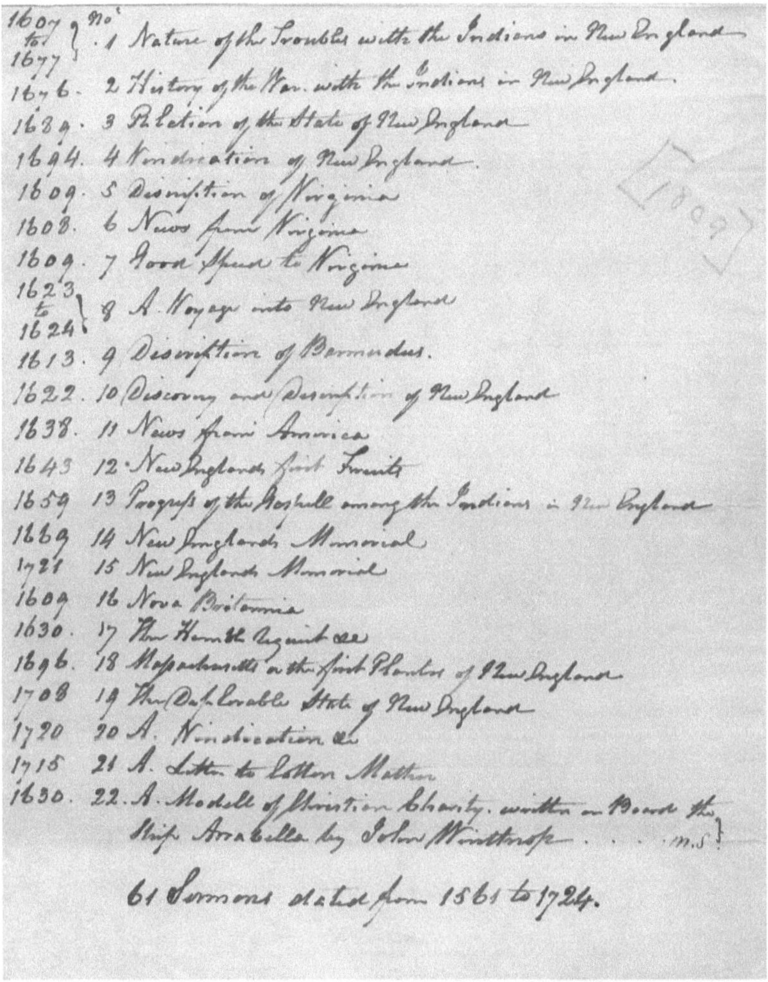

1607 to 1677 } No. 1 Nature of the Troubles with the Indians in New England
1676. 2 History of the War with the Indians in New England.
1689. 3 Relation of the State of New England
1694. 4 Vindication of New England.
1609. 5 Description of Virginia
1608. 6 News from Virginia
1609. 7 Good Speed to Virginia
1623 to 1624 } 8 A Voyage into New England
1613. 9 Description of Bermudas.
1622. 10 Discovery and Description of New England
1638. 11 News from America
1643 12 New Englands first Fruits
1659 13 Progress of the Gospell among the Indians in New England
1689 14 New Englands Memorial
1721 15 New Englands Memorial
1609 16 Nova Britannia
1630. 17 The Humble Request &c
1696. 18 Massachusetts or the first Planters of New England
1708 19 The Deplorable State of New England
1720 20 A Vindication &c
1715 21 A Letter to Cotton Mather
1630. 22. A Modell of Christian Charity. written on Board the Ship Arrabella by John Winthrop . . . . M.S.}

61 Sermons dated from 1561 to 1724.

[1809]

FIGURE 9. Francis Bayard Winthrop's "Donation List" (1809). New-York Historical Society General Correspondence (NYHS-RG 2). Photograph: Collection of the New-York Historical Society.

Because the final ellipsis shows that Winthrop wanted to indicate missing text at the end, one wonders why he didn't give a medial ellipsis for the dropped line. The answer seems to be that the line wasn't there when he copied the title into the donation list. Indeed, if one examines the manuscript headnote closely, one can see what its design and orthography disclose. First of all, the headnote was consciously scripted to imitate the typical layout of title pages of colonial pamphlets and sermons—sermons such as, for instance, John Cotton's 1630 farewell *Gods Promise to His Plantations* (see fig. 10).

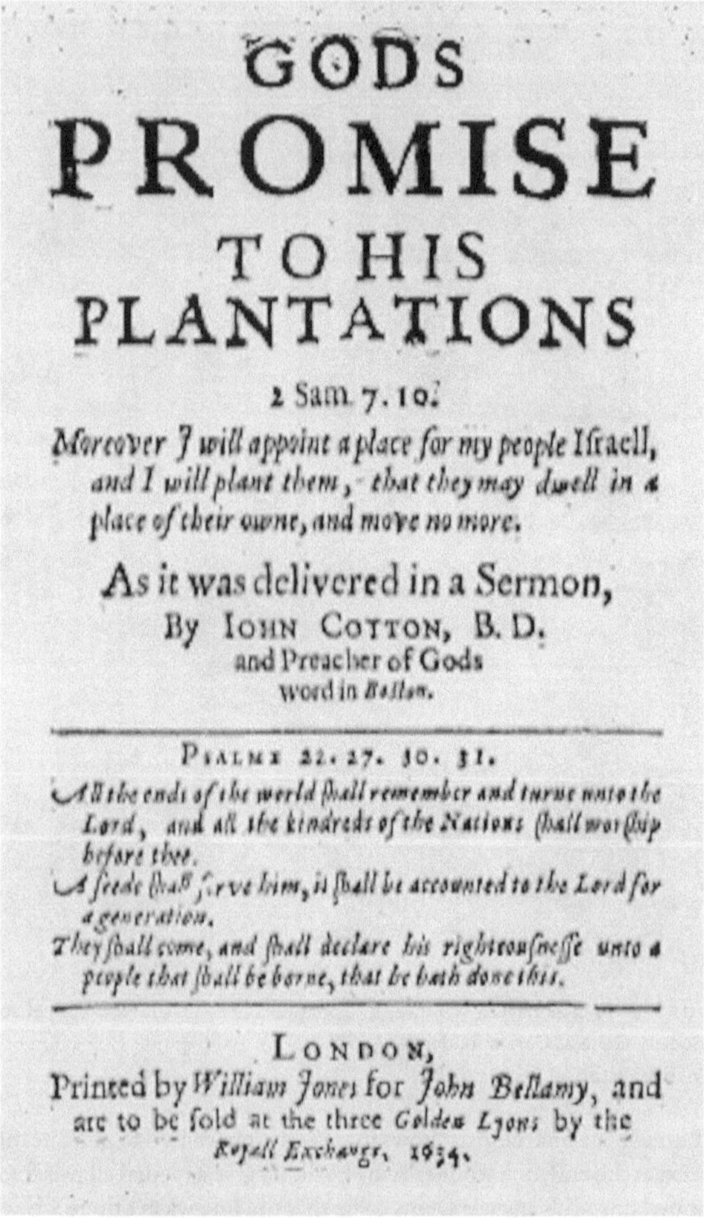

GODS PROMISE TO HIS PLANTATIONS

2 Sam. 7. 10.

Moreover I will appoint a place for my people Israell, and I will plant them, that they may dwell in a place of their owne, and move no more.

As it was delivered in a Sermon,
By IOHN COTTON, B. D.
and Preacher of Gods
word in *Boston*.

PSALME 22. 27. 30. 31.

All the ends of the world shall remember and turne unto the Lord, and all the kindreds of the Nations shall worship before thee.

A seede shall serve him, it shall be accounted to the Lord for a generation.

They shall come, and shall declare his righteousnesse unto a people that shall be borne, that he hath done this.

LONDON,
Printed by *William Jones* for *John Bellamy*, and are to be sold at the three *Golden Lyons* by the *Royall Exchange*. 1634.

FIGURE 10. *Gods Promise to His Plantations as it was Delivered in a Sermon, by Iohn Cotton, B. D. and Preacher of Gods Word in Boston* (London, 1634). Photograph: Early English Books Online.

There's a good example of the most common format for the title pages of early seventeenth-century Puritan sermons. That is to say, in addition to giving the immediate occasion of the sermon, the title page set down the scriptural passages that supplied its homiletic point of reference. Later in the seventeenth century the conventional format changes slightly, as one sees in figure 11, an example from an Isaac Ambrose sermon of 1674.

While this is much closer to the layout that is echoed in "Christian Charity," we can see that the manuscript headnote was certainly composed and designed with these print models in mind. Recognizing the presence of that model, however, we may notice as well how the headnote's lineation deviates. A printer would not have broken the lines in the way they are broken in the New-York Historical Society manuscript. But the appearance of the headnote as we see it now is different from the way it appeared when it was first written. Then it mirrored very nicely the balanced form of a seventeenth-century title page.

That fact becomes apparent when we realize that the headnote was built up in three compositional stages, thus:

First stage: A / Modell of X.tian Charity. / Written / On Board th. Arrabella / On th. Attlantick. / By the Honr.bl John Winthrop Esqr. / In his passage / to New-England in th. North America. / *Anno 1630.*

Second stage: A / Modell of X.tian Charity. / Written / On Board th. Arrabella / On th. Attlantick. / By the Honr.bl John Winthrop Esqr. / In his passage, (w.th th. Great / Company of Religious people of w.ch he was th. / Gov.r,) from th. Island of Great Brittaine, / to New-England in th. North America. / *Anno 1630.*

Third (final) stage: A / Modell of X.tian Charity. / Written / On Board th. Arrabella ! / On th. Attlantick. Ocean! / By the Honr.bl John Winthrop Esqr. / In his passage , (w.th th. Great / Company of Religious people of w.ch Xtian Tribes he was th. / Brave leader & famous Gov.r!,) from th. Island of Great Brittaine, / to New-England in th. North America. / *Anno 1630.*

The revision process helps us grasp the importance of those exclamation points. The general form of the headnote signals that it wants to be read as a true account of the following document—a statement of relevant contextual facts. But the headnote's documentary features reveal that an aggressive interpretive view has shaped—and in one crucial respect, has *mis*shaped—the explanation it offers. The author of the headnote is far removed historically from the events that it represents—mistakenly, in at least two respects—as fact.

Our inquiry has left us with the essential questions about the New-

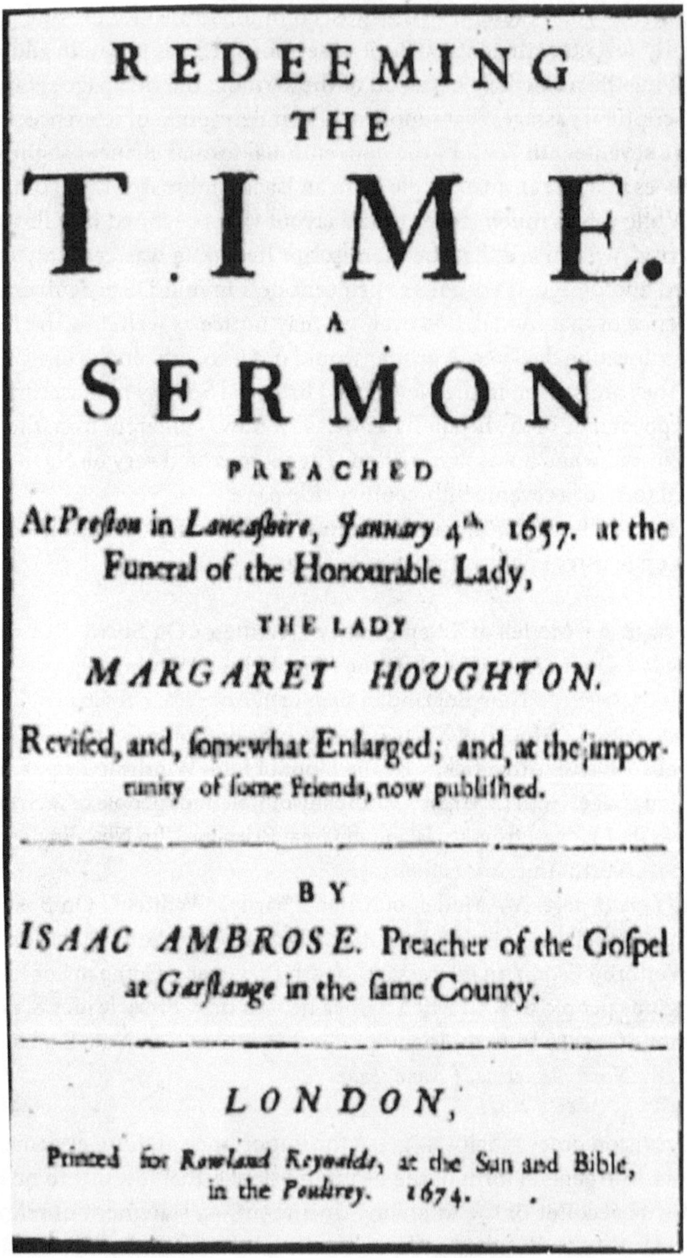

REDEEMING THE T.IME.

A SERMON

PREACHED

At *Preston* in *Lancashire*, *January* 4th 1657. at the Funeral of the Honourable Lady,

THE LADY

MARGARET HOUGHTON.

Revised, and, somewhat Enlarged; and, at the importunity of some Friends, now published.

BY

ISAAC AMBROSE. Preacher of the Gospel at *Garstange* in the same County.

LONDON,

Printed for *Rowland Reynolds*, at the Sun and Bible, in the *Poultrey*. 1674.

FIGURE 11. *Redeeming the Time. A Sermon Preached at Preston in Lancashire, January 4th, 1657, at the Funeral of the Honourable Lady, the Lady Margaret Houghton ... by Isaac Ambrose* (London, 1674). Photograph: Early English Books Online.

York Historical Society manuscript still unanswered: Who wrote the headnote? Who commissioned the secretarial copy? Who made that copy? And of course, who wrote "A Modell of Christian Charity"? But now our ignorance has turned to a kind of scholarly bliss. Now we know more about what we don't know. Now we know that, without an answer to the first question, we can't begin to have confidence about an answer to the last. "A Modell of Christian Charity" will remain a textual version of what Churchill called Russia in 1939: "a riddle, wrapped in a mystery, inside an enigma."

But the documentary evidence allows us to propose an answer to that first question: who wrote the headnote. Because it was consciously scripted to imitate the title-page format of a seventeenth-century sermon, identifying its authorship through the handwriting is seriously compromised.[33] But we don't need to identify the headnote script with a specific person's calligraphy. The answer to the question is supplied by another script on the cover page—the number "22" at the top. That number above the headnote was written by the person who wrote the headnote, and as we can see from the donation list, that number was apparently written by the man who donated the manuscript to the New-York Historical Society, Francis Bayard Winthrop.[34]

So perhaps Governor Winthrop did not write the work. He was a lawyer and an administrator, not a minister, and no lay sermons by Winthrop are extant. On the other hand, perhaps a "Christian Charity" sermon was actually written "heere in England" and even delivered "On Boarde the Arrabella! / On the Attlantick ! Ocean!" if the author was someone other than the "Brave Leader & famous Gov.r!" And perhaps Governor Winthrop himself actually commissioned the secretarial document that lay undiscovered in his papers until the nineteenth century.[35]

Those surmises gain purchase when we resurrect the likely authors of such a sermon: the two ministers who sailed on the *Arbella*, John Wilson (1575–1648) and George Phillips (1593–1644). Both were known semi-separatists, and both would figure prominently in the Bay colony: Wilson at Salem, where he served as assistant minister, and Phillips at Watertown, where he led the congregation. Phillips was curate at Boxted in 1629 when, late that year, he determined to emigrate and asked John Maidstone, Winthrop's nephew and an important figure in Boxted, to recommend him to Winthrop, which Maidstone did (*The Winthrop Papers*, 2:164–65). When they met, Winthrop must have been impressed with Phillips since he installed him as the presiding minister on the *Arbella*.[36] He called Phillips "our minister" and praised his preaching and catechetical work on the voyage.[37]

Soon after landing in the New World Phillips, left Boston with Sir Richard Saltonstall and a small company of separatists and semi-separatists to found Watertown, where he served as the settlement's minister and continued his much-admired preaching. He remained in close contact with Winthrop and, at the outset of the voyage, was one of the signatories to the *Humble Request* letter that declared allegiance to "the Church of England [...] our dear mother."[38]

That Phillips and not Wilson was signatory is important. Although William Hubbard long ago named John White as the author of *A Humble Request*, Phillips is far more likely, as his biographer Henry Wilder Foote plausibly argued.[39] White did not sign the letter, never actually emigrated, and was associated not with the *Arbella* at all but with the *Mary and John*, whose passengers he recruited. Phillips was thus far and away the best-positioned signatory to express the ecclesiastical and theological issues at the heart of *A Humble Request* so as to persuade the Crown and established church authorities of the loyalty of Winthrop's emigrants. The same is even more true for *A Humble Request*'s cognate work, "Christian Charity," since Phillips's homiletic skills were so celebrated. What Foote says of *A Humble Request*, then, might also be said of "Christian Charity": "Winthrop might have written it, but Phillips, as the only minister on board, would have been the person to whom the task [...] would naturally have fallen."[40] Though Wilson was also aboard the *Arbella*, he was not a signatory. Did Phillips write and perhaps even deliver the sermon "heere in England"? Did Winthrop possess an imperfect copy and have that copied? What are the other possibilities? What difference would it make to know?

As Watertown's minister, Phillips would have written that church's eloquent covenantal decree, as Foote argues he did.[41] Though himself semi-separatist, his congregation had many separatist members, and some were not pleased that Phillips was preaching "that the churches of Rome were true churches."[42] Protesting to the Boston authorities, they called Winthrop and other Boston authorities to Watertown in 1631 to adjudicate their charges. Although the committee ruled that Phillips was "in error," the decision had no practical effect on Phillips's ministry or semi-separatist convictions. He remained close to Winthrop and was Watertown's elected minister till his death.

Besides the documentary evidence of authorship, stylistic evidence sheds further light on the matter. Two signal features of "A Modell of Christian Charity" align it with Winthrop's most important commitments. The first is its insistence on establishing "a place of Cohabitation and Consorteshipp vnder a due forme of Government both ciuill and ecclesiasticall." But the sermon avoids any detailed discussion of institutional issues and makes only a brief declaration of Crown allegiance. In this connection, two of Winthrop's works are particularly revealing:

his exploration of the "Reasons to be Considered for [...] the Intended Plantation in New England" (1629), written at the outset of the venture, and the so-called "Little Speech on Liberty" (1645), which he delivered after the General Court acquitted him of malfeasance in a dispute about a militia election.[43] Both of these works illustrate how Winthrop expresses himself on public occasions and questions, and they differ sharply in style from "A Modell of Christian Charity." Winthrop was a lawyer and a magistrate, not a minister or a theologian, and his formal prose reflects an executive and managerial attitude toward colonial issues and problems that is far from the clerical and strongly pastoral approach of the sermon. A severe man, he was also notably generous because he knew the duty he owed to those in need. But nothing he ever wrote handled the issue of community love as it is dealt with in the sermon, and the sermon's final inspiring appeal is the pastoral rhetoric of a minister, not of a brave leader and famous governor like Winthrop.

All of Winthrop's 1629 "Reasons" fall into the following general categories: "to help on the coming of the fullness of the Gentiles [i.e., Reformed Religion], and to raise a bulwark against the kingdom of Antichrist which the Jesuits labor to rear up in those parts" ("Reasons," 138). Emigration is driven by the political conditions in Europe and England that "are grown to that height of Intemperance in all excess of Riott [...] that all artes & Trades are carried in [...] deceiptfull & unrighteous course" ("Reasons," 139). Like "A Modell of Christian Charity," "Reasons to be Considered" looks forward to the founding of uncorrupted civil and ecclesiastical institutions. But unlike the "Modell," "Reasons to be Considered" frames the issues in pragmatic and worldly terms.

Starting with the legal question of what right the emigrants have to the land in America, Winthrop proposes a series of ten "Objections" to the "enterprise" and then gives multiple "Answers" for each one. The land claim is established in the standard European way: "That which lies common, and has never been replenished or subdued, is free to any that possess and improve it" ("Reasons," 140). The other objections are similarly either ethical or instrumental: "[i]t [is] wrong to our Church and Country to take away the good people" (141); "[w]e have feared a judgment a great while, but yet we are safe. It were better therefore to stay till it comes" ("Reasons," 142); "[t]he ill success of the other Plantations may tell us what will become of this" ("Reasons," 142); the adventure "is attended with many and great difficulties" ("Reasons," 142); and so forth. Thinking in particular of Virginia's "ill success," Winthrop doesn't mince words: "for first their mayne end which was proposed was carnal and not religiouse they aymed chiefly at profitt and not the propagation of religion: secondly they vsed vnfitt instruments viz: a multitude of rude and misgoverned persons the very scumme of the land: 3. They did not establysh a right forme of gover[n]ment" (*The Winthrop Papers*, 2:114). When he passes to the objection that "[i]t is a work above the power of the undertakers" ("Reasons," 143), he appeals to historical examples that would resonate with the Puritan company: "The Waldenses weare scattered into the Alpes and mountaines of Piedmont by small companies but they became famous Churches whereof some remaine to this day, and it is certaine that the Turckes, Venetians, and other States weare very weake in their beginninges" (*The Winthrop Papers*, 2:143). The emigrants are to be inspired by the (oft-cited Reformers') example of the proto-Protestant twelfth-century Waldensians, on one hand, and shamed by the example of the "paynim" Turks and papal Venetians, on the other.

As I've already discussed in detail Winthrop's "Little Speech on Liberty" (1645), here I merely point out how closely it recalls the managerial rhetoric of his 1629 "Reasons to be Considered for [. . .] the Intended Plantation in New England," and how unlike is the pastoral address of the *Arbella* sermon. Ministers and governors alike are concerned with preserving the bonds of their communities, but in the one case the bond is forged by "love" and strengthened by pastoral work, in the other it is established and maintained by "the Authoritye of the magistrates" and the submission of the people to that authority. So Winthrop will argue in his "Little Speech" that "if your magistrates should erre," if their quotidian social and political judgments should prove wrong or even "evill," "your selues must beare it (*J*, 587)." The full depth of his commitment to such municipal control is exposed in a small but telling revision he made to the text of the speech that he copied into his *Journal*. He changed "this Libertye we are to stand for" to "this Libertye you are to stand for" (*J*, 588 n. 3). Certain persons do not "stand for" such liberty—they define and administer it.

II

All of the scholars who have engaged with this work have, it seems to me, acted in good faith, not least of all Folsom and Savage in 1838. Our hindsight throws the context of their work into relief. The rise of Unitarianism in the early nineteenth century exacerbated the critique of Puritan Congregational history that had begun in the late seventeenth century. Given the cultural situation in the age of Emerson, one can appreciate the enthusiasm with which the discovery of "A Modell of Christian Charity" was greeted by scholars sympathetic to the legacy of the Puritan errand. Their attention was understandably focused on the dramatic occasion of the work, its remarkable discovery, and its message of love, rather than on its documentary status.⁴⁴ The sermon projected a view of John Winthrop and the Puritans that would stand against the voices of William Ellery Channing and William Cullen Bryant, the critical fictions of Lydia Child (*Hobomok*, 1824) and James Fenimore Cooper (*The Wept of Wish-Ton-Wish*, 1829), and especially such severe works as John Neal's *Rachel Dyer* (1828). It was a reminder that if the Puritan adventure climaxed in the bad eminence of 1792 Salem, it began very differently.⁴⁵ That early antiquarian approach to "Christian Charity," as we know, grew and prevailed through the next 150 years, mutating into the important recent work of scholars like Perry Miller, Sacvan Bercovitch, and Andrew Delbanco.

But the success of that approach came at a cost, though not to the ideas presented in "Christian Charity," however we assess those ideas and whoever wrote the work. For 150 years scholars—literary scholars in particular—did not give their undivided and unbiased attention to a foundational work of American cultural memory. Enspelled by the local (Puritan) ideological conflicts preserved in that memory, we neglected what has always been our special vocation: philological truth, the source and end and test of all historical and cultural interpretation. And in neglecting to seek that truth we have failed to appreciate the significance—the *meaning*—of the work's two-hundred-year disappearance on one hand, or, on the other, the meaning of the meanings it acquired when it was finally made public.

CHAPTER ELEVEN

The American Scholar in the Twenty-first Century

I have imagined a man who might live as the coldest scholar on earth.
JOHN HAINES, *The Stars, the Snow, the Fire* (1989)

And all that has existed in the space of six thousand years:
Permanent, & not lost not lost nor vanishd, & every little
act, Word. work. & wish. that has existed, all remaining
WILLIAM BLAKE, *Jerusalem*, chapter 1, plate 13

In 1934 the classical scholar Milman Parry reformulated what he judged one of the most significant convictions of the ancient world: that "there is nothing at the same time finer and more practical than the truth."[1] He was glossing the Greek word *aletheia*—usually translated "truth" but meaning more specifically the disclosure of obscured or hidden reality. Parry advanced the idea knowing that in 1934 it would have struck many people, not least his powerful public contemporaries, as quaint. The formulation can seem even less pertinent in our contemporary world of complex knowledge industries and networked digital research and communicative exchange.[2] But that vast mediated context is exactly what exposes the importance of its demanding simplicity and philological inflection.

Consider where we are. The institutional effort to save, share, augment, and engineer knowledge and information with digital resources, now in full-blown development, is alternately lamented and extolled by humanist scholars, and in each case with good reason. On the plus side: digitization is already promoting research that would not have been possible using traditional so-called analog tools, and we are only beginning to explore the capabilities of this technology. It is also providing public access to vast amounts of data and documentary corpora, much of it free.

But there are serious downsides, as we know. The technologies are far from universally available. For those who do have access, privacy is radically compromised and, more ominous, falsified information is rampant. Of course all technologies have always been machines of Enlightenment, as the history of the book and other textual technologies themselves testify. But of all those Faustian technologies perhaps none has been more powerful or more dangerous than the digital. It promotes to an unprecedented degree the myth of mastery and control that was the great subject of Max Horkheimer and Theodor Adorno's *Dialectic of Enlightenment*. We can now data-mine just about everything and everyone we've never heard of. But of course that is precisely the problem. Perhaps never before have we been able to "know about" so much and yet know so little of what we know. Gaining a certain kind of power, we become alienated from our weaknesses, according to the mighty working that Thomas Hardy long ago sketched in his reflections on the *Titanic*:

And as the smart ship grew
In stature, grace, and hue,
In shadowy, silent distance, grew the iceberg too.[3]

That is our situation today, as Paul Connerton, among many others, has helped us to see.[4] But it is a situation with a long history, perhaps as long as human history itself. It was Parry's situation in 1934, just as it was Emerson's one hundred years before when he delivered a lecture to the Phi Beta Kappa Society in Cambridge. The lecture would be America's most influential manifesto for the scholar's vocation.

Working from an image of "the Soul erect and unconquered still" (*Journal*, May 21, 1837), Emerson elaborated what he called "a theory of the Scholar's office": "to read in all books . . . the one incorruptible text of truth" (*Journal*, July 29, 1837).[5] At the theory's core was the view he had introduced in the previous year with his Transcendentalist testimonial, *Nature*. What that essay called the "transparent eyeball" became in the lecture "Man Thinking." Emerson was proposing an Enlightenment ideal of intellectual freedom as it was modified through Romantic ideas about organic energy: "Free should the scholar be,—free and brave. Free even to the definition of freedom, 'without any hindrance that does not arise out of his own constitution.'"[6] Not the least significant feature of Emerson's lecture was the public context in which it was delivered. Three months earlier, in mid-May, the United States had begun its long plunge into the depression that historians call the Panic of 1837, an economic crisis that would last for seven years. Reflecting on that "emphatic and universal calamity," Emerson thought it presented him with a singular opportunity:

to expose what he saw as the true "bankruptcy" of the nation. Now that "the boasted world [of money and material wealth] had come to nothing" (*Journal*, May 21, 1837), Emerson decided "to inquire if the Ideal might not be tried" as an inspiration to a "generation . . . bankrupt of principles and hope." That inquiry became his famous lecture of August 29, "The American Scholar."

Emerson was exaggerating when he suggested that the "commodity" world of the United States had "come to nothing" in the financial collapse. More exactly, the crash had exposed yet again one of the more dismal laws driving the country's political economy. So Emerson moved to make Transcendental capital from the legacy of those quotidian laws. He wanted Americans to embrace what he called in a later lecture the "Spiritual Laws" (1841) of the sovereign individual. The custodian of those higher laws is Emerson's American Scholar, whose mission is to "master"—that is Emerson's keyword—the brute circumstances of daily life. As he majestically declares, "The true scholar [is] the only true master": "He learns that he who has mastered any law in his private thoughts, is master to that extent of all men whose language he speaks, and of all into whose language his own can be translated" (*Essays and Lectures*, 64). Emerson saw the Panic of 1837 as the recurrent legacy of the commodity masters of America. Yet that commercial power was for Emerson not masterful but anarchic. To escape subjection to its anarchs, one must first recognize how "Nature" is "the first in importance of the influences" upon the American Scholar, or Man Thinking. This is the lecture's initial move.

And the question is definitely *how* rather than *why*, for Emerson's Nature is a force field of dynamic action. It is not a congeries of empirical objects—"rocks and stones and trees"—but an ideal system obeying "a law which is also [the] law of the human mind" that works to discover its law. Man Thinking turns a reciprocal attention to the arresting pressure of the impinging material world. In that act of attention, the American Scholar and Nature are reciprocal agents, "beholding and beholden": "To the young mind, every thing is individual, stands by itself. By and by, it finds how to join two things, and see in them one nature; then three, then three thousand; and so, tyrannized over by its own unifying instinct, it goes on tying things together, diminishing anomalies, discovering roots running under ground, whereby contrary and remote things cohere, and flower out from one stem" (*Essays and Lectures*, 55). In the interchange with Nature, Emersonian Man discovers the "principle" that gives him mastery. It is the idea of an implicate order realized as Idea before it ever need be or even could be realized in fact. For Emerson, Man Thinking is, like Great Creating Nature, "a becoming creator": "Every day, the sun; and after sunset, Night and her stars. Ever the wind blows, ever the grass grows" (*Essays and Lectures*, 55). Those are, for the American Scholar, the very first examples of Emersonian Nature. They are perfectly chosen because they define Nature, shaping it as an idea of a comprehensive and recurrent order. The natural world is for Emerson the manifestation of its subsisting idea.

Emerson will spend a lifetime generating further figures to show how "[Nature's] laws are the laws of his own mind." But his ideal conviction concealed a real problem. Once Man Thinking had seized the idea, what need of an empirical pursuit? Might Man Thinking—Emerson Thinking—actually not know his own mind, or for that matter, Nature? Indeed, might the mind's sovereign idea rather be—this was Edgar Allan Poe's darkly comic thought—the pursuit of its illusions, of how it is "a becoming creator" of illusions? These are the kinds of questions lying behind the persistent judgments initially brought against Emerson by Poe and reinforced by later readers: that he made a false homology between the human condition and the state of nature.

Poe was Emerson's Blakean Contrary—far less a critic of his limitations than, like Herman Melville, the dark interpreter of his genius. The best critic of Emerson is his best and most assiduous student, Henry David Thoreau. We now see pretty clearly how Thoreau moved "gradually, partially, and self-conflictedly beyond the program" of Emersonian Transcendentalism and the scholarly ideas it promoted: "Thoreau became increasingly interested in defining nature's structure, both spiritual and material, for its own sake, as against how nature might subserve humanity, which was Emerson's primary consideration."[7] In the late journals and the so-called late natural history writings such as "The Dispersion of Seeds" and *Wild Fruits*, we track Thoreau's painstaking efforts to put acts of attention well before acts of invention—or the human encounter with the material world before reflection on the order of that world.[8]

And I say "painstaking" because in Thoreau we read the story of a person learning how to learn by submitting to a far more demanding master than Emerson. It was a teacher who, Thoreau came to understand, spoke an entirely foreign language. Bradley P. Dean called it "the language of trees," because Dean focused on a dialect that Thoreau came to study more closely than its other dialects: for instance, the language of fauna, of stones, of water. But Thoreau was well acquainted with Nature's entire family of languages, and in his Walden experiment he proved so arrested by those languages that one or another of Nature's native speakers would sometimes even address him directly.

For example, Walden Pond itself, according to Thoreau, speaks many dialects. All are in communion with the dialects of the other ponds in Walden's neighborhood. Fishermen nearby, Thoreau reports, "say that the 'thundering of the pond' scares the fishes and prevents their biting," but neither they nor Thoreau is certain what the ponds are saying in their winter words, or even if it is the ponds and not some other communicant who are speaking to the fish. But Thoreau senses that he is fronting, is immersed in, a scene of complex communicative action that he doesn't understand. "The pond does not thunder every evening, and I cannot tell when to expect its thundering; but though I may perceive no difference in the weather, it does."[9]

Nature, so to speak, speaks a different language, or perhaps many different dialects of a single language. So foreign is this family of languages to human persons, however, that a true and useful acquaintance only begins when you realize you will never master any of them. Consider Thoreau's famous encounter with Mount Ktaadn.

> Vast, Titanic, inhuman Nature has got him at disadvantage, caught him alone, and pilfers him of some of his divine faculty. She does not smile on him as in the plains. She seems to say sternly, Why came ye here before your time. This ground is not prepared for you. Is it not enough that I smile in the valleys? I have never made this soil for thy feet, this air for thy breathing, these rocks for thy neighbors. I cannot pity nor fondle thee here, but forever relentlessly drive thee hence to where I am kind. Why seek me where I have not called thee, and then complain because you find me but a stepmother? Shouldst thou freeze or starve, or shudder thy life away, here is no shrine, nor altar, nor any access to my ear.
> "Chaos and ancient Night, I come no spy With purpose to explore or to disturb The secrets of your realm, but. . . .
> . . . . . as my way Lies through your spacious empire up to light."[10]

Thoreau summons Milton's Satan for a language and fit reply to the obdurate language of Ktaadn. And Thoreau isn't quoting Milton—he is translating the passage to an alienated context and occasion. The translation signals a scholarly attitude toward Nature that is decisively different from Emerson's.

Thoreau can translate Milton because Milton and Thoreau speak the same language. Thoreau cannot translate Ktaadn because Ktaadn has no knowable language. So Ktaadn's words here are not Thoreau's translation, but rather his commentary on his encounter with the natural world. Translation is out of the question because there is no book of Nature. Ktaadn's words are thus Thoreau's representation of an alien encounter, and Milton is invoked to annotate the scene.

The Emersonian scholar—Man Thinking—proves his "mastery" when he realizes the correspondence between mind and Nature. As *Walden* shows, Man Thinking is equally the pivot point of Thoreau's work. But Thoreau's figural flights keep colliding with the intransigence of minute and material particulars. The inorganic world—Ktaadn, the ponds of Walden, seasonal weather, the "clay and sand ... flowing down the sides of a deep cut on the railroad"—all are Thoreau's brute and eloquent neighbors whose grace is to overthrow the higher laws of the Transcendental program. In Emerson, Man Thinking takes communion with a mysterious Nature and discovers the mastery of metaphoric translation. But in Thoreau communion leads finally to translational and metaphoric breakdown. He is pleading for an Adamic language through "which all things and events speak without metaphor" ("Sounds," *Walden*, 411).

> The distant rumbling of wagons over bridges ... the baying of dogs ... the trump of bullfrogs ... vainly bellowing troonk from time to time, and pausing for a reply ... wild cockerels crow[ing] on the trees, clear and shrill for miles over the resounding earth ... sturdy pitch-pines rubbing and creaking against the shingles ... a scuttle or a blind blown off in the gale—a pine tree snapped off or torn up by the roots. ...
> ("Sounds," *Walden*, 422 and 424)

So education for Thoreau is not a progress in knowledge but a repetition of primary encounters. The cycle of the seasons and the diurnal round locate his passage through "Chaos and ancient Night" on his journey to primal Earth. The ice on Walden Pond melts in a very particular pattern every year, but each year the pattern unfolds so uniquely that each year it has to be rediscovered: "In 1845 Walden was first completely open on the 1st of April; in '46, on the 25th of March; in '47, the 8th of April; in '51, the 28th of March; in '52, the 18th of April; in '53, the 23rd of March; in '54, about the 7th of April" ("Spring," *Walden*, 564). Such a cunning move, to climax his statistical record with that word "about." Besides, Thoreau does not time-stamp this record by minute and hour. And what exactly does it mean to say, or to think, that the pond was "first completely open"?

Or what of those red squirrels he will soon meet—creatures who, "[a]t the approach of spring" each year, would

> [get] under my house two at a time, directly under my feet as I sat reading or writing, and kept up the queerest chuckling and chirruping and vocal pirouetting and gurgling sounds that ever were heard; and when I stamped they only chirruped the louder, as if past all fear and respect in their mad pranks, defying humanity to stop them. No, you don't—chickaree—chickaree. They were wholly deaf to my argu-

ments, or failed to perceive their force, and fell into a strain of invective that was irresistible. ("Spring," *Walden*, 669)

That is Thoreau making a reprise on one of his most celebrated reports in all of *Walden*: his encounter with the loon in "Brute Neighbors." When he glosses the loon's cry as a derisory laugh, the figure is itself derisory, marking a scene of contact where misunderstanding appears all on one side (Thoreau's). So too with the red squirrels, who are, Thoreau imagines, too busy and preoccupied to pay any notice to their noisy neighbor upstairs. All he registers is a scene of existential repletion, as remote in its way as stern Ktaadn. "While he was thinking one thing in his brain," Thoreau writes of the loon, "I was endeavoring to divine his thought in mine" ("Brute Neighbors," *Walden*, 510). With the verb "divine," Thoreau registers the sublunar divinity of his brute neighbors, who mock and tease him for the deficiency of his understanding. In the poverty of his report he also reports how the implicate order of the loon's world will always remain to be discovered.

Where Emerson proposes "going down into the secrets of his own mind," Thoreau's catalog of particulars is outward bound to "the necessity of being forever on the alert": "Instead of no path to the front-yard gate in the Great Snow—no gate—no front-yard—and no path to the civilized world" ("Sounds," *Walden*, 424). That out-of-bounds thought climaxes the chapter appropriately devoted to sounds, where Thoreau invokes an order of communication that dispenses with semantics, syntax, and the cognitions of Man Thinking.

But the decisive anti-Transcendentalist move is made in the paired chapters "Higher Laws" and "Brute Neighbors." Explicitly invoking Emerson's essay "Spiritual Laws" (1841), where Emerson argues that "a higher law...regulates events," Thoreau's study of these "Higher Laws" turns out to be a wrestling match with his Emersonian angel. The struggle makes him realize that "[t]here is unquestionably this instinct in me which belongs to the lower orders of creation" ("Higher Laws," *Walden*, 493).

The uncertainties climax in the chapter's final paragraph, where Thoreau tells the story of John Farmer. Like Thoreau in his prose, John Farmer struggles to realize his desire "to recreate his intellectual man," to find his sovereign Emersonian way. But John Farmer's high hopes come to an uncertain end:

> A voice said to him—Why do you stay here and live this mean moiling life, when a glorious existence is possible for you? Those same stars twinkle over other fields than these.—But how to come out of

this condition and actually migrate thither? All that he could think of was to practise some new austerity, to let his mind descend into his body and redeem it, and treat himself with ever increasing respect. ("Higher Laws," *Walden*, 499)

The investigation of "Higher Laws" ends in this disturbed finale, where the impulse to redeem the brute body is thrown into question. The move from "Higher Laws" to "Brute Neighbors" signals a sharp course reversal in the quest romance of *Walden*.[11]

Redemption, it turns out, is not a descent from above. The chapter opens when a certain "Poet" unexpectedly arrives to invite Thoreau—who calls himself "Hermit"—to leave his reflective isolation and come "a-fishing." The invitation sets Hermit thinking once again on higher and lower things: "Shall I go to heaven or a-fishing?" he wonders. When he decides against heaven and for fishing, the event delivers him from new austerities to the wonders of the imbruted world: "[t]he mice which haunted my house," "[a] phoebe . . . a robin . . . the partridge [leading] her brood past my windows" ("Brute Neighbors," *Walden*, 503).

These brief encounters draw him out further and in deeper, through the chaos and ancient night of the embattled ants to the "demoniac" loon. A less extravagant person than Thoreau might have climaxed his sojourn among the brutes with that famous encounter. But the episode of the loon is actually anticlimactic, for "Brute Neighbors" has one more paragraph of brutish revelation.

Once again "on the alert," Thoreau "watch[es] the ducks cunningly tack and veer and hold the middle of the pond, far from the sportsman." Wise ducks, Thoreau is thinking. But the thought is quickly trumped when he thinks again that these are "tricks which they will have less need to practice in Louisiana bayous" ("Brute Neighbors," *Walden*, 511). Beyond these thoughts of Man Thinking lie the astonishing wisdom of the ducks. What depths of knowledge must they possess that they understand so well how to manage the shifting circumstances of their migrating lives! If hunters are everywhere, Walden Pond and a Louisiana bayou are worlds elsewhere, and so are the hunters, and so are the ducks. Besides, some hunters are just going fishing.

Thoreau marks his decision to go fishing with a memorandum: "Mem. There never is but one opportunity of a kind" ("Brute Neighbors," *Walden*, 502). The apothegm has the form of generalization or law, but its focus is entirely on differentials and variants. Opportunities are one of a kind, and so are experiences and all the singularities that comprise them.

Thoreau's studies of nature kept drawing him toward what Alfred Jarry would soon call a "science of exceptions."[12] Today we may be surprised to recognize Jarry's "pataphysical science" as the shaping spirit of environmental studies. Listen to Barry Lopez: "The world of variables... is [so] astonishingly complex [that it] seems a reflection of that organization of energy that quantum mechanics predicts for the particles that compose an atom."[13] An "evaluation... of a stretch of land," Lopez observes, "no matter how profound or accurate," will always seem "inadequate," for "the land retains an identity of its own, still deeper and more subtle than we can know" (228). So too for all the earth's creatures: not just flora and fauna but weather and water and perduring Pangaea, where knowledge and power abide beyond the range of our knowledge and power, if not beyond the range of our attention. Of the ways of the polar bear, Lopez remarks, "No matter how long you watch, you will not see all it can do" (96). And so a warning goes forth across the whole of his book: "The imposed view, however innocent, always obscures" (176). This is Lopez channeling Thoreau, man on the alert, not Emerson, the man who thought thinking was "mastery."

Arctic Dreams is thus an extended reflection on disciplines of knowledge, on truth and method. Its recurrent message is "no country, finally, is just like another. The generalities are abstractions" (259). But more than that, Lopez discovers that no country, finally, is just like itself. Arctic natives who are constantly dealing with their elusive, volatile, and shape-shifting world possess that understanding. They practice a science that is "less formal" than traditional European science but "not necessarily less rigorous" on that account. It is a science of exceptions that is "reluctan[t] to extrapolate from the individual" (269 n.): "They know they can be very precise about what they do, but that does not guarantee that they will be accurate. They know the behavior of an individual animal may differ strikingly from the generally recognized behavior of the species, and that the same species may behave quite differently from place to place, from year to year" (269). So when a "man from Anaktuvuk Pass [was asked] a question about what he did when he visited a new place," he responded: "'I listen.' That's all. I listen, he meant, to what the land is saying... before I, myself, ever speak a word" (257).

Here the land and its brute individuals cast such a cold eye on Man Thinking that a scholar like me receives a shock of recognition. *Arctic Dreams* is an allegory for a scholar's life where our Emersonian commitments to "mastery" make a further commitment to meet their master. We are to follow "The Course of a Particular" and "the cry of leaves that do not transcend themselves."[14] We are to cultivate "a mind of winter" and zero-degree encounters with our culture, its *Umwelt*, its material documents. Here is what that mind of winter looks like:

A tundra botanist once described to me her patient disassembly of a cluster of plants on a tussock, a tundra mound about 18 inches high and a foot or so across. She separated live from dead plant tissue and noted the number and kind of the many species of plants. She examined the insects and husks of berries, down to bits of things nearly too slight to see or to hold without crushing. The process took hours, and her concentration and sense of passing time became fixed at that scale.

Then "at one point" her fixed attention broke and "she remembered looking up ... at the tundra that rolled away in a hundred thousand tussocks toward the horizon" (259–60). The enormity of her studies came so sharply into focus that she could not resume her work, "not for long minutes." When she left the tundra for home, we know the stories she would tell and how she would tell them. If she wrote them in a book it would be called *Arctic Dreams*.

That botanist was a scholar who understood both the wonder and the difficulty of her vocation. Only a student honoring that implacable land and its little tussocks has any chance of approaching the land's secrets. Mastery is out of the question. Few of us have been to the Arctic, much less submitted to its rigorous demands. Yet not a few will understand that botanist and the commitment to truth she represents. The subjects of the commitment are a secondary matter. No one learns to prepare good meals, or even some favorite dishes, without a study and care that may well turn to a lifelong endeavor. There are baseball fans who exhibit that botanist's habit of mind, as do many gardeners, carpenters, and musicians—professional and amateur.

Lopez fashioned his Arctic botanist to an image I am especially familiar with. She recalls the scholar focused for hours or days on some book, some document, some passage or word that opens to a formidable horizon. Tennyson glimpsed "all experience" of this kind as "an arch where through / Gleams that untraveled world whose margin fades / For ever and for ever when I move" ("Ulysses," 19–21).[15] If you travel there, you pledge allegiance to truth: to accuracy, thoroughness, and all their stipulated costs. As a matter of social practice, when that scholar leaves the tundra to join her neighbors in the human world, her commitment to truth is called troth, which is every bit as demanding.

We humans will climb Mount Ktaadn and take our measure of her measure. We will explore the poles, go to the moon or Jupiter, and imagine—if only in our children's toys—traveling, like Buzz Lightyear, "to infinity and beyond." But our measures will fall short, as ancient wisdom has always known. That truth is disclosed yet again—will we never learn?—by physicists and bioastronomers who reflect on these human endeavors and the second law of thermodynamics. Exploring nature, then, we may find ourselves and take our Socratic measure. Or not.

Arctic exploration and the quest for a Northwest Passage have furnished an archive of documents of "inestimable" value because the documents "expose in startling ways the complacency of our thoughts about land in general." Arctic land is important because it "is irritatingly and uncharacteristically uncooperative" (12), so Lopez offers chastening examples of how to read the accounts of others who were smitten with Arctic dreams: Martin Frobisher, Robert Peary, Knud Rasmussen, Sir John Franklin, British Petroleum, Exxon Mobile.

But if the work is important for reading the records of wilderness encounter, it has even greater relevance for what Walter Benjamin called the "documents of civilization." *Arctic Dreams* was written to wake up its "temperate-zone" neighbors—we who are accustomed to imagine the world as a place "where the sun actually sets on a summer evening, where cicadas give way in the twilight to crickets, and people sit on porches—none of which happens in the Arctic." *Arctic Dreams* brings enlightenment to those kinds of temperate illusion, which our Anthropocene minds have recently begun to see—"Thank Somebody," as Swinburne liked to say—as "irritatingly and uncharacteristically uncooperative" (12).

Emerson dreamed of an American Scholar who would stand against the dismal American Dream of money and paths to wealth. Those longstanding American dreams have mutated in our contemporary era of mediated illusions. I have an Arctic Dream that educators and educated citizens might take that tundra botanist as a figure for thoughtful address. Here are a few stories about why I have that dream.

When Megyn Kelly of Fox News interviewed Dick Cheney on June 18, 2014, she began by asking him to respond to the following passage from a recent article in the *Washington Post* by Paul Waldman: "'There is not a single person in America who has been more wrong and more shamelessly dishonest on the topic of Iraq than Dick Cheney, and now as the cascade of misery and death and chaos, he did so much to unleash raises anew, Mr. Cheney has the unadulterated gall to come before the country and tell us that it's all someone else's fault.' The suggestion is that you caused this mess, Mr. Vice President. What say you?" Cheney replied: "Well, obviously I disagree . . . I think we went into Iraq for very good reasons." He added that President Obama was responsible for destroying what he called a "very positive" situation that he and his people had created in Iraq. When Kelly pressed him about the fearful consequences of the invasion, he stood his ground: "I just fundamentally disagree, Megyn. You've got to go back and look at the track record. We inherited a situation where there was no doubt in anybody's mind about the extent of Saddam's involvement in weapons of mass destruction."

"I just fundamentally disagree." The phrase is disturbing partly because it dodges what Cheney knew was the truth. Well over 100,000 Iraqi civilians were killed between 2003 and 2008. But beyond that, to say that "there was no doubt in anybody's mind about the extent of Saddam's involvement in WMDs [weapons of mass destruction]" was definitely not true. Many people at the time, as the vice president knew, expressed their doubts often and publicly, and some—the United Nations, most notably—tried to verify what was or wasn't true about the American administration's charges. But the administration did not allow Hans Blix's inspection team to make a report that might have, could have, prevented the ensuing disaster by telling the truth.

As instructive as Cheney's 2014 interview with Kelly is Ron Suskind's interview with Karl Rove in the summer of 2002 when final preparations for the invasion of Iraq were being made. Promoting what he judged a "creative" approach to reality, Rove told Suskind that the "judicious study of discernible reality" was hopelessly out of date. You are laboring, Rove told Suskind,

> "in what we call the reality-based community [of] people who believe that solutions emerge from your judicious study of discernible reality." I nodded and murmured something about enlightenment principles and empiricism. He cut me off.
> "That's not the way the world really works anymore.... We're an empire now, and when we act, we create our own reality. And while you're studying that reality—judiciously, as you will—we'll act again, creating other new realities.... We're history's actors... and you, all of you, will be left to just study what we do."[16]

Several things need to be pointed out here. First of all, no document, not even a poem, is a passive act in the world, and certainly not polemical journalism like Suskind's. In 2002 Rove could dismiss Suskind's work—this very report—because the administration's policy dossier was still being written. But beginning in March 2003, reality would work drastic changes in the practical realities these two men were discussing. Other realities than our own are always in play in the theaters of reality, and when we move to "create our own," we call them out. Besides, the force of circumstance always has a stake in all these events. So Rove—like Cheney, bewitched by the dream of imperial power—scorned Suskind's "reality-based skepticism" as a kind of academic pedantry.

A "judicious study of discernible reality" is a prerequisite for responsible social action. But "discernible reality" is usually (always?) a can of worms. That's why the vocation of educators and scholars—journalists among them—and the work that they do, the documents they make, are so consequential. They model the fiendish complexity of the records that ground both our understanding and our actions, trying to turn a crush of factual detail to truthful account.

Contrary to the tired cliché, scholars do not live in ivory towers. We live in ordinary space-time where we meet day-to-day obligations. Our special vocation shapes our contributions to society at large. In a period like ours, when technical skills command such attention, the educational value of humanist disciplines versus STEM disciplines—C. P. Snow's "two cultures"—can seem problematic and unclear. Humanists used to lay special claim to "critical thinking," but surely everyone now can see that that oft-cited virtue is not the special province of humanist studies or a humanist education. Indeed, to the degree that critical thinking demands procedural rigor, humanist scholars can be as sloppy as the best, or the worst.

Because Cheney and Rove took a blithe attitude to matters of fact, they could take their "creative" approach to matters of consequence, matters of life and death. Both practiced what Hannah Arendt called "defactualization," a habit of public dishonesty that has, since her essay was published in 1971, become brazen and shameless.[17] Cheney and Rove would have been wiser had they read *Arctic Dreams* and taken seriously one of Barry Lopez's running themes: "The imposed view, however innocent, always obscures" (176). Not even the vice president would argue that his views were innocently imposed. So in 2002–3 both made dreadful mistakes. In 2014 Cheney lied about what he knew was true about the reality of 2002–3.

But matters of fact, our brute neighbors, can be dismissed from attention in a very different way. This other way became widespread when humanities scholarship shifted from its traditional grounding in history and material culture toward literary philosophy and interpretive theory. For my generation, the name Paul De Man would be totemic for that shift. Listen to what he had to say about literary studies in 1970 as the theory movement in humanities was in serious liftoff: "There is no room . . . for notions of accuracy and identity in the shifting world of interpretation."[18] Or, as he remarked a few years earlier in an essay on the poetry of Keats, we must not think, when studying the poems, that they have any "positive existence."[19] History was not "bunk" for De Man, as a famous American entrepreneur once said, but accuracy and matters of fact were no longer "notions" for which the humanist scholar had any room.

That retreat from philology to theory is a dangerous move for anyone charged with monitoring and preserving our cultural record. Because documentary witnesses fairly demand a science of exceptions, we recognize how and why the imposed theoretical view, however innocent, always obscures. The book of nature is difficult and mysterious, but so are the books of men and women. The records of positive actions and singular events comprise both natural history and human history, but the two are very different. Nature is mysterious because it is absolute; human records are mysterious because they're not. Fallible human beings—scientists, as we now say—study the book of nature and make both wonderful discoveries and terrible mistakes. But the book of nature, their subject, is itself perfect. Nature does not change, it mutates, as the humanly devastated state of nature around Chernobyl reminds us. Or the melting of the polar ice caps, or the pollution of the seas, or the deforestations of the land.

Fallible human beings study the books and records that were made by other fallible human beings. Data are records, and they are as prone to error as any other record. Worse yet, all these imperfect records are always fallibly preserved and imperfectly passed along to other fallible beings. Skeptics might call that a house built on sand. It's actually more like a house resting on the backs of those turtles that go, as someone famously once said, all the way down. You need a lot of honesty, patience, and sympathy when you practice the human sciences. For the humanist, it's human beings—natural, mortal—all the way down through our "[c]haos and ancient night."

Socrates proposed that knowledge should be understood and pursued as complete self-reflection. That was an impossible proposal, as he knew. He thought he was wise because he knew he knew nothing for certain. We call his knowledge program the Hellenic vision of truth. In the West we know its complement as the (equally impossible) Hebrew or Christian or Islamic vision. These are the visions of the people of the Book, who practice an equally impossible task. The Bible is our normative book for studying human history. Why? Because as a book of truth it is also an imperfect book, full of error and evil—what Poe called "the good and the bad and the worst and the best."

But like the hard sciences, the human sciences have systematic methods, and you can see why. Humanists need as much rigor and system as we can muster because everything we study, including ourselves, is so unreliable. The book of nature is rock-solid. The Word of God is turtles all the way down. So are the humanities, which have to be prosecuted as an art: that is, less under the rule of theory or idea, and more as a regimen of careful practice.

Asked about the method of philology, one of its greatest practitioners, Ulrich von Wilamowitz-Moellendorff, quipped:

"'Philological method'? There simply isn't any—any more than a method to catch fish.... And hunting? I suppose there is something like method there? [But] there is a difference between hunting lions and catching fleas."

Wilamowitz leaves unexpressed the clear moral of his maxim: that there are different procedures for different kinds of fishing and hunting. There are, we will add, great differences between fishing for trout and fishing for sheepshead, though each is exceedingly difficult, requiring great care and long experience. Or fishing for trout in Utah v. fishing for trout in Virginia. Or again:

> It is far more to the point that the ancient poet speak, not some modern professor. We perform our task correctly only when we don't force our own mind into every ancient book... but rather read out of it what is already there. That is precisely the philological task of comprehending a different individual.... In the self-sacrifice of our own individuality lies our strength. We philologists... ought to carry something of the actor in ourselves, not of the virtuoso who sets his own idiosyncratic touches onto the role; but of the true artist, who gives life to the dead through his own heart's blood.[20]

Scrupulous attention to the specific and "positive existence" of the human record, past as well as ongoing present. Mark Twain called all of that *Life on the Mississippi*. You have to know the land, the river, the seasonal shifts, the weather conditions, and all their unpredictable history. And like Twain's river pilots, scholars have to know it at first hand, in actual contact with the documentary record. And you have to know it repeatedly because, like that river, the documents change over time as they pass through the hands of those who transmit them. Finally, you have to know it through the firsthand knowledge of others whom you know to have long-standing experiential credentials. Those are the people you go fishing with. Those are the people whose scholarship makes a difference. In the shifting world of the human sciences, accuracy is imperative, as much as you can manage. We can't make reliable judgments without being confident that we have accurate information—that is to say, reports that mean to be candid, honest, and as thorough as possible.

People with a commitment to knowledge and truth—people from every quarter of the social and political landscape—recognize dishonesty. The recognition is nonpartisan and interdisciplinary, a function of a common, if differently shaped, vocation to truth. But to give that vocation force you need more than the commitment of a sovereign individual—as

Emerson, perhaps more than Thoreau, understood. The scholar has a pastoral office to fulfill. It's not all theology and shop talk. If it were, we wouldn't be troubled that people who recognize and deplore dishonesty often give it a pass.

I like to think that De Man would have been appalled at Cheney's cavalier attitude toward accuracy and factual truth.[21] But De Man's skepticism about human knowledge—about the testimonial record—was, if not dishonest, misguided. It set an unreliably narrow model for human studies. I know a better model, or at least a story about a better model. It's the story I began with. Parry died a year after he delivered his 1934 lecture. Though a young assistant professor—he was thirty-three when he died—he had already achieved considerable reputation. That was why he was invited to speak to Harvard's Board of Overseers. And while his lecture had a singularly unprepossessing title—"The Historical Method in Literary Criticism"—he delivered it because he was troubled by a crisis in the humanities.

Even in 1934 there was a crisis in the humanities? Alas, yes, as there was in 1837, when Emerson engaged the crisis in his lecture to the Phi Beta Kappa Society. In truth, the humanities have been in a regular state of crisis at least since the eighteenth century. Crisis has become the modern fate of humanist studies, whose vocation is the pursuit of social, historical, and personal truth and the preservation of the record of those pursuits. These are obligations that humanists undertake knowing they are impossible to fulfill. The historical record that comes down to us makes a small fractional recollection of the human past, and even that fraction is riven with holes and fragmentary, disfeatured remains. And as for the data glut of the present, it is being mined but not mastered. Data mining, we may recall, was what led Cheney and his accomplices to their misjudgment about Saddam Hussein and WMDs (though it had nothing to do with their lying).

Parry did not know about Big Data, but he didn't have to. His little data was trouble enough for someone interested in fishing for the truth. And that is what he made the subject of his lecture. As with Emerson, the important context of his lecture is signaled by its date, 1934, when "propaganda . . . social changes and confusion" were taking such hold of bewildered people throughout Europe and America.[22] Stalin had assumed control of the Soviets in 1923, Hitler of the Weimar Republic in 1933, and a freewheeling American capitalism had plunged the United States into a tormented social condition, worse even than the Panic of 1837. Parry reflected on that situation:

> The chief emotional ideas to which men seem to be turning at present . . . are those of nationality—for which they exploit race—and

class. . . . Anyone who has followed the history of the use of propaganda for political purposes, with its extraordinary development of intensity and technique in the past fifty years [recognizes how] those who were directing that propaganda expressed their lack of concern, or even contempt, for what actually was so, or actually had been so.[23]

Parry went on quietly to suggest that "the European humanistic tradition" had something important to contribute to these benighted societies.[24] He wasn't thinking of what Poe called "the glory that was Greece, and the grandeur that was Rome." On the contrary, he was thinking about humanist scholars who spend their lives trying to give accurate reports about such worlds, so dead and far gone from the modern present, as he was reminding the Harvard overseers. He was also fully aware how insignificant—how pedantic—such academic pursuits often appear to living people bewitched by propagandistic dreams of national glory and exceptional virtue.

Parry's heroes are not Achilles or Hector, nor even Socrates or Plato. They are far more minor and modest. They are people who believe "that there is nothing at the same time finer and more practical than the truth," and who will spend their days acting on that belief. You want to know what such days are like? They are days spent on a vast tundra studying a document few people read or perhaps have ever heard of—perhaps written in a strange or even a dead language—trying to say something accurate and truthful about it. I knew a scholar who set all his other research work aside for months trying to write a footnote that told the truth about a sentence in a letter by the poet Tennyson—a sentence that mentioned, but didn't identify, Tennyson's tooth powder. Whether the document being searched has ideas with current social relevance is, for these adepts of truth, beside the point. Indeed, apparent irrelevance might be exactly to the point for people surrounded by the defactualizations of our fiercely just-in-time present.

What, then, is the point? Simply, in Parry's words, "that there is nothing at the same time finer and more practical than the truth." That would be the truth as such. Accuracy and truth are not well characterized as "notions" that we have—De Man's characterization. Better to know them as commitments that we make. The strength of a commitment—and therefore its practicality—rests in how out far and how in deep it goes. The turtles of truth go all the way down to where there is, we trust, something we will never have and never know, though we pledge it our allegiance: the truth, the whole truth, and nothing but the truth.

No more trenchant account of philological truth and method exists than Parry's three-paragraph discussion of a brief passage in book 12 of the

Iliad: Sarpedon's call to "his friend Glaucus to follow him to the assault on the Greek wall."[25] Parry's account shows that the horizon for a philological truth-telling must recover the particulars of the entire composition and reception history of the work being studied, from its *fons et origo* down to the present (every present) moment. So of course "[t]he work upon it will never be done."[26] But it is work that, truth to tell, must proceed nonetheless. And so Parry summarized in nine brilliant words philology's *Wahrheit und Methode*: "I make for myself a picture of great detail."[27]

This is a succinct statement of the four premises of philological truth and method: even if the document being studied is a text, it should be read as a picture (so that the picture, though a gestalt, flaunts its negative space, where a universe of other related pictures invisibly hovers); the picture will be as detailed as I can make it (on the understanding that it could never be made detailed enough); the picture is my particular date-stamped construction (understanding that it can and will be read by others who will have their own pictures to make, including a picture—it could never be detailed enough—of the picture I have made); and finally, it is therefore a picture in fractal dimensions (so that Parry's sentences about the passage in the *Iliad*, understood as making "a picture of great detail," resemble what mathematicians conceive as a one-dimensional line with the functional character of a surface).

Scholars are thus pledged to a kind of impossible truth. Making the pledge is one of the two public functions of the humanist scholar. The other—it is closely related—is the obligation to protect human memory from neglect and erasure—as much of it as possible. Both commitments resist the pressure of the consuming present, where illusions of sovereignty are fashioned from memories of convenience, truthiness, or even depraved purposes.

The public world does not naturally cultivate habits of accuracy, thoroughness, and candor, and it may even—as Parry remarked and as we know only too well—hold them in contempt. In the fugitive and cloistered world of the scholar, however, these are predominant values. They monitor all quests for sovereignty and power because they recognize the seductive uncertainty of higher laws and the uncanny intransigence of brute fact. It is difficult to tell the truth, the whole truth, and nothing but the truth about a Tennyson letter. Yet to be in a habit of attempting it is both sobering and superb. We touch the vast implicate order of things only by a close acquaintance with the most insignificant objects that make it up.

Before the scholar's art comes the slipping-down life of the world. To uphold that world's dubious honor asks a mind of winter and a faithfulness unto all generations. What another poet devoted to loss called "a light to lesson ages and voluptuous princes."

ACKNOWLEDGMENTS

Like Tim Robinson's *Stones of Aran*, this "book that is committed to failure" has only learned to make its way with the guidance and wise example of many people.

While I can't name here the hundreds of students who helped me bring my scholar's life home to America during the past ten years, I want to call out and thank a small recent group who have been their second selves: James Ascher, Shalmi Barman, Thomas Berenato, Alex Buckley, Matt Martello, Annie Persons, Lloyd Sy, and Annie Thompson.

They are the younger lights of a bright company, many of them friends, who have enlightened American literature and culture for me for some time: Charles Bernstein, Anna Brickhouse, Ryan Cordell, Steve Cushman, Jonathan Elmer, Jennifer Greeson, Susan Howe, Myra Jehlen, Jerry Kennedy, Alan Liu, Emily Ogden, Sam Otter, Michael Pickard, George Quasha, Jeffrey Robinson, Marion Rust, Reiner Smolinski, Elisa Tamarkin, Alan Taylor, Abram Van Engen, and Marta Werner.

And among them I have to single out certain close and guiding persons, a few now gone into the world of light: Steve Arata, Virgil Burnett, Adriana Craciun, Lisa Goff, Jeffrey Herrick, Janet Kauffman, Cecil Lang, Beth Nowviskie, John O'Brien, Andy Stauffer, Patricia Spacks, Michael Suarez, Chip and Betsy Tucker, Cindy Wall, John and Maggie Unsworth, and my sister, Lorraine Holton.

For special help with this book I am also deeply grateful to Barbara Norton, Randy Petilos, and David Rumsey; and to the librarians of the University of Virginia and the University of California, Berkeley, of the Massachusetts Historical Society, and of the Watertown Free Library. And for permissions of various kinds I thank the New-York Historical Society, particularly Michael Ryan and Ted O'Reilly; the Field Museum of Natural

History in Chicago; and three scholarly journals, *New Literary History*, *Scholarly Editing*, and *Textual Cultures*.

It has been a special pleasure for me to see this book published by the University of Chicago Press, where my first academic works were published. Most of all I have been blessed with the support of Alan Thomas, the press's editorial director, for his commitment to me and to this book.

Finally, there are the shaping spirits of my imagination: my wife Anne, my family, and especially my grandchildren, to whom this backward-looking work is dedicated. When Faulkner wrote that "The past is never dead—it's not even past," he was thinking in the present of the future.

* * *

An earlier version of chapter 7 appeared in *New Literary History* 50, no. 2 (Spring 2019): 171–95, © 2019 *New Literary History*, The University of Virginia; an earlier version of chapter 10 appeared in *Textual Cultures* 12, no. 1 (2019): 27–52; and an earlier version of chapter 11 appeared in *Scholarly Editing* 37 (2016): 1–22.

NOTES

PREFACE

1. Claude Lévi-Strauss, *Tristes Tropiques* (New York: Athenaeum, 1975), 393.
2. Ibid., 393.
3. John Modern, *Secularism in Antebellum America* ... (Chicago: University of Chicago Press, 2011), 289.
4. "Outside time and space." Lévi-Strauss, *Tristes Tropiques*, 392.
5. August Boeckh, *Enzyklopädie und Methodologie der gesamten philologischen Wissenschaften*, ed. Ernst Bratuschek (Leipzig: B. G. Teubner, 1877). And see below, pp. 4ff.
6. William Gustav Gartner, "An Image to Carry the World Within It: Performance Cartography and the Skidi Sky Chart," in *Early American Cartographies*, ed. Martin Brückner (Chapel Hill: University of North Carolina Press, 2012), 169–239, at 178. More specifically as to method, and in homage to his mentor, the cartographer David Woodward, Gartner writes that "to understand maps on their own terms" requires "integrating the form, content, and context of the artifact itself" (177). That simple formula launches Gartner upon a close study of the materials, means, and modes of production of the Sky Chart over time through its ceremonial functions. The star map is estimated to have been made sometime between approximately 1600 and 1800; it is housed in the Chicago Field Museum, which acquired it in 1906.
7. Ibid., 202.
8. Ibid., 239.
9. Ibid., 188.
10. Ibid., 213 and 224–25.
11. Ibid., 235.
12. Ibid., 232.
13. Ibid., 233.
14. Ibid., 209.
15. Ibid., 236.
16. Among the most interesting of Gartner's observations is that the Sky Chart "was painted in multiple sittings and perhaps over long periods of time ... and that each individual act of production was meaningful" (ibid., 188). Indeed, Gartner believes "that the Skidi Star Chart at the Field Museum," which is reliably dated to sometime before 1867, "is merely the latest version of an ancient map" (ibid., 192).

17. William Wordsworth, *The Prelude*, Book 3, 63–64; *William Wordsworth: The Prelude, 1799, 1805, 1850*..., ed. Jonathan Wordsworth, M. H. Abrams, and Stephen Gill (New York: W. W. Norton, 1979), 95.

18. "The American Scholar," *Ralph Waldo Emerson: Essays and Lectures*, ed. Joel Porte (New York: Library of America, 1983),

19. Wallace Stevens, "Poetry is the scholar's art": "Adagia," in *Collected Poetry and Prose* (New York: Library of America, 1997), 906; "major man": "Notes toward a Supreme Fiction" ("It Must Be Abstract," VIII), ibid., 334. See Laura Riding, *Poems: A Joking Word* (London: Cape, 1930), and *The Telling* (New York: Harper & Row, 1973), 66 ("the common risks of language, where failure stalks in every word"). Her major philological work is *Rational Meaning: A New Foundation for the Definition of Words* (with Schuyler B. Jackson), ed. William Harmon and with an afterword by Charles Bernstein (Charlottesville: University Press of Virginia,1997), but a large corpus of her unpublished work on language is being collected and published in posthumous editions.

20. Samuel Beckett, *Worstward, Ho* [1983], in *Poems—Short Fiction—Criticism* (New York: Grove Press, 2006), 4:471.

CHAPTER ONE

1. See Paul Guyer, *Kant and the Experience of Freedom: Essays on Aesthetics and Morality* (Cambridge: Cambridge University Press, 1993); and Brian Donahue, "An Examination of Moral Action and Aesthetic Judgement in Kant's Critical Philosophy," *Janus Head* 1, no. 3 (1999), at http://www.janushead.org/JHSpg99/donohue.cfm. On axiology, see Nicholas Rescer, *Value Matters: Studies in Axiology* (Frankfurt: Ontos Verlag, 2005). Kenneth Burke, *A Grammar of Motives* (New York: Prentice-Hall, 1945), and Burke's various associated writings offer a distinctively American approach to an axiology of literary and artistic discourse.

2. Here I am recalling, and slightly revising, the argument first set down in my *Social Values and Poetic Acts: The Historical Judgment of Literary Work* (Cambridge, MA: Harvard University Press, 1988); see preface, viii.

3. Hugh Amory, "The Trout and the Milk: An Ethnobibliographical Talk," *Harvard Library Bulletin*, n.s., 7, no. 1 (1996): 50–65; William Charvat, *The Profession of Authorship in America, 1800–1870: The Papers of William Charvat*, ed. Matthew J. Bruccoli, foreword by Howard Mumford Jones (Columbus: Ohio State University Press, 1968); Boeckh, *Enzyklopädie und Methodologie*, 11; and D. F. McKenzie, *Bibliography and the Sociology of Texts*, The Panizzi Lectures, 1985 (London: British Library, 1986). See also the introduction to my *A New Republic of Letters: Memory and Scholarship in the Age of Digital Reproduction* (Cambridge, MA: Harvard University Press, 2014), esp. 2–8 and chap. 3 ("Memory, History, Philology").

4. Quentin Skinner, "Motives, Intentions, and the Interpretations of Texts," reprinted from *New Literary History* in *Meaning and Context: Quentin Skinner and His Critics*, ed. James Tully (Oxford and New York: Oxford University Press, 1988), 76.

5. Quentin Skinner, "Introduction: Seeing Things Their Way," in *Visions of Politics: Regarding Method* (Cambridge: Cambridge University Press, 2002), 1:3.

6. James Sidbury and Jorge Cañizares-Esguerra, "Mapping Ethnogenesis in the Early Modern Atlantic," *William and Mary Quarterly* 68, no. 2 (2011): 182.

7. Roger Shattuck, introduction to Alfred Jarry, *Exploits and Opinions of Dr. Faustroll, Pataphysician*, trans. Simon Watson Taylor (Boston: Exact Change, 1996), xi.

8. The Society was created under the auspices of University of Virginia's Rare Book School, founded by Terry Belanger and since carried forward by Michael Suarez.

9. Matt Cohen, *The Networked Wilderness: Communicating in Early New England* (Minneapolis: University of Minnesota Press, 2010); Matt Cohen and Jeffrey Glover, eds., *Colonial Mediascapes: Sensory Worlds of the Early Americas* (Lincoln: University of Nebraska Press, 2014); and Lisa Brooks, *The Common Pot: The Recovery of Native Space in the Northeast* (Minneapolis: University of Minnesota Press, 2008). The scholarship regularly printed in the journal *Early American Literature* has been especially influential in restoring the authority of philological methods, for which Edward W. Said pleaded toward the end of his life. See Said, "The Return to Philology," in *Humanism and Democratic Criticism* (New York: Columbia University Press, 2004), 57–84, and my *A New Republic of Letters*.

10. Marta Werner, *Writing in Time: Emily Dickinson's Master Hours* (Amherst, MA: Amherst University Press, 2021), is perhaps the most brilliant of Werner's brilliant series of books. For Cordell's *Viral Texts Project* see https://viraltexts.org.

11. Michael Ditmore, "What Do We Know about the New England Puritans, and When Did We Know It? Twenty-first Century Reconsiderations of William Bradford and John Winthrop," in *American Literature and the New Puritan Studies*, ed. Bryce Traister (Cambridge: Cambridge University Press, 2017), chap. 12. The volume as a whole gives a useful picture of the state of Puritan studies to date, though for my purposes the essay by Abram C. Van Engen and Traister's introduction and afterword have been most important.

12. See Alexander X. Byrd, "Eboe, Country, Nation, and Gustavus Vassa's *Interesting Narrative*," *William and Mary Quarterly* 63, no. 1 (2006): 123–48; and Vincent Carretta, "Olaudah Equiano or Gustavus Vassa? New Light on an Eighteenth-Century Question of Identity," *Slavery and Abolition* 20, no. 3 (1999): 96–105.

13. See chap. 10.

14. Thomas McElwain, "'Then I Thought I Must Kill Too': Logan's Lament; A 'Mingo' Perspective," in *Native American Speakers of the Eastern Woodlands: Selected Speeches and Critical Analyses*, ed. Barbara Mann (Westport, CT: Greenwood Press, 2001), 107–21.

15. In a fundamental sense, this double-phased American Enlightenment perfectly illustrates what Theodor W. Adorno and Max Horkheimer meant by the *dialectic* of Enlightenment: that under certain stressed social conditions, myth and instrumental reason fall into a reciprocal relation. The core thesis of their *Dialectic of Enlightenment* (1944) is that "myth [= religion] is already enlightenment, and enlightenment [= instrumental reason] reverts to mythology" (Adorno and Horkheimer, *Dialectic of Enlightenment: Philosophical Fragments*, ed. Gunzelin Schmid Noerr, trans. Edwund Jephcott [Stanford, CA: Stanford University Press, 2002], xviii).

16. Charles Bernstein, "The Truth in Pudding," in *Recalculating* (Chicago: University of Chicago Press, 2013), 4.

17. See the discussion in chap. 4 of Mather's *Magnalia*.

CHAPTER TWO

1. John Lardas Modern, *Secularism in Antebellum America* (Chicago: University of Chicago Press, 2011), 7.

2. Ibid., 282–83.

3. The study of Indian treaties should begin with the following two works: *Indian*

Treaties Printed by Benjamin Franklin, 1736–1762, with an introduction by Carl Van Doren and historical and bibliographical notes by Julian P. Boyd (Philadelphia: Historical Society of Pennsylvania, 1938), and Francis Jennings, William N. Fenton, Mary A. Druke, and David R. Miller, eds., *The History and Culture of Iroquois Diplomacy: An Interdisciplinary Guide to the Treaties of the Six Nations and Their League*, new ed. (Syracuse, NY: Syracuse University Press, 1995), cited hereafter as *Iroquois Diplomacy*, with the relevant page number. Citations of the Franklin folios will be to *Indian Treaties*, using a double pagination system, the first number referring to the page in the individual folio, the second to the page number in the edition with notes by Boyd. From time to time reference will also be made to the useful, modernized transcriptions in Susan Kalter, *Benjamin Franklin, Pennsylvania, and the First Indian Nations: The Treaties of 1736–1762* (Urbana: University of Illinois Press, 2006). For an incisive general introduction to this aspect of Franklin's work, see James N. Green and Peter Stallybrass, *Benjamin Franklin, Writer and Printer* (Philadelphia: Oak Knoll Press, and London: British Library, 2006). Other important works on the Indian treaties are, in chronological order: Lawrence C. Wroth, "The Indian Treaty as Literature," *Yale Review* 17 (1928): 749–66; Constance Rourke, *The Roots of American Culture and Other Essays*, ed. and with a preface by Van Wyck Brooks (New York: Harcourt, Brace, 1942), 60–75; A. M. Drummond and Richard Moody, "Indian Treaties: The First American Dramas," *Quarterly Journal of Speech* 39 (1953): 15–24; Francis Jennings, *The Ambiguous Iroquois Empire: The Covenant Chain Confederation of Indian Tribes with English Colonies from Its Beginnings to the Lancaster Treaty of 1744* (New York: W. W. Norton, 1984); Colin G. Calloway, *Dawnland Encounters: Indians and Europeans in Northern New England* (Hanover, NH: University Press of New England, 1991); Robert A. Williams, Jr., *Linking Arms Together: American Indian Treaty Visions of Law and Peace, 1600–1800* (Oxford and New York: Oxford University Press, 1997); James H. Merrell, "A Sort of Confusion: Treaties," in *Into the American Woods: Negotiators on the Pennsylvania Frontier* (New York: W. W. Norton, 1999), 253–301; Bruce E. Johansen, ed., *Enduring Legacies: Native American Treaties and Contemporary Controversies*, foreword by Vine Deloria Jr. (Westport, CT: Praeger, 2004); Colin G. Calloway, *Pen and Ink Witchcraft: Treaties and Treaty Making in Native American History* (Oxford and New York: Oxford University Press, 2013), 12–48, and 96–120; Jeffrey Glover, *Paper Sovereigns: Anglo-Native Treaties and the Law of Nations, 1604–1664* (Philadelphia: University of Pennsylvania Press, 2014); Anthony F. C. Wallace and Timothy Powell, "How to Buy a Continent: The Protocols of Indian Treaties as Developed by Benjamin Franklin and Other Members of the American Philosophical Society" (2015), Departmental Papers (Religious Studies), 15, http://repository.upenn.edu/rs_papers/15; Lisa Brooks, *Our Beloved Kin: A New History of King Philip's War* (New Haven, CT: Yale University Press, 2018); and Matthew J. Hill and Jon Parmenter, *The Fort Stanwix Treaties: An Ethnohistory of Iroquois Diplomacy and Dispossession* (Lowell, MA: Northeast Region Ethnography Program, National Park Service, 2018).

4. Marshall Sahlins, *Islands of History* (Chicago: University of Chicago Press, 1985).

5. Karl Marx, *The Eighteenth Brumaire of Louis Bonaparte* (1852; New York: International, 1994), 13.

6. One of the best studies of this idea is Abram C. Van Engen, *City on a Hill: A History of American Exceptionalism* (New Haven, CT: Yale University Press, 2020). His book is not concerned, however, with the exceptional event that is my primary interest: the encounter between neolithic and early modern civilizations under conditions that were in great measure determined by the former.

7. Rourke, *The Roots of American Culture*, 63.

8. Jon Parmenter, "The Meaning of *Kaswentha* and the Two Row Wampum Belt in Haudenosaunee (Iroquois) History: Can Indigenous Oral Tradition Be Reconciled with the Documentary Record?," in "Early Iroquoian-European Contacts: The Kaswentha Tradition, the Two Row Wampum Belt, and the Tawagonshi Document," special issue, *Journal of Early American History* 3, no. 1 (2013): 82–109, at 83.

9. Marshall Sahlins, *Stone Age Economics* (Chicago: Aldine-Atherton, 1972), 171–82. And see Thomas Hobbes, *Leviathan*, book 1, chap. 14: "The first and fundamental law of Nature, which is, 'to seek peace, and follow it.' The second, the sum of the right of Nature, which is, 'by all means we can, to defend ourselves.' From this fundamental law of Nature, by which men are commanded to endeavour peace, is derived this second law, 'that a man be willing, when others are so too, as far-forth as for peace and defence of himself he shall think it necessary, to lay down this right to all things, and be contented with so much liberty against other men as he would allow other men against himself.' For as long as every man holdeth this right of doing anything he liketh, so long are all men in the condition of war. But if other men will not lay down their right as well as he, then there is no reason for any one to divest himself of his; for that were to expose himself to prey, which no man is bound to, rather than to dispose himself to peace."

10. Ibid., 171.

11. Ibid., 177.

12. Ibid.

13. Ibid., 182.

14. Helen Hunt Jackson, *A Century of Dishonor* (New York: Harper & Bros., 1881).

15. Two excellent general treatments of the tensions and conflicts are Richard White, *The Middle Ground: Indians, Empires, and Republics in the Great Lakes Region, 1650–1815* (Cambridge: Cambridge University Press, 1991); and Alan Taylor, *The Divided Ground: Indians, Settlers, and the Northern Borderland of the American Revolution* (New York: Random House, 2006).

16. Frederick Jackson Turner, *The Frontier in American History* (New York: Henry Holt, 1921), esp. chap. 1, "The Significance of the Frontier in American History"; and Richard Slotkin, *Regeneration through Violence: The Mythology of the American Frontier, 1600–1860* (Middletown, CT: Wesleyan University Press, 1973).

17. This study is much in debt to the exponential growth since the 1960s of the literature on the native context of English colonial settlement. The materials that have been most important for my argument are cited throughout.

18. Kathleen Donegan, *Seasons of Misery: Catastrophe and Colonial Settlement in Early America* (Philadelphia: University of Pennsylvania Press, 2013), shines an impressively severe light on the early English explorers and settlers—more severe than the view I take in this book. While many incidents and players involved seem to me to deserve her stern commentary, I am moved by the fatal inheritances that the British and other Europeans labored under—one that, in my view, we have scarcely escaped. I deeply admire Donegan's refusal of the pieties that still pervade colonial studies, often in subtle ways.

CHAPTER THREE

1. The validity of the document was closely questioned in Charles Gehring, William Starna, and William N. Fenton, "The Tawagonshi Treaty of 1613: The Final Chapter,"

New York History 68, no. 4 (1987): 373–93. But whatever the status of the document, the treaty event (or events) seems certain: see Jon Parmenter, *Edge of the Woods: Iroquoia, 1534–1701* (Lansing: Michigan State University Press, 2010), 22–24, and, for a more extensive discussion, Parmenter, "The Meaning of *Kaswentha*." See also Robert Venables, "An Analysis of the 1613 Tawagonshi Treaty" (2012), published online in four parts (https://encyclopediavirginia.org/entries/treaty-ending-the-third-anglo-powhatan-war-1646/), an extensive article in which the author gives a useful presentation of the different texts, in Dutch as well as in English translation; and "Early Iroquoian-European Contacts: The Kaswentha Tradition, the Two Row Wampum Belt, and the Tawagonshi Document," special issue, *Early American History* (2013).

2. Gehring, Starna, and Fenton, "The Tawagonshi Treaty of 1613," 385.

3. Though Venables wrote "1622 in Massachusetts," he is referring to the 1621 treaty with the Plymouth colony; Venables, "An Analysis of the 1613 Tawagonshi Treaty."

4. William Fenton, "The Earliest Recorded Description: The Mohawk Treaty with New France at Three Rivers—Rituals of Peace Making," in *Iroquois Diplomacy*, 127–53.

5. Ibid., 137–44.

6. Ibid., 143.

7. Ibid., 144–49.

8. Ibid., 146.

9. In this connection see Richard Cullen Rath, "Hearing Wampum: The Senses, Mediation, and Limits of Analogy," in *Colonial Mediascapes: Sensory Worlds of the Early Americas*, ed. Matt Cohen and Jeffrey Glover (Lincoln: University of Nebraska Press, 2014), 290–321, esp. 302–4. Other key scholarly works that investigate these crucial matters are Hilary E. Wyss, "Land and Literacy: The Textualities of Native Studies," *American Literary History* 22, no. 2 (2010): 271–79; Andrew Newman, *On Records: Delaware Indians, Colonists, and the Media of History and Memory* (Lincoln: University of Nebraska Press, 2012); Sarah Rivett, *Unscripted America: Indigenous Languages and the Origins of a Literary Nation* (Oxford and New York: Oxford University Press, 2017); and Angela Calcaterra, *Literary Indians: Aesthetics and Encounter in American Literature to 1920* (Chapel Hill: University of North Carolina Press, 2018).

10. Fenton, "The Earliest Recorded Description," 149–53.

11. Ibid., 150.

12. Ibid., 151.

13. Unless otherwise noted, my citation text for Winthrop's journal throughout this book is John Winthrop, *The Journal of John Winthrop, 1630–1649*, ed. James Savage, Richard S. Dunn, and Laetitia Yeandle (Cambridge, MA: Harvard University Press, 1996). Further citations of this work will be abbreviated as *J*, followed by the relevant page number.

14. Other entries to note are *J*, 191–92, 280, 341, 409, and 462.

15. Jon Parmenter, "'L'Arbre de Paix': Eighteenth-Century Franco-Iroquois Relations," *French Colonial History* 4 (2003): 65.

16. Philip L. Barbour, ed., *The Complete Works of Captain John Smith*, 3 vols. (Chapel Hill: University of North Carolina Press, 1986), 1:151; see also Alfred A. Cave, *The Pequot War* (Amherst: University of Massachusetts Press, 1996), 54–73.

17. Cave, *The Pequot War*, 57.

18. For the ways in which "deteriorating exchange-based relations" undermined the settlement efforts at Ajacan, Roanoke, and Jamestown, see Seth Mallios, *The Deadly Politics of Giving: Exchange and Violence in Ajacan, Roanoke, and Jamestown* (Tuscaloosa:

University of Alabama Press, 2006), 23. But as the author shows (21, 61, 69, and 101–3), the "exchange-based relations" were weak and uncertain from the outset. For good extended treatments of the conflicted situation in Virginia, see Jean B. Russo and J. Elliott Russo, *Planting an Empire: The Early Chesapeake in North America* (Baltimore, MD: Johns Hopkins University Press, 2012), esp. chaps. 1 and 2; and Frederick W. Gleach, *Powhatan's World and Colonial Virginia* (Lincoln: University of Nebraska Press, 1997), chap. 2.

19. Barbour, *The Complete Works of Captain John Smith*, 301.

20. Ibid., 299 and 298.

21. Ibid., 300.

22. See W. Stitt Robinson, ed., *Virginia Treaties, 1607–1722*, vol. 4 of *Early American Indian Documents: Treaties and Laws, 1607–1789* (Washington, DC: University Publications of America, 1979–),8–9 and 28; see also Mallios, *The Deadly Politics of Giving*, 108–10. Following previous anthropological studies, Mallios argues that the famous story of Smith and Pocahontas represents an "extended adoption ritual" (88) that temporarily helped to mitigate hostilities between natives and settlers.

23. Barbour, *The Complete Works of Captain John Smith*, 298. For a shrewd discussion of these passages in Smith's *Generall Historie*, see John G. Read, *New World, Known World: Shaping History in Early Anglo-American Writing* (Columbia: University of Missouri Press, 2005), 30–31. Read's entire treatment of Smith's book in his first chapter is one of the best we have. He teases out the various ways the *Generall Historie* "speaks not with one voice but with many voices" (41).

24. For the treaty text see *The Statutes at Large; Being a Collection of All the Laws of Virginia from the First Session of the Legislature in the Year 1619*, ed. William Waller Hening (New York: R. & W. & G. Bartow, 1814), 1:323–26, https://encyclopediavirginia.org/entries/treaty-ending-the-third-anglo-powhatan-war-1646/.

25. No text of the 1634 Pequot treaty survives, though Winthrop discusses it in his November 1634 entry (J, 133–35). Winthrop wrote up a text of the 1636 treaty with the Narragansetts in his October 1636 entry (J, 191–92).

26. See Cave, *The Pequot War*, 104–13.

27. See the text at the Indian Papers Project, https://findit.library.yale.edu/yipp. The different colonial texts of the treaty are well addressed in Daragh Grant, "The Treaty of Hartford (1638): Reconsidering Jurisdiction in Southern New England," *William and Mary Quarterly*, 3rd ser., 72, no. 3 (2015): 461–98.

28. The text of the treaty is reprinted in William Bradford, *Of Plymouth Plantation, 1620–1647*, ed. Samuel Eliot Morison (New York: Alfred A. Knopf, 1949), 437–40.

29. The New England colonies' approach to treaty-making with the Indians was not that different from its approach to the often extreme religious divisions that all the colonies, but especially the dominant Massachusetts Bay Colony, had to negotiate. Like the American nations, the Puritan emigrants came in many flavors. The famous "Middle Way" adopted by Massachusetts worked hard to accommodate the differences its own commitments accepted and even fostered, but there were limits to what it would permit as actual social and religious practice.

30. Standard treatments of these events are Jennings, *The Ambiguous Iroquois Empire*, and *Iroquois Diplomacy*. See also Daniel K. Richter and James H. Merrell, eds., *Beyond the Covenant Chain: The Iroquois and Their Neighbors in Indian North America, 1600–1800* (Syracuse, NY: Syracuse University Press, 1985).

31. The legend of the amity between William Penn and Tamenend (aka Tammany

or Tamenund) and the land cessions is the focus of Benjamin West's famous painting *Treaty with the Indians* (1771–72). That the relations between the two were more difficult is now clear, however. In 1684, three years after Tamenend gifted lands to Penn, the sachem took a very different line, and Penn, then back in England, wrote to his surveyor that Tamenend should be handled with severity. See Nicholas Varga, "America's Patron Saint: Tammany," *Journal of American Culture* 10, no. 4 (1987): 45–51 ("In 1685 after Penn returned to England, Tammany apparently regretted the cession of territory and warned the new settlers to vacate the land. Some reportedly took his threats seriously and moved to New Jersey. To still the panic, Penn ordered measures taken to bring Tammany to order"). Varga cites C. A. Weslager, *The Delaware Indians: A History* (New Brunswick, NJ: Rutgers University Press, 1972), 169; and *William Penn's Own Account of the Lenni Lenape or Delaware Indians*, ed. Albert Cook Myers (Moylan, PA: A. C. Myers, 1937), 24–25 and 83–91.

32. Lawrence H. Leder, ed., *The Livingston Indian Records, 1666–1723* (Gettysburg, PA: Pennsylvania Historical Association, 1956).

33. The Eastern Gate of Iroquoia is the Hudson Valley and the Lake Champlain/Lake George watershed to the north.

34. Leder, *The Livingston Indian Records*, 29.

35. Ibid., 29–49.

36. Ibid., 43.

37. Ibid., 45–46.

38. Ibid., 46.

39. This is Bradford's spelling. Hereafter I will use the modernized form *Of Plymouth Plantation* unless I am quoting from a document.

40. "By 1753 the [Canajoharie] Mohawks considered the Covenant Chain broken.... The harsh realities of a changing frontier economy had pushed the Mohawks into a corner, eroding their subsistence and threatening their land.... New Yorkers had also defaulted in their diplomacy, failing to observe ceremonies" (Timothy J. Shannon, *Indians and Colonists at the Crossroads of Empire: The Albany Congress of 1754* [Ithaca, NY: Cornell University Press, 2000], 48–50). See also John C. Newbold, *The Albany Congress and the Plan of Union of 1754* (New York: Vantage, 1955).

41. The Indians were arrested for trespassing on a land tract that Myles Standish declared to be his property: see *The Plymouth County Directory and Historical Register* (Middleboro, MA: Stillman B. Pratt, 1867), 38.

42. See also Brooks, *Our Beloved Kin*, 29; Bruce Elliott Johansen, *Encyclopedia of Native American Economic History* (Westport, CT: Greenwood Press, 1999), 211–12; and William Marder, *Indians in the Americas* (San Diego: The Book Tree, 2005), 101–10. For a more general perspective on this important matter, see William Cronon, *Changes in the Land: Indians, Colonists, and the Ecology of New England* (New York: Hill and Wang, 1983); Frank Waters, *Brave Are My People* (Santa Fe, NM: Clear Light, 1993); and George S. Snyderman, "Concepts of Land Ownership among the Iroquois and Their Neighbors," in *Symposium on Local Diversity in Iroquois Culture*, ed. William N. Fenton, Bureau of American Ethnology Bulletin 149 (Washington, DC: U.S. Government Printing Office, 1951), 15–34. See also interchap. 1, nn. 10 and 23.

43. See Anthony F. C. Wallace and Timothy Powell, "How to Buy a Continent: The Protocols of Indian Treaties as Developed by Benjamin Franklin and Other Members of the American Philosophical Society," *Proceedings of the American Philosophical Society* 159, no. 3 (September 2015): 251–81. In their otherwise excellent introduction to colo-

nial treaty-making (and beyond), the authors fail to maintain the crucial distinction between treaty-making and treaty records—largely, I believe, because their account is so heavily influenced by Benjamin Franklin's ideas and his treaty folios. See also interchaps. 1 and 2 passim.

44. A detailed account of the event is given in Saliha Belmessous, "Wabanaki versus French and English Claims in North America, c. 1715," in *Native Claims: Indigenous Law against Empire, 1500–1920*, ed. Saliha Belmessous (Oxford and New York: Oxford University Press, 2012), 107–28.

45. That they sent a letter and not a petition was itself a declaration of their sovereignty, as Belmessous observes. Furthermore, that it was sent in four languages—French, Wabanaki, Latin, and English—was "meant to make clear that, despite earlier English claims that the Jesuits controlled their speeches, they were the true authors of their letter" (ibid., 115).

46. Ibid., 116. The French text reads: "isse vivre in paix aveq mois de me prendre ma terre malgre mois ma terre que jais recue du Dieu seul, ma terre de lacquelle aucun Roi in aucun puissance estranger na peut in ne peut disposer malgre mois." The English, however, reads thus, dropping the key phrase "que jais recue du Dieu seul": "Is it to live in peace with me to take away my land? Which no King nor strange power has been able, nor is able to dispose of against my will" (*Colonial Office Records* 5/869, fols. 106 and 108). As usual, the native claim is double: that the land is inalienable, and that the Wabanaki have the authority from God to make determinations about its disposition—to allow the English to use it or not.

47. John G. Reid, *Essays on Northeastern North America, Seventeenth and Eighteenth Centuries* (Toronto: University of Toronto Press), 155.

48. See Newbold, *The Albany Congress*, and Shannon, *Indians and Colonists at the Crossroads of Empire*. I quote from Frederick Jackson Turner, "The Significance of the Frontier in American History" (1894), reprinted in Frederick Jackson Turner, *Frontier and Section: Selected Essays of Frederick Jackson Turner*, ed. and with an introduction by Ray Billington (Englewood Cliffs, NJ: Prentice-Hall, 1961), 37–62, at 43 and 38.

49. Turner, *Frontier and Section*, 46.

50. Turner's "frontier" is the source of all orthodox "tradition[s] of interpretation of American exceptionalism": that is, "a zone of free land ... where ... a sociocultural furnace forged a new Americanism embodying democracy, individualism, pragmatism, and a healthy nationalism." See Brook Thomas, "Turner's Frontier Thesis as a Narrative of Reconstruction," in *Centuries' Ends, Narrative Means*, ed. Robert Newman (Stanford, CA: Stanford University Press, 1996), 117–37, at 118.

51. Karl Polanyi, *The Great Transformation* (New York: Farrar & Rinehart, 1944).

52. John Grenier, *The First Way of War: American War Making on the Frontier, 1607–1814* (Cambridge and New York: Cambridge University Press, 2005); and Nicholas P. Canny, "The Ideology of English Colonization: From Ireland to America," *William and Mary Quarterly*, 3rd ser., 30 (1973): 575–98.

53. Letter to Major General John Sullivan, May 31, 1779. See Barbara Alice Mann, *George Washington's War on Native America* (Westport, CT: Praeger, 2005), 51–110. Mann's study examines the general policy of "Total War" against the eastern tribes after 1775. For Washington's letter see *Founders Online*, https://founders.archives.gov.

54. See my discussion of the title page of *The Pioneers* in *A New Republic of Letters*, chap. 9, and my earlier essay "Fenimore Cooper's Anti-aesthetic and the Representation of Conflicted History," *Modern Language Quarterly* 73, no. 2 (2012): 123–56.

55. "Edgar Poe's Significance," *Specimen Days*, January 1, 1880 (citing from *The Walt Whitman Archive*, https://whitmanarchive.org/published/other/CompleteProse.html #leaf081v1).

56. See J. Gerald Kennedy, *Strange Nation: Literary Nationalism and Cultural Conflict in the Age of Poe* (Oxford and New York: Oxford University Press, 2016).

57. Dickinson was reflecting on the tensions that were fracturing the Whig party as it was about to open its convention in June 1852. See *Letters of Emily Dickinson*, ed. Thomas H. Johnson and Theodora Ward (Cambridge, MA: Harvard University Press, 1958), 1:211–12. See as well Betsy Erkkila's comprehensive assessment of Dickinson's social and political views in "Dickinson and the Art of Politics," in *A Historical Guide to Emily Dickinson*, ed. Vivian R. Pollack (Oxford and New York: Oxford University Press, 2004), 133–74.

PART I PROLOGUE

1. Isaac Ambrose, *Media: The Middle Things in relation to the first and last things* (Glasgow: Printed for Archibald Ingram [etc.], 1637).

2. Ibid., 281.

3. Andrew Delbanco, *The Puritan Ordeal* (Cambridge, MA: Harvard University Press, 1989).

4. I quote, respectively, ibid., 72; and Sacvan Bercovitch, "New England Epic: Cotton Mather's *Magnalia Christi Americana*," *ELH* 33, no. 3 (1966): 337.

5. Arnold's touchstones were the pivot of his essay "The Study of Poetry," first published as the introduction to T. H. Ward's anthology *The English Poets* (London: Macmillan, 1880); see also "The Function of Criticism at the Present Time," the lead piece in Matthew Arnold, *Essays in Criticism*, 1st ser. (London: Macmillan, 1865), for his famous critical dictum "to see the object as in itself it really is." Walter Benjamin's apothegm comes in the seventh of his "Theses on the Philosophy of History," written in 1940.

6. Delbanco, *Puritan Ordeal*, 74.

7. Ambrose, *Media*, 11.

8. There is a large body of literature on the topic of the city on a hill. An exceptionally fine example is Engen, *City on a Hill*. See also this volume, chap. 10 and notes.

9. Ambrose, *Media*, 15.

CHAPTER FOUR

1. In *Mourt's Relation*, where the diary is printed, it is headed "A Relation or Journall of the Proceedings of the Plantation settled at Plimoth in New England"; Winslow's letter is headed "A Journey to *Packanokik*, the habitation of the Great King Massasoyt. As also our message, the answere and intertainment wee had of Him." These headings were editorially added when the manuscript documents were printed. *Mourt's Relation* is in fact the editorial creation of George Morton, working in concert with Robert Cushman, the author of the last of the texts printed in the 1622 book: "Reasons and Considerations touching the lawfulness of removing out of England unto the parts of America." Morton and Cushman were agents for the pilgrims who were managing their financial affairs with the company of colonial investors and the London Council of New England, which issued patents for settling New World plantations. *Mourt's Relation* was published in London in 1622 by John

Bellamie with an elaborately historiated title page that also bore an "Argument" and summary of the book's contents. *Mourt's Relation*, where Bradford's daybook/diary was first printed in 1622, was not reprinted in its entirety until Alexander Young's 1841 edition (from a copy discovered in the Harvard library). Bradford's manuscript is housed in the State Library of Massachusetts, and a facsimile is available online: https://www.mass.gov/info-details/bradfords-manuscript-of-plimoth-plantation. My reference text is the typescript facsimile of Bradford's manuscript published for the Commonwealth of Massachusetts (Boston: Wright & Potter, 1898). Cited henceforth in text and notes as *OPP*, it is available online, prepared by Ted Hildebrand, at http://faculty.gordon.edu/hu/bi/ted_hildebrandt/nereligioushistory/bradford-plimoth/bradford-plymouthplantation.pdf. My reference text for Bradford's journal and daybook is *Mourt's Relation or Journal of the Plantation at Plymouth*, with an introduction and notes by Henry Martyn Dexter (Boston: J. K. Wiggin, 1865), available online from the Hathi Trust; hereafter cited in text and notes as *MRJPP* with the page number. But I have followed Morison's modernized spelling for the reader's convenience (see chap. 3, n. 28: Bradford, *Of Plymouth Plantation*, ed. Morison).

2. Commenting on these new settlers, Bradford wrote that many were "very useful persons and became good members to the body; and some were the wives and children of such as were here already. And some were so bad as they were fain to be at charge to send them home again the next year" (*OPP*, 171).

3. The *Of Plymouth Plantation* manuscript, which disappeared for two centuries, was discovered in 1855 and first privately printed in Boston in 1856, edited by Charles Deane (available online from the Hathi Trust).

4. The condolence ceremony was a key feature of *kaswentha* treaty-making. Although *kaswentha* was created by the Iroquois League, probably in the fifteenth century, it greatly influenced Indian treaty-making across the entire eastern littoral. The eastern Algonquian tribes, including the Wampanoag tribes, adopted the Iroquois *kaswentha* ceremonials: see Frank Speck, "The Functions of Wampum Among the Eastern Algonkian," *American Anthropological Association Memoirs* 6 (1919): 3–71, and Parmenter, "The Meaning of Kaswentha."

5. As Dexter indicates in his notes (*MRJPP*, 112 n.), in the original diary there seems to be some confusion about the dates of the trip to Pokanoket and the search for John Billington, which Dexter reasonably surmises happened at the end of July or early in August. In any case, the search mission came after the visit to Pokanoket.

6. Betty Booth Donohue, *Bradford's Indian Book: Being the True Roote and Rise of American Letters as Revealed by the Native Text Embedded in "Of Plimoth Plantation"* (Gainesville: University Press of Florida, 2011), 15–18.

7. Ibid., 17.

8. Young's *Of Plimouth Plantation* edition footnotes the treaty with Jeremy Belknap's eighteenth-century commentary: "This treaty, the work of one day, being honestly intended on both sides, was kept with fidelity as long as Massasoit lived, but was afterwards, in 1675, broken by Philip, his successor" (Young, 193–94). Needless to say, this is far from an accurate gloss. The treaty was not "the work of one day" and it was not "kept with fidelity" by the colonials up to 1675.

9. Cohen, *The Networked Wilderness*, 4.

10. See *The Plymouth County Directory*, 38.

11. For a good account of the main lines of interpretation, see Walter P. Wenska, "Bradford's Two Histories: Pattern and Paradigm in *Of Plymouth Plantation*," *Early*

American Literature 13, no. 2 (1978): 151–64. See also Jesper Rosenmeier, "'With my owne eyes': William Bradford's *Of Plymouth Plantation*," in *The American Puritan Imagination: Essays in Revaluation*, ed. Sacvan Bercovitch (London: Cambridge University Press, 1974), 77–106; as a tale of "loss and failure," 105–6. Douglas Anderson, *William Bradford's Books: "Of Plimmoth Plantation" and the Printed Word* (Baltimore, MD: Johns Hopkins University Press, 2003), is a useful study of Bradford's work and its possible literary models.

12. Commenting on these new settlers, Bradford wrote that many were "very useful persons and became good members to the body; and some were the wives and children of such as were here already. And some were so bad as they were fain to be at charge to send them home again the next year" (*OPP*, 171).

13. The quotation is from Francis Jennings, *The Invasion of America: Indians, Colonialism, and the Cant of Conquest* (New York: Norton, 1976), 189; for detailed explication of the parts played in the destruction of the Pequots by the Narragansetts and the Massachusetts Bay Colony, see Cave, *The Pequot War*, 104–13.

14. It's probable that Winthrop himself was aware that the Narragansetts were not candid or honest in reporting the treachery of the Pequots. But Winthrop's fear of regional violence and his annoyance at the "insolence" of the Pequots seem to have moved him to choose sides.

15. I quote Charles Deane's description from the introduction to his edition of William Bradford, *Dialogue . . . concerning the Church and the Government Thereof* (Boston: John Wilson & Son, 1870), iv. The work was apparently written around 1652, and Deane later edited it for the Massachusetts Historical Society.

16. See this volume, chaps. 7 and 10, for more evidence of Phillips's authorship. It is a striking fact that the only positive evidence we have of Winthrop's authorship, universally accepted, is a title page composed many years after the sermon by someone who was plainly wrong about what he set down there.

17. See *J*, 672 and 677–80.

18. The Hebrew studies feeding that desire are also apparent throughout Bradford, *Dialogue . . . concerning the Church and the Government Thereof*. See Isadore S. Meyer, *The Hebrew Exercises of Governor William Bradford* (Plymouth, MA: Pilgrim Society, 1973), and Karen J. Goldstein, *A History of Jewish Plymouth* (Charleston, SC: History Press, 2013). The Hebrew Exercises are laid in as a kind of introduction to *Of Plymouth Plantation*.

19. Bradford scripted this text to mirror the page design, a technique often used to give a climactic signal of the end of a printed or manuscript book. See figs. 10 and 11.

20. For a good overview of Bradford's late views and their historical context, see M. L. Sargeant, "The 'Log of the Mayflower': Memory and Desire in the Winter of William Bradford" (2006), https://www.gordon.edu/page.cfm?iPageID=3196.

CHAPTER FIVE

1. Edmund S. Morgan, *The Puritan Dilemma: The Story of John Winthrop* (New York: Little, Brown, 1958), 31.

2. Ibid., 7.

3. Ibid.

4. John Winthrop, *The History of New England from 1630 to 1649 by John Winthrop*, ed. James Savage (Boston: Printed by Phelps & Farnham, 1825–26).

5. Lee Sweninger, *John Winthrop* (Boston: Twayne, 1990), 71. While my term "Journal/History" is useful in the present context, it would introduce other reading problems if it were set as the title for an edition.

6. Winthrop, *The History of New England*, ed. Savage, x.

7. After the Great Migration of the 1630s, the population of the Massachusetts Bay Colony grew to some twenty thousand. Plymouth remained small—somewhere between fifteen hundred and two thousand is the standard estimate.

8. As the religious struggle began to get seriously engaged in the late 1630s, the distinction took on greater prominence. See William Hooke, *New England's Tears for Old England's Fears* (London, 1641), and Anne Bradstreet, "A Dialogue between Old England and New" (1642).

9. It's surprising that presentations of the original charter to this day regularly drop the opening five paragraphs, where the franchise rights of all the chartered colonists are set forth, and where ultimate authority is vested in the king and his ministers, with secondary authority being deputed to the colonial authorities.

10. For a thorough presentation of the different allegiance oaths, especially the changes to the Massachusetts Bay Oath, see Charles Evans, *Oaths of Allegiance in Colonial New England* (Worcester, MA: American Antiquarian Society, 1922).

11. Ibid., 32.

12. Winthrop reports on each of these incidents in his "Journal/History": see *J*, 148, 177, 291–92, 332–33, and 624–79 passim, esp. 624–25, 648, 662, 677, and 679.

13. See J. D. Neff, "Roger Williams: Pious Puritan and Strict Separationist," *Journal of Church and State* 38, no. 3 (1996): 529–46; and Stephen Philips, "Roger Williams and the Two Tables of the Law," *Journal of Church and State* 38, no. 3 (1996): 547–69.

14. The "Little Speech on Liberty" is at *J*, 584–89; the other two documents are in *The Winthrop Papers*, vol. 4 (Boston: Massachusetts Historical Society, 1863–92), 380–92 and 468–88. For the most accurate readings, the reader should consult the Winthrop Papers Digital Edition, https://www.masshist.org/publications/winthrop/index.php/search.

15. Winthrop and the church magistrates insisted that "natural" (secular) "Libertye is incompatible & inconsistant with Authoritye" (*J*, 587). Winthrop termed it "Civill or foederall," by which he means—in our terms—the authority of the colony's religious leaders. The event, the so-called Hingham Trial, is laid out in *J*, 575–93; for further commentary see Robert Emmet Wall, Jr., *Massachusetts Bay: The Crucial Decade, 1640–1650* (New Haven, CT: Yale University Press, 1972), chap. 3.

16. Winthrop shared the Reformers' view that the immigrants should work to convert the natives from their allegiance to "the divell": see the 1629 colony's seal and the *Reasons to be Considered...* (see Massachusetts Historical Society, ed., *The Winthrop Papers* [Boston: The Society, 1929–31; henceforth cited as *The Winthrop Papers*, followed by the relevant volume and page number], 2:145), though the seal strongly emphasizes the natives' economic importance. The most comprehensive treatment of the widely held belief that Satan set up a kingdom in America is in the millenarian scholar Joseph Mede's (1586–1639) "Epistle XIII," posthumously published (see *The works of the pious and profoundly-learned Joseph Mede, B.D....* (London: Roger Norton for Richard Royster, 1672).

17. See Winthrop's entry for September 22, 1642, *J*, 414–16.

18. "Less than half of the Anglican Prayer Book leaves are nibbled, and then only at the tips of the lower right-hand corners" (*J*, 341 n.).

19. Satan "persuaded her ... to break the neck of her child, that she might free it from future misery" (J, 272).

20. It was not the first printed work, however. A press was established in 1639 by the locksmith Stephen Daye, the first works of which were *The Oath of a Freeman* and an almanac. No copies of either survive.

21. More worldly ministers than John Cotton criticized both the Bay Psalm Book's obscurities and the encouragement it gave to free-form singing. See Amy Morris, "The Art of Purifying: The Bay Psalm Book and Colonial Puritanism," *Early American Literature* 42, no. 1 (2007): 123.

22. John Cotton, *Singing of Psalmes a Gospel-Ordinance*... (London: Printed by M.S. for Hannah Allen [etc.], 1647), 56.

23. Ibid., 56.

24. Ibid., 60–61.

25. Zoltán Haraszti, *The Enigma of the Bay Psalm Book* (Chicago: University of Chicago Press, 1956), 55. This remains the standard introduction to the *Bay Psalm Book*. But see also Morris, "The Art of Purifying."

CHAPTER SIX

1. The two contemporary editions of Bradstreet's works are *The Tenth Muse Lately sprung up in America*... ("Printed at London for Stephen Bowtell at the signe of the / Bible Head-Alley, 1650") and *Several poems compiled with great variety of wit and learning*... ("Boston, printed by John Foster, 1678"). Both are available in good online editions: *The Tenth Muse* at https://quod.lib.umich.edu/e/eebo2/A77237.0001.001/1:13?rgn =div1;view=toc; and *Several Poems*... at https://quod.lib.umich.edu/e/eebo/A29149 .0001.001?view=toc. My texts are taken from the 1678 collection, though the citations indicate in which book the specific poem first appeared. A recent scholarly edition is available with apparatus and notes: Anne Bradstreet, *The Complete Works of Anne Bradstreet*, ed. Joseph R. McElrath Jr. and Allan B. Robb (Boston: Twayne, 1981). The standard teaching edition is Anne Bradstreet, *The Works of Anne Bradstreet*, ed. Jeannine Hensley (Cambridge, MA: Harvard University Press, 1967), though it is, as Margaret Olofson Thickstun has recently made clear, inadequate; see Thickstun, "Contextualizing Anne Bradstreet's Literary Remains: Why We Need a New Edition of the Poems," *Early American Literature* 52, no. 2 (2017): 389–422. A new edition by Thickstun is in press.

2. The phrase was attributed to Plato by an anonymous Hellenistic epigrammatist, after which it became a cultural commonplace. Plato called her "the lovely Sappho" in *Phaedrus* 235c. See Angela Gosetti-Murrayjohn, "Sappho as the Tenth Muse in Hellenistic Epigram," *Arethusa* 39, no. 1 (2006): 21–45.

3. Woodbridge took Bradstreet's manuscripts with him when he went to England in 1647, but the book was not published until 1650.

4. See her ironic reflections on what her brother-in-law had brought about ("The Author to her Book," in *Several Poems*, 236).

5. Bradstreet is working from a view of fame as ancient as Homer and as contemporary as Milton and beyond: e.g., "Fame is no plant that grows on mortal soil" ("Lycidas," 78); "Short is my date, but deathless my reknown" (Homer, *Iliad* 9.535, Pope translation). The wit of Bradstreet's argument means to free the idea of fame from, for example, this other ancient judgment: that "posthumous fame [is] altogether vanity" (Marcus Aurelius, *Meditations*).

6. Rosamond Rosenmeier, *Anne Bradstreet Revisited* (Boston: Twayne, 1991), 105. See also Rosamund [*sic*] R. Rosenmeier, "'Divine Translation': A Contribution to the Study of Anne Bradstreet's Method in the Marriage Poems," *Early American Literature* 12, no. 2 (1977): 121–35.

7. Bradstreet seems to have made a triple distinction among flesh, spirit, and soul. See her dialogue "The Flesh and the Spirit," where "Spirit" is represented struggling with the "Flesh" toward the poetic soul's *"fantastic"* world of the "Gates of Pearl" and the "Chrystal River."

8. In the "Salmanasser" section of "The Four Monarchies" (*The Tenth Muse; Several Poems*, 77) and, just below, in the discussion of "A Dialogue between Old *England* and New."

9. Ann Stanford, "Anne Bradstreet," in *Major Writers of Early American Literature*, ed. Everett Emerson (Madison: University of Wisconsin Press, 1976), 33. This volume comprises an influential collection of essays.

10. Though I will not elaborate the matter here, Bradstreet is working with a typological view even within those late tender, pained, and personal works. God the father, the bridegroom Christ, the bride of the Church, and the promise of a new life are all deftly mapped to her father, her husband, herself, and her children and grandchildren.

11. I am working out of Michael Ditmore, "Bliss Lost, Wisdom Gained: Contemplating Emblems and Enigmas in Anne Bradstreet's 'Contemplations,'" *Early American Literature* 42, no. 1 (2007): 31–72, in which fine essay the author usefully summarizes the history of recent commentary. He shows how the work is not "a seamlessly integrated and artistic 'whole'—a systematically unified, coherent, and symbolically coordinated literary expression" (33). As a meditative or devotional work, it is "discordant," and he explicates its "three" most prominent instances (33). I would add a fourth: the poem's stumbling transitions. But in my judgment, all of these are deliberated moves, and the poem's devotional "anomalies" (32) are essential to its rejection of normative structure. The text is in *Several Poems*, 221–29.

12. Ditmore, "Bliss Lost, Wisdom Gained," 37.

13. For that author, imagining a world elsewhere was specifically, characteristically American (Richard Poirier, *A World Elsewhere: The Place of Style in American Literature* [Oxford and New York: Oxford University Press, 1966]). Baudelaire's famous phrase, though taken from an English poet (Thomas Hood's "The Bridge of Sighs"), is itself a distinctly "American" reflection that was nourished by his study and admiration of Poe.

14. Bradstreet's dialogue is surely recalling William Hooke, *New England's Tears for Old England's Fears* (London, 1641). The "parliament" at the end of Bradstreet's's poem references the Long Parliament, which was pressing for massive church reform and had arrested Bishop Laud and would soon execute him. See Francis J. Bremer, *Building a New Jerusalem: John Davenport, a Puritan in Three Worlds* (New Haven, CT: Yale University Press, 2012), chap. 16.

15. Byron, *Childe Harold's Pilgrimage*, canto 4, stanza 125.

CHAPTER SEVEN

1. After the first edition of 1702, the complete work was printed only three times: first in 1820 (Hartford, CT: Silas Andrus, Roberts & Barr), from which printing two subsequent ones were made (1853 and 1855); then in 1972 (New York: Arno Press); and finally in 1978 in a facsimile of the 1702 edition (Ann Arbor, MI: University

Microfilms). There is also a severely abridged edition: Cotton Mather, *Magnalia Christi Americana, or The Ecclesiastical History of New England*, ed. and abridged Raymond J. Cunningham (New York: Frederick Ungar, 1970). The first two books were published in a good critical edition (see n. 9 of this chapter). None of these editions reproduces 1702's important foldout map of New England. For readers' convenience I cite here from the 1978 facsimile edition (hereafter cited in text and notes as *M* with the volume and page numbers), except when discussing the foldout map, when I cite the first (1702) edition.

2. Sacvan Bercovitch, "New England Epic: Cotton Mather's *Magnalia Christi Americana*," *ELH* 33, no. 3 (1966): 337–50.

3. The phrase became famous because of Ernest Lee Tuveson's three important studies of American history of ideas: *Millennium and Utopia: A Study in the Background of the Idea of Progress* (Berkeley and Los Angeles: University of California Press, 1949); *The Imagination as a Means of Grace: Locke and the Aesthetics of Romanticism* (Berkeley and Los Angeles: University of California Press, 1960); and *Redeemer Nation: The Idea of America's Millennial Role* (Chicago: University of Chicago Press, 1968).

4. Reiner Smolinski, "'Seeing Things Their Way': The Lord's Remembrancers and Their New England Histories," in "Massachusetts and the Origins of American Historical Thought," special issue, *Massachusetts Historical Review* 18 (2016): 18–63. "The privilege of historical backwardness" is one of the leading ideas in Leon Trotsky, *The History of the Russian Revolution*, trans. Max Eastman (Chicago: Haymarket Books, 2008), 24.

5. Sacvan Bercovitch, *The Puritan Origins of the American Self* (New Haven, CT: Yale University Press, 1975), 86, 87, and 88–89; and Smolinski, "'Seeing Things Their Way,'" 44. Bercovitch's important revisionist work has been regularly reflected on by scholars; see the forum on his work in *Early American Literature* 47 (2012): 377–441. Because I want to keep the methodological issues front and center, I scant various interpretive essays on the *Magnalia* that would distract from the focus I am bringing.

6. The other three are the histories by William Hubbard (*A General History of New England*, 1680), Edward Johnson (*The Wonderworking Providence of Sion's Savior in New England*, 1654), and Daniel Neal (*The History of New England*, 1720). This is Smolinski's general argument: "Whereas Johnson's history is largely formed by his belief in an imminent millennium taking shape in Oliver Cromwell's England, Hubbard's is governed by his mild skepticism and the parameters of the General Court, Mather's by his irenicist endeavor to unite Congregationalists and Presbyterians under the umbrella of the United Brethren, and Neal's by his preoccupation to pillory religious persecution in all its forms, especially among his American confreres" (Smolinski, "'Seeing Things Their Way,'" 21).

7. The *Magnalia* is painfully aware that the first Quaker meetinghouse and the first Anglican chapel were both established in Boston in 1688. Equally significant for Smolinski's *Magnalia* were the portentous comets that appeared in the skies at the outset of the decade in 1680 and 1682. Increase Mather meditated on their religious import in sermons delivered in 1681 and 1682 and again in a 1683 treatise. Cotton Mather worked up a remarkable almanac for 1683 in which he underscored the divine significance of the comets as heavenly signs (Increase Mather, *Heaven's Alarm to the World* [1681]; *The Voice of God in Signal Providences* [1682]; *A Discourse Concerning Comets* [1683]; and *The Boston Ephemeris: An Almanack for the [Dionysian] Year of the Christian Aera M DC. LXXX III* [1683]). See Andrew P. Williams, "Shifting Signs: Increase Mather and the Comets of 1680 and 1682," *Early Modern Literary Studies* 1, no. 3 (1995): 1–34. Mather's almanac commentary called attention to his father's analyses and to the unusual conjunction of

Saturn and Jupiter in Leo in May 1683, an event seen by many as portentous. Mather was notably contemptuous of almanacs. Cotton Mather, *Diary of Cotton Mather, 1681–1708*, foreword by Worthington Chauncey Ford (Boston: Massachusetts Historical Society Collections, 1911), 7:276.

8. Milman Parry, "The Historical Method in Literary Criticism," in *The Making of Homeric Verse: The Collected Papers of Milman Parry*, ed. Adam Parry (Oxford: Clarendon Press, 1971), 411.

9. The standard accounts are Michael J. Mages, *Magnalia Christi Americana: America's Literary Old Testament* (San Francisco: International Scholars, 1999), 8–43; the introduction and notes to Cotton Mather, *Magnalia Christi Americana, Books I and II*, ed. Kenneth B. Murdock (Cambridge, MA: Harvard University Press, 1977); and Thomas James Holmes, *Cotton Mather: A Bibliography of His Works in Three Volumes* (Cambridge, MA: Harvard University Press, 1940), 2:573–96. See also Chester N. Greenough, "A Letter Relating to the Publication of Cotton Mather's *Magnalia*," *Publications of the Colonial Society of Massachusetts* 26 (1926): 296–312; and D. N. Deluna, "Cotton Mather Published Abroad," *Early American Literature* 26, no. 2 (1991): 145–72. Mages says that "by 1697 the *Magnalia* was complete . . . except for those additions and revisions Mather made right up until the manuscript went to press" (*Magnalia Christi Americana: America's Literary Old Testament*, 1). Those were so extensive, however, that to call the *Magnalia* complete without them is seriously misleading. Holmes dates the completion to 1696. Some key general points of reference for dating the composition history: Mather, "General Introduction" ("[a] little more than two years . . . have rolled away since I began it": *M* 1:32); and John Higginson, "Attestation" of January 1697 (*M*, 1:13–18); William Turner, *Compleat History of the Most Remarkable Providences . . . in This Present Age* (1697) announced that Mather's work "is now almost finished" and covers a period "down to . . . 1696"; Cotton Mather, *Johannes in Eremo* (Boston: Michael Perry, 1695), 31; Mather, *Diary*, entry of August 1697 declaring the work "finish[ed]" (1:229); and finally, Robert Calef, *More Wonders of the Invisible World* (written 1696; London and Salem, MA: William Carlton, 1700), and John Hale, *A Modest Enquiry Into the Nature of Witchcraft* (written 1697; Boston: Benjamin Eliot, 1702) (hereafter cited in text and notes as *ME*, followed by the relevant page number), both read by Mather in mid- to late 1697.

10. It seems likely that before 1697, and perhaps even later, book 7, chap. 7 only extended through the Twelfth Example. The long Ninth Example is the retelling from *Memorable Providences* (1689) of the "Four children of John Goodwin" (*M*, 2:456); the Eleventh Example is an excerpt Mather lifts from his sermon *The Cause and Cure of a Wounded Spirit* (published in December 1692); and the Twelfth Example is the Joseph Beacon passage lifted from *The Wonders of the Invisible World* (1692). The Tenth Example seems to date from late 1695, which suggests when Mather may have been composing these sections of chap. 7. The new material would have included, however, besides "Sadducismus Debellatus" (the Fourteenth Example), the Thirteenth Example.

11. The best account of *Pietas in Patriam* and its relation to the *Magnalia* is Mather, *Magnalia Christi Americana, Books I and II*, ed. Murdock, 1–48 and 459–80.

12. Besides Holmes, *Cotton Mather: A Bibliography*, 2:573–96, three essential works that deal with the history of the *Magnalia*'s publication are Greenough, "A Letter Relating to the Publication of Cotton Mather's *Magnalia*"; Deluna, "Cotton Mather Published Abroad"; and Mages, *Magnalia Christi Americana: America's Literary Old Testament*, 8–43. The map is not reproduced in the later American editions. On the map, see Lloyd A. Brown, "Notes on the Magnalia Map" (Holmes, *Cotton Mather: A Bibliography*, 2:592–

96), an essay that has been superseded since its publication; and Jefferson Dillman, "Defending the 'New England Way': Cotton Mather's 'Exact Mapp of New England and New York,'" *Historical Journal of Massachusetts* 38, no. 1 (2010): 111–31. On Parkhurst as a publisher, see Harold Love, "Preacher and Publisher: Oliver Heywood and Thomas Parkhurst," *Studies in Bibliography* 31 (1978): 227–35.

13. Citing John Quick's letter, Dillman claims that Mather authorized the map. But that is unlikely, and when he says that Quick's letter implies that he did, he misrepresents what the letter actually says. This judgment has been corroborated for me in correspondence with the cartographer David Rumsey and between Rumsey and the cartographer Matthew Edney. Referring to the "additional prints" that Mather sent to Quick for *Magnalia*, Dillman says they are "unknown" ("Defending the 'New England Way,'" 117 n. 7). But this is not correct. These "prints" were the various print publications that Mather had issued separately—certainly the ones that did not appear until 1700 and perhaps some others as well—and that were eventually included—as just noted—in books 6 and 7. Nothing suggests that Mather had such a careful map printed for him or that he had access to the exemplar maps that he would have needed. However, such materials were ready to hand for a publisher like Parkhurst.

14. That is, from the founding of separatist Plymouth to the first year of peace following King William's War. The date should have been 1699. Before he sent his manuscript of the *Magnalia* to London for publication, Mather added materials that hadn't been written before 1699, including the long "Letter" on the "imposter" Samuel May/Samuel Axel (*M*, 2:546–51). Mather published the whole of Book 7, chap. 5 as a separate pamphlet in 1700.

15. See Barbara McCorkle, *New England in Early Printed Maps, 1513–1800: An Illustrated Carto-Bibliography* (Providence, RI: John Carter Brown Library, 2001), 44 and 71.

16. Paul E. Cohen and Robert T. Augustyn, *Manhattan in Maps, 1527–2014* (1997; Mineola, NY: Dover, 2014), 34.

17. Oddly, Parkhurst's map corresponds most closely to the centralized and short-lived (1686–89) Crown "Dominion of New England." There is no question that the *Magnalia* projects—tentatively, it is true—a less insular view of New England than the Massachusetts Bay Colony had long cultivated (as the model Congregational church community). By the mid-1690s, for example, Anglicans were no longer forbidden to live in the colony. One notes that the map does not specifically identify each of the colonies that the Dominion had amalgamated. It may well be that Parkhurst's map is an effort to represent that emerging and less exclusive Massachusetts Bay Colony idea.

18. See also the earlier attack on the Quakers in the appendix to Cotton Mather, *A Discourse of Witchcraft*; this work was published together with the *Memorable Observations* (Boston: R[ichard] P[ierce], 1689).

19. In Sacvan Bercovitch, "'Nehemias Americanus': Cotton Mather and the Concept of the Representative American," *Early American Literature* 8, no. 3 (1974): 220–38, the author argues that the physical "locale" of the New World was not "just another plot of ground in a fallen world" but, "like Canaan of old, belonged wholly to God" (224). Nowhere is his Romantic reading of Mather more surely declared. Canaan for Mather is a place to be wiped clean of its devils and their institutions—he subscribed to Joseph Mede's view of the New World—so that the saints can prepare it for the City of God.

20. I strongly suspect that Mather wrote the *Magnalia*'s Hannah Swarton text from her oral report. The style, particularly the telling use of biblical citations, seems to me clearly Matherian.

21. In his final remarks on the war in *Decennium Luctuosum*, Mather includes documents that are dated January 1699 (*M*, 2:642–43).

22. See Holmes, *Cotton Mather: A Bibliography*, 1:222.

23. See the discussion of Calef below, pp. 95–100 passim.

24. "Prints" is the word that Quick used for these materials. I suspect that Dillman misread Quick's letter to Mather because he thought this word meant engravings, like the map that he thought Mather had authorized and sent.

25. Mather declares that "these new Quakers cover their sentiments with such fallacious and ambiguous expressions, that all Fox's gross Quakerism can be at once asserted or denied" (*M*, 2:527).

26. The text reads "best" but that seems an erratum for "least," though not one recorded in the *Magnalia*'s list of errata or in George W. Robinson, *Errata in Cotton Mather's "Magnalia"* (Cambridge, MA: Privately printed, 1943).

27. "Wolves in Sheeps Cloathing" was originally titled "Warning to the Flocks" (Holmes, *Cotton Mather: A Bibliography*, 3:1196–97).

28. Kenneth Silverman, *The Life and Times of Cotton Mather* (New York: Harper & Row, 1984), 159. Lorraine Daston and Peter Galison, *Objectivity* (New York: Zone Books, 2007), is an incisive critical survey of the philosophic tradition; see esp. 372–74. Steven Shapin, *A Social History of Truth: Civility and Science in Seventeenth-Century England* (Chicago: University of Chicago Press, 1994), connects "Trust and the Order of Society" (8) to Foucault's "regimes" of knowledge.

29. In his life Mather seems to have met only one Quaker of whom he could approve, George Keith, who later turned against the Society (see *M*, 2:645–46). He is probably the Quaker Mather refers to but does not name in book 3 (*M*, 2:243).

30. Mather began his *Biblia Americana* when he began the *Magnalia*. Five volumes of the projected ten have been published. See *Cotton Mather: Biblia Americana...*, ed. Reiner Smolinski, vols. 1, 3, 4, 5, and 9 (Tübingen: Mohr Siebeck, and Grand Rapids, MI: Baker Academic, 2010).

31. This is a general Reformation formulary. I quote from the *Second Helvetic Confession* (1562 and 1566), chap. 11 (available from the *Christian Classics Ethereal Library* of Calvin College at https://www.ccel.org/creeds/helvetic.htm). See Jaroslav Pelikan, *Interpreting the Bible and the Constitution* (New Haven, CT: Yale University Press, 2004), esp. chaps. 1 and 2.

32. The Mason, Underhill, Vincent, and Gardener accounts are reprinted in Charles Orr, *History of the Pequot War: The Contemporary Accounts of Mason, Underhill, Vincent and Gardener* (Cleveland, OH: Helman-Taylor, 1897).

33. The best account of Mather's laudatory "Plutarchan" biographies is David Levin, *Cotton Mather: The Young Life of the Lord's Remembrancer, 1663–1703* (Cambridge, MA: Harvard University Press, 1978), chap. 6. See also Silverman, *The Life and Times*, 159–65, and the more elaborate treatment in Mages, *Magnalia Christi Americana: America's Literary Old Testament*, 56–108.

34. Calef's postscript on Mather's biography is the earliest account of Governor Phips to point out the "mistakes in [Mather's] book; as also those miscarriages wherewith Sir William was chargeable" (see Calef, *More Wonders*, 144–55). For authoritative critical accounts of Governor Phips see Viola F. Barnes, "The Rise of William Phips," *New England Quarterly* 1, no. 3 (1928): 271–94; Barnes, "Phippius Maximus," *New England Quarterly* 1, no. 4 (1928): 532–53; and Jane Donahue Eberwein, "'In a Book, as in a Glass': Literary Sorcery in Mather's Life of Phips," *Early American Literature* 10, no. 3 (1975–76): 289–300.

35. Juvenal, *Satires*, book V, Satire 14, 242–43.

36. For less sensational accounts see Eve LaPlante, *American Jezebel: The Uncommon Life of Anne Hutchinson, the Woman Who Defied the Puritans* (San Francisco: Harper Collins, 2004); and Francis J. Bremer, *Anne Hutchinson: Troubler of the Puritan Zion* (Huntington, NY: Robert E. Krieger, 1981), 1–8.

37. Virgil, *Aeneid*, book III, 658.

38. Silverman, *The Life and Times*, 158–59.

39. Jan Stievermann, "Writing 'To Conquer All Things': Cotton Mather's *Magnalia Christi Americana* and the Quandary of 'Copia,'" *Early American Literature* 39, no. 2 (2004): 271, 279.

40. Stievermann, "Writing 'To Conquer All Things,'" 279–80.

41. Calef charged that Mather spoke ambiguously about the trials and executions; i.e., while Mather warned against the possibility of error, he yet insisted that the trials proceed and supported their verdicts and death sentences. See Silverman, *The Life and Times*; and Calef, *More Wonders*, 143–44.

42. Silverman, *The Life and Times*, 117. Silverman gives a good account (83–137) of the witch-trial controversies as they reflect Mather's work.

43. See Silverman's discussion of one of Mather's most unfortunate "ambidexter" documents, *The Return of Several Ministers* (1692) (Silverman, *The Life and Times*, 100).

44. See Silverman, *The Life and Times*, 135–37.

45. Mather quotes verbatim from *ME*, 23–38.

46. "Shew us what we know not, and help us wherein we have done amiss, to do so no more ... [and] humble us therefore, and pardon all the errors of his Servants & People, that desire to love his Name, and be attoned to his land" (*ME*, 167).

47. Calef, *More Wonders*, 179.

48. This was the view of those "other" Puritans who sympathized with antinomian ideas, especially Anne Hutchinson and Roger Williams. In Bercovitch's view, none of these are "representative Americans" (Bercovitch, "'Nehemias Americanus,'" 236).

49. Silverman, *The Life and Times*, 159.

50. Laura Riding Jackson, *The Telling* (New York: Harper & Row, 1973), 66.

INTERCHAPTER ONE

1. See interchap. 2, "The End of Kaswentha."

2. There are thirteen Franklin folios that commence with the Treaty of 1736, convened in Philadelphia, and stop with the Treaty of 1762, held in Lancaster.

3. Rourke, *The Roots of American Culture*, 10.

4. Merrell, *Into the American Woods*, 256–58.

5. "Quasi-official" because with one exception—the Treaty of 1757—they have been incorporated in Donald H. Kent, ed., *Pennsylvania and Delaware Treaties, 1629–1737*, vol. 1 of *Early American Indian Documents: Treaties and Laws, 1607–1789* (Washington, DC: University Publications of America, 1979).

6. Besides Boyd, Kalter, and Merrell, notable exceptions are Jack M. Sosin, *Whitehall and the Wilderness: The Middle West in British Colonial Policy, 1760–1775* (Lincoln: University of Nebraska Press, 1961), Michael N. McConnell, *A Country Between: The Upper Ohio Valley and Its Peoples, 1724–1774* (Lincoln: University of Nebraska Press, 1992); Sandra Gustafson, *Eloquence Is Power: Oratory and Performance in Early America* (Chapel Hill: University of North Carolina Press, 2000), 112–15; Thomas Hallock, *From the Fallen*

Tree: Frontier Narratives, Environmental Politics, and the Roots of a National Pastoral, 1749–1826 (Chapel Hill: University of North Carolina Press, 2003), 90–95; and Lisa Brooks's two books, *The Common Pot* and *Our Beloved Kin*.

7. James H. Merrell, "'I Desire All That I Have Said... May Be Taken Down Aright': Revisiting Teedyuscung's 1756 Treaty Council Speeches," *William and Mary Quarterly*, 3rd ser., 63, no. 4 (2006): 777–826, at 816.

8. In an "Examination of the Council Books" for 1742, Patrick Baird—the secretary for the Treaty of 1742—had failed "to enter several Messages... between the Governor & Assembly," so the Council record had to be corrected. See *Minutes of the Provincial Council of Pennsylvania...* (Harrisburg, PA: Theo Fenn, 1851), 5:67.

9. For an especially useful recent exploration of these matters, see Cohen, *The Networked Wilderness*, 1–29.

10. Some useful points of departure for studying these matters are: Frank Speck, "The Functions of Wampum among the Eastern Algonkian," *American Anthropological Association Memoirs* 6 (1919): 3–71; George S. Snyderman, "The Functions of Wampum," *Proceedings of the American Philosophical Society* 98, no. 6 (1954): 469–94, at 470; Snyderman, "The Function of Wampum in Iroquois Religion," *Proceedings of the American Philosophical Society* 105, no. 6 (1961): 571–608; Michael K. Foster, "Another Look at the Function of Wampum in Haudenosaunee-White Councils," in *Iroquois Diplomacy*, 99–114; Lynn Ceci, "The Value of Wampum among the New York Iroquois: A Case Study in Artifact Analysis," *Journal of Anthropological Research* 38, no. 1 (1982): 97–107; Marshall Joseph Becker and Thomas F. Doerflinger, "Lenape Land Sales, Treaties, and Wampum Belts," *Pennsylvania Magazine of History and Biography* 108. no. 3 (1984): 351–66; Gregory Schaaf, *Wampum Belts and Peace Trees: George Morgan, Native Americans, and Revolutionary Diplomacy* (Golden, CO: Fulcrum, 1990); Tehanetorens, *Wampum Belts and the Iroquois* (Summertown, TN: Book Publishing, 1999); Germaine Warkentin, "In Search of 'The Word of the Other': Aboriginal Sign Systems and the History of the Book in Canada," *Book History* 2, no. 1 (1999): 1–27; Angela Haas, "Wampum as Hypertext: An American Indian Intellectual Tradition of Multimedia Theory and Practice," *Studies in American Indian Literatures* 19, no. 4 (2007): 77–100; Kathryn V. Muller, "The Two Mystery Belts of Grand River: A Biography of the Two Row Wampum and the Friendship Belt," *American Indian Quarterly* 31, no. 1 (2007): 129–64; and Penny Kelsey, *Reading the Wampum: Essays on Hodinöhsö:ni' Visual Code and Epistemological Recovery* (Syracuse, NY: Syracuse University Press, 2014).

11. Besides the sources just cited, one of the most useful recent essay collections on native forms of expression is Barbara Alice Mann, ed., *Native American Speakers of the Eastern Woodland: Selected Essays and Critical Analyses*, Contributions to the Study of Mass Media and Communications 60 (Westport, CT: Greenwood Press, 2001).

12. In his oft-cited early essay, Wroth rightly says that these were not official documents but were published "as private ventures at the charge of the printer," i.e., that they were Franklin's ventures (Wroth, "The Indian Treaty as Literature," 750).

13. This point is central to the important essay by Foster, "Another Look at the Function of Wampum," n. 7: "The common thread running through the non-native accounts [of the function of wampum] is a focus primarily on the *retrospective* uses... i.e., as a device for recalling past events." But every bit as important was that it "function[ed] *prospectively*, i.e., as a device for organizing present and future events [and] to maintain or prolong communication" (108).

14. Ibid., 110.

15. See Parmenter, "The Meaning of Kaswentha."

16. Alfred Taiaiake, *Peace, Power, Righteousness: An Indigenous Manifesto* (Oxford and New York: Oxford University Press, 1999), 51.

17. Fenton, "The Earliest Recorded Description," 127.

18. Ibid.

19. The Virginia situation is well analyzed in Mallios, *Deadly Politics*.

20. For good references see Keven Kenny, *Peaceable Kingdom Lost: The Paxton Boys and the Destruction of William Penn's Holy Experiment* (Oxford and New York: Oxford University Press, 2009): 11–14 and 45–49; Steven Craig Harper, *Promised Land: Penn's Holy Experiment, the Walking Purchase, and the Dispossession of the Delawares, 1600–1763* (Bethlehem, PA: Lehigh University Press, 2006); and Jennings, *The Ambiguous Iroquois Empire*, 236–48, 322–42.

21. William N. Fenton, "Structure, Continuity, and Change in the Process of Iroquois Treaty Making," in *Iroquois Diplomacy*, 29.

22. Ibid., 29 and 27.

23. The point is now widely understood: a lucid and succinct account is given in Anthony F. C. Wallace, "Women, Land, and Society: Three Aspects of Aboriginal Delaware Life," *Pennsylvania Archaeologist* 17 (1947): 2. See also Snyderman, "Concepts of Land Ownership," 101–10; Cronon, *Changes in the Land*, chap. 4; and Jenny Hale Pulsipher, *Subjects unto the Same King: Indians, English, and the Contest for Authority in Colonial New England* (Philadelphia: University of Pennsylvania Press, 2005).

24. See the discussion of Maussian gift exchange ("total prestation") in Marshall Sahlins, *Stone Age Economics* (Chicago: Aldine-Atherton, 1972), 171–82.

25. This is the only folio record that underscores how crucial the condolence ceremony was for the treaty-making. Because the Indians refused to begin at all until the proper ceremonial gift forms were prepared, treaty-making was delayed for an unspecified period. See *Indian Treaties*, 3/125, and the *Autobiography* (*Writings*, 1421).

26. See n. 10 of this interchapter above, especially the essays by Speck, Snyderman, Foster, and Muller, and the pamphlet by Tehanetorens.

27. Citations to this folio will be made in the text and notes as *A Treaty of Friendship*, followed by the pertinent page number.

28. See the discussion in Bruce E. Johansen, "'By Your Observing the Methods Our Wise Forefathers Have Taken, You Will Acquire Fresh Strength and Power': Closing Speech of Canassatego, July 4, 1744, Lancaster Treaty," in Mann, *Native American Speakers of the Eastern Woodlands*, 83–106.

29. (London: A. Sowle, 1683), 7. Available online from the Internet Archive at https://archive.org/details/aletterfromwill00penngoog.

30. For the official record see Kent, *Pennsylvania and Delaware Treaties, 1629–1737*, 341–58.

31. This treaty was first recorded in the *Jesuit Relations*; for an English translation, see Reuben Gold Thwaites, ed., *The Jesuit Relations and Allied Documents* (Cleveland, OH: Burrows Brothers, 1896–1901), 27:247–305, reprinted in *Iroquois Diplomacy*, 137–53. See the discussion in the introduction above.

32. How eager the English were to ingratiate themselves with the Iroquois is also clear from Weiser's subsequent remarks. The opening ceremonies took place at Logan's house in Stenton, which was not then, as it is now, within Philadelphia. Speaking through Weiser, Penn offered to keep treatying at Stenton since "a Small Pox are there" in the city. The Indians declined the offer, adding that they "*were much obliged ... for the Care we took of them*" (*A Treaty of Friendship*, 5).

33. These are named the "Fire, Road, and Chain of Friendship" articles; *A Treaty of Friendship*, 7).

34. The Indian names given and accepted by the colonial authorities—Brother Onas (Pennsylvania), Corlear (New York), Assaragoa (Virginia), Tocarry-Hogan (Maryland), and Onontio (French Canada)—underscore how important it was to foreground the native character of the treatying.

35. The treatying that continued through July 9 included more ceremonial feasting as well as Canasatego's assurance that certain native acts of violence would be dealt with in order to "aid [our] Brethren the white People in obtaining Justice."

36. Canasatego's intention to make a forceful display of League authority was apparent from his first words at the 1742 treaty, when he "rebuk[ed] ... severely" the Iroquois warriors who entered into "Publick Business" (*Indian Treaties*, 4/18).

37. The phrase used by the Ottawa chief Egushawa (*Minutes of Debates in Council, on the Banks of the Ottawa River, November, 1791* [Baltimore, MD: Warner & Hanna, 1800], 11), which Calloway used for the title of his important study *Pen and Ink Witchcraft*.

38. In attempting to vindicate the Delaware, scholars correctly point out that, according to the League's political habitus, "women" signified a social function (see, e.g., Jennings, *The Ambiguous Iroquois Empire*, 198): to act as "peacemakers and mediators between the Iroquois and other tribes" (Kalter, *Benjamin Franklin, Pennsylvania, and the First Indian Nations*, 85 n. 9). Kalter's long note goes on to bring further clarity to the invidious implication of Canasatego's speech, though she does not mention that the Delaware would throw off that League responsibility as the social balance between native and non-native interests descended into the chaos and violence in the mid-1750s.

39. Speaking for the League at the Treaty of 1761, the Seneca chief Tokahaio declared, "We would have you make some Satisfaction to our Cousins here, the *Delawares*, for their lands" (*Indian Treaties*, 16/260). Kalter underscores what an "extraordinary shift in Iroquois policy" was being expressed in Takahaio's words (*Benjamin Franklin, Pennsylvania, and the First Indian Nations*, 357 n. 6).

40. "By 1853 the [Canajoharie] Mohawks considered the Covenant Chain broken": Shannon, *Indians and Colonists at the Crossroads of Empire*, 48; "The harsh realities of a changing frontier economy had pushed the Mohawks into a corner, eroding their subsistence and threatening their land.... New Yorkers had also defaulted in their diplomacy, failing to observe ceremonies. ...." (ibid., 49). See also Newbold, *The Albany Congress*.

41. On the renunciation of their role as peacemakers, see Kenny, *Peaceable Kingdom Lost*, 70–71. At the Treaty of 1762, Tamaqua (Beaver), the spokesman for the Ohio Delaware, worked to restore peace and friendship between his people and Pennsylvania. When he was asked to speak to the land claims of the eastern Delaware—the still unresolved Walking Purchase dispute—he declined to make a judgment.

42. There were two 1757 treaties, one convened at Lancaster (March, April, and May), where Teedyuscung was not present, and the second at Easton (July and August), where he was the key native presence, having been requested to gather "the ten following Nations," including the League, to that conference. Although not actually present at the first of the 1757 treaties, he was a strong, even dominating, absent presence. Indeed, the chief upshot of the first 1757 treaty was to decide, on Teedyuscung's advice and—with the support of the Mohawk Little Abraham, the Oneida Shickallemo, and the Shawnee Sacsidora—to convene the second 1757 treaty (at Easton) where "we shall settle all Differences between them and us" (*Indian Treaties*, 5/171). The

focus was to be the free use of "that very Land we look upon to be our own" (9/175). It is also important to see that the 1756 treaty at Easton, which began in late July, had an extended three-month runup from late April, with meetings in Philadelphia and Teaogan (Tioga). Once those preparations had been completed, "Teedyuscung, *King* of the Delawares, *attended by several Chiefs and Deputies of the Ten Nations*" (3/191), arrived at Easton in late July to begin the conference.

43. For the foundational expectation of sincerity in treaty-making, see Snyderman, "The Function of Wampum in Iroquois Religion," 603; and Michel Foster, "When Words Become Deeds: An Analysis of Three Iroquois Longhouse Speech Events," in *Explorations in the Ethnography of Speaking*, ed. Richard Bauman and Joel Sherzer (Cambridge: Cambridge University Press, 1989), 364.

44. See the discussion of Conrad Weiser's failed attempt at the 1757 treaty to have Teedyuscung's charges about land fraud expunged from the record, and the Delaware chief's unusual—indeed, unique—insistence that "his words be recorded and . . . 'openly and publickly declared and published to the province or provinces under the Government of the Great King,'" in Brooks, *The Common Pot*, 233.

45. "At a time when all the other major towns in America had forts and walls, and when King Philip's War in New England and Bacon's war against the Virginia Indians were recent memories, Penn laid out his capital city [Philadelphia] as if to prove that it occupied the most peaceful corner of the world" (Mary Maples Dunn and Richard S. Dunn, "The Founding, 1681–1701," in *Philadelphia: A 300 Year History* [New York: W. W. Norton, 1982], 6).

46. Franklin commented on this in 1747 in his *Plain Truth* pamphlet (Philadelphia, 1747): "*Pennsylvania*, indeed, situate in the Center of the Colonies, has hitherto enjoy'd profound Repose; and tho' our Nation is engag'd in a bloody War, with two great and powerful Kingdoms, yet, defended, in a great Degree, from the French on the one Hand by the Northern Provinces, and from the Spaniards on the other by the Southern, at no small Expence to each, our People have, till lately, slept securely in their Habitations" (4).

47. It was fragile for two familiar reasons, as pointed out in Dunn and Dunn, "The Founding," 5–6. First, Penn's attitude to the Indians was "essentially patronizing"; second, he did not "understand that the Delaware had no conception of land ownership, and imagined that in their land 'sales' they were "merely affirming the right of the white men to share the use of the land."

48. Robert L. D. Davidson, *War Comes to Quaker Pennsylvania, 1682–1756* (New York: Columbia University Press, 1957), esp. chaps. 3–6.

49. There is a long and useful discussion of the term in Kalter, *Benjamin Franklin, Pennsylvania, and the First Indian Nations*, 84–85. See also Francis Jennings, "Brother Miquon: Good Lord!," in *The World of William Penn*, ed. Richard S. Dunn and Mary Maples Dunn (Philadelphia: University of Pennsylvania Press, 1986), 195–214, at 198, and Harper, *Promised Land*, 80–85.

50. Unlike the notorious "memorial reconstructions" of Shakespeare's plays, the special reliability of these documents—what they reveal about Franklin's colonial view—is more certain.

CHAPTER EIGHT

1. Although unreferenced here, my work on Franklin is much indebted to Mitchell Breitwieser, Christopher Looby, and Michael Warner. Breitwieser's and Looby's meth-

odologies, however, are very different. Warner's historicism, on the other hand, has long been a strong influence on my work, as was explicitly clear in a previous version of this book. See Michael Warner, *Letters of the Republic: Publication and the Public Sphere in Eighteenth-Century America* (Cambridge, MA: Harvard University Press, 1992); Mitchell Breitwieser, *Cotton Mather and Benjamin Franklin: The Price of Representative Personality* (Cambridge and New York: Cambridge University Press, 1984); and Christopher Looby, *Voicing America: Language, Literary Form, and the Origins of the United States* (Chicago: University of Chicago Press, 2006).

2. Franklin called this work his "Memoirs" and never agreed to its publication. The term "Autobiography" has become standard, though it is misleading on many levels, as Jill Lepore suggests in her introduction to the Everyman edition *The Autobiography and the Writings* (New York: Alfred A. Knopf, 2015). It was first applied in the heavily expurgated edition of Jared Sparks, *The Works of Benjamin Franklin* (Boston: Tappan, Whittemore, & Mason, 1840), 10 vols. Unless I indicate otherwise, and for the reader's convenience, I cite from the excellent Benjamin Franklin, *Writings*, ed. J. A. Leo Lemay (New York: Library of America, 1987), cited in the text and notes as *Writings*, followed by the relevant page number. But indispensable for all serious readers is the genetic edition of J. A. Leo Lemay and P. F. Zall, *The Autobiography of Benjamin Franklin: A Genetic Text* (Knoxville: University of Tennessee Press, 1979). In quoting from Franklin's other writings, because most are available in excellent online editions, I cite from those sources whenever possible, and chiefly from the Franklin Papers Online (https://franklinpapers.yale.edu). The other most useful online source is the archive *Founders Online*, https://founders.archives.gov/?q=%20Author%3A%22Franklin%2C%20Benjamin%22&s=1111211121&r=1.

3. *Indian Treaties*, 304.

4. I quote from the title of a Crown-commissioned pamphlet: Charles Thomson, *An Enquiry into the Causes of the Alienation of the Delaware and Shawanese Indians from the British Interest ... Written in Pennsylvania* (London: J. Wilkie, 1759).

5. Lemay and Zall, *The Autobiography of Benjamin Franklin: A Genetic Text*, xx.

6. How closely Franklin associates his pursuit of a "tolerable" character and his printer's work is underscored in the passage where he discusses being improved by his failures: "yet I was, by the endeavour, a better and a happier man than I otherwise should have been if I had not attempted it; as those who aim at perfect writing by imitating the engraved copies, tho' they never reach the wish'd-for excellence of those copies, their hand is mended by the endeavor, and is tolerable while it continues fair and legible" (*Writings*, 1391).

7. As his publications in Great Britain from 1758–62 show, Franklin was determined to make his long-standing enthusiasm for the British Empire a matter of public record. Of those many writings, probably the most decisive was *The Interest of Great Britain Considered, With Regard to her Colonies, And the Acquisitions of Canada and Guadaloupe: To which are added, Observations concerning the Increase of Mankind, Peopling of Countries, &c.* (London: T. Becket, 1760). He had published the *Observations* in 1751 and again in 1755 with another pamphlet (and a coauthor, William Clarke) that bore an equally imperialist title: *Observations On the late and present Conduct of the French, with Regard to their Encroachments upon the British Colonies in North America* (Boston : Printed and sold by S. Kneeland, 1755). The most thorough treatment of Franklin's imperialism is Carla J. Mulford, *Benjamin Franklin and the Ends of Empire* (Oxford and New York: Oxford University Press, 2013), esp. chaps. 3–6.

8. I am summarizing the judgment of the historians and biographers. See, e.g., Walter Isaacson, *Benjamin Franklin: An American Life* (New York: Simon & Schuster, 2003), 172–74, 184, 205. "His goal, at least initially, would be to lobby the Proprietors to be more accommodating to the Assembly over taxation and other matters, and then, if that failed, to take up the Assembly's cause with the British Government" (173). For Franklin's relevant writings, see his parodic article "The Jesuit Campanella's Means of Disposing the Enemy to Peace," which he published as "A BRITON" in *The London Chronicle* (August 13, 1761), reprinted in *Writings*, 535–39. Since 1747, when Franklin saw "War . . . rag[ing] over a great Part of the known World," he had become increasingly concerned that the colonists take a broader view of their circumstances and interests: see his related 1747 writings "Form of Association" (in the *Pennsylvania Gazette*) and the pamphlet *Plain Truth*, the latter specifically referenced in the *Autobiography* (*Writings*, 1411).

9. See part 3 of the *Autobiography* (*Writings*, 1405).

10. It's important to remember that although William remained a Loyalist when war broke out, he and his father both judged Whitehall's policies toward the colonies after 1763 to be seriously misguided.

11. In 1773 Franklin was accused of seeking to undermine British authority in the colonies by helping to publish certain inflammatory letters written earlier by the governor and lieutenant governor of Massachusetts. See Edmund Morgan, *Benjamin Franklin* (New Haven, CT: Yale University Press, 2003), 180–202 passim, and Kenneth Penegar, *The Political Trial of Benjamin Franklin* (New York: Algora, 2011).

12. Franklin was not even aware that the manuscript had been lost since 1777, when it was removed from his home because of invading British troops.

13. *Writings*, 1381. Compare the example in part 1 of the *Autobiography* where his friend Ralph asks Franklin to help protect him from Osborne's "envy" (*Writings*, 1340–42).

14. "Benjamin Franklin to —— [December 13, 1757]": http://franklinpapers.org/framedVolumes.jsp.

15. Franklin's important outline for the *Autobiography* is not printed in *Writings*, though it is available in most good editions, and a thorough presentation is given in Lemay and Zall, *The Autobiography of Benjamin Franklin: A Genetic Text*. The text is available in the online Franklin Papers project at the end of its text of the *Autobiography*: see Franklin Papers Online (https://franklinpapers.yale.edu).

16. See William's letter to his father of August 14, 1775, at Franklin Papers Online.

17. For a good account of the relationship between father and son, see Daniel Mark Epstein, *The Loyal Son: The War in Ben Franklin's House* (New York: Ballantine Books, 2017).

18. The two letters are available in the online Franklin Papers.

19. Benjamin Franklin, *The Writings of Benjamin Franklin*, ed. Albert H. Smyth, vol. 10 (New York: Macmillan, 1907), 493. Though the document is dated June 1789, Franklin wrote it in the summer of 1788, just before he resumed work on part 3 of his *Autobiography*.

20. Leonard W. Larabee, ed., *The Papers of Benjamin Franklin* (New Haven, CT: Yale University Press, 1962), 5:456–63.

21. Letter to Peter Collinson, June 26, 1755. The letters next quoted to Whitefield (July 2, 1756) and Lord Kames (January 3, 1860) are also available through the online Franklin Papers.

22. Sosin, *Whitehall and the Wilderness*, 141. The story of this event has been often told, but Sosin's is the most extensive and authoritative account. It is the focus of chaps. 6–9,

esp. chaps. 7–8. William J. Campbell, *Speculators in Empire: Iroquoia and the 1768 Treaty of Fort Stanwix* (Norman: University of Oklahoma Press, 2012), has a good account of the treaty-making (chap. 5) as well as some interesting commentary on the involvement of the two Franklins (114–16). The two standard earlier accounts are Thomas Perkins Abernethy, *Western Lands and the American Revolution* (New York: D. Appleton-Century, 1937), and Kenneth P. Bailey, *The Ohio Company of Virginia and the Westward Movement, 1748–1792* (Glendale, CA: Arthur H. Clark, 1939). Besides the two Franklins, the key players were George Croghan, Sir William Johnson, Richard Jackson, Joseph Galloway, George Morgan, Samuel and Thomas Wharton, and the Walpole Associates, especially Thomas Walpole.

23. He first sketched it ironically in *Poor Richard*'s Casuist pieces, which extended over a period of nearly two years, January 1831–December 1832: see Franklin Papers Online.

24. Rhode Island and a few delegates from other states did not sign the Constitution, and soon after it was published a vigorous antifederalist opposition emerged. Nine months passed before the required nine states ratified the document and made it law. Two more states, Virginia and New York, ratified before the end of 1788, but only on condition that it be amended. That process went forward the following year and produced the Bill of Rights and the original set of amendments, after which North Carolina ratified. Rhode Island's ratification did not come until 1790. In 1791 Vermont ratified and requested admission as a new state.

25. Edward Lear, "The Pelican Chorus," in *The Complete Nonsense of Edward Lear*, ed. Holbrook Jackson (London: Faber & Faber, 1998), 232–33.

26. These details might be a gloss on the proposals implicit in Father Abraham's speech in *Poor Richard improved: Being an Almanack and Ephemeris... for the Year of our Lord 1758...*, By Richard Saunders, Philom. (Philadelphia: Printed and Sold by B. Franklin, and D. Hall).

27. This was Franklin's convention speech against executive-branch government Salaries (*Writings*, 1131).

28. *The Papers of Benjamin Franklin*, ed. Ellen R. Cohn (New Haven, CT: Yale University Press, 2014), 41, 412–23, and 597–608.

29. This came as a cool but scathing letter-essay from Passy to his daughter Mrs. Sally Franklin Bache (January 26, 1784): http://franklinpapers.org/framedVolumes.jsp. Franklin was hardly alone in objecting to the Society at the time. Washington himself—who was named president of the Society—conferred with Jefferson, who was appalled at the idea of such a society. Washington threatened to resign unless its primogeniture rule was removed. See also Frank E. Grizzard Jr., "George Washington and the Society of the Cincinnati," Washington Papers: https://washingtonpapers.org/resources/articles/george-washington-and-the-society-of-the-cincinnati/.

30. McHenry's diary is available online from the Yale Law School's Avalon Project: see https://avalon.law.yale.edu.

CHAPTER NINE

1. The standard print edition for many years was Thomas Jefferson, *Notes on the State of Virginia*, ed. William Peden (Chapel Hill: University of North Carolina Press, 1954). While it remains reliable, it has been superseded by Thomas Jefferson, *Notes on the State of Virginia*, ed. Frank Shuffleton (New York: Penguin Books, 1999), which

has significant additional materials and features; hereafter cited as Jefferson, *Notes*, ed. Shuffleton, followed by the relevant page number. David Tucker, *Enlightened Republicanism: A Study of Jefferson's "Notes on the State of Virginia"* (Lanham, MD: Lexington Books, 2008), further illuminates the work's ideas and rhetorical strategies (see esp. chaps. 1 and 2), and the classic essays by Robert Ferguson ("'Mysterious Obligation': Jefferson's *Notes on the State of Virginia*," *American Literature* 52, no. 3 [1980]: 381–406) and Susan Manning ("Naming of Parts; or, The Comforts of Classification: Thomas Jefferson's Construction of America as Fact and Myth," *Journal of American Studies* 30 [1996]: 345–64) remain pertinent. An especially useful commentary on Jefferson is Jay Fliegelman, *Declaring Independence: Jefferson, Natural Language, and the Culture of Performance* (Stanford, CA: Stanford University Press, 1993). Two other essays I found particularly useful were Mark D. McGarvie, "'In Perfect Accordance with His Character': Thomas Jefferson, Slavery, and the Law," *Indiana Magazine of History* 95, no. 2 (1999): 142–77; and Douglas L. Wilson, "The Evolution of Jefferson's 'Notes on the State of Virginia,'" *Virginia Magazine of History and Bibliography* 112, no. 2 (2004): 98–133.

2. Jefferson to James Madison, May 11, 1785, text from Founders Online (https://founders.archives.gov/).

3. See in particular Jefferson's letter of June 7, 1785 to the Marquis de Chastellux, reprinted in Jefferson, *Notes*, ed. Shuffleton, 266–69; see also Jefferson, *Notes*, ed. Shuffleton, Query XI.

4. An excellent online edition of that Massachusetts Historical Society manuscript is available; see https://www.masshist.org/thomasjeffersonpapers/notes/.

5. See Jefferson, *Notes*, ed. Shuffleton, 102 and n. 144.

6. Charles M. Johnston, ed., *The Valley of the Six Nations: A Collection of Documents on the Indian Lands of the Grand River* (Toronto: Champlain Society for the Government of Ontario, University of Toronto Press, 1964), xxix–xxx.

7. Tony C. Brown, "The Barrows of History," *Studies in Eighteenth-Century Culture* 37 (2008): 41–65, takes an approach to the barrows passage that is similar to the one I develop here. Because the mounds exhibit—indeed, actually build—an ethos of transtemporal temporality, Brown argues that Jefferson's "historicist" approach "appears unable to face up to" what they represent. Jefferson's object is to deracinate the mounds by means of the "disciplinary frameworks of archaeology and historiography" (Jefferson, *Notes*, ed. Shuffleton, 58). See also Jonathan Elmer, "The Archive, the Native American, and Jefferson's Convulsions," *Diacritics* 28, no. 4 (1998): 5–24.

8. See McElwain, "'Then I Thought I Must Kill Too,'" in Mann, *Native American Speakers of the Eastern Woodlands*, 107–21.

9. See the letter to the Marquis de Chastellux: "I believe the Indian, then, to be, in body and mind, equal to the white man. I have supposed the black man, in his present state, might not be so; but it would be hazardous to affirm, that, equally cultivated for a few generations, he would not become so" (Jefferson, *Notes*, ed. Shuffleton, 268).

10. For a good brief account of both Hemings and Jefferson's overseers, see Lucia C. Staunton, "'Those Who Labor for My Happiness': Thomas Jefferson and His Slaves," in *Jeffersonian Legacies*, ed. Peter S. Onuf (Charlottesville: University Press of Virginia, 1993), 158–60.

11. Danielle Allen, *Our Declaration: A Reading of the Declaration of Independence in Defense of Equality* (New York: W. W. Norton, 2014).

12. Ibid.

13. Ibid., 92–93.

14. Ibid., 43.
15. Ibid.
16. *Selected Poems of Rainer Maria Rilke*, trans. Robert Bly (New York: Harper & Row, 1981), 146–47.

INTERCHAPTER TWO

1. Letter of February 13, 1818, in *The Selected Writings of John and John Quincey Adams*, ed. Adrienne Koch and William Peden (New York: Alfred A. Knopf, 1946), 203–5.

2. See J. Hector St. John de Crèvecoeur, *More Letters from the American Farmer: An Edition of the Essays in English Left Unpublished by Crèvecoeur*, ed. Dennis D. Moore (Athens: University of Georgia Press, 1995), especially the eight last essays printed by Moore (163–335) and the essays "An Happy Family Disunited by the Spirit of Civil War," "Susquehanna," "Landskapes," "A Grotto," and "The Man of Sorrow."

3. There was widespread hatred of the writs of assistance as well—the court orders for searching warehouses for smuggled goods. Smuggling, which was rampant in the northern ports, cut seriously into imperial revenue.

4. See above, 141–43, and Thomas D. Curtis, "Riches, Real Estate, and Resistance: How Land Speculation, Debt, and Trade Monopolies Led to the American Revolution," *American Journal of Economics and Sociology* 73, no. 3 (2014): 474–626.

5. Dorothy Jones, *License for Empire: Colonialism by Treaty in Early America* (Chicago: University of Chicago Press, 1982).

6. See Michael N. McConnell, *A Country Between: The Upper Ohio Valley and Its Peoples, 1724–1774* (Lincoln: University of Nebraska Press, 1992), 253.

7. "Minutes of the Southern Congress at Augusta, Georgia. Georgia; North Carolina; Cherokee Indian Nation; Catawba Indian Nation; et al. October 01, 1763–November 21, 1763," hereafter cited as "Minutes" followed by the relevant page number. The treaty parties were the Chickasaw, Choctaw, Creek, Cherokee, and Catawba nations and the governors of Georgia, the Carolinas, and Virginia (represented by the lieutenant governor), with the proceedings directed by the Crown superintendent John Stuart. See *The Colonial and State Records of North Carolina* 11:156–207 (treaty text available online: http://docsouth.unc.edu/csr/index.html/document/csr11-0084).

8. E. B. O'Callaghan, ed., *Documents Relative to the Colonial History of the State of New York* ... (Albany, NY: Weed, Parsons, 1857), 7:648–58; available online at https://babel.hathitrust.org/cgi/pt?id=umn.31951002213919 5;view=1up;seq=664.

9. On this famous—not to say infamous—treaty, already discussed, see Hill and Parmenter, *The Fort Stanwix Treaties*, passim; McConnell, *A Country Between*, chaps. 10–11; Sosin, *Whitehall and the Wilderness*, 172–93; Nicholas B. Wainwright, *George Croghan, Wilderness Diplomat* (Chapel Hill: University of North Carolina Press, 1959), chap. 11; and Peter Marshall, "Sir William Johnson and the Treaty of Fort Stanwix, 1768," *Journal of American Studies* 1 (1967): 149–79. As these scholars make clear, speculators and traders all the way from central and western New York to Virginia were working to exploit the treaty by shifting the Proclamation Line to the west. In my discussion, however, I focus entirely on the special interests of the Franklins, who were "deeply committed" to their Vandalia speculation (Marshall, "Sir William Johnson and the Treaty of Fort Stanwix," 167). It was known at the time that Johnson had "deliberately conducted part of the negotiations in secret" (150).

10. O'Callaghan, *Documents Relative to the Colonial History of the State of New York*, 8:111–37; available online at http://treatiesportal.unl.edu/earlytreaties/treaty.00007.html.

11. For an explication of the interesting distinction the Indians at the Fort Stanwix treaty-making drew between "buy[ing] the land" and exploiting its resources, see *Diary of David McClure*, ed. Franklin B. Dexter (New York: Privately printed, Knickerbocker Press, 1899), 83–85.

12. See *Indian Affairs: Laws and Treaties*, ed. Charles J. Kappler (Washington, DC: Government Printing Office, 1904), 2:3–5. The treaty text is online at https://babel.hathitrust.org/cgi/pt?id=uiug.30112039509200;view=1up;seq=8 and http://avalon.law.yale.edu/18th_century/del1778.asp. Chief White Eyes negotiated the treaty for the Delaware. He and probably his wife were murdered by patriot militia in November 1778. Shortly thereafter his people broke with the patriot forces. See Joseph Henderson Bausman and John Samuel Duss, *History of Beaver County, Pennsylvania* (New York: Knickerbocker Press, 1904), 1:32.

13. Some two thousand Indians attended the meetings in two broad deputations: one made up of the Iroquois League nations and their dependents, led by Joseph Brant, the other a group of "Lake Indians" led by the Wyandot chief Sindatton (variously spelled).

14. The treaty-making events carried over the months from May 6 to September 6, when a final agreement was signed. For the Haldimand Papers see *Historical Collections* (Lansing: Michigan Pioneer and Historical Society, 1892), vols. 19–20, hereafter cited as Haldimand Papers, *Historical Collections*, followed by the relevant volume and page number. The materials relevant to my discussion are in vol. 20, available online at https://babel.hathitrust.org/cgi/pt?id=mdp.39015071219581&view=2up&seq=14&size=125. On Ephraim Douglas, see Clarence C. Burton, ed., *Ephraim Douglas and His Times: A Fragment of History* (New York: William Abbatt, 1910).

15. See Haldimand Papers, *Historical Collections*, 20:177.

16. See Robert N. Clinton, "Treaties with Native Nations: Iconic Historical Relics or Modern Necessities?," in *Nation to Nation: Treaties between the United States & American Indian Nations*, ed. Suzan Shown Harjo (Washington, DC: Smithsonian Books, 2014): 17.

17. The most comprehensive examination of the Haldimand Proclamation is Charles M. Johnston, ed., *The Valley of the Six Nations: A Collection of Documents on the Indian Lands of the Grand River* (Toronto: Champlain Society for the Government of Ontario, University of Toronto Press, 1964). When British authorities moved swiftly to undo the Proclamation, reducing the grant by two-thirds, they began a series of disputes over the land cession that carried into the twentieth-century. For the Proclamation, see Johnston, *The Valley of the Six Nations*, 50.

18. For a text of the treaty, see *Treaties between the United States of America and the Several Indian Tribes, from 1778 to 1837* (Washington, DC: Langtree & O'Sullivan, 1837), 54–62; available online at http://avalon.law.yale.edu/18th_century/greenvil.asp.

19. A variant of the standard formula. This is taken from "The Great Treaty of 1722" (O'Callaghan, *Documents Relative to the Colonial History of the State of New York*, 5:657–81 and 679; available online at http://treatiesportal.unl.edu/earlytreaties/treaty.00001.html?q=rivers.

CHAPTER TEN

1. The sermon has been a regular focus of readers and scholars since its first appearance in 1838, most recently in Daniel T. Rodgers, *As a City on a Hill: The Story of America's*

Most Famous Lay Sermon (Princeton, NJ: Princeton University Press, 2018). Given the textual problems that continue to bedevil readings of this work, my point of reference and citation is the online facsimile made available by the New-York Historical Society at http://cdm16694.contentdm.oclc.org/cdm/ref/collection/p16124coll1/id/1952.

2. For the first 1838 printing of the New-York Historical Society's manuscript edited by Folsom and Savage, see their "Model of Christian Charity, by Gov. Winthrop," in *Collections of the Massachusetts Historical Society*, 3rd ser., (Boston: Massachusetts Historical Society, 1838), 7:31–47. The volume is available online through the Hathi Trust at https://babel.hathitrust.org/cgi/pt?id=njp.32101076467495;page=root;seq=7;view =image;size=100;orient=0. In 1929 the Society published an improved and annotated version (see chap. 5, n. 16) that corrects all but one of the text's errors. The Winthrop Papers were made available online in 2019; see Winthrop Papers Digital Edition, http://www.masshist.org/publications/winthrop/index.php/view/PWF02d270.

3. A parenthetical note at the foot of the page was added in 1838 or soon afterward by an archival agent of the New-York Historical Society.

4. For the most recent (at the time of this writing) study of the *Arbella* sermon, see Rodgers, *As a City on a Hill*, chap. 1, esp. 18–20, 22–23, and 29. Based on verbal similarities between one passage in the sermon and John Winthrop's "Address . . . to the Company of Massachusetts Bay," and a short list of biblical citations in an appended page in Winthrop's *Journal*, Rodgers speculates that the work was written in four sections at different times. He develops his theory in order to avoid certain contradictions that arise from the bibliographical and historical evidence. See also *The Winthrop Papers*, 2:174–77, and *J*, 726.

5. See Hugh J. Dawson, "John Winthrop's Rite of Passage: The Origins of the Christian Charity Discourse," *Early American Literature* 26, no. 3 (1991): 219–31.

6. "Apparently contemporary" is the judgment made in the introductory editorial note to *The Winthrop Papers*.

7. See Dawson, "John Winthrop's Rite of Passage," 228–29 n. 6. Those 1991 judgments about the paper have been recently corroborated for me by Heather Wolfe, Curator of Manuscripts, Folger Library. In addition, Fenella France, Acting Director of Preservation, and her staff at Library of Congress have completed a thorough analysis of the inks used in the manuscript. Except for the 1838 notation at the bottom of the title/ headnote page, all the ink is iron gall, which was in common use throughout the West, even into the twentieth-century; see Fenella France et al., "John Winthrop Christian Charity Manuscript and Other Corresponding Documents: Optical Analyses for Baseline Characterization and Comparison of Inks and Assessment of Congruency between Documents for the Purpose of Provenance" (Washington, DC: Library of Congress, 2018), 1–30.

8. See a discussion of the revision in a New-York Historical Society blog posting at http://blog.nyhistory.org/21991-2/.

9. In 1991 Dawson accepted Winthrop's authorship. Seven years later he was less certain: see Hugh J. Dawson, "Winthrop's Sermon in Its English Context," *Early American Literature* 33, no. 2 (1998): 117–48.

10. Dawson, "John Winthrop's Rite of Passage" (229 n.), notes that this transcription error was corrected in some later reprintings, but it has nonetheless been perpetuated in much of the literature, not least in the standard online and often-cited Massachusetts Historical Society version. Even the most distinguished Puritan scholars continue to insist that the sermon was delivered at sea (e.g., Michael Colacurchio, *Godly Letters: The*

Literature of the American Puritans [Notre Dame, IN: University of Notre Dame Press, 2006], 151).

11. See Dawson, "John Winthrop's Rite of Passage," 229 n. The persistence of the error is largely the result of its presence in the important Massachusetts Historical Society edition of the Winthrop Papers, where a variant of the mistaken 1838 text is reprinted. Of the available school texts—in print or online—that print the document, the only anthology with the correct reading is Myra Jehlen and Michel Warner, eds., *The English Literatures of America, 1500–1800* (New York: Routledge, 1996). All the other general American or specialized Puritan anthologies either do not print the relevant section or, when they do, misprint it.

12. Dawson, "John Winthrop's Rite of Passage," 223.

13. See *J*, 57. For Winthrop as a lay sermonist, see Francis J. Bremer, *Lay Empowerment and the Development of Puritanism* (Basingstoke: Palgrave Macmillan, 2015), 76–83.

14. See Francis J. Bremer, *John Winthrop: America's Forgotten Founding Father* (Oxford and New York: Oxford University Press, 2003), 174–75; he discusses the work at length at 173–84.

15. Jacie mentions "Christian Charity" in his letter to John Winthrop Jr., in the Winthrop Papers Digital Edition, 3:188–89, where it is dated, incorrectly, ca. 1634–35. Roger Williams, writing to John Winthrop Jr. on May 28, 1864, refers to "the Winthrops and their Modells of Love" in drawing an invidious contrast between the first- and second-generation puritans; see *The Correspondence of Roger Williams*, ed. Glenn W. LaFantasie (Hanover, NH: Brown University Press for the Rhode Island Historical Society, 1988), 2:527–28.

16. See Malcolm Freiberg, "The Winthrops and Their Papers," *Collections of the Massachusetts Historical Society*, 3rd ser., 80 (1968): 55–70. Edward O'Reilly, of the New-York Historical Society pointed out to me that in a letter to Nathaniel Green (March 18, 1780), John Adams wrote that "America is the City, set upon a Hill." He must have been thinking of the source text in Matthew 5:14, for it is unimaginable that he would have seen or read the Winthrop manuscript. It is nonetheless striking that he would have made the same connection the sermon makes of America to the city on a hill.

17. Dawson, "John Winthrop's Rite of Passage," 222.

18. See Abram C. Van Engen, "Origins and Last Farewells: Bible Wars, Textual Form, and the Making of American History," *New England Quarterly* 86, no. 4 (2013): 543–92.

19. Van Engen, "Origins and Last Farewells," 549–50. The author observes, "It matters which Bible—which particular physical object—Winthrop held and read when he composed his sermon, and it is no accident that the Geneva, not the KJV, stands behind his text. His was 'an adversarial Bible,' the Bible of both resistance and renewal" (555–56). Van Engen's work here revised the received view that "Christian Charity" quotes from both Geneva and the King James Version; see also Harry S. Stout, "Word and Order in Colonial New England," in *The Bible in America: Essays in Cultural History*, ed. Nathan O. Hatch and Mark A. Noll (Oxford and New York: Oxford University Press, 1982), 19–38, esp. 29.

20. Van Engen notes that "Puritan sermons were typically composed of six elements—scripture, elucidation of the verse, doctrine, reasons, application, and exhortation. The last four are elaborated in 'Christian Charity,' but the first two parts—the opening verse and its initial elucidation—are lacking" ("Origins and Last Farewells," 557).

21. Ibid., 557.

22. Others who have noted the truncated character of the manuscript have decided to treat the document not as a sermon but as a "discourse"—the term used in the manuscript itself; see Richard Gamble, *In Search of the City on a Hill: The Making and Unmaking of an American Myth* (London and New York: Continuum:, 2012). As Van Engen has noted, "The reason Gamble and others want it to be a 'discourse' is in part because they want a governor, not a minister, to be the author of it" (personal communication, May 4, 2018).

23. See Brian C. Wilson, "KJV in the USA: The Impact of the King James Bible in America," *Comparative Religion Publications* 2 (2011), http://scholarworks.wmich.edu/religion_pubs/2; see also Francis J. Bremer, "John Winthrop and the Shaping of New England History," in "Massachusetts and the Origins of American Historical Thought," special issue, *Massachusetts Historical Review* 18 (2016): 1–17.

24. Most records now spell his name "Jessey." I have retained the spelling he used when he signed his letters.

25. H. Kingsburie is either Henry Kingsbury, from Groton, Suffolk, who emigrated in 1630 with his wife and son, or his father (see *The Winthrop Papers*, 2:188). *A Treatise of Faith* could be any one of four possible works all bearing this title: John Ball's (1631), Ezekiel Culverwell's (1625), George Throgmorton's (1624), or John Fisher's (1605); Ball, Culverwell, and Fisher were multiply reprinted, as was John Rogers, *The Doctrine of Faith* (1629). The other books mentioned are William Perkins, *The foundation of Christian religion: gathered into sixe principles [...]* (1591), and *A sweet Posie for God's Saints [...] gathered out of [...] the Holy Scriptures* (1642), by J. O. As for the materials specifically related to Winthrop, "Mr. Higginson's letter" is Rev. Francis Higginson, *True Relacion of the Last Voyage to New England* (1629) (or perhaps his *New England's Plantation* [1630]). The "Petition" requested is *The Humble Request of His Majesties Loyall Subjects, the Governour and the Company Late Gone for New England; to the Rest of Their Brethren, in and of the Church of England* (1630; *The Winthrop Papers*, 2:231–33). The "Map" is probably Winthrop's "Chart of the Coast from Gloucester to Marblehead," reproduced in *The Winthrop Papers*, 2: after p. 280. Finally, Jacie mentions the "sermon."

26. See the records of the British National Archives: http://discovery.nationalarchives.gov.uk/results/r?_q=Overton+stationer.

27. "Within a few months of sailing [i.e., late 1629], he had employed in private correspondence the same maternal figure later favored by [John] Cotton and [John] White in telling of his trust that, by their migration, the 'members of that Churche [in America] may be of better vse to their mother Churche heere'" (*The Winthrop Papers*, 2:132).

28. Dawson, "Winthrop's Sermon in Its English Context," 122.

29. Ibid., 135.

30. For a good account of the Jacobite Church, semiseparatism, and the relation of the semiseparatists to the colonial Congregational movement, see Murray Tolmei, *The Triumph of the Saints: The Separate Churches of London, 1616–1649* (Cambridge: Cambridge University Press, 1977), chap. 1 ("The Jacob Church"), esp. 12–19 ("The Jacob-Lathrop-Jessey Church"). For an earlier look at the English and the colonial scene, see Perry Miller, *Orthodoxy in Massachusetts, 1630–1650: A Genetic Study* (Cambridge, MA: Harvard University Press, 1933) esp. chaps. 3–5.

31. See Dawson, "Winthrop's Sermon in Its English Context," 141 n. 1. But here Dawson still writes as if Winthrop were the author of "Christian Charity."

32. It is numbered "22," which is the number written at the top of the manuscript

page bearing the document's title/headnote. But Bayard Winthrop's final note on the donation list, referring to "61 Sermons dating from 1561 to 1724," does not specify whether they are manuscript or print documents.

33. That is to say, the title/headnote parodied such a design in its first stage. The changes made in the stage 2 and stage 3 revisions obscured the initial page design.

34. The scripting of the numbers on the two documents is the same, and the donation list was prepared by Francis Bayard Winthrop perhaps as late as 1809. Spectral curve analysis of the iron gall inks on the title/headnote page and the donation list corroborate the relation: according to the 2018 report prepared by the Library of Congress, both "have the same shape and inflection points, though we cannot definitively say it is the exact same pen/author, just similar type of ink." The report concludes that "given the similarity of the curve [. . .] there is a high probability" that they are the same (France et al., "John Winthrop Christian Charity Manuscript and Other Corresponding Documents," 12).

35. Remarking on the biblical citations in *J*, 726), Van Engen first thought what Rodgers thinks (Van Engen, "Origins and Last Farewells," 557): that Winthrop was sketching out the texts for his sermon. He now judges that "it makes better sense to see him sitting there *listening* to a sermon and jotting down the scriptural verses that Phillips is using to preach. We have loads of sermon notes from the seventeenth century, and these could be Winthrop's shipboard sermon notes as he listened to Phillips preach. This actually seems to make more sense, especially since while on board the ship, the journal was very much a journal still (not the 'History of New England' it later self-consciously became)" (personal correspondence, May 4, 2018). See also Meredith Neuman, *Jeremiah's Scribes: Literary Theories of the Sermon in Puritan New England* (Philadelphia: University of Pennsylvania Press, 2013).

36. Maidstone's recommendation is effusive: "His exelency in matters of divinity is such (as I make noe question but experience will make good,) as that hee is inferiour to very few, if to any: for proofe wheareof, I stande not vpon mine owne slender conceipte, but refer my selfe to the judgemente of all the eminenteste Christians that ever have exercised familiarity with him: of whome many are encouraged to goe for his sake, and others to follow, so soone as god shall so dispose: neither doe I at all doubte, but your owne iudgemente (good sir) is so sounde and peircinge, as it will with shorte experience finde out the truth of this relation. If therefore I may bee so bolde, I desire that in the choyce of your pastor, you would bee mindefull of him, if your selfe shall see it meete. I seeke not any thinge herein (if my worde may bee credited) but the promotion of Christes cause" (*The Winthrop Papers*, 2:165).

37. See *J*, 10 and 730 and n.

38. *The Winthrop Papers*, 2:231–33.

39. See Henry Wilder Foote, "George Phillips, Minister of Watertown," *Proceedings of the Massachusetts Historical Society*, 3rd ser., 63 (1930): 197–201. As Foote points out, the subscription to *A Humble Request* implies that it was "written on board ship" (199).

40. Ibid., 199.

41. Ibid., 206–7.

42. Ibid., 211.

43. See *The Winthrop Papers*, vol. 2. The large body of the "Reasons to be Considered for [. . .]" manuscript materials, including drafts, revisions, and related copies, is collected and edited in *The Winthrop Papers*, 2:106–42.

44. See Folsom and Savage, "Model of Christian Charity, by Gov. Winthrop," 31–32.

45. For useful discussions of these matters, see Lindsay Dicuirci, "Reviving Puritan History: Evangelicalism, Antiquarianism, and Mather's *Magnalia* in Antebellum America," *Early American Literature* 45, no. 3 (2010): 565–92; Philip Gould, "New England Witch-Hunting and the Politics of Reason in the Early Republic," *New England Quarterly* 68, no. 1 (1995): 58–82; Peter Carafoil, "The Constraints of History: Revision and Revolution in American Literary Studies," *College English* 50, no. 6 (1988): 605–22; Nina Baym, "Early Histories of American Literature: A Chapter in the Institution of New England," *American Literary History* 1, no. 3 (1989): 459–88; Stanley K. Schultz, *The Culture Factory: Boston Public Schools, 1789–1860* (Oxford and New York: Oxford University Press, 1973); and Kermit Vanderbilt, *American Literature and the Academy* (Philadelphia: University of Pennsylvania Press, 1986). Two key works of antiquarian defense are Abdiel Holmes, *American Annals*, 2 vols. (Cambridge, MA: W. Hilliard, 1805), and James Grahame, *History of the Rise and Progress of the United States*, 2 vols. (London: Longman, Rees, Orme, Brown, & Green, 1827). Like George Bancroft, *History of the United States* (Boston: Little, Brown, 1844–75), both were unabashedly pro-Puritan (see in Bancroft esp. vol. 1, chap. 12, "The Pilgrims").

CHAPTER ELEVEN

1. Though not published until 1936, the comment came in his lecture of 1934, "The Historical Method in Literary Criticism," in Parry, *The Making of Homeric Verse: Collected Papers*, 412.

2. For important context, see *Application of Big Data for National Security: A Practitioner's Guide to Emerging Technologies*, ed. Babak Akhgar, Gregory Saathoff, Hamid Arabnia, Richard Hill, Andrew Staniforth, and Petra Saskia Bayerl (Oxford: Butterworth-Heinemann, 2015).

3. Thomas Hardy, "The Convergence of the Twain," in *The Variorum Edition of the Complete Poems of Thomas Hardy*, ed. James Gibson (London: Macmillan, 1979), 307, lines 22–24.

4. Paul Connerton, *How Modernity Forgets* (Cambridge and New York: Cambridge University Press, 2009). This is the sequel to his important *How Societies Remember* (Cambridge and New York: Cambridge University Press, 1989).

5. Ralph Waldo Emerson, *Journals of Ralph Waldo Emerson*, vol. 4: 1820–1872, ed. Edward Waldo Emerson and Waldo Emerson Forbes (Boston: Houghton Mifflin, 1910), 242, 259. The subsequent quotation is from p. 259.

6. This "definition" actually comes from Kant, and while the quotation marks suggest Emerson is quoting, he's actually synthesizing passages from *The Critique of Pure Reason* and *The Philosophy of Right*. This is what the lecture called "going down into the secrets of his own mind," where Thinking Man "descend[s] into the secrets of all minds" and even into the secrets of nature itself. Before Kant was, Emerson is saying, I AM.

7. Lawrence Buell, "Thoreau and the Natural Environment," in *The Cambridge Companion to Henry David Thoreau*, ed. Joel Myerson (Cambridge: Cambridge University Press, 1995), 172.

8. Henry David Thoreau, *Faith in a Seed: The Dispersion of Seeds and Other Late Natural History Writings*, ed. Bradley P. Dean (Washington, DC: Island Press and Shearwater Books, 1993); and Thoreau, *Wild Fruits*, ed. Bradley P. Dean (New York: W. W. Norton, 2000).

9. Henry David Thoreau, "Spring," in *Walden*, in *A Week on the Concord and Merrimack*

Rivers; Walden; The Maine Woods; Cape Cod, ed. Robert F. Sayre (New York: Library of America, 1985), 563.

10. Thoreau, *The Maine Woods*, 641.

11. "Higher Laws" is the most stuttering episode in the book, veering repeatedly between the contradictory instincts of his mortal being.

12. Shattuck, introduction to Jarry, *Exploits and Opinions of Dr. Faustroll*, xi.

13. Barry Lopez, *Arctic Dreams* (New York: Scribner, 1986), 177. Further citations to *Arctic Dreams* appear in parentheses in the text.

14. Wallace Stevens, *Collected Poetry and Prose*, ed. Frank Kermode and Joan Richardson (New York: Library of America, 1997), 460.

15. Alfred Tennyson, *The Major Works*, ed. Adam Roberts (Oxford and New York: Oxford University Press, 2000), 81.

16. Ron Suskind, "Faith, Certainty, and the Presidency of George W. Bush," *New York Times Magazine*, October 17, 2004: http://www.nytimes.com/2004/10/17/magazine/faith-certainty-and-the-presidency-of-george-w-bush.html.

17. Hannah Arendt, "Lying in Politics: Reflections on the Pentagon Papers," *New York Review of Books*, November 18, 1971.

18. Paul De Man, *Blindness and Insight: Essays in the Rhetoric of Contemporary Criticism* (Oxford and New York: Oxford University Press, 1971), 110.

19. Paul De Man, introduction to *Selected Poetry of John Keats* (New York: New American Library, 1966), xi.

20. See William M. Calder III, "How Did Ulrich Von Wilamowitz-Moellendorff Read a Text?" *Classical Journal* 86, no. 4 (April–May 1991): 350–51.

21. Though in this matter, Evelyn Barish, *The Double Life of Paul De Man* (New York: Liveright, 2014), does give one pause.

22. Parry, "The Historical Method in Literary Criticism," 412.

23. Ibid.

24. Ibid., 413.

25. Ibid., 408–9.

26. Ibid., 409.

27. Ibid., 411.

INDEX

aborigines, 154–55, 157
Achilles, 216
Adams, Henry, 30
Adams, John, 79, 163, 166, 167
Adorno, Theodor, 201; *Dialectic of Enlightenment*, 201, 223n15
Aeneid (Virgil), 94, 125
Africa, 160
Agricola (Tacitus), 166, 179
Ahab, 101
Albany (New York), 23, 108, 112; Council Fire of (1677), 23, 24, 112
Albany Congress (1754), 25, 27, 130
Albany Plan, 11, 130, 134
aletheia, 200. *See also* truth
Allegheny Mountains, 142
Allen, Benjamin, 188
Allen, Danielle, *Our Declaration*, 163–64
Ambrose, Isaac, 33; *Media*, 31; *Redeeming the Time* (sermon), 193–94
American Dream, 30, 131, 210; the American Scholar vs., 210; as exceptional, 30
"American Scholar," the, xiv, 6, 210
"American Scholar, The" (Emerson), 201–3
Amory, Hugh, 4
Anabaptists, 88, 92
Anaktuvuk Pass, 208
Andros, Edmund, 22–23
Anglo-Dutch War (final), 22
Anthropocene, 210
Antichrist, the, 197

Antinomian controversy of 1637, 58
Antinomians, 88
Arbella (ship), 47, 52, 185, 186, 195, 196
Arbella sermon, the, 3, 5, 6, 32, 53, 57, 58, 78
"Arctic Dream," 210
Arctic Dreams (Lopez), 207, 210, 212
Arendt, Hannah, on "defactualization," 212
Aristotle, 95
Arnold, Matthew, 32, 151, 163; on cultural "touchstones," 32; on the "dialogue of the mind with itself," 151, 163
Articles of Confederation, 143
"as long as the sun shall shine," 169
Assaragoa, 117, 243n34. *See also* Virginia
Augustine, Saint, 69; *The City of God*, 70
Autobiography (Franklin), 3, 129–49
Axel, Samuel, 90, 238n14
axiology, vs. aesthetics, 3, 222n1

Bache, Sally Franklin, 247n29
Bacon's Rebellion, 22, 123, 168, 169
Bailey, John, 82, 92, 96
Baird, Patrick, 241n8
Baker, J. A., *The Peregrine*, 183
Ball, John, 253n25
Banneker, Benjamin, 152, 159, 162, 163
Barbé-Marbois, François, 150
Barlow, Joel, 163
Battle of Fallen Timbers, 178
Baudelaire, Charles, 77
Bay Psalm Book, The, 3, 65–66, 69, 234n21

Beacon, Joseph, 95, 237n10
Beckett, Samuel, xv, 165
Belanger, Terry, 223n8
Belknap, Jeremy, 231n8
Belmessous, Saliha, 27
Benjamin, Walter, 32, 160, 210; on "documents of barbarism," 160; on "documents of civilization," 32, 210
Bercovitch, Sacvan, 79–81, 94, 199, 240n48
Bernstein, Charles, v
Berryman, John, 67; *Homage to Mistress Bradstreet*, 67
Bible, the, 213
Big Data, 215
Billington, John, 40
Bill of Rights, 163
bishop of St. Asaph. *See* Shipley, William
Blake, William, 200, 203
Blix, Hans, 211
Boeckh, August, xi; *Sachphilologie* of, 4
"book of nature" (natural history), 213
"books of men and women" (human history), 213
Bradford, William, 6, 13, 35–50, 52, 60, 76, 78; daybook or diary of, 35–42; "Hebrew Exercises" of, 42, 48–49, 77; *Of Plimoth [Plymouth] Plantation*, 25, 35, 38–39, 41–48, 50, 53
Bradstreet, Anne, 3, 4, 6, 66, 67–78; "Contemplations," 66, 73; "Dialogue between Old *England* and New; concerning their present Troubles, Anno, 1642, A," 76–77; *In Honour of that High and Mighty Princess, Queen Elizabeth*, 70; "Meditations Diuine and morall," 73; *Several Poems...*, 67; *The Vanity of All Worldly Things*, 69; Woodbridge and Bradstreet's *The Tenth Muse*, 67
Bradstreet, Simon, 73
Brant, Joseph (Mohawk chief), 175, 177, 250n13
Breitwieser, Mitchell, 150, 244n1
Bremer, Francis, 186
Brewster, William, 45, 47
British Indian Department (Northern and Southern Districts), 168, 169, 171
British Petroleum, 210

Brockden Brown, Charles, 11
Bryant, William Cullen, 199
Buffon, Comte de, 158
Burroughs, George, 97

Calcagus, 166, 179
Calef, Robert, 7, 88, 95, 96, 237n9, 239n34, 240n41; on "prejudice of education," 7
Calvinism, 64, 65, 189
Cambridge (Massachusetts), 201
Cambridge Platform (1648), 52, 53, 55, 59, 64, 65, 77
Cambridge Synod, 64
Canaanites (colonial name for Indians), v, 49, 58, 78, 81, 99, 238n19
Canada, 23, 113, 142, 169, 176, 178
Canajoharie (Mohawks), 228n40, 243n40
Canasatego (Onondaga chief), 105, 111, 112, 115, 116, 117, 118, 119, 124, 243nn35–36, 243n38
Cañizares-Esguerra, Jorge, 4
Canoncet (Narragansett chief), 22
Cape Fear River, 22
Carlyle, Thomas, xiv
Carolinas, 113, 167, 249n7
Carretta, Vincent, 5
Carrollton (Kentucky), 142
Carver, John, 39, 44
Casaubon, xiv
Casco Bay, 22, 84
Cather, Willa, *My Ántonia*, 30
Cato, 136
"Causes of the Alienation of the Delawares and Shawanese from the British Interest, The" (Benjamin Franklin), 130
Cave, Alfred, 18
Champlain, Lake, 228n33
Channing, William Ellery, 199
Charles I (king), 188
Charvat, William, 4
Chastellux, Marquis de, 248n9
Cheapside (London), 83
Cheney, Dick, 210–12, 215
Chernobyl, 213
Child, Lydia Maria, *Hobomok*, 30, 199
Child, Robert, 56; "Remonstrance and Petition... to Massachusetts General Court," 56

INDEX 259

Churchill, Winston, 195
Church of England (Anglican), 189, 196, 236n7, 238n17
Cicero, 136
Cincinnati (Ohio), 142
Collinson, Peter, 140
Comets of 1680 and 1682, 236n7
Concord (Massachusetts), 166
condolence ceremony/ritual, 10, 17, 30, 107, 139, 170, 171. See also *kaswentha*
Condorcet, Marquis de, 163
Congregational Church, 53, 54, 56, 58, 59, 64, 65, 81, 89, 188, 198, 236n6, 238n17; in England, 189; non-separating Congregationalists, 186; semi-separating Congregationalists, 187, 188, 189, 253n30
Congregational General Court, 54, 55, 197, 236n6
Connecticut, 142
Connerton, Paul, 201
Constitutional Convention, 145, 147, 148, 153
Constitution of the United States, the, 3, 145, 152, 163; ratification of, 162, 247n24; slavery institutionalized in, 162
"Contemplations" (Anne Bradstreet), 66, 73, 76
Continental Congress, 135
Cook, Captain James, 9
Cooke, Francis, 36, 38
Cooper, James Fenimore, 11, 29, 30, 199; *The Crater*, 30; *The Last of the Mohicans*, 29, 30; *The Pioneers*, 29; *The Wept of Wish-Ton-Wish*, 199
Cordell, Ryan, Viral Texts Project of, 5
Coriolanus, 77
Corlear, 117, 243n34. See also New York
Cotes, R., 188
Cotton, John, 63, 66, 100, 186, 189, 191, 234n21; his sermon *Gods Promise to His Plantation*, 186, 191–92
Covenant Chain treaties, 6, 23, 24, 25, 27, 102–25, 129, 243n40; treaty-making, 17, 26, 166–79, 228n40
Crane, Hart, 66
Crater, The (Cooper), 30
Cresap, Michael, 158

Crèvecoeur, Michel Guillaume Jean de, 11, 249n2; *Letters from an American Farmer*, 11, 148, 166
Croghan, George, 142, 247n22
Cromwell, Oliver, 47, 236n6
Cromwell, Thomas, 47
Crown (English), the, 12, 27, 54, 134, 167, 169, 171, 175
Culverwell, Ezekiel, 253n25
Cushman, Robert, 35, 230n1

Davenport, John, 63
Dawson, Hugh J., 185, 186, 189, 190
Daye, Stephen, 234n20
Dean, Bradley P., 203
Declaration of Independence, the, 3, 79, 152, 159, 162, 163, 164, 175
"defactualization" (Arendt), 212, 216
Delaware (Leni Lenape), 13, 25, 112, 115, 117, 118, 119, 120, 121, 124, 125, 174, 175, 177, 243n38, 243n41
Delbanco, Andrew, 32, 199
Denny, William, 121–22, 134
de Man, Paul, 212, 215–16
Detroit, 175
Dialectic of Enlightenment (Adorno and Horkheimer), 201, 223n15. See also enlightenment
"Dialogue between Old *England* and New; concerning their present Troubles, Anno, 1642, A" (Anne Bradstreet), 76–77
Dickinson, Emily, 30, 66, 155
Dickinson, Susan Huntington Gilbert, 30
Dillman, Jefferson, 238n13, 239n24
"Discourse on Arbitrary Government" (John Winthrop), 57
"Dispersion of Seeds, The" (Thoreau), 203
Ditmore, Michael, 5, 76
Dogood, Silence, 130
Donohue, Betty Booth, 40
Douglas, Ephraim, 175
Du Bartas, Guillaume de Salluste, 68–69
Dudley, Thomas, 68
Dunn, Richard, 51, 57, 58
Dürer, Albrecht, xiv
Dustan, Hannah, 88, 99

Dutch, the, 23, 24
Dyer, Mary, 62, 88, 93, 94, 95
Dyonquat (Delaware chief), 177

"earthly kingdom of Messiah," 50, 59, 65, 71
Easton (Pennsylvania), 102, 108, 110, 119–23, 125, 240n5, 243n42, 244n42
Ecclesiastes, xiii
"Edge of the Woods" ceremonial negotiations, 106
Edney, Matthew, 238n13
Egremont, Earl of, 171
Egushawa (Ottawa chief), 243n37
Eliot, T. S., 25
Elizabeth I, 69–72
Emerson, Ralph Waldo, xiv, xv, 6, 188, 198, 201, 210, 215; "The American Scholar," 201–3; *Journal*, 201–2; on "mastery," 202; "Nature," 201
enlightenment, 5, 6, 12, 13, 79; American, two phases of, 5, 12, 13; discoveries of, 164; faith/piety of, 158–59; mind of, 162
Episcopal Church, 57
Erkkila, Betsy, 230n57
"errata," 133, 136, 138, 152
"error," 134, 136, 139, 145, 148, 213
Essais (Montaigne), 153
Everyman, 100
exceptionalism, 9, 13, 30
Exxon Mobile, 210

failure, xv, 8, 13, 32, 101, 163, 219
Farmer, John (in *Walden*), 206
Father Abraham, 148
Father William, 144
Faulkner, William, 220
Faust, 201
Fenton, William, 16, 108
Field Museum (Chicago), 221n6
Fisher, John, 253n25
Fisher, Samuel, 89
Floridas, 142, 167, 169
Folsom, George, 183, 198
Foote, Henry Wilder, 196
Ford, Henry, on history as "bunk," 212
forgiveness, 170, 174
Foucault, Michel, 239n28

Fox, George, 86, 239n25
Fox News, 210
France, 81, 88, 120, 132, 134, 167, 168, 169
Franklin, Benjamin, 3, 11, 102–25, 129–49, 150, 151, 163; Albany Plan of, 11, 130; *Autobiography*, 3, 11, 129–49; "The Causes of the Alienation of the Delawares and Shawanese from the British Interest," 130; "Information to those who would remove to America," 148; *Plain Truth* pamphlet, 244n46; *Plan for Settling Two Western Colonies*, 140; *Poor Richard Improved*, 136; *Poor Richard's Almanac*, 149; "Remarks Concerning the Savages of North America," 148; "Sidi Mehemet" hoax of, 148; Treaty Folios of, 6, 11, 79, 102–25, 129
Franklin, Elizabeth, 139
Franklin, Sir John, 210
Franklin, William, 131, 132, 133, 135, 138, 139, 140, 141, 142, 143, 172
Freeman's Oath ("Oath of a Freeman"), 55, 233n10
Frobisher, Martin, 210

Galilei, Galileo, xiv
Galloway, Joseph, 247n22
Gartner, William Gustav, xii, xiv, xv
Geneva Bible, 50, 65, 76, 186, 187, 189, 252n19
George (Seneca spokesman), 110
George, Lake, 228n33
George III (king), 12, 152, 167, 170, 177, 178
Georgia, 135, 148, 169, 249n7
Gods Promise to His Plantation (Cotton), 186, 191–92
Goodwin, John, 237n10
Goodwin family, 100
Gorton, Samuel, 95
Grand River, the, 178
Great Depression, 215
Great Migration, 55, 233n7

"habits of truthfulness," 7. See also truth
Haines, John, 200
Haldimand, Sir Frederick, 175, 176, 177, 178
Haldimand Proclamation, 178

Hale, John, 83, 96, 97, 98, 99, 237n9
Hall, David, 108
Hamilton, James, 110
Haraszti, Zoltán, 66
Hardy, Thomas, 201
Hartford (Connecticut), 20, 21
Hartley, L. P., 1
Harvard College, 90, 99
Harvard University, Board of Overseers of, 215–16
"haunting of America," the, 178
"Hebrew Exercises" (Bradford), 42, 48–59, 77
Hebrew-language verse/poetry, 66, 69
Hemings, Sally, 159
Henry, Patrick, 167
Hetaquantegechty (Seneca spokesperson), 114
Hett, Anne Needham, 62
Higginson, Francis, 253n25
Higginson, John, 237n9
Hingham Trial, 233n15
"Historical Method in Literary Criticism, The" (Parry), 215
historicism, 4, 5
historicist method, xii
Hitler, Adolf, 215
Hobomok (Lydia Maria Child), 30, 199
Hobbes, Thomas, 10, 225n9
Homer, 234n5
Hooke, William, 235n14
Hooker, Thomas, 63, 94
Hope Leslie (Sedgwick), 30
Hopkins, Ann, 67
Hopkins, Stephen, 37, 40
Horkheimer, Max, 201; *Dialectic of Enlightenment*, 201, 223n15
House of Mirth, The (Wharton), 30
Howe, Susan, 66
Hubbard, William, 186, 196, 236n6
Hudson River vValley, 84, 228n33
humanities, crisis of, 215
"Humble Petition to Lords Commissioners for Foreign Plantations" (John Winthrop), 56
Humble Request of His Majesties Loyall Subjects, The, 53, 188, 196
Hunt, Thomas, 37, 38, 39

Hussein, Saddam, 211, 215
Hutchinson, Anne, 56, 59, 62, 63, 76, 88, 92, 93, 95, 240n48
Hutchinson Affair, 135, 138

"ideology," 8
Iliad, 217
Indians, nullification of, 164
Indian Tribes: Abenaki (Wabanaki), 27; Algonquin, 16; Catawba, 249n7; Cherokee, 169, 171, 172, 173; Chickasaw, 249n7; "Chippewey," 176; Choctaw, 171, 249n7; Creek, 169, 171, 176, 249n7; Delaware (Leni Lenape), 13, 27, 112, 115, 117, 118, 119, 120, 121, 124, 125, 174, 175, 176, 177, 243n38, 243n41; Huron, 176; Iroquois Confederacy/League (Haudenosaunee), 10, 13, 15, 16, 22, 23, 25, 28, 29, 106, 107, 110–20, 124, 129, 134, 139, 155, 169, 171, 172, 173, 174, 175, 176, 178, 242n32, 243n36, 243n39, 243n42, 250n13; Maquas (Mohawk), 23, 111, 228n40, 243n40, 243n42; Mingo, 176; Mohawk (Maquas), 23, 24, 25, 175; Mohegan, 20, 21, 22, 45; Narragansett, 13, 19, 20, 21, 22, 25, 43, 45, 88, 91, 107, 232n13; Nauset (Nausite), 37, 38, 39, 40; Niantic, 21, 22; Oneida, 174, 243n42; Onondaga, 24, 108, 115, 116, 172, 173; Ottawa, 176; Pequot, 13, 19, 20, 21, 25, 43, 45, 88, 91, 107, 232n13; "Poutteawatamie," 176; Powhatan Confederacy, 18, 19, 25, 107; Seneca, 24, 110, 112, 243n39; Shawnee (Shawanese), 112, 125, 176, 243n42; Tuscarora, 174; Wabanaki (Abenaki), 27, 37, 229nn45–46; Wampanoag Confederacy, 16, 22, 26, 36, 37, 38, 40; Western Confederacy of Indian nations, 178; Wyandot, 176, 250n13
In Honour of that High and Mighty Princess, Queen Elizabeth (Anne Bradstreet), 70
"inner standing point," 8
intention, 4
Interesting Narrative of the Life of Olaudah Equiano, The (Vassa), 5
Intolerable Acts, 174
Ipswich (England), 186
Iraq, 210

Irish, as "savage," 28
Iroquoia, 228n33

Jacie, Henry, 186, 187, 188, 189, 254n25
Jackson, Helen Hunt, on the "Century of Dishonor," 11
Jackson, James, 148
Jackson, Richard, 247n22
Jacob, Henry, 189
Jacobite Church, 187, 189, 253n30. *See also* Jacob, Henry
James, Abel, 131, 132, 135
James, Henry, *The American Scene*, 30
James I (king), 41, 43
Jamestown, 16, 18
Jarry, Alfred, the "science of exceptions" (pataphysics) of, 5, 207–8
Jefferson, Thomas, 3, 4, 5, 11, 79, 141, 150–65; on "merciless Indian savages," 152–53, 175; *Notes on the State of Virginia*, 3, 5, 6, 11, 150–65; "Report" to the Virginia Assembly for revising the laws of Virginia, 159
Jerome, Saint, xiv, 92
Jesuits, 16, 197, 229n45
Jesus (Christ), xiv, 63, 97, 136
Jewell (ship), 60
Jews, 64
Johansen, Bruce E., 112
Johnson, Edward, 236n6
Johnson, Sir William, 142, 168, 171, 172, 173, 174, 177, 247n22
Johnston, Charles, 155
Jones, Dorothy, 167
Journal (Emerson), 201
Journal (John Winthrop), 17, 42, 45, 77, 91, 186, 198
Judas, 89
Junto (Leather Apron Club), 133, 146–47
Jupiter, 209
jus absconditus, 159
Juvenal, 92

Kames, Lord (Henry Home), 141
Kanickhungo (Seneca spokesman), 112, 114
Kant, Immanuel, 255n6
kaswentha, 10, 13, 15, 23, 26, 28, 30, 107, 108, 110, 114, 120, 139, 166–79, 231n4. *See also* condolence ceremony/ritual
Keats, John, 212
Keith, George, 239n29
Kelly, Megyn, 210–11
Kentucky River, 142
King George's War, 115, 124
King James Bible, 186, 252n19
King Philip's War (Great Narragansett War), 22, 88, 91, 107, 123
Kingsberry, Eleazer, 90
Kingsbury, Henry, 253n25
King William's War, 28, 81, 83, 84, 87, 88, 89, 238n14
Kiotseaeton (Iroquois spokesperson), 16
Ktaadn, Mount, 204, 209

"Lake Indians," 250n13
Lancaster (Pennsylvania), 105, 108, 111, 240n2, 240n5, 243n42
Last of the Mohicans, The (Cooper), 29, 30
Lathropp, John, 189
Laud, Bishop William, 188, 189, 235n14
Lazarus, Emma, v
Lea, Phillip, 84, 85
Lear, Edward, 146
Lee, Thomas, 167
Lepore, Jill, 245n2
Letter from William Penn . . . to the committee of the Free society of traders . . . , 112
Lévi-Strauss, Claude, xi
Lexington (Massachusetts), 166
Library of Alexandria, xi
Library of America, 79
"License for Empire," 168
Life on the Mississippi (Twain), 214
Lightyear, Buzz, 209
Lilly, Gabriel, 159
Lincolnshire, 92
Litchfield jail, 139
Little Abraham (Mohawk chief), 243n42
"Little Speech on Liberty" (John Winthrop), 57, 197
Livingston Indian Records, 1666–1723, The, 23, 24
Livy, 69
Logan (Native American speaker), 5, 158, 159

Logan, James, 111, 112, 130
Looby, Christopher, 244n1
Lopez, Barry, 207, 210, 212; *Arctic Dreams*, 207, 210, 212
Loyalists, 178

Machiavelli, 175
Maclean, General Allan, 175, 176
Madison, James, 163, 164
Mages, Michael, 81
Magnalia Christi Americana (Mather), 3, 32, 79–101, 150; *Decennium Luctuosum*, 88, 89; "Ecclesiastical History of New-England, from its first planting, in the year 1620, unto the year of Our Lord 1698," 80; *An Exact Mapp of New England and New York* (Thomas Parkhurst), 83–84, 86; *Pietas in Patriam*, 83; "Sadducismus Debellatus," 83; schedule of revisions of the *Magnalia*, 82
Maidstone, John, 195
"major man," xv
"Man Thinking" (Emerson), xiv, 201
Mapp of New England, A (John Sellers), 84
Marcus Aurelius, 234n5
Martin, Luther, 158
Marx, Karl, "The Eighteenth Brumaire of Louis Bonaparte," 9
Mary and John (ship), 196
Maryland, 23, 24, 86, 111, 115, 116, 119, 124
Mason, George, 167
Massachusetts Bay Colony, 17, 18, 19, 20, 21, 22, 25, 26, 27, 32, 43, 44, 49, 50, 52, 53, 54, 55, 58, 59, 60, 65, 76, 79, 88, 92, 93, 135, 183, 185, 189, 195, 227n29, 232n13, 232n15, 233n7, 238n17
Massachusetts Historical Society, 185, 232n15
Massasoit, 17, 22, 23, 25, 36, 37, 38, 39, 40, 41, 43, 44, 77, 123; arrest of, 25
Masters, John, 60
"mastery," 161, 201–2
Mather, Cotton, 3, 6, 7, 13, 79–101, 129, 150, 151, 186, 237n9; "The Bostonian Ebenezer" sermon, 82, 87; *Magnalia Christi Americana*, 3, 6, 13, 79–101
Mather, Increase, 236n7

Maule, Thomas, 89; *Truth Held Forth and Maintained*, 89
Mauss, Marcel, 10, 107, 120, 178
May, Samuel, 90, 238n14
Mayflower (ship), 47
McElwain, Thomas, 5
McHenry, James, 149
McKee, Alex, 177
McKenzie, Donald Francis, 4
"meaning of the meanings," the, 199
Mede, Joseph, 233n13, 238n19
Media (Ambrose), 31
"Meditations Diuine and morall," 73; *Several Poems*... (Anne Bradstreet), 67
Mellon Foundation, Andrew W., 5
Melville, Herman, 30, 101, 203
Merrell, James H., 102–5
Metacom (Wampanoeg chief), 22
Miantunnomoh (Narragansett sachem), 20, 21, 22
Middle Passage, 160
Milborne, Peter, 59
Miller, Perry, 199
Milton, John, 204, 234n5
Mississippi, 141, 167, 168
Mississippi River, 169, 214
Moby-Dick (Melville), 101
"modell of Xtian Charity, A," v, 32, 57, 58, 78, 183–99. See also *Arbella* sermon, the
Modern, John Lardas, 8, 23
Montaigne, Michel de, 153
Monticello, 159
Moore, Marianne: "The Steeplejack," 5
Morden, Robert, 84, 85
Morgan, Edmund, 50
Morgan, George, 247n22
Morison, Samuel Eliot, 46
Morton, George, 35, 230n1
Mourt's Relation, 35
"Munster tragedy," 92
Murie, James, xiii
My Ántonia (Cather), 30
Mystic massacre, 20

Nature (Emerson), 201
Neal, Daniel, 236n6
Neal, John, 199; *Rachel Dyer*, 199
Necotowance (Powhatan chief), 19

"Negative Vote" (John Winthrop), 57
neolithic civilization, 28, 163
New England, 18, 23, 25, 28, 52, 64, 107, 123; Confederation, 18, 20, 21, 65
New France, 12, 16, 113, 117
New Hampshire, 142, 167
New Map of New England New York New Iarsey Pensilvania Maryland and Virginia, A (Thornton, Morden, and Lea), 84
New Netherland, 15, 22
Newton, Isaac, xiv
New York, 22, 112, 114, 117, 129, 151, 243n40
New-York Historical Society, 184, 186, 190, 191, 193, 195, 251nn1–2
Nietzsche, Friedrich, xiv, 80; *The Birth of Tragedy*, 80
Niles, Hezekiah, 166
Notes on the State of Virginia (Jefferson), 3, 5, 6, 150–65; on Indian barrows, 156–57; Logan's speech in, 5, 158
Northwest Passage, 210

Obama, Barack, 210
Ohio, 113, 119
Ohio Company, 167
Ohio Country (Indian Reserve of), 174, 175, 176, 178
Ohio River, 140, 142
Oldbuck, Jonathan, xiv
Onas (Brother Onas), 114–15, 118, 243n34. See also Pennsylvania
Onontio (French Canada), 243n34
Ontario, 178
Opechancanough (Powhatan chief), 18–19
Our Declaration (Danielle Allen), 163–64
Overton, Richard (or John), 187, 188
Owen, John, 89

Packanokik (Pokanoket), 40
Palatine Germans, 111, 117
Pangaea, 208
Panic of 1837, 201, 215
Parkhurst, Thomas, 83–84, 86, 238n12, 238n17; *An Exact Mapp of New England and New York*, 83–84, 86
Parliament, 54, 167, 171; the Long Parliament, 188, 235n14

Parmenter, Jon, 10
Parry, Milman, 81, 200, 201, 215–17; "The Historical Method in Literary Criticism," 215; "I make for myself a picture of great detail," 217
Passy (France), 132
Paul, Saint, 33, 93
Paxinosa (Shawnee chief), 125
Paxton Boys, 171
pays d'en haut, 106, 113, 124, 174
Peary, Robert, 210
pedant, as hero, xiv
"pen-and-ink magic," 174
"pen and ink witchcraft," 26, 27, 112, 118
Penn, Thomas, 112, 113, 116, 123, 129, 130, 140
Penn, William, 6, 29, 86, 89, 107, 108, 111, 114, 118, 120, 123, 125, 134, 227n31; *Letter from William Penn . . . to the committee of the Free society of traders . . .* , 112
Pennsylvania, 23, 86, 112, 114, 115, 116, 117, 118, 119, 120, 123, 124, 129, 135, 139, 143, 151, 172, 243n41
Pennsylvania Abolition Society, 148
Pennsylvania Council, 105
Penn Treaty Elm, 23
Pequod, 101
Perkins, William, 253n25
Peters, Richard, 112, 130
Phi Beta Kappa Society, 201, 215
Philadelphia (Pennsylvania), 86, 108, 112, 113, 114, 124, 131, 132, 134, 244n42
Phillips, George, 47, 58, 195, 196
philological method, xi; its *Warheit und Methode*, 217
"philological truth," 199. See also truth
philology, xi, 5, 8, 80, 212, 217
Phips, William, 83, 92, 98, 239n34
Pioneers, The (Cooper), 29, 229n54
Pittsburgh (Pennsylvania), 142
Plain Truth pamphlet (Benjamin Franklin), 244n46
Plan for Settling Two Western Colonies (Benjamin Franklin), 140
Plantation Commission, 55
Plato, 68, 90, 216, 234n2
Plimoth [Plymouth] Plantation, Of (Bradford), 25, 35, 38–39, 41–48, 50, 53

Plutarch, 239n33
Plymouth (colony), 16, 18, 22, 25, 52, 58, 59, 107, 123, 183, 188, 232n7, 238n14
Pocahontas, 18
Poe, Edgar Allan, 30, 66, 203, 213, 216
Poirier, Richard, 77
Polanyi, Karl, 28
Poor Richard, 130, 142
Poor Richard Improved (Benjamin Franklin), 137
Poor Richard's Almanac (Benjamin Franklin), 149
Pope, Alexander, 234n5
Popes-head-Alley (London), 188
Powhatan Wars, 19, 25, 91, 107
"practical" character of North American colonial literature, 3, 9, 12, 13, 79, 108, 129, 130, 164, 197, 200
Presbyterian Church, 57, 236n6
Prince Rupert's Land, 168
Proclamation Line (Boundary Line), 12, 134, 141, 142, 167, 168, 169, 171, 172, 173, 175, 176, 177, 178; legacy of, 250n17
Proprietors, 111, 115, 140
providence, 52, 59
Puritan adventure, 199
Puritan Dilemma, 50, 56
Puritan discourse, 91
Puritan emergency, 151
Puritan ethos, 80
Puritan homiletics, 193, 252n20
Puritan Ordeal, 32
Puritans, 25, 79, 107, 138, 185, 188, 199
Puritan treaties, 19–20

Quakers, 32, 55, 86, 88, 89, 91, 95, 136, 236n7, 238n18, 239n25
Quebec, 174, 175, 176
Quebec Act, 174, 175
Queen Anne's War (War of the Spanish Succession), 27
Quick, John, 238n13, 239n24

Rachel Dyer (Neal), 199
racism, 13
rage for order, the, 80
Randolph, Peyton, 167
Rare Book School, 5

Rasmussen, Knud, 210
"Reasons to be Considered for [. . .] the Intended Plantation in New England" (John Winthrop), 197, 198
Redeeming the Time (Ambrose), 193–94
redemption, 207
Reformation, 81, 87–88, 91
Reformed Church, 86, 90, 197
"Remonstrance and Petition . . . to Massachusetts General Court" (Robert Child), 56
Revolution, American, 28, 120, 156, 166, 167
Rhode Island, 53, 55, 56, 64, 65, 93, 142
Riding, Laura, xv
Rilke, Rainer Maria, 164
Roaming Scout (Pawnee), xiii
Robinson, Tim, *Stones of Aran*, 219
Rogers, John, 253n25
Roman Catholic Church, 17, 64, 90, 91, 196
Romanticism, 94, 101
Rosenmeier, Rosamond, 72
Rourke, Constance, 9, 102; *The Roots of American Culture*, 9
Rousseau, Jean-Jacques, xi
Rove, Karl, 211–12
Royal Exchange (London), 188
Rule, Margaret, 100
Rumsey, David, 238n13
Russia (Soviet Union), 195, 215

Sachphilologie, of August Boeckh, 4
Sacsidora (Shawnee chief), 243n42
Sahlins, Marshall, 9, 10, 163; *Stone Age Economics*, 10
Salem (Massachusetts), 32, 62, 96, 195, 199; witch trials of, 32, 79, 81, 83, 95
Saltonstall, Sir Richard, 195–96
Samoset, 37, 38, 39, 123
Sandwich Islands, 9
Sappho, 68
Sarpedon, 217
Satan, 61, 62, 63, 65, 80, 98, 100, 137, 204, 233n16
Savage, James, 51, 52, 183, 198
"savages," 11, 28, 35, 152–53, 163, 175
"scholar's art," the, xv

"science of exceptions," the, 5
Scott, Sir Walter, xiv
Scrooby separatists, 42–43, 45
"secular imaginary," the, 8
Sedgwick, Catharine Maria, 30; *Hope Leslie*, 30
Sellers, John, 84, 85
Seven Years' War, 12, 25, 107, 121, 130, 167, 169
Shickallemo (Oneida chief), 243n42
Shipley, Catherine, 144
Shipley, William (bishop of St. Asaph), 132, 135, 143
Shute, Samuel, 27
Sidbury, James, 4
Sidney, Sir Philip, 69, 95; "The Defence of Poesy," 95
Silverman, Kenneth, 94, 96
Sindatton (Wyandot chief), 176, 250n13
Skidi Sky Chart, xii
Skinner, Quentin, 4
slavery, 8, 13, 30, 146–48, 152, 160, 163, 164; abolition of, 148; American scandal of, 8; emancipation from, 160; institutionalized in the Constitution, 162; Roman vs. American, 160
slave trade, the, 13
Slotkin, Richard, 12
Smith, John, 18–19, 76
Smolinski, Reiner, xii, 80
Snow, C. P., the "two cultures" and, 212
Society of Fellows in Critical Bibliography, 5
Society of the Cincinnati, 148, 247n29
Society of the Free and Easy, 148
"sociology of texts," the, 4
Socrates, xiv, 136, 210, 213, 216
Solomon, 136
"so long as the grass is green," 15
"so long as the mountains & Rivers & the sun & moon shall endure," 179
"so long as the sun and moon shall last," 14, 25, 174
"so long as the sun shines," 15
Sosin, Jack, 141
Southampton (England), 186, 188
Southwark (London), 189
Spain, 167, 169

Spenser, Edmund, 69
Squanto (Tisquantum), 39, 41
Stalin, Josef, 215
Standish, Myles, 36, 38, 228n41
Stanford, Ann, 73
STEM disciplines, 212
Stenton (Pennsylvania), 242n32
Stevens, Wallace, xv, 5, 152
Stievermann, Jan, 94, 95
Stiles, Ezra, 186
Stamp Act, 167
Stamp Act Resolutions, 167
"St. Laurence," 141
Strabo, 86
Strafford, 1st Earl of (Thomas Wentworth), 188
Stuart, Captain John, 168, 169, 171, 249n7
Suarez, Michael, 223n8
Sugar Act, 167
Sullivan Campaign, 29
Suskind, Ron, 211
Swarton, Hannah, 88, 99, 238n20
Swayn, Dick, 90
sweet Posie for God's Saints, A, 187, 188
Sweninger, Lee, 52
"swerve," the (Lucretian), 5
Swinburne, Algernon Charles, 210

Tacitus, *Agricola*, 166, 179
Talby, Dorothy, 62, 63
Tamaqua (Beaver), 243n41
Tamenend, 23, 26, 29, 30, 227n31
Teaogan (Tioga), 244n42
Teedyuscung (Delaware chief), 119–22, 125, 243n42, 244n42
Tennyson, Alfred, Lord, 209, 216–17; "Ulysses," 209
Tenth Muse, The (Woodbridge and Bradstreet), 67
Tertullian, 92; *Prescription against Heretics*, 92
Teufelsdröckh, xiv
Thanksgiving, the "First," 40, 123
theorization, over- vs. under-, 4–5
thick description, 81
Thickstun, Margaret Olofson, 234n1
Thomson, Charles, 157
Thoreau, Henry David, 29, 203, 215; "The

Dispersion of Seeds," 203; *Walden*, 205–7; *Wild Fruits*, 203
Thornton, John, 84, 85
Throgmorton, George, 253n25
Thyatira, 93
Tirawahat, xiii
Tisquantum (Squanto), 39, 41
Titanic (ship), 201
Tocarry-Hogan, 117, 243n34. *See also* Maryland
Tokahaio (Seneca chief), 243n39
traders, on the American frontier, 171
trans-Appalachian Indian Reserve, 167, 171, 176
Transcendentalism (Emersonian), 203
"transparent eyeball" (Emerson), 201
treaties: vs. documents fashioned from them, 26; Paris, 138, 148, 167, 168, 174, 175, 176, 177; Ryswick, 87; Utrecht, 27
treaties, Indian: Augusta, 168, 169, 170, 171, 172, 173; Carlisle, 109, 130; Easton, 102, 108, 110, 119–23, 125, 240n5, 243n42, 244n42; Fort Niagara, 168, 169, 171, 172; Fort Pitt, 27, 102, 174; Fort Stanwix, 12, 142, 167, 169, 171, 172, 173, 174, 175, 177, 250n11; Greenville, 168, 178; Hard Labor, 169, 171, 172; Lancaster, 105, 111, 240n2, 240n5, 243n42; Lochaber, 169; Middle Plantation, 20; Mohawk, 24, 118, 124; Plymouth (Massasoit), 27, 107, 109; Puritan, 19–20; Sandusky, 171, 175, 176, 177, 178; Tawagonshi, 15, 23; Treaty of 1682, 112; Treaties of 1683–1701, 112; Treaty of 1701, 108, 112; Treaty of 1722, 250n19; Treaty of 1732, 112, 113, 129; Treaty of 1736, 112, 113, 123, 129, 240n2; Treaty of 1742, 120, 124, 241n8, 243n36; Treaty of 1744, 120; Treaty of 1756, 244n42; Treaty of 1761, 243n39; Treaty of 1762, 243n41; Trois-Rivières, 16, 113; Wampanoag, 22, 102
Treaty held with the Indians of the Six Nations, at Philadelphia, in July, 1742 (Benjamin Franklin), 102–3, 115–19
Treaty of Friendship Held with the Chiefs of the Six Nations, at Philadelphia, in September and October, 1736, A (Benjamin Franklin), 111–15, 123

Trojan War, 125
Trotsky, Leon, 236n4
truth, v, 3, 7; correspondence vs. coherence theory of, 3; Hellenic vision of, 213; speaking truth vs. power to, 7. *See also aletheia*
Trump, Donald, 7, 148
Turks, 198
Turner, Frederick Jackson, 12, 27, 28
Turner, William, 237n9
"turtles all the way down," 213
Tuveson, Ernest Lee, 79
Twain, Mark, 30, 214; *Life on the Mississippi*, 214
Twyford (England), 132, 135

Umwelt, 208
Uncas (Mohegan chief), 20, 21, 22, 30
Unitarianism, 188, 198
United Brethren, 236n6
United Colonies of New England, 43, 52, 53, 59, 64
United Nations, 211
United States Army, 178
Utah, 214
"*utile*" function of North American colonial literature, 3

Vandalia, 131, 139, 142, 143, 148, 173, 249n9
Van Engen, Abram C., 186, 187, 190
Vanishing American, the, 157
Vanity of All Worldly Things, The (Anne Bradstreet), 69
Vassa, Gusatvus, 5
Vaughan, Benjamin, 131, 132, 135
Venables, Robert, 16
Venetians, 198
Vermont, 142
Vetus Latina, xiv
Virgil, 80, 94, 125; *Aeneid*, 125
Virginia, 16, 18, 21, 23, 24, 25, 28, 53, 86, 107, 115, 116, 119, 123, 142, 167, 168, 172, 173, 177, 183, 197, 214, 249n7; House of Burgesses of, 167

Walden (Thoreau), 205–7; John Farmer in, 206
Walden Pond, 203

Waldensians, 198
Waldman, Paul, 210
Walking Purchase fraud/swindle, 108, 115, 116, 117, 119, 120, 123, 124, 130, 243n41
Walpole, Thomas, 247n22
Walpole Associates/Company, 142, 247n22
wampum, 105, 110, 114, 119–20, 170, 171, 173, 176
Ward, T. H., 230n5
Warner, Michael, 244n1
Washington, George, 29, 167, 247n29
Washington Post, 210
Watertown (Massachusetts), 60, 195, 196
weapons of mass destruction, 211, 215
Weimar Republic, 215
Weiser, Conrad, 111, 112, 113, 114, 115, 117, 119, 123, 242n32, 244n42
Wept of Wish-Ton-Wish, The (Cooper), 199
Werner, Marta, 5
werowance, 19
Wessagusett (colony), 44
West, Benjamin, 228n31
Westminster Confession, 55
Weston, Thomas, 44
Weymouth (Massachusetts), 61
Wharton, Edith, 30; *The House of Mirth*, 30
Wharton, Samuel, 247n22
Wharton, Thomas, 247n22
Wheelwright, John, 63
Whig Party (America), 30
White, John, 189, 196
White Eyes (Delaware chief), 174, 250n12
Whitefield, George, 140, 141
Whitehall, 134, 142, 168, 172
Whitman, Walt, 30, 130, 152; "Crossing Brooklyn Ferry," 130–31; "Edgar Poe's Significance," 30; *Song of Myself*, 152

Wigglesworth, Michael, 3
Wilamowitz-Moellendorff, Ulrich von, 213–14
Wild Fruits (Thoreau), 203
William and Mary, College of, 150
Williams, Roger, 53, 54, 56, 57, 59, 63, 65, 88, 186, 240n48
Wilson, John, 195, 196
Winslow, Edward, 35, 39, 40, 47, 49
Winthrop, Francis Bayard, 190–91, 195, 254n32, 254n34
Winthrop, John, 4, 6, 13, 20, 21, 32, 42, 47, 50–66, 67, 73, 76, 91, 92, 93, 150, 183–99; *Arbella* sermon, the, 3, 5, 6, 32, 53, 57, 58, 78, 83, 183–99, 253n25; "Discourse on Arbitrary Government," 57; *The History of New England from 1630 to 1649*, 50–65, 91; "Humble Petition to Lords Commissioners for Foreign Plantations," 56; *Journal*, 17, 42, 50–65, 77, 91, 186, 198; "Little Speech on Liberty," 57, 197, 198; "Negative Vote," 57; "Reasons to be Considered for [. . .] the Intended Plantation in New England," 197, 198
Winthrop, John, Jr., 187
Winthrop Papers, 186
witch trials, 83, 95
Wittgenstein, Ludwig, xi
Woodbridge, John, 67–68; Woodbridge and Bradstreet's *The Tenth Muse*, 67–68; *The Vanity of All Worldly Things*, 69
Woodward, David, 221n6
Wordsworth, William, xiv
Wright, James, 169–70

Yeandle, Laetitia, 51, 58
Yeats, William Butler, 125

www.ingramcontent.com/pod-product-compliance
Lightning Source LLC
Chambersburg PA
CBHW022042290426
44109CB00014B/943